C++ AND C TOOLS, UTILITIES, LIBRARIES, AND RESOURCES

FREE AND COMMERCIAL SOFTWARE TOOLS

DAVID SPULER

**Prentice Hall PTR
Upper Saddle River,
New Jersey 07458**

For book and bookstore information

http://www.prenhall.com

Library of Congress Cataloging-in-Publication Data

Spuler, David
    C++ and C tools, utilities, libraries, and resources / David
  Spuler.
      p. cm.
    Includes index.
    ISBN 0-13-226697-0 (acid-free paper)
    1. C++ (Computer program language) 2. C (Computer program
  language) I. Title.
  QA76.73.C153S6985 1996
  005.13--dc20   96-13567
                                                CIP

Editorial/production supervision: *Diane Heckler Koromhas*
Cover director: *Jerry Votta*
Cover design: *Design Source*
Manufacturing buyer: *Alexis R. Heydt*
Acquisitions editor: *Paul Becker*
Editorial assistant: *Maureen Diana*
Editorial Liaison: *Patti Guerrieri*

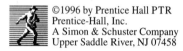

The publisher offers discounts on this book when ordered in bulk quantities.
For more information, contact;
    Corporate Sales Department
    Prentice Hall PTR
    One Lake Street
    Upper Saddle River, NJ 07458
    Phone: 800-382-3419; Fax: 201-236-7141
    e-mail: corpsales@prenhall.com

Printed in the United States of America

10 9 8 7 6 5 4 3 2 1

ISBN 0-13-226697-0

Prentice-Hall International (UK) Limited, *London*
Prentice-Hall of Australia Pty. Limited, *Sydney*
Prentice-Hall Canada Inc., *Toronto*
Prentice-Hall Hispanoamericana, S.A., *Mexico*
Prentice-Hall of India Private Limited, *New Delhi*
Prentice-Hall of Japan, Inc., *Tokyo*
Simon & Schuster Asia Pte. Ltd., *Singapore*
Editora Prentice-Hall do Brasil, Ltda., *Rio de Janeiro*

To Anita, with my deepest love, for making each day worthwhile.

Contents

Preface

*T*his book began with the perplexing question of "I wonder what's out there?" that I found myself asking on too many occasions. Whenever some programming task annoyed me, I wondered if there was a tool out there to reduce the burden. Far too many times have I searched textually for the string "->something" and then changed the structure member name because having the compiler complain about any I missed was the "easiest" method. There must be a tool for this, but how would you find it?

Hence I set myself the task of documenting all the tools I could find archived or advertised on the Internet, advertised in trade magazines, or demonstrated at conferences. I have discovered a great many gems, including a number of cross-referencing tools to solve the aforementioned structure use problem. Although there are no doubt many more tools than covered in these pages, all of the major classes of tools are examined and I am proud to offer this book as a broad survey of the major tools for C and C++ programming.

WHO THIS BOOK IS FOR

This book will benefit people in a number of positions. The discussion of the purpose of tools and how they work ensures that this book is not just a catalog of wares. Many readers will learn a lot about tools, and start to think of ways they could be using tools in their daily programming sessions. Some of the people whom this book will benefit include:

Programmers: As a professional programmer myself, this research into tools has strengthened my own skills and reading the material will strengthen yours too. Programmers will benefit from knowledge of what types of tools they should be using, information on how tools work, and tips on using tools to their best advantage.

Development Managers: Educating a team of programmers to better use their time through new tools and techniques is an excellent productivity improvement method. Every advantage to the individual from using new tools pays off many-fold if the entire team buys into the techniques.

Software Engineering Process Group (SEPG) members: Nothing scales up like education. Introducing new tools and techniques on a company-wide basis will offer immense benefit across the board. The material in this book will aid SEPG members in finding the best tools and in focusing efforts on those types of tools that will offer the greatest payoff in terms of productivity and quality.

Instructors: Educational courses on programming tend to focus on learning the features of a programming language such as the syntax and semantic structure. Although this is unavoidable to a large extent since students must learn the basics, any studies on the techniques and tools they should use for real-world programming would be of great benefit. To this end, this book should aid the instructor as supplementary reading for an intermediate or advanced C/C++ course. Alternatively, a more adventurous idea would be a course or specialized section on programming tools for which this book would be ideal.

Graduate students: While this book is not a treatise on the state-of-the-art of the theoretical aspects of programming tools, there are certainly subject areas in this book where a masters or doctoral thesis would be possible. There are some references to academic papers throughout the book, but they are certainly not a substitute for a full literature search. The "wish" sections in some chapters give indications of areas where the current generation of tools is lacking. Some of the more interesting areas of research include source code analysis via dataflow analysis, code reformatting theory, space usage profiling, source code instrumentation versus object code instrumentation, and automated documentation generation.

PLATFORMS COVERED BY THE BOOK

This book covers tools for all major operating system and compiler platforms. There are reviews of tools on many platforms and the coverage is intentionally one addressing all major development environments. In addition, the techniques and technology behind the various tools applies to software development in general, independent of the particular flavor to which you are accustomed.

The multiplatform nature of the C and C++ programming languages carries across into the tools that are needed. A memory stomp is a program failure regardless of whether it causes a GPF, hung program, or a core dump. Hence, a memory allocation checker is a valuable tool wherever you are coding.

How to Read this Book

There is no real order imposed on the topics in the book, and hence the chapters may be perused in any order. Most chapters begin with a discussion of what the class of tool is used for, the technology used to achieve this, and hints on the best features to look for. The body of the chapter is typically a discussion of a number of the free or commercial tools in that class.

Overall, the book is logically separated into three major parts, each with a separate focus. These parts are not dependent on each other, nor are individual chapters dependent on other chapters.

Part I: Tools — This part examines all the various classes of tools that help the programmer write code faster or produce code of better quality. The general rule is that a "tool" is a utility or command that is launched, not a piece of code that is incorporated into the project. In various cases this is a gray area as many tools require code changes or linkage with code libraries.

Part II: Libraries — This part covers the numerous C function libraries and C++ class libraries that can be added to your project. Libraries allow the reuse of code written by another individual or commercial vendor. Programmers can leverage the code already written by using it in a particular component of a project.

Part III: Resources — The last part covers various resources in C and C++ programming that are not tools or techniques in the programming process. Instead this section addresses sources of informational material such as news groups, books, magazines and online archives.

The primary focus of the book is on how programmers can *use* tools and libraries, rather than how to design better tools. However, readers interested in the technological aspects of software tools should examine the introductory sections of most chapters, the various "wish" sections in some chapters, and the appendix on tool design issues. There are also references to academic and trade publications that examine some design issues in detail.

Commercial Tool Listings

The listings of commercial tools contained in this book are those of an independent reviewer. I am not affiliated with any of the companies listed. Furthermore, no fee was charged to vendors for inclusion in the book. Vendors of products that I was aware of and considered appropriate to the book's scope were approached to participate in the review scheme by provision of promotional material, product documentation and evaluation copies of the product. My aim with all the listings was to offer a fair representation of product features and limitations.

All addresses and phone numbers are within the USA unless otherwise stated. Price and platform listings for products are intended as a guide only. Please contact the vendor of a product for the most up-to-date information.

COMMON SENSE WHEN PURCHASING TOOLS!

A large number of commercial, shareware and public domain tools, utilities, libraries and resources have been mentioned and/or reviewed in these pages. To the best of my knowledge at the time of writing all the information presented here in the book is correct and provided in good faith — however, due to the constantly changing nature of tools and to the type of research involved, it is possible some inaccuracies in details may occur. Furthermore, it was not possible to verify all the product feature claims made by vendors in product marketing material, nor to fully test the product in all real-world conditions to verify its stability and the true extent of its value to the user over a period of time. As with any purchasing decision, the reader should take care in gathering all necessary information, including that marketing, business and technical information available from any commercial vendors, before committing to any obligations, financial or otherwise.

LEGAL ISSUES

In many places I have attempted to give an indication as to the legal status of a tool or code library by marking them as "commercial", "shareware", or "free". However, as every product has its own unique set of legal issues, the reader would be wise in seeking professional counsel to verify the status of these issues. Some of the issues that may arise include whether a product is commercial, shareware, and the details of the licensing agreements, royalties, support, and so on.

Even the so called "free" tools examined in this book are often subject to specific licensing constraints. For example some "free" tools require various conditions to be met for use of the product such as acknowledgment of their use in product documentation. Some tools may even restrict commercial distribution either explicitly or by the absence of any stated position. Legal advice should be sought when deciding upon the use of any tool, library or product.

BOOKS BY THE SAME AUTHOR

If you enjoy reading this book you might also be interested in my earlier books. I have two other books available in the Prentice Hall PTR series covering professional programming techniques:

> SPULER, David A., *C++ & C Debugging, Testing, and Reliability: The prevention, detection and correction of program errors*, Prentice Hall, New Jersey, 1994. ISBN 0-13-308172-9.

This book covers numerous debugging and testing techniques, software quality assurance, and reliability techniques including exception handling and defensive programming. There are also ten chapters forming a catalog of the various common pitfalls that a C/C++ programmer must beware. An appendix maps failure symptoms back to possible causes.

SPULER, David, *C++ & C Efficiency: How to improve program speed and memory usage*, Prentice Hall, New Jersey, 1992. ISBN 0-13-096595-2.

Many performance improvement techniques are examined, including micro-optimizations such as using the & operator instead of the % operator, code transformations such as loop code motion, C++ tricks including avoidance of temporary objects, and algorithm changes such as precomputation and lazy evaluation. Space efficiency is examined for reduction of static, stack and heap storage needs. The book is rounded off with coverage of topics such as measurement, estimation, compiler optimization issues, data structures and abstract data types, and a number of examples including a super-optimized tic-tac-toe player.

PLATFORM INFORMATION

Each of the product listings has a list of supported "platforms" covering the hardware and/or operating system on which the software will run. The following abbreviations are commonly used throughout this book:

Abbreviation	Hardware/operating system
Win16,Windows 3.1	Microsoft Windows version 3.1 or earlier.
NT, Windows NT	Microsoft Windows NT (for 80x86, DEC Alpha RISC or MIPS).
Win95, Win32	Microsoft Windows 95 operating system.
Solaris	Sun MicroSystems workstations running the Solaris operating system on Sun-SPARC processors.
Solaris-x86	Solaris OS from Sun Microsystems on 80x86 hardware.
SunOS	SunOS operating system from Sun MicroSystems on SunSPARC processors.
SGI, IRIX	Silicon Graphics Inc. hardware with the IRIX operating system.
AIX, RS/6000	IBM workstation RS/6000 running AIX operating system.
ICL	Hardware from ICL Personal Systems.
Bull, BOS	Bull hardware running Bull Operating System (BOS).
Linux	Free UNIX-like operating system for 80x86 hardware.
Mac, Macintosh	Apple Corporation's Macintosh or Power Macintosh hardware.
PowerPC	IBM Power PC running Macintosh OS or Windows NT.
Amiga	Amiga hardware running the Amiga operating system.
Atari	Atari hardware running the Atari operating system.
DOS, MSDOS	Microsoft Disk Operating System on 80x86 hardware.
SCO	Santa Cruz Operation (SCO) hardware with SCO UNIX OS.

Abbreviation	Hardware/operating system *(Continued)*
OSF/1, Digital	Digital Equipment Corporation (DEC) Alpha RISC hardware running the Open Systems Foundation (OSF) operating system. Now formally known as Digital UNIX.
IIP, IIP-UX	Hewlett-Packard hardware with the HP-UX operating system.
VMS, OpenVMS	Digital Equipment Corporation (DEC) VAX or Alpha hardware running the VMS operating or OpenVMS system.
MVS	IBM mainframe hardware running the MVS operating system.
Ultrix	Digital Equipment Corporation (DEC) RISC hardware running the Ultrix operating system.
DG	Data General hardware running the DG-UX operating system.
OS/2	IBM Operating System/2 running on 80x86 hardware.
Sequent, ptx	Sequent hardware running the ptx operating system.
NCR, AT&T	AT&T hardware with AT&T operating system (formerly NCR).
Pyramid	Pyramid hardware running the Pyramid operating system.
QNX	QNX Software Systems realtime operating system for 80x86.
NEC, NEC UNIX	NEC computers running the NEC UNIX operating system.

CONTACTING THE AUTHOR — FUTURE EDITIONS

Correspondence regarding new free, shareware, or commercial C/C++ tools can be sent to the address below. Letters should include a brief description of the product, contact details (including fax number) and the person to contact regarding any future reviews. Please do not send promotional material, product documentation or product evaluations to this address. I am also interested to receive book corrections and suggestions for new areas to cover. Finally, I have a long-standing interest in software development tools from an academic and commercial point of view. I would like to hear about any tool projects, and might be available to contribute. All correspondence can be sent to this postal address:

David Spuler: Tools Book

P.O. Box 1262

Aitkenvale, QLD 4814

AUSTRALIA

TYPESETTING

This book was typeset using FrameMaker version 5 for Windows, from Frame Technology Corporation (phone: 1-800-U4-FRAME or 408-975-6000; fax: 408-975-6799; email: comments@frame.com; web: http://www.frame.com). This is an excellent piece of software that far exceeds the capabilities of the cheaper well-known Windows word processor packages. The design of FrameMaker scales easily to large documents with its updating facilities allowing each chapter to be edited independently with up-to-date pages and cross-references. I recommend it to anyone who is serious about rapidly producing high-quality documents.

TRADEMARKS

A large number of names and symbols that are trademarks or registered trademarks have been used herein. The trademarks shown below were derived from various sources. All product, service, or company names or service marks not listed below are trademarks, service marks, registered trademarks, or registered service marks of their respective holders.

UNIX is a registered trademark licensed exclusively through X/Open Company Ltd. PostScript is a registered trademark of Adobe Systems, Inc. AT&T is a registered trademark of American Telephone & Telegraph. Apple, AppleTalk, Mac, Macintosh, and Power Macintosh are trademarks or registered trademarks of Apple Computer, Inc. NetWare 3, NetWare 4, and NLM are trademarks of Novell, Inc. dBASE, ObjectWindows, Turbo C, Turbo C++, Borland C++, and CodeGuard are trademarks or registered trademarks of Borland International, Inc. CompuServe is a registered trademark of CompuServe, Inc. Epsilon is a trademark of Lugaru Software, Inc. Compaq is a registered trademark of Compaq Computer Corporation. DEC, Alpha AXP, VAX, DIGITAL, ULTRIX and VMS are trademarks or registered trademarks of Digital Equipment Corporation. Gupta is a registered trademark of Gupta Technologies, Inc. Hewlett-Packard, and HP are registered trademarks of Hewlett-Packard Company. Intel is a registered trademark, and 286, 386, and Pentium are trademarks of Intel Corporation. Cantata is a trademark of Information Processing Limited. AIX, IBM, OS/2 and DB/2 are registered trademarks and PowerPC, Presentation Manager, RISC System/6000, and VisualAge are trademarks of International Business Machines Corporation. Microsoft, Microsoft Access, MS, Windows, CodeView, Visual Basic, MS-DOS, Visual C++, Visual SourceSafe, QuickC, Microsoft C, Win32, Win32s, and Windows NT are trademarks or registered trademarks of Microsoft Corporation. Motorola is a registered trademark of Motorola Corporation. NCR is a registered trademark of NCR Corporation. NEC is a registered trademark of NEC Corporation. ORACLE is a registered trademark of Oracle Corporation. Motif and OSF/Motif are registered trademarks of Open Software Foundation, Inc. SCO is a registered trademark of Santa Cruz Operations, Inc. Silicon Graphics is a registered trademark of Silicon Graphics, Inc. NFS and Solaris are registered trademarks of Sun Microsystems, Inc. SunOS and SunSoft are trademarks of Sun Microsystems, Inc. SYBASE is a registered trademark of Sybase, Inc. Watcom, Watcom C, and Watcom C++ are trademarks of Watcom Systems, Inc. Wind/U is a registered trademark and HyperHelp a trademark of Bristol Technology, Inc. Premia is a registered trademark and Codewright, a trademark of Premia Corporation. BugBase is a trademark of Archimedes Software. PCYACC and CodeCheck are registered trademarks of Abraxas Software, Inc., Visual SlickEdit is a registered trademark of MicroEdge, Inc. Symantec, NetBuild and OPTLINK are trademarks or registered trademarks of Symantec Corporation. Rogue Wave and .h++ are registered trademarks and Tools.h++ is a trademark of Rogue Wave Software. Pure Software, Purify, and Quantify are registered trademarks, and PureCoverage and PureLink trademarks of Pure Software, Inc. Nu-Mega Technologies and BoundsChecker are trademarks of Nu-Mega Technologies. The C Shroud, PC-lint and FlexeLint are trademarks of Gimpel Software, and C-Vision is a trademark of John Rex and Gimpel Software. WinScope and Periscope are registered trademarks of The Periscope Company, Inc. Blue Sky Software and Visual Programmer are trademarks or registered trademarks of Blue Sky Software Corporation. C++VS is a trademark of Perennial, Inc. Track Record is a registered trademark of UnderWare, Inc. EnhancementPak, Epak, DBPak, DatabasePak, DX, Database Xcessory, BX, Builder Xcessory, and ViewKit ObjectPak are trademarks or registered trademarks of Integrated Computer Solutions, Inc. SENTINEL and Object Module Transformation are trademarks of AiB Software Corporation. Apogee-C/C++ is a trademark of Apogee Software, Inc. MKS, MKS Code Integrity, MKS Lex & Yacc, and MKS Source Integrity are trademarks or registered trademarks of Mortice Kern Systems, Inc. C-Index, C-Index/II, and Trio Systems are trademarks of Trio Systems. HeapAgent, SmartHeap, and SwapTuner are trademarks of MicroQuill Software Publishing, Inc. M++ is a trademark of Dyad Software Corporation. FOR_C, FOR_C++, FOR_STRUCT, FOR_STUDY and Cobalt Blue are registered trademarks of Cobalt Blue, Inc. C/Database Toolchest and Power C are trademarks of Mix Software, Inc. Raima, Raima Database Manager, Velocis, and Raima Object Manager are trademarks of Raima Corporation. Insure++ is a trademark of ParaSoft Corporation. SAS is a registered trademark of SAS Institute, Inc. CC-RIDER and C++-RIDER are trademarks of Western Wares. Yacc++ is a registered trademark of Compiler Resources, Inc. High C/C++ is a trademark of MetaWare, Inc. MIPS is a registered trademark of MIPS Computer Systems, Inc. CCC is a registered trademark of Softool Corporation. X Window System is a trademark of The Massachusetts Institute of Technology. QA Partner is a registered trademark of Segue Software, Inc. INTERSOLV and PVCS are registered trademarks of Intersolv, Inc.

DISCLAIMER

The author and publisher have used their best efforts in developing this book, associated software and associated CDROM distribution. The information, software and CDROM in this book distribution are provided on an "as is" basis and the author and publisher hereby disclaim all warranties, express or implied, including those of merchantability and fitness for any particular purpose. The author and publisher make no warranties or representations regarding the accuracy or completeness of the information. In no event shall the author or publisher be liable for any special, indirect, incidental or consequential damages, lost profits, lost data, or any indirect damages, arising out of or in connection with the use or performance of this information or software, even if the author or publisher have been informed of the possibility thereof.

ACKNOWLEDGMENTS

There are a number of people who deserve my thanks for their help in bringing this book to market. First and foremost, a very special thanks to Anita who was easily the largest contributor and responsible for typesetting, proofing, and administrating the product review process. Mike brought many a tool and Internet site to my attention. Mark contributed much information about advanced tools including emacs and TCL tips. Thanks also to the larger number of friends and colleagues, too numerous to mention, who have contributed either to the quality of the book or to keeping me sane during the writing of this book.

Prentice Hall has seen this book through from start to finish with the early impetus from Andrew Binnie and Kaylie Smith, and very useful reviews by Bernie Goodheart, Peter Jones and the other anonymous reviewers. Tim Chambers was a great technical reviewer, providing me with useful information and intelligent discussion of many book aspects. Thanks to Paul Becker, who carried the book from early development through to final production. Credit also goes to Sophie Papanikolaou, Maureen Diana and Mike Hays for their involvement. Hearty thanks to Diane Koromhas for her prompt and professional handling of all production issues.

Thanks to all of the many companies that offered information and demonstration product versions. And finally, my thanks and encouragement to the many inspired programmers who have developed the variety of advanced development tools that are freely available today.

1

TOOLS

This first part of the book examines all the various classes of tools that a programmer may use. A tool is loosely defined as something that helps the programmer "do something" in order to create a better program. Programming tools by this definition range from the basic compiler to the various debugging, testing, profiling and documentation tools available. This definition distinguishes this part from the second part of the book which examines a slightly different programming aid, the library, which is more like a ready-made building block than a tool to create new blocks.

All tools have their particular place in the software development process. The modern market offers tools for almost every conceivable task confronting the programmer. All of the phases of software development from design through implementation to maintenance now have a variety of tools that ease the process.

The value of a tool is that it extends the programmer's ability by automating manual tasks. This allows the programmer to handle larger and more complicated software. Tools are a central part of the advances in the software market and have a direct impact on the complexity, functionality and quality of the software under development. Without tools we would still be struggling with the complexity of even moderate software programs. With increasingly sophisticated tools, there is no limit to the advances possible in software technology.

Introduction

*T*ools are what distinguishes humans from apes. So too, do programming tools distinguish real programmers from ape programmers. The maturity of a programmer can be measured by the level of comfort in using advanced programming tools as part of his or her personal software development habits. Programmers who use good tools are likely to have a much higher level of productivity than they would if they didn't use the tools.

The aim of this book is to help you, the programmer, to discover the many, many different tools that are available. This book grew out of the many times I asked myself "I wonder if there's a tool out there to do...", and whilst writing this book I've been amazed at the broad tool offerings available freely and commercially.

This book's purpose does not end with discussing existing tools because of the annoying problem that not all the tools I want actually exist. I have a long "wish list" of tools that would be useful to C and C++ programmers, but which no-one seems to have built yet. Hence there are a number of "wish" sections throughout the book as encouragement to software vendors to produce some fancy tools.

Choosing and Using the Right Tools

One point that became immediately obvious is the impossibility of using all the tools available. It just isn't feasible to learn them all. A more practical solution is to use a small number of tools that solve specific problems, probably one from each of the major tool classes: editor, debugger, memory checker, source code checker, etc. Used this way, it is possible to achieve a deep level of understanding of your tools and put them to their best effect. This is the strategy I employ in my personal coding practices while at the same time attempting to achieve a reasonable understanding of the other many, many tools.

But one should also be willing to investigate and learn new tools. Adding a new tool to your repertoire or learning the deeper features of a tool is a sure road to better programming. Here are some typical uses of good tools you should aspire to:

- fast location of function definitions in your editor
- enabling and examining compiler warnings
- regular use of any runtime memory allocation checker
- single-stepping through code with your debugger
- regular use of a source code checker

The conversion from one familiar tool to a "better" tool is another way to ramp up your programming productivity, but it is usually a difficult task in the short-term. The day-to-day coding habits that form your programming style are formed over the years and can often be slow to change.

Market Trends for Software Development Tools

Maybe you're a true C/C++ programmer and you haven't noticed, but the dominance of C and C++ for application development is definitely under attack from rapid application development tools. Some examples are Microsoft's Visual Basic and Borland's Delphi. These are basically new programming languages combined with powerful environments. While I can't predict the long-term dominance of programming languages, it's fairly obvious that C and C++ already have large support bases and will be widely used for years to come. In addition, the sophistication of C and C++ tools continues to grow and is still mounting a good defense against the other development language options.

The state-of-the-art for C and C++ compilers and integrated development environments continues to press the envelope. Graphical information presentation seems to be the order of the day. Environments are continually extending the level of visual information heading toward visual debuggers, graphical reports from profilers, and GUI-based third-party tools.

As usual, the quality of C/C++ compilers available for DOS and Windows platforms continues to be impressive, with major players such as Microsoft, Borland, Watcom and Symantec offering excellent integrated software development environments. The competition in this "low-end" hardware market has continually led to the easy availability of good technology in software development tools. These platforms have had good quality graphical integrated development environments for quite some time, making the text-based offerings on UNIX in the past appear somewhat lacking.

Some hardware vendors for UNIX platforms are also strengthening their software development tool suites. Hardware companies such as Hewlett-Packard, Sun Microsystems, Inc. and Silicon Graphics Inc., seem to be setting the standard with a variety of software tools. In addition, there are a number of third-party tools offering integrated development environments and various advanced facilities.

However, the market for UNIX software development environments continues to meet resistance from users content with using free tools such as the `emacs` editor and the `gcc`/`g++` GNU C and C++ compiler for software development. Although these free tools are not at the state-of-the-art level in graphical presentation, they do offer the advantages of a low price tag and multiplatform availability.

In general, the number of third-party C/C++ software development tools available has sky-rocketed over the past few years. The market for third party tools has become well established and many companies have prospered. The future of third-party tools appears secure but only quality tools are likely to thrive. The multi-vendor nature of the market ensures that good tools available on a multitude of platforms will survive improvements in the offerings of individual vendors. On the other hand, major vendors are continually improving their offerings and might begin to squeeze out some common forms of third-party tools. For example, compilers could begin to offer built-in functionality, as has already happened to some extent with profilers and debuggers, and could further extend to source code checking or runtime error diagnosis. Another possible direction is that compiler vendors may start to provide explicit support for third-party tools rather than reinventing the technology. Whatever the future, the third-party tool market is currently massive, and it comprises the majority of commercial tool entries in this book!

Unix Tools

Every UNIX implementation brings its own bag of tools and many are relevant to C and C++ programming. The majority of these tools also have perhaps the best feature of all: price. Most UNIX tools are effectively free as they come bundled with the operating system. Although some vendors are charging for the "larger" tools for development (e.g., C or C++ compilers), the "smaller" tools are quite valuable and it is worth the effort to familiarize yourself with what is available.

A summarized list of some of these tools is given in Table 1–1. Note that UNIX variants differ, and these tools may not all be available on your UNIX platform. An interesting and educational exercise is to surf your man pages. Try using the "`man`" utility to browse the list of UNIX tools. There are many that are relevant to programming, far more than are listed.

Table 1–1 Standard UNIX tools

Tool	Purpose
cc	C Compiler
cpp	C preprocessor
make	Compile multiple file C/C++ programs

Table 1–1 Standard UNIX tools *(Continued)*

Tool	Purpose
lint	Static checker for C errors
ar, ranlib	Create archives (libraries)
cb, indent	Pretty print C/C++ programs
cexpl, cdecl	Explain C declarations
vgrind	Typeset C programs
sccs	Version management for large projects
ctrace	Debugging output program tracing tool
cflow	Call graph of function calls and external references
cxref	Cross-reference listing of C files
dbx	Debugger
nm	Object file analysis
sdb	Debugger
adb	Low-level debugger
trace	Trace system calls at run-time

Also note that many of the other "free" tools discussed in this book could well have already been installed on your UNIX system. If you're searching for a particular tool, look in the manuals and even if it's not there, try running it. If it really isn't there, buy your system administrator a copy of this book.

In addition to these particular tools, other basic features of UNIX can be used to great effect. Script files of commands are very useful. Redirection of input and output is a very powerful feature which can be combined with all the usual file manipulation utilities such as `cat`, `more` `cp`, `mv`, `head` and `tail`.

WINDOWS, WINDOWS NT AND DOS TOOLS

Microsoft Windows platforms have a rapidly growing list of tools. In addition to Microsoft's many offerings in the various tool categories, many other third-party vendors have added high-quality tools to the market. Some of the tools for Windows platforms are listed in Table 1–2. The review of each tool can be examined for details of platform availability and the features that are available.

Table 1–2 Tools for DOS, Windows 3.1, Windows 95, and Windows NT

Tool Category	Tool Names
Compilers:	DJGPP, Apogee-C/C++, MetaWare High C/C++, C++/Views, Watcom C++, Symantec C++, Microsoft Visual C++, Borland C++, NDP C/C++
Source Code Checkers:	PC-lint, CodeCheck, MKS Code Integrity, CMT++, CLINT
Memory Debugging:	MemCheck, HeapAgent, Bounds Checker, CodeGuard, Purify
Debuggers:	Dr Watson, WinSpector, MultiScope, Turbo Debugger, Code-View, Periscope, Soft-ICE
Tracing Tools:	Spy, DDE Spy, WinSight, DBWin, WinScope, Footprints, TrackDeck
Editors:	RimStar Programmer's Editor, Visual SlickEdit, CodeWright
Browsers/Document:	CC-Rider, c2man, C-XREF, C-TREE
Coverage:	CTC++, STW/Coverage, C-Cover
Testing Tools:	WinSatellite, QA Partner, Cantata, SoftTest, Panorama C/C++, Automated Test Facility, STW/Regression, McCabe ToolSet, CTB
Parser Tools:	PCYACC, Yacc++, MKS lex & yacc, Visual Parse++

OS/2 Tools

A number of software development tools are available for IBM's OS/2 operating system. Some of those covered in this book are listed in Table 1–3. The list includes both free and commercial tools, with offerings from IBM and other third-party vendors. There are also ports of the GNU toolset, including gcc/g++, discussed later in this chapter.

Table 1–3 OS/2 tools

Tool Category	Tools Names
Compilers:	VisualAge C++, MetaWare High C/C++, Liant C++/Views, Watcom C/C++, NDP C/C++, gcc/g++
Source Code Checkers:	PC-Lint, CodeCheck, CMT++
Memory Debugging:	MemCheck
Debuggers:	MultiScope, Periscope
Tracing Tools:	Footprints
Pretty Printers:	indent, cPost, C-Vision,
Editors:	RimStar Programmer's Editor, Visual SlickEdit

Table 1–3 OS/2 tools *(Continued)*

Tool Category	Tools Names
Browsers/Document:	CC-Rider, c2man
Testing Tools:	Cantata, SoftTest, Automated Test Facility, QA Partner
Parser Tools:	Yacc++, Visual Parse++, MKS lex & yacc

VMS TOOLS

This section shows a list of VMS tools discussed elsewhere in the book. In addition, readers can find VMS ports of free GNU software discussed later in the chapter.

Table 1–4 VMS tools

Tool Category	Tool Names
Source Code Checkers:	FlexeLint, CodeCheck, QualGen
Memory Debugging:	MemCheck
Pretty Printers:	C Printer
Language Conversion:	cfortran.h, FOR_C, FOR_C++
Documentation:	DocGen/C, CDADL
Testing Tools:	Cantata, McCabe ToolSet
Parser Tools:	PCYACC
Preprocessors:	Decus cpp
Porting Tools:	Wind/U

MACINTOSH TOOLS

A number of software development tools for Macintosh and Power Macintosh are listed in Table 1–5. Compiler offerings include native compilers and cross-platform development tools. There are also a variety of additional software tools of interest.

Table 1–5 Macintosh tools

Tool Category	Tool Names
Compilers:	Symantec C++ for Macintosh, Liant C++/Views, Absoft C/C++, Visual C++ Cross Development Edition
Source Code Checkers:	FlexeLint, CodeCheck
Memory Debugging:	MemCheck

Table 1–5 Macintosh tools *(Continued)*

Tool Category	Tool Names
Testing Tools:	QA Partner
Parser Tools:	PCYACC
Versioning:	Visual SourceSafe

FREE TOOLS — GNU SOFTWARE

GNU software is freely available software for many platforms that is written and maintained by many authors. An organization called the Free Software Foundation (FSF), founded by Richard M. Stallman, started the ball rolling and continues to play the central role in the creation and distribution of GNU software. The distribution rights of GNU software are unique, using a legal form commonly called "copyleft" that preserves the rights to free redistribution by preventing the creation of a proprietary version through modification.

Product Name:	GNU software
Company:	Free Software Foundation
Address:	59 Temple Place, Suite 330, Boston, MA 02111-1307, USA
Phone:	617-542-5942
Fax:	617-542-2652
Email:	gnu@prep.ai.mit.edu, fsf-orders@gnu.ai.mit.edu

GNU software covers many aspects of computer usage, and some of the tools apply to software development in C and C++. Note that a few of the tools in Table 1–6 are not actually produced by the FSF, but are additions to GNU tools.

Table 1–6 GNU-related free tools

Tool	Purpose
gdb	Symbolic debugger
xxgdb	X windows front-end for gdb
Duel	Enhanced commands for gdb
gcc/g++	C/C++ compiler
protoize	Convert K&R C to ANSI C
unprotoize	Convert ANSI C to K&R C
DejaGnu	Automated testing facility

All GNU tools are freely available via FTP from one of the sites shown in Table 1–7; the relevant directory is also shown. Additionally, the FSF offers CDROMs, disks and tapes con-

Table 1–7 GNU software FTP archive sites

Site	Directory	Country
archie.au	/gnu	Australia
ftp.uu.net	/packages/gnu	USA
gatekeeper.dec.com	/pub/GNU	USA
nic.funet.fi	/pub/gnu	Finland
plaza.aarnet.edu.au	/gnu	Australia
prep.ai.mit.edu	/pub/gnu	USA (main site)
src.doc.ic.ac.uk	/gnu	United Kingdom
utsun.s.u-tokyo.ac.jp	/ftpsync/prep	Japan

taining GNU software for sale, and, since this is the primary source of support for the FSF's continued creation of free software, you should consider this alternative. The ordering address is given above. In addition, the FSF offers t-shirts, books, and product documentation. Donations to the FSF are also tax deductible in the United States.

GNU software has been ported to numerous platforms as shown in Table 1–8 below. Some are maintained by the FSF directly, and others are supported by various community-spirited programmers.

Table 1–8 FTP sites of GNU ports not found in the central GNU archives

Platform	FTP site	Directory
Amiga	ftp.funet.fi	/pub/amiga/gnu
Atari	atari.archive.umich.edu	/atari/Gnustuff
OS/2	ftp-os2.cdrom.com	/pub/os2/unix
VMS	ftp.vms.stacken.kth.se	/GNU-VMS and /GNU-VMS/contrib
VMS (gcc binaries)	flash.acornsw.com	VS0169:[LT94A.GNUC_VMS]

FREE TOOLS — COAST TO COAST REPOSITORY (SIMTEL)

The repository is primarily for DOS and Microsoft Windows 3.1, 95 and NT software for IBM PCs and compatibles. There is quite a large number of C/C++ programming tools and libraries archived there and it has mounted up over the years that these archives have been collecting material. The repository is maintained by Coast to Coast Telecommunications,

Inc., which relies on sales of CDROMs containing the archives for support. Ordering information is presented below:

Product Name:	Coast to Coast Software Repository
Company:	Coast to Coast Telecommunications, Inc.
Address:	5850 Dixie Highway Clarkston, MI 48346, USA
Phone:	1-800-900-9960, 810-623-6700
Fax:	810-623-1469
Email:	cdrom@Mail.Coast.NET, or service@coast.net
Web:	http://www.coast.net/

The Coast to Coast Repository can be accessed freely via anonymous FTP at a variety of different mirror sites as shown in Table 1–9. World Wide Web users can also access SimTel files via *http://www.coast.net/* or *ftp://ftp.coast.net/* and Gopher users can use the access path *Gopher.Oakland.Edu.*

Table 1–9 SimTel archive sites

Archive site (IP address)	Directory	Country
archie.au (139.130.23.2)	/micros/pc/SimTel	Australia
ftp.iniaccess.net.au (203.6.129.17)	/pub/SimTel	Australia
ftp.tornado.be (193.121.0.3)	/SimTel	Belgium
ftp.linkline.be (194.51.224.5)	/mirror/simtel	Belgium
ftp.unicamp.br (143.106.10.54)	/pub/simtel	Brazil
ftp.agt.net (198.80.55.1)	/pub/Simtel	Canada
sunsite.dcc.uchile.cl (146.83.4.11)	/pub/Mirror/simtel	Chile
ftp.pku.edu.cn (162.105.129.30)	/pub/simtel	China
pub.vse.cz (146.102.16.9)	/pub/simtel	Czech R.
micros.hensa.ac.uk (194.80.32.51)	/mirrors/simtel	England
src.doc.ic.ac.uk (155.198.1.40)	/pub/packages/simtel	England
ftp.demon.co.uk (158.152.1.44)	/pub/mirrors/simtel	England
ftp.funet.fi (128.214.248.6)	/mirrors/simtel.coast.net	Finland
ftp.grolier.fr (194.51.174.67)	/pub/pc/SimTel	France
ftp.ibp.fr (132.227.60.2)	/pub/pc/SimTel	France
ftp.tu-chemnitz.de (134.109.2.13)	/pub/simtel	Germany

Table 1–9   SimTel archive sites   *(Continued)*

Archive site (IP address)	Directory	Country
ftp.uni-mainz.de (134.93.8.129)	/pub/pc/mirrors/simtel	Germany
ftp.uni-paderborn.de (131.234.10.42)	/SimTel	Germany
ftp.uni-tuebingen.de (134.2.2.60)	/pub/simtel	Germany
ftp.cs.cuhk.hk (137.189.4.110)	/pub/simtel	Hong Kong
ftp.hkstar.com (202.82.0.48)	/pub/simtel	Hong Kong
ftp.unina.it (192.132.34.17)	/pub/simtel	Italy
cnuce-arch.cnr.it (131.114.1.10)	/pub/msdos/simtel	Italy
ftp.flashnet.it (194.21.12.5)	/mirror/simtel	Italy
ftp.riken.go.jp (134.160.41.2)	/pub/SimTel	Japan
ftp.saitama-u.ac.jp (133.38.200.1)	/pub/simtel	Japan
ftp.crl.go.jp (133.243.18.20)	/pub/pc/archives/simtel	Japan
ftp.kornet.nm.kr (168.126.63.7)	/pub/SimTel	Korea
ftp.nowcom.co.kr (203.238.128.34)	/pub/SimTel	Korea
ftp.nuri.net (203.255.112.4)	/pub/Simtel	Korea
ftp.omnitel.net (205.244.196.3)	/pc/simtel	Lithuania
ftp.nic.surfnet.nl (192.87.46.3)	/mirror-archive/software	Netherlands
ftp.vuw.ac.nz (130.195.2.193)	/simtel	New Zealand
ftp.bitcon.no (193.69.224.22)	/pub/micro/pc/SimTel	Norway
ftp.cyf-kr.edu.pl (149.156.1.8)	/pub/mirror/simtel	Poland
ftp.man.poznan.pl (150.254.173.3)	/mirror/simtel	Poland
ftp.icm.edu.pl (148.81.209.3)	/pub/simtel	Poland
ftp.ua.pt (193.136.80.68)	/pub/simtel	Portugal
ftp.is.co.za (196.4.160.8)	/SimTel	S. Africa
ftp.sun.ac.za (146.232.212.21)	/pub/simtel	S. Africa
ftp.uakom.sk (192.108.131.12)	/pub/SimTel	Slov. Rep.
ftp.arnes.si (193.2.1.72)	/software/SimTel	Slovenia
ftp.sunet.se (130.238.127.3)	/pub/pc/mirror/SimTel	Sweden
ftp.switch.ch (130.59.1.40)	/mirror/simtel	Switz.
ftp.ncu.edu.tw (140.115.1.71)	/SimTel	Taiwan
ftp.nectec.or.th (192.150.251.33)	/pub/mirrors/SimTel	Thailand

Table 1–9 SimTel archive sites   *(Continued)*

Archive site (IP address)	Directory	Country
ftp.metu.edu.tr (144.122.1.101)	/pub/mirrors/simtel	Turkey
ftp.cdrom.com (192.216.191.11)	/pub/simtel	CA, USA
uiarchive.cso.uiuc.edu (128.174.5.14)	/SimTel	IL, USA
OAK.Oakland.Edu (141.210.10.117)	/SimTel	MI, USA
wuarchive.wustl.edu (128.252.135.4)	/SimTel	MO, USA
ftp.uoknor.edu (129.15.2.20)	/SimTel	OK, USA
ftp.orst.edu (128.193.4.2)	/pub/mirrors/simtel	OR, USA
ftp.pht.com (198.60.59.5)	/pub/mirrors/simtel	UT, USA

FREE TOOLS — USENET SOURCE ARCHIVES

There are numerous C and C++ tools available in the archives of newsgroups, especially *comp.sources.unix, comp.sources.reviewed* and *comp.sources.misc*. These *comp.sources* groups are archived in many FTP sites around the world. A good place to start is to try the main sites listed in Table 1–10 for any of the sources archives.

Table 1–10 comp.sources archive sites

Archive site (IP address)	Directory	Country
archie.au (139.130.23.2)	/usenet	Australia
ftp.uu.net (192.48.96.9)	/usenet	Falls Church, VA, USA
wuarchive.wustl.edu (128.252.135.4)	/usenet	MO, USA
gatekeeper.dec.com (16.1.0.2)	/pub/usenet/	USA
rtfm.mit.cdu (18.181.0.24)	/pub/usenet	USA

FREE TOOLS — X WINDOWS DISTRIBUTIONS

The X Windows system is a freely available windowing package maintained by the X Consortium. It is available for use on almost any UNIX platform and a number of non-UNIX platforms. In addition to the free source for each X Windows release, there is a suite of tools available in the "contrib" distributions. Although these tools are provided on an "as is" basis, there are quite a few gems available. The archive is quite general, though there are a few development tools of interest as shown in Table 1–11 below.

The X Windows distributions, contributed tools and documentation are distributed on a variety of media by the X Consortium for reasonable prices. The tools are also freely available via FTP to *ftp.x.org* which belongs to the X Consortium. Naturally, this is a busy

Table 1–11   Examples of X11 contribution tools for X Windows

Tool	Purpose
ddd	Graphical front-end for gdb and dbx debuggers
xxgdb	Graphical front-end for gdb debugger
xdbx	Graphical front-end for dbx debugger
xmon	Tracing tool for the X protocol
xcoral	Editor and C/C++ browser

machine and there are a variety of mirror sites. The file "GettingR6" details various methods of obtaining the distributions, including the purchase of CDROMs and FTP mirror sites. This file can be retrieved via FTP from *ftp.x.org*, via the Web as *http://www.x.org/consortium/ GettingX11R6.html*, and by sending the message "send R6 sales" to *xstuff@x.org* via email. An abridged list of mirror sites is shown in Table 1–12 below. The contributed tools are usually in a "*contrib*" or "*R5contrib*" subdirectory.

Table 1–12   Short list of X11 mirror sites for X Windows distributions

FTP site (IP address)	Directory	Location
ftp.x.org (198.112.44.100)	/contrib *or* /R5contrib	MA, USA
ftp.crl.research.digital.com (192.58.206.2)	/pub/X11/contrib	MA, USA
ftp.cs.columbia.edu (128.59.26.5)	/archives/X11R6/contrib	NY, USA
ftp.uu.net (192.48.96.9)	/systems/window-sys/X/	VA, USA
ftp.cs.purdue.edu (128.10.2.1)	/pub/X11/R6	IN, USA
gatekeeper.dec.com (16.1.0.2)	/pub/X11/contrib	CA, USA
ftp.austria.eu.net (192.92.138.34)	/pub/x11/x11r6/contrib	Austria
ftp.eunet.be (192.92.130.1)	/contrib	Belgium
ftp.zel.etf.hr (161.53.65.13)	/pub/X11/contrib	Croatia
ftp.eunet.cz (193.85.1.11)	/pub/x11/R6/contrib	Czech Republic
ftp.denet.dk (129.142.6.74)	/pub/X11/contrib	Denmark
ftp.eunet.fi (192.26.119.1)	/X11R6/contrib	Finland
ftp.inria.fr (192.93.2.54)	/X/contrib-R6	France
ftp.germany.eu.net (192.76.144.75)	/pub/X11/XConsortium/	Germany
sunserv.sztaki.hu (192.84.227.1)	/pub/R6-contrib	Hungary
ftp.ieunet.ie (192.111.39.3)	/pub/R6/contrib	Ireland
ftp.iunet.it (192.106.1.6)	/X11/contrib	Italy

Table 1–12 Short list of X11 mirror sites for X Windows distributions   *(Continued)*

FTP site (IP address)	Directory	Location
ftp.eunet.no (193.71.1.7)	/pub/X11/contrib	Norway
relay.puug.pt (193.126.4.65)	/pub/X11R6/contrib	Portugal
ftp.kiae.su (144.206.136.10)	/x11/X11R6/contrib	Russia
ftp.luth.se (130.240.18.2)	/pub/X11/contrib	Sweden
ftp.switch.ch (130.59.1.40)	/mirror/X11/contrib	Switzerland
ftp.nl.net (193.78.240.13)	/pub/windows/X/contrib	The Netherlands
ftp.britain.eu.net (192.91.199.5)	/pub/X11R6-contrib	UK
ftp.cs.cuhk.hk (137.189.4.57)	/pub/Xcontrib	Hong Kong
ftp.iij.ad.jp (192.244.176.50)	/pub/X/contrib	Japan
sunsite.sut.ac.jp (133.31.30.7)	/pub/archives/X11/R6contrib	Japan
nctuccca.edu.tw (140.111.1.10)	/X/contrib	Taiwan
archie.au (139.130.23.2)	X11/contrib	Australia

FREE TOOLS — LINUX ARCHIVE SITES

Linux is a UNIX-like operating system for 80x86 IBM PC platforms that is freely available. The archive contains a great deal of free software including sources for the operating system, X Windows system, and various utilities. Naturally, there are various C/C++ development tools relevant to this book including ports of GNU tools, X11 *contrib* archives, and various other contributed utilities.

The main archive site for FTP is *sunsite.unc.edu/pub/Linux*. This is a busy machine and there are a variety of mirror sites with an abridged list shown in Table 1–13 and the full list available as file */pub/Linux/MIRRORS* from *sunsite.unc.edu*. The main *sunsite* archive is also available through the Web via *http://sunsite.unc.edu/pub/Linux/welcome.html*. Various commercial vendors also offer CDROMs containing distributions of Linux sources.

Table 1–13 Abridged list of FTP mirror sites for sunsite.unc.edu/pub/Linux

FTP site	Directory	Location
ftp.io.org	/pub/systems/linux/sunsite/	Canada
sunsite.unc.edu (Main site)	/pub/Linux/	Chapel Hill, NC, USA
ftp.cdrom.com	/pub/linux/sunsite/	Concord, CA, USA
ftp.sun.ac.za	/pub/linux/sunsite/	South Africa
ftp.cs.cuhk.hk	/pub/Linux/	Hong Kong
ftp.spin.ad.jp	/pub/linux/sunsite.unc.edu/	Japan

Table 1–13 Abridged list of FTP mirror sites for sunsite.unc.edu/pub/Linux *(Continued)*

FTP site	Directory	Location
ftp.nuri.net	/pub/Linux/	Korea
ftp.nus.sg	/pub/unix/Linux/	Singapore
ftp.nectec.or.th	/pub/mirrors/linux/	Thailand
bond.edu.au	/pub/OS/Linux/	Australia
ftp.univie.ac.at	/systems/linux/sunsite/	Austria
ftp.fi.muni.cz	/pub/UNIX/linux/	Czech Republic
ftp.funet.fi	/pub/Linux/sunsite/	Finland
ftp.loria.fr	/pub/linux/sunsite/	France
ftp.germany.eu.net	/pub/os/Linux/Mirror.SunSITE/	Germany
ftp.kfki.hu	/pub/linux/	Hungary
ftp.italnet.it	/pub/Linux/	Italy
ftp.nvg.unit.no	pub/linux/sunsite/	Norway
sunsite.icm.edu.pl	/pub/Linux/sunsite.unc.edu/	Poland
ftp.cs.us.es	/pub/Linux/sunsite-mirror/	Spain
ftp.switch.ch	/mirror/linux/	Switzerland
ftp.metu.edu.tr	/pub/linux/sunsite/	Turkey
unix.hensa.ac.uk	/mirrors/sunsite/pub/Linux/	United Kingdom

Compilers

*T*he compiler is the most important tool for C or C++ programming. It is so fundamental that it is often not really thought of as a tool in its own right. However, most of the compilers in existence today, commercial or free, have a great many features and are generally of high quality. Making the most of these features is the key to using your compiler effectively as a programming tool.

There is also another important matter to consider: price. In the current market, the value in terms of features that you get for your money seems to depend on the platform. Compilers for DOS and Microsoft Windows have traditionally offered more in the way of an integrated environment at a reasonable price. UNIX platforms typically offer a command-line compiler for batch compilation and programmers often use the free GNU editor "emacs" as a substitute for an integrated environment. Some hardware vendors and third-party software vendors offer integrated graphical development environments for UNIX, and the prices, although typically higher than Windows products, are reasonable if you take into account the higher cost of the underlying hardware.

In addition to commercial tools, there are free compilers for many platforms including UNIX, DOS and Windows, and a number of these compilers are mentioned in the following pages. Although you might fear that you "get exactly what you pay for" when you use a free compiler, a number of these tools are of very high quality. For example, the GNU gcc/g++ compiler from the Free Software Foundation is impressive within the UNIX realm, although perhaps less so in comparison with some of the integrated environments offered by compiler vendors such as the various commercial compilers for Microsoft Windows.

WHAT FEATURES DOES A GOOD COMPILER HAVE?

The term "compiler" is often synonymous with the more general issues of a suite of tools for program development of which the actual *compiler* (i.e., the translating tool that converts C or C++ source code to machine code) is only one of the parts. Thus, the first major feature to look for when evaluating a "compiler" package is whether the compiler is part of an integrated development environment (IDE) including other component tools such as an editor, debugger, browser, visual GUI prototyper, libraries, and many more. Some of these components of an IDE are considered in more detail below.

Editor: The text editor provided for source code editing has a big impact on your productivity as a programmer. Some of the better features to seek include color syntax highlighting and syntax-smart editing (automatic indentation modes, or even fixing typos such as missing parentheses while you code). See Chapter 11 for more on editors.

Browser: Once a project reaches a certain critical mass it outgrows the capabilities of one person to visualize all of its design components. At this point, it is the "browser" tool for source code that aids the programmer in viewing the source code and the overall design. The simplest browser is nothing more than an easy way to skip around source code to find certain variables and functions. This is certainly a powerful feature in itself, but nothing compared to the wonderful graphical views available from a good browser. Some of the graphical views of a program include hierarchy of C++ class inheritance, function call graphs and function flow graphs. Chapter 12 contains a further discussion of browsers.

Debugger: In an analogous manner to a browser displaying views of the nature of source code, a debugger can provide information about the runtime nature of a program's execution. A debugger allows you to go "under the hood" and see exactly what is happening to your program's execution sequence and to the data in variables. This is often the easiest way to identify the cause of a bug. See Chapter 5 for more detailed coverage of debuggers.

Profiler: For performance improvement, a profiler is a necessary tool for programmers to make educated choices rather than guessing (often wrongly) where a program should be optimized. Launching a profiler tool within the IDE is the preferred way of using such a tool. (See Chapter 7.)

Visual programming features One of the major trends in software development is towards "visual" programming — where the developer uses a graphical interface to program instead of typing text. The visual prototyping tools now widely available as part of C/C++ programming environments are a step toward this style of visual programming for one specific component of an application: the GUI. Developing any graphical application is cumbersome via textual means and its inherent graphical nature makes it an obvious target for visual programming. These visual GUI builder components have been well received in the market and greatly ease the GUI development process. For the C/C++ compilers these visual tools typically involve graphical specification of the GUI, and the visual tool will then automatically generate the C/C++ code for the interface, with the appropriate "hooks" back to the non-GUI application code.

Project definition features: The best IDEs offer one-click building of a full project by saving source files, detecting dependencies and compiling all files into the final executable. Project definition features are those that allow you to specify which files are to be included as part of the project. UNIX programmers use the "make" utility for this purpose but a good GUI for doing this is usually more efficient and easier to use.

In addition to the various advanced features of an IDE discussed above, there are a number of features of the compiler itself. These should be taken into account when deciding upon which compiler to use to generate executable files for your project. Some of these features of the compiler (i.e., the translator) include:

C++ features: The changes during the ANSI/ISO C++ standardization process have left many compiler vendors playing catch-up. Make sure the compiler you choose has all the C++ language features that you need. Some of the areas to check include: exceptions, templates, namespaces, casting notations, RTTI, and the boolean type. On the other hand, you might want to avoid some of these areas in the code you write to avoid making your C++ code non-portable to less compliant compilers.

Compilation warnings: The warning messages produced by the compiler can be highly effective in improving code quality and reducing errors — it is like running a static checker every time you compile. Modern C and C++ compilers usually have a large array of warnings, and these should be enabled rather than suppressed.

Run-time error checks: Another useful debugging feature often available in modern compilers is run-time error detection. Compilers often support run-time checking of errors such as stack overflow, NULL pointer dereference, etc. These options should be enabled during the development phase of the program so as to trap any such errors. The options can be disabled when producing the final version to improve efficiency.

Compilation speed: Slow compilation times will reduce your productivity by making you wait for a build to complete. Precompiled headers and changing other compiler options (such as disabling optimizations) can speed up the process for some compilers.

Optimization: The performance of your application at run-time will depend on two factors: your ability to write efficient code, and the compiler's ability to generate fast machine code. Many compiler vendors promote their "global optimization" techniques. Certainly a better optimizer can improve runtime performance, but I would caution against using optimization as the solution to poor performance when code improvement techniques combined with profiling tools will often yield order-of-magnitude improvements. However, optimization is easier to enable than code rewriting, is usually reasonably safe with fewer optimizer bugs in modern compilers, and a little extra speed never hurts!

GCC/G++ — FREE GNU C/C++ COMPILER

The GNU C/C++ compilers, gcc and g++, are a superb free compiler suite for most UNIX platforms. The DOS platform is also supported through the DJGPP port of the GNU compilers. The source for gcc/g++ is freely available from any GNU archive site or redistributor. It is also available on the book's companion CDROM in the gcc directory (also the CDROM djgpp directory).

In my experience, gcc is usually superior to native UNIX C compilers in areas such as conformance to the standard, quality of compiler warnings, execution speed of generated code, and overall reliability (i.e., fewer compiler bugs!). In addition to higher quality, it is also usually substantially cheaper than vendor released compilers!

In early releases, the g++ compiler for C++ was separate from gcc, but now both C and C++ support is available via gcc, and g++ is just another front-end for gcc. Although it isn't currently completely up-to-date with the draft ANSI C++ standard, g++ is still a good choice for programming in the well-defined areas of C++. I expect that g++ will rapidly catch up in the areas of C++ conformance where it is currently lagging. Overall, g++ is a professional quality C++ compiler provided you don't need the newly added fancy features of the C++ language, and usually you don't.

Another important aspect of gcc/g++ is that they offer versions of the standard C and C++ libraries. Complete source code is available, and the C library is quite comprehensive, supporting not only ANSI standard C functions, but also POSIX standard functions and other common semi-standard UNIX library functions. The C++ library, libg++, is also what you would expect from a library of C++ classes, supporting issues like boolean types, strings, etc.

TIP: gcc extensions to C

An interesting feature of gcc is that it offers a number of extensions to ANSI C that can be used to overcome various limitations of standard C. For example, variable argument macros are supported, as is an __FUNCTION__ macro for the current function (similar to the ANSI C macros __LINE__ and __FILE__). There are numerous other small improvements — consult the gcc documentation for details. If you are developing only using gcc and never a platform's native compiler then these improved features are available. The sacrifice is, of course, portability of source code, should you ever wish to support a platform for which gcc is not available (not that there are many).

DJGPP — GNU C/C++ COMPILER FOR DOS

DJGPP is a port of the GNU C/C++ compiler version 2.6.0 to DOS by DJ Delorie. It retains all the features of the GNU compiler with full ANSI C and C++ support. DJGPP is available

Product Name:	DJGPP
Purpose:	Free C/C++ compiler for DOS
Author:	DJ Delorie
Availability:	GNU archive sites as files djgpp*
Mailing List:	Mail to djgpp-request@sun.soe.clarkson.edu

from GNU archive sites and redistributors. It is also to be found on the book's companion CDROM in the `djgpp` directory.

In addition to the basic compiler, there are ports of various other GNU development utilities such as `flex`, `bison`, `gas` and `binutils`. Hence, DJGPP represents a free development environment for those who do not mind using the DOS command-line interface rather than a Windows GUI.

GNU C/C++ FROM FREE SOFTWARE FOUNDATION

Product Name:	GNU tools (gcc, gdb, etc)
Purpose:	Compiler, debugger and related tools
Platforms:	Many including: Solaris, SunOS, AIX, HP-UX, OSF/1, Linux
Languages:	C++, ANSI C, K&R C, Objective-C
Status:	Copyleft
Price:	Free but CDROM prices range $20-$240
Company:	Free Software Foundation
Address:	59 Temple Place, Suite 330, Boston, MA 02111-1307, USA
Phone:	617-542-5942
Fax:	617-542-2652
Email:	gnu@prep.ai.mit.edu, fsf-orders@gnu.ai.mit.edu

The software produced by the GNU project is available from the Free Software Foundation. Since GNU software is free (covered by the GNU General Public License), you pay only for the media costs of the CDROMs. The main advantages to this method of obtaining the GNU tools are avoiding Internet searching and download time, prebuilt binaries, and the availability of commercial support.

CYGNUS SUPPORT — GNU SOFTWARE SUPPORT

Product Name:	GNU Pro Toolkit
Purpose:	Commercial and custom support for GNU development
Platforms:	DOS, Mac, PowerPC, Solaris, SunOS, AIX, HP-UX, OSF/1
Company:	Cygnus Support
Address:	1937 Landings Drive, Mountain View, CA 94043, USA
Phone:	1-800-CYGNUS-1, 415-903-1400
Fax:	415-903-0122
Email:	info@cygnus.com
Web:	http://www.cygnus.com

Cygnus provides commercial support for software produced by the GNU project including prebuilt tested binaries, documentation and various support services. Their claim is to "make free software affordable" by avoiding developer time wasted on building and fixing GNU tools. Cygnus staff include many major GNU contributors — notably the *DejaGnu* automated testing tool developed by Cygnus. Because of this, Cygnus quickly wraps improvements to the GNU tools into fully tested maintenance releases. The GNU tools most fully supported by Cygnus include the gcc/g++ compiler, the gdb debugger, and the *DejaGnu* testing tool.

APOGEE C/C++ COMPILER PACKAGE

Product Name:	Apogee C/C++ Compiler Package
Purpose:	Optimizing compilers for C and C++
Platforms:	Solaris, SunOS, PowerPC (AIX, Windows NT)
Languages:	ANSI C, C++, K&R C
Status:	Commercial Product
Price:	C: $795; C++: $895; both: $1,095
Company:	Apogee Software, Inc.
Address:	1901 South Bascom Ave., Suite 325, Campbell, CA 95008-2207, USA
Phone:	1-800-854-6705; 408-369-9001
Fax:	408-369-9018
Email:	sales@apogee.com

Apogee offers high performance optimizing compilers for C and C++ with particular emphasis on SPARC platforms. Apogee-C supports both ANSI and K&R C, and Apogee-C++ offers an ANSI C++ mode and cfront 2.1/3.0 compatibility modes. Optimization is one of Apogee's strengths with numerous optimizations available. Although the optimizations are too numerous to mention in full, the list includes: constant and copy propagation, dead code elimination, hoisting, strength reduction, loop unrolling, and various inter-procedural optimizations. There is also a parallelizing KAP preprocessor available with Apogee-C.

METAWARE HIGH C/C++ MULTIPLATFORM COMPILER

Product Name:	High C/C++
Purpose:	Optimizing compiler for C and C++
Platforms:	DOS, Extended DOS, Solaris, Solaris-x86, SunOS, PowerPC, RS/6000, HP, NCR/AT&T, embedded-x86
Languages:	ANSI C, C++, K&R C
Status:	Commercial Product
Price:	$595-$2,895
Company:	MetaWare Incorporated
Address:	2161 Delaware Avenue, Santa Cruz, CA 95060- 5706, USA
Phone:	408-429-6382 (429-META)
Fax:	408-429-9273 (429-WARE)
Email:	techsales@metaware.com
FTP:	ftp.metaware.com
Web:	http://www.metaware.com

MetaWare's High C/C++ compiler is an advanced product that is ported to a variety of systems including 32-bit Extended DOS and various UNIX platforms. The Extended DOS version is a 32-bit compiler and includes a source level debugger. The UNIX versions include the GNU gdb debugger which is specially modified to support High C/C++ allowing source level debugging and various C++ debugging features. Finally, High C/C++ versions are also available for cross platform development for embedded PowerPC processors by developing on RS/6000, Sun SPARC, HP or Intel 386/486 and embedded x86 targets.

High C/C++ tracks the ISO C and C++ standards, and the advanced C++ language features that are supported include exception handling, RTTI, new cast notations, namespaces, and templates. There is also special support for C to C++ migration with four levels of C++ support ranging from ANSI C through weak C++ support to full C++ enforcement. Optimization is another strength with eight levels of global optimization including techniques such as loop strength reduction, loop unrolling, function inlining, and global common subexpression elimination, to name a few. The Tools.h++ class library from Rogue Wave is also distributed with High C/C++ — another attractive feature.

EPC ANSI C AND C++ PORTABLE COMPILERS

Product Name:	EPC ANSI C; EPC C++
Purpose:	Compilers for C and C++
Platforms:	Solaris, Solaris-x86, Sequent, SGI, ICL, DG, Unisys, SVR4, NCR/AT&T, Pyramid, NEC, Tandem
Languages:	C++, ANSI C, K&R C
Status:	Commercial Product
Price:	ANSI C from $895; C++ from $995
Company:	Edinburgh Portable Compilers
Address:	1906 Fox Drive, Champaign, IL 61820-7334, USA
Phone:	1-800-372-1110; 217-398-5787
Fax:	217-398-6386
Email:	info@epc.com

EPC offers compilers for a variety of languages including C and C++ that are ported to most UNIX platforms. EPC ANSI C supports both ANSI and K&R C with warnings for constructs where behavior differs. Profiling is available via support for prof and lprof profilers. Performance of generated code is enhanced by offering three levels of optimization: a global optimizer for high-level transformations, code level optimizations and a global instruction scheduler.

EPC C++ is a native-code compiler that tracks the ANSI C++ standard with support for templates, exception handling and RTTI. Bundled with EPC C++ are the AT&T class libraries and Rogue Wave tools.h++ class libraries.

EPC also offers an advanced Motif-based graphical debugger for C and C++ called edb that is bundled with the compilers. There is also sdb support in EPC ANSI C for SVR4 die-hards. Part of the debugger is integration between the compiler, editor and debugger called Code-It. This allows high productivity during the compile-edit-debug cycle. Overall, EPC ANSI C and EPC C++ are strong offerings that have a good reputation.

C++/VIEWS FROM LIANT SOFTWARE CORPORATION

C++/Views is more than a compiler — it is an application development environment supporting many platforms using C++ classes. Included in the product is the C++/Views Constructor

Product Name:	C++/Views
Purpose:	Multi-platform C++ Application Framework
Platforms:	Windows 3.1, Windows NT, OS/2, Mac, PowerPC, Solaris, SunOS, RS6000, DEC Alpha, OSF/1, SGI
Languages:	C++
Status:	Commercial Product
Price:	Windows, NT, OS/2, Mac: $1,499; Motif: $2,499
Company:	Liant Software Corporation
Address:	959 Concord Street, Framingham, MA 01701, USA
Phone:	1-800-833-3678; 508-872-8700
Fax:	508-626-2221
Email:	support@lpi.liant.com
BBS:	508-626-0681

for visual building of interfaces and class browsing. The visual interface builder is a WYSI-WYG tool including a dialog editor, menu editor and bitmap editor. The class browser includes features such as a graphical view of the class inheritance hierarchy graph. Portability of the GUI to the various platforms is achieved through the use of a C++ class library that abstracts visual elements of a GUI, and is mapped to native primitives without the user needing to be concerned with the details. This makes C++/Views an alternative to using different compilers and environments for development of multi-platform application GUIs.

UNIX TOOLS FOR OBJECT FILES, LIBRARIES AND EXECUTABLES

There are a variety of tools available for creation and analysis of UNIX object files, libraries and executables. These tools are listed in Table 2–1.

Table 2–1 UNIX object file tools

Command	Purpose
ar	Archiver for creating libraries
size	Size in bytes of various code segments for object files, libraries and executables
nm	Names of symbols in object files, libraries of executables
lorder	Show linking dependency order for modules
tsort	Topological sort (useful in conjunction with lorder)

Table 2–1 UNIX object file tools *(Continued)*

Command	Purpose
ld	Loader used as the last phase by most compilers
ldd	List dynamic libraries required by an executable
strip	Strip debugging symbols from object files and executables
strings	List all string data in a binary file

The `size` utility is useful for examining the actual size of code for object files, libraries or executables. The output usually consists of a breakdown of the sizes into various segments such as text (executable code), static data, bss (zero-initialized static data), and a total. Writing a simple script to compute the sizes of parts of your project can offer a better metric than SLOC measurement tools.

The nm utility has a number of applications and a perusal of its manual page is well worth the effort. It can be used to report the number of functions and global variables and/or the size of individual functions or global variables. A useful example is finding in which library an undefined identifier is called (if you are on a platform where the linker doesn't report this). The simple idea is to use the "-u" option to report undefined references, and the "-R" option presents the archive name and object file name in the output:

```
nm -R -u *.a | grep myfunc
```

The lorder utility reports on the dependencies of object files. It generates a set of ordered pairs on standard output, which can then be piped to the `tsort` utility to find a topological order. In theory, the sequence

```
lorder *.c | tsort
```

will generate the correct order to list object files in the link phase of compilation; however, I've never heard of any real need for this.

The `ld` command is the linker on most UNIX platforms, and is not limited to use with C/C++ object files. There is not much to say in general about `ld` since it is highly platform specific. Usually it has options for issues like static or dynamic loading, and stripping of object files. Refer to the manual pages.

The `strip` command removes symbol information from object files, libraries and executables. This information is mainly useful for symbolic debugging of an executable and is not crucial to execution. However, stripping an executable mainly serves to decrease disk usage, and does not have much effect, if any, on the size of the image during execution.

The `strings` command is a general tool for handling binary files, but can be useful for dealing with executable files. The output of `strings` is a list of all ASCII strings in the binary file. Although there is usually a lot of noise in the output, it is possible to see string literals or other string data that are part of the executable.

PURELINK FROM PURE SOFTWARE

Product Name:	PureLink
Purpose:	linker tool: replacement for the standard linker
Platforms:	Sun SPARC with SunOS 4 or Solaris 2
Languages:	ANSI C, C++, K&R C
Status:	Commercial Product
Company:	Pure Software, Inc.
Address:	1309 S. Mary Avenue, Sunnyvale, CA 94087, USA
Phone:	408-720-1600, 1-800-353-7873
Fax:	408-720-9200
Email:	info@pure.com, support@pure.com
Web:	http://www.pure.com/

Designed to reduce compilation times, PureLink is a commercial UNIX linking tool that replaces the default "ld" linker. The advantage is faster linking during the final stage of compilation. PureLink is an incremental linker that works by caching information on disk about each object file so that each incremental link has better performance with only the changed object files being analyzed again. In this way, PureLink trades disk space for link speed, and does so quite successfully with noticeable speedup of the link stage for large executable files.

WATCOM C/C++ COMPILER FOR WINDOWS, OS/2 AND NETWARE

Product Name:	Watcom C/C++ compiler
Purpose:	Compiler for Windows and other PC platforms
Platforms:	DOS, Windows 3.1, Windows 95, Windows NT, OS/2, Novell NetWare, Extended DOS
Price:	$350; upgrade — $129; competitive upgrade — $199
Company:	Powersoft Corporation
Address:	415 Phillip St., Waterloo, Ontario, Canada N2L 3X2
Phone:	1-800-265-4555, 519-886-3700
Fax:	519-747-4971
Web:	http://www.watcom.com/ or http://www.powersoft.com

Watcom C++ is one of the "big four" C/C++ compilers for Windows platforms with its advanced IDE for rapid development. The integrated tool suite includes compiler, linker, text editor, debugger, profiler, resource editors and browser. Every aspect of C/C++ application development is available within the Watcom IDE, thereby allowing high productivity. Watcom has a history of advanced optimizing code generation while lagging behind in the area of integrated tools, but this limitation seems to be in the past while the optimization technology remains. The IDE's GUI is more than adequate for effective development with all the components a programmer requires.

The integrated debugger is simple to use with all the usual features such as step into, step over, breakpoints, etc. There is a GUI version for Windows 3.1, Windows NT, and OS/2, and a character mode interface for other platforms. One of its most advanced features is a replay feature to trace applications back to a previous state.

The execution profiler offers advanced features such as bar graph presentation of gathered results. As with the debugger, there is a GUI version for some platforms and a character mode interface for others.

The browser allows analysis of functions and classes but does not allow editing methods directly. There are displays of the inheritance hierarchies and the function call tree that allow visual navigation through the various views of the application.

The IDE has hooks for version control tools such as Intersolv PVCS and RCS or Source Integrity from Mortice Kern Systems. These are independent products that are available from separate vendors.

Watcom supports native code development for Windows 16-bit and 32-bit operating systems. Watcom C++ also distinguishes itself with its broad range of platform support by not being limited to Windows operating systems.

Watcom C++ includes Visual Programmer (from Blue Sky Software) as a visual application prototyping tool. This allows rapid creation of applications by building the visual elements and attaching code blocks to events. The generated code uses MFC and can be modified for the desired functionality.

Project development is also enabled by a variety of resources editors for Windows and Windows NT resources. These allow creation and modification of resources such as dialogs, icons, bitmaps, and cursors.

Windows message spying is supported by a number of features. Messages to windows can be monitored and filtered based on message type and window destination. DDE messages can also be monitored with tracking of registered strings, servers and conversations.

Postmortem debugging is supported by the Dr Watcom feature. This allows analysis of the stack trace leading up to a program fault. Dr Watcom also allows attaching the debugger to a running task, and analysis of NT threads for a task.

SYMANTEC C++ COMPILER FOR WINDOWS

Product Name:	Symantec C++
Purpose:	C/C++ compiler for Windows
Platforms:	Windows 3.1, Windows 95, Windows NT

Price:	$399; competitive upgrade — $199
Company:	Symantec Corporation
Address:	10201 Torre Ave., Cupertino, CA 95014, USA
Phone:	1-800-441-7234, 503-334-6054
Fax:	503-334-7400
AutoFax:	1-800-554-4403, Menu Option #1
Web:	http://www.symantec.com

Symantec C++ is an advanced product featuring a full IDE for application development. The IDE features a full suite of tools including editor, compiler, browser, profiler and debugger. The compiler supports advanced C++ features such as exceptions, templates and RTTI. An advanced feature of the IDE is a BASIC-like scripting language that controls many IDE features and allows customizations of the environment to improve productivity even further.

The integrated browser offers the usual browsing of functions, classes, and methods with the convenient feature that editing is fully supported. Inheritance can be edited in the Hierarchy Editor by clicking and dragging in the tree hierarchy view of the application. The browser is also state-of-the-art in that the views are always available without compilation due to incremental parsing performed by the compiler.

The MultiScope Debugger is fully integrated into the environment. This is a highly advanced debugger with features such as thread views, hardware breakpoints, and a graphical view of data structures. The MultiScope Debugger is discussed more fully in the chapter on debuggers.

The OPTLINK linker is a 32-bit linker that enables fast link times. On top of this, Symantec C++ offers the new NetBuild capability that distributes work across a LAN to other networked machines to offer even faster build times.

Rapid development of applications is supported in a number of ways. The Class Editor and Hierarchy Editor make it easy to create new classes from existing ones. The MFC library is provided without extra charge as part of Symantec C++ and is fully supported. Symantec C++ also supports ODBC, OLE 2.0 and OCX custom controls. The Resource Studio allows editing of all Windows resources including icons, dialogs, bitmaps, menus and fonts. A number of "express agents" ease the developer through various development tasks. ProjectExpress takes the programmer through the IDE steps needed to create a new project. ClassExpress simplifies MFC usage by allowing rapid customization of MFC behavior, such as mapping events to member functions.

SYMANTEC C++ COMPILER FOR MACINTOSH

Product Name:	Symantec C++
Purpose:	C/C++ compiler for Macintosh

Platforms:	Macintosh, Power Macintosh
Price:	$499; upgrade: $149.95
Company:	Symantec Corporation
Address:	10201 Torre Ave., Cupertino, CA 95014, USA
Phone:	1-800-441-7234, 503-334-6054
Fax:	503-334-7400
AutoFax:	1-800-554-4403, Menu Option #1
Web:	http://www.symantec.com

Symantec C++ is available for the Macintosh and Power Macintosh. This is not a port of the Windows version and although the two product lines undoubtedly share some technology, the product feature sets are independent. Symantec C++ for Macintosh offers a full IDE suite of tools including compiler, editor, browser, and prototyping components. The compiler supports multiple inheritance, templates and exceptions. The built-in editor offers color syntax highlighting and automatic indentation modes for rapid code development. The smart incremental linker enables rapid build times.

The Visual Architect feature offers rapid prototyping of GUI applications. This permits visual development of an interface using the GUI elements with automatic generation of the required source code.

The advanced project management system organizes large and complicated projects. The Project Manager tracks changes to files for dependency analysis for rapid builds. There is support for both graphical and scripted control over all aspects of the project.

The built-in class browser allows analysis of classes, members and source code. Editing of source code is possible without leaving the browser. The built-in debugger is also enabled to the source code level and tightly integrated with the compiler to offer full expression evaluation capabilities.

MICROSOFT VISUAL C++ COMPILER FOR WINDOWS

Product Name:	Visual C++
Purpose:	C/C++ compiler for Windows
Platforms:	Windows 3.1, Windows 95, Windows NT, NT Alpha, NT MIPS, NT PowerPC
Price:	$499; upgrade — $299; competitive upgrade — $349
Company:	Microsoft Corporation
Address:	1 Microsoft Way, Redmond, WA 98052-6399, USA
Phone:	1-800-426-9400, 1-800-727-3351

Fax:	206-635-2222, 206-936-7329
AutoFax:	1-800-426-9400
Web:	http://www.microsoft.com/

Visual C++ is an advanced environment for C++ development available from Microsoft. Visual C++ offers an advanced IDE called the Developer Studio that has all the tools a developer requires including compiler, linker, editor, browser, and debugger. The editor provides advanced programmer features such as color syntax highlighting, auto-indentation and multi-file search capabilities. The Developer Studio also offers hooks for other Microsoft tools such as Microsoft Visual Test (automated testing tool) and Microsoft SourceSafe (source code versioning tool), and also for third-party vendors to integrate their tools into the environment.

A lot of effort has gone into making re-use of code and components easier. The Component Gallery is a central store of components including C++ classes and OLE custom controls, that can be dragged and dropped into your application. Visual C++ comes with a lot of already written source code. The Microsoft Foundation Classes (MFC) library offers over 150 classes including basic container classes and Windows GUI programming classes. The MFC library has become a well-accepted library with other vendors such as Watcom and Symantec including it with their compilers, although Borland still offers Object Windows Library (OWL) as an alternative. The Data Access Objects (DAO) classes are also available for object-oriented access to the built-in Jet database engine. Database applications are also enabled through support for Open Database Connectivity (ODBC) for databases such as Microsoft SQL Server, Microsoft Access and ORACLE.

The Visual C++ compiler has advanced support for the latest C++ language features including namespaces, RTTI, templates, exceptions and full Standard Template Library (STL) support. An incremental compiler and linker pair offer fast build times by avoiding recompilation of functions and files that are not really affected by a change, such as a header file modification affecting a class. The only limitation is that the compiler cannot generate both 16-bit and 32-bit code, and so DOS and Windows 3.1 programs need to be compiled by a separate compiler.

The Developer Studio includes an integrated debugger component. The debugger offers source-level debugging and also low-level debugging of assembly, memory and registers. Inspecting values is supported in a few ways by dragging objects into the watch window, by typing the name, or via a DataTip window if you pause the mouse over source code.

The browser provided in the Developer Studio is called ClassView. This presents graphical views of classes and global variables in the project. An important improvement is that these views are available at all times without the need for compilation.

VISUAL C++ CROSS-DEVELOPMENT EDITION FOR MACINTOSH

Product Name:	Visual C++ Cross-Development Edition
Purpose:	C/C++ cross-compiler for Macintosh

Price:	$1,999
Platforms:	Macintosh, Power Macintosh
Company:	Microsoft Corporation
Address:	1 Microsoft Way, Redmond, WA 98052-6399, USA
Phone:	1-800-426-9400, 1-800-727-3351
Fax:	206-635-2222, 206-936-7329
AutoFax:	1-800-426-9400
Web:	http://www.microsoft.com/

The Visual C++ Cross-Development Edition extends the Visual C++ IDE with extra features for creating and debugging Macintosh applications. Use of the Cross-Development Edition requires a Windows host connected to a Macintosh target machine via an ethernet connection using Ethernet AppleTalk or TCP/IP. Development is performed through the Visual C++ Developer Studio running on the Windows host. Debugging is performed by remote execution on the Macintosh target machine with the controlling IDE remaining on the Windows host.

The aim is to migrate your code to Macintosh and use a single source code base for both Windows and Macintosh versions of your application. The application can still use the MFC library or the Microsoft Win32 API and these will be mapped by the portability library to work for the Macintosh version. The goal is up to 90% reuse of the source code, according to Microsoft, with the remainder being code to exploit Macintosh-specific features or code porting those Win32 APIs that are not mapped by the portability library. The Visual C++ resource editor can be used to create resources native to both Windows and Macintosh.

BORLAND C++ COMPILER FOR WINDOWS

Product:	Borland C++ (version 4.5)
Purpose:	C/C++ compiler for Windows
Platforms:	DOS, Windows 3.1, Windows 95, Windows NT
Price:	$499; upgrade — $149.95
Company:	Borland International
Address:	100 Borland Way, Scotts Valley, CA 95066, USA
Phone:	800-233-2444, 510-354-3828
Web:	http://www.borland.com/

Borland C++ is the top-of-the-line C++ compiler offering from Borland for professional developers. Borland C++ includes a full IDE with all the components needed by developers including editor, compiler, project manager, browser, debugger and profiler. The editor is convenient to use and has programming features such as color syntax highlighting, regular expression search, auto-indent, brace matching and multiple undo.

The built-in project manager component allows easy GUI specification of the project. It analyzes dependencies and has support for multiple targets including the ability to create executables, DLLs and libraries in one build.

The compiler supports advanced C++ language features such as templates, exceptions, and RTTI. Borland C++ offers full support for all the major 16-bit and 32-bit Windows platforms in the one box. Applications that run under DOS, Win16 or Win32 can be created within the same IDE.

Borland includes the ObjectWindows Library (OWL) for application prototyping, and thus distinguishes itself by not lining up behind Microsoft to support the MFC library. Borland C++ also includes the OCF library for OLE 2.0 support. It is also possible to use a modified version of MFC with Borland C++ but this is not bundled with the compiler.

There is an integrated debugger in the Borland C++ environment, but I personally prefer the standalone Turbo Debugger product. This debugger is fully featured and discussed in detail in the chapter on debuggers (see page 98).

Borland C++ also has a number of other relevant tools as part of the package, or as separate tools. The memory error detection tool called CodeGuard is discussed on page 85. The postmortem debugging tool WinSpector is examined on page 97.

VISUALAGE C++ FOR OS/2 FROM IBM

Product Name:	VisualAge C++
Platform/s:	OS/2
Company:	International Business Machines Corporation (IBM)
Phone:	1-800-IBM-3333, 520-574-4600, Canada 1-800-IBM-4YOU
Email:	askibm@info.ibm.com
Web:	http://www.ibm.com or http://www.software.ibm.com

VisualAge C++ is a fully integrated development environment for OS/2 using a Presentation Manager (PM) GUI. The major components are the editor, debugger, class browser, compiler, performance analyzer, and a visual GUI builder.

The editor is language sensitive with color syntax highlighting and auto-indentation. The editor is also customizable with control over key mappings, external commands, tool bar configurations, and an emulation mode for the OS/2 EPM editor.

The integrated debugger is a source-level debugger with a PM GUI interface. The source code window can display source code, assembly code, or a mixture. The flow of control commands include facilities to step, run, and set breakpoints. The data display facilities include showing the function call stack, watching variables, and low-level displays of hardware registers, threads, and memory storage. There is automatic heap overwrite checking whenever the debugger restarts the application. Support for debugging PM GUI features includes a 3-D display of all windows showing characteristics and relationships, and a Message Queue Monitor to show current messages.

The browser offers various views of the project. There are graphical displays of the C++ class inheritance hierarchy, function call graph, and file inclusion dependencies. These graphs can show the entire project, or be limited to a particular class such as the view of all ancestor classes of a given class. It is also possible to list program objects by type, by content and by component.

The compiler supports modern C++ features such as templates and exceptions. The output is optimized 32-bit code with optimizations including: instruction scheduling, code hoisting, global register allocation, user code inlining, and various intermodule optimizations. The compiler also permits the coexistance of 16-bit and 32-bit code. VisualAge C++ also includes the IBM Open Class Library that includes Standard (I/O stream, Complex), Data type and Exception, Collection (container classes), Database access (for DB2/2 databases), and User Interface (PM) classes.

The IDE includes a performance analyzer for tuning programs. This creates a trace file during execution that records function calls and returns with the time spent on the stack. This trace file can be analyzed to present a function call graph where each node is sized according to the number of calls to the function, and arc sizes are proportional to the number of calls down that path. This scaling can be turned off to get a simple view of the call graph. Another view of the same data is the "timeline" view that shows the progression of execution time with the function name marked against each point. The simplest view is a listing of each function and the percentage of time spent and the number of calls.

There is a visual GUI builder incorporated as part of the IDE. This allows the visual creation of an interface with automatic generation of C++ code. There is also a Data Access Builder for visually creating classes for DB2/2 database access. This will generate the C++ source, SOM IDL, and SQL scripts, and automatically generate add, update, delete, and retrieve methods for each class.

IBM's System Object Model (SOM) is strongly supported by VisualAge C++ via the Direct-to-SOM (DTS) component. This allows the generation of SOM objects directly from the compiler, with debugger support for SOM objects, and the browser showing them in different color. The data access builder also allows generation of SOM classes or IDL code.

ABSOFT C/C++ COMPILER FOR MACINTOSH

Product Name:	Absoft C/C++
Platforms:	Macintosh, Power Macintosh, Windows NT/PowerPC, AIX
Price:	from $399
Company:	Absoft Corporation
Address:	2781 Bond St, Rochester Hills, MI 48304, USA
Phone:	810-853-0050

Fax:	810-853-0108
Web:	http://www.absoft.com

Absoft C/C++ compiler is a native Macintosh compiler and development environment for Macintosh and Power Macintosh, supporting C++ with templates, exceptions and STL, and ANSI C and K&R C. Optimizations include code hoisting, strength reduction, code motion and subexpression elimination. The compiler has a native Macintosh GUI interface, and good support for Macintosh toolbox and libraries. Apple Events, Publish, Subscribe, and Scripting are supported.

There are a number of additional tools provided with Absoft C/C++ including a Create-Make utility, an optimizing Power-Link linker, the Fx debugger, and debug trace support. The Fx debugger also offers a native Macintosh GUI interface.

NDP C/C++ FROM MICROWAY

Product Name:	NDP C/C++
Platforms:	DOS, Windows 3.1, Windows 95, Windows NT (80x86 and DEC Alpha), OS/2, Linux, PowerPC, DEC
Price:	$695-$1,295
Company:	Microway, Inc.
Address:	Research Park Box 79, Kingston, Mass. 02364, USA
Phone:	508-746-7341
Fax:	508-746-4678
Email:	info@microway.com

NDP C/C++ is a compiler that generates native code for a variety of platforms that are based on the Pentium and DEC Alpha processors. Supported languages include K&R C, ANSI C, and C++ with strict or soft ANSI compliance. NDP C/C++ offers fast numeric code and assembly language access via register aliased variables.

SAS/C CROSS-PLATFORM UNIX TO MVS COMPILER

Product Name:	SAS/C Cross-Platform Compiler
Platforms:	MVS, Sun, RS/6000, HP
Company:	SAS Institute, Inc.

Address:	SAS Campus Drive, Cary, NC 27513, USA
Phone:	919-677-8000
Fax:	919-677-4444

The SAS/C Cross-Platform Compiler is a compiler that offers the advantages of cross-platform development for mainframe software. The compiler runs on a UNIX workstation and generates code for the MVS and CMS mainframe environments. Programmers work using the tools of the UNIX environment and the SAS/C compiler to create prelinked output files, and then use TCP/IP to transfer files to the mainframe for link-edit processing in conjunction with the mainframe-based SAS/C Compiler.

The advantages offered by cross-platform development include convenience and reduced cost. Programmers working under UNIX can use all the traditional development tools. By doing all development work away from the mainframe, the amount of costly mainframe CPU usage is significantly reduced.

SNiFF+ DEVELOPMENT ENVIRONMENT FROM TAKEFIVE SOFTWARE

Product Name:	SNiFF+
Platforms:	UNIX — Solaris, Solaris-x86, SunOS, HP-UX, DEC, AIX, DG, SGI, Ultrix, Linux, Windows support planned
Price:	$2,990 (single user floating license)
Languages:	C, C++, Java, CORBA IDL, Fortran
Company:	TakeFive Software
Address:	20823 Stevens Creek Blvd, Suite 440, Cupertino, CA 95014, USA
Phone:	1-800-418-2535, 408-777-1440 (Europe: +43-662-457915)
Fax:	408-777-1444 (Europe: +43-662-4579156)
Email:	info@takefive.com (Europe: info@takefive.co.at)
Web:	www.takefive.com

SNiFF+ is an integrated development environment for UNIX C/C++ programming that uses an original approach. Rather than reinventing all the various components, SNiFF+ integrates with existing compilers, debuggers and other tools through the use of a powerful "adaptor" feature called "sniffaccess" for integrating third-party tools. Based on this technology, SNiFF+ is designed to automate many aspects of development of large projects with the tools already used by developers in the project.

Project management is the central aim of SNiFF+. Hence, the primary task when employing SNiFF+ is to define the extent of the project. This is achieved through the GUI by specifying the various files and their type. There are many file types with in-built support including C source, header file and more complicated types such as `lex` and `yacc` input files. SNiFF+ uses this project information as the basis for most of its project management tasks.

Build management is an important area that can be controlled by SNiFF+. Existing compilers and `make` utilities are used to do the build, and SNiFF+ can automatically generate additional files such as dependencies and macro files to support the `make` process.

The editors supported are a built-in editor provided as part of SNiFF+ and integration with various `emacs` variants. The built-in editor offers powerful features such as multiple undo/redo, bracket and quote matching, and comment/uncomment commands. SNiFF+ also supports `emacs` 19 and `xemacs` and `lemacs` variants as integrated editors. The editor is integrated to offer features such as automatic jumping to the source from compilation errors in the build process.

Versioning and configuration management is another major area of features. SNiFF+ offers integrations with various versioning tools including SCCS, CVS, GNU RCS, IBM CMVC, Atria Clear Case, and others via the powerful adaptor technology. This places a GUI front-end over whatever versioning and configuration management tool you currently use. There is built-in diff/merge support for two-way and three-way file version analysis.

Debugging is supported by a GUI front-end on top of various existing debuggers. The GUI shows the command-line dialog in the window with various menus and dialogs for performing various activities. The debugger is synchronized with the editor to display the current source code. Common actions such as printing values can be performed by selecting identifiers in the window and applying menu commands. A convenient Attach dialog shows all running processes to simplify attaching to a running process. Breakpoints are also displayed and managed through a separate convenience dialog. The debuggers currently supported include `gdb`, `dbx`, `xdb`, HP `dde`, SCO `dbxtra` and DEC `ladbx`.

Code browsing is supported by various features based on an in-built "fuzzy" parser for C and C++ code. The parser examines source code to gather information about the project and its fuzzy nature comes into play in that it does not need complete macro definitions or header files to be workable, although supplying them will improve accuracy. Symbols in a project can be browsed in a list with filtering based on regular expression and the category of the symbol (i.e., variable, macro, `typedef`, etc). A class browser facility allows viewing of class components such as methods and members. The C++ class inheritance hierarchy can be shown graphically for the project or limited to a particular root class. The Retriever component is available to find all uses of a given symbol based on text matches and more complicated built-in patterns such as assignments. The cross-referencing component is highly featured with presentation of symbol uses based on many attributes. For example, it can distinguish between reads and writes, and between various categories of symbols such as macros, type names and variables.

Documentation is another important aspect of the project that can be managed using SNiFF+. There are features for automatic generation of internal project documentation based on source code. Documentation about symbols can be automatically generated based on a documentation "frame" that specifies the format of the output. This documentation can be exported to various formats including PostScript, HTML, RTF, and MIF.

WISH — SUPER DEBUGGING COMPILER WISH LIST

Have you ever noticed how most of the compilers available have marketing information making a big deal out of their super-duper global optimizer without mentioning any debugging features? Well, my number one wish as a C/C++ programmer is a compiler that saves MY time rather than the processor's, and the biggest waste of my time is debugging. Compilers are in an incredibly powerful position for providing useful error reduction features to improve overall productivity and it is time they started flexing some of that muscle. Some of the areas where the compiler could protect the programmer from pitfalls include:

1. compile-time warnings
2. link-time warnings
3. run-time error checking
4. debugging libraries

Let's look at each of these issues in turn.

Compiler warnings: There are literally hundreds of common coding errors that can be caught during compilation. Checker tools are just half-implemented compilers, so there's no reason your compiler can't be a checker. Some warnings could even be errors (!) since they are so obviously wrong — for example, does your compiler permit you to run a program containing `fprintf("Hello World\n")`? Admittedly, compilers tend to be rather unintelligent robot-like beings and attempting to get them to prevent compilation might cause them to accidentally disallow valid code. Nevertheless, at least a warning would be helpful and thankfully the quality of compiler warnings is gradually increasing across the board.

Link-time warnings: Object files already contain a lot of information and most linkers do catch some common errors (e.g., function and global variable multiple definitions). However, there are a great many error checks that would help. The most obvious check is lint-like error checking of the types of global variable and function uses and definitions across modules. As another example, how many run-time crashes or segmentation faults have you had from adding a struct field and then forgetting to re-compile some source files or to rebuild your dependencies? A linker could check structure definitions in each object file for consistency. Similarly, a number of other inconsistencies could be detected: different compile-time options on each file (e.g., DOS memory model), inconsistent C++ inline function definitions or C++ class definitions.

Run-time error checking: Most compilers already provide a small number of run-time error checks such as stack overflow checking. However, there are so many more run-time error checks that could be performed. A short list includes array bounds checking, pointer validation, uninitialized variables, and even NULL pointer dereferences (is the typical DOS compiler's "null pointer write" message at the end of a program really much use in tracking down the error?). An interesting point to note is that many of these forms of run-time checking are currently available from third-party software vendors as specialized tools.

Debugging libraries: I wish that compiler vendors would provide two versions of their standard C libraries, an ordinary version and a debug version. The debug version should detect a variety of common run-time errors such as `malloc/free` mismatches, invalid file operations (e.g., write on a file opened for read) and bad arguments to any library functions. In addition, it would be useful to have the ability to be informed, via a window of run-time warnings or something similar, of anomalous but not necessarily erroneous events such as memory allocation failure, library errors that set `errno`, library errors that don't set `errno` (e.g., some mathematical functions underflowing) and low level resource failures such as file write failed.

The main argument against these various error detection features seems to be along the lines of efficiency (surprised?) — slower compilation, slower execution. While this may be true to a certain extent of compilation and link-time warnings, a huge number can be detected with only trivial slow-down. As for run-time checking and debugging library versions, there's no need to leave the debugging code in the final shipped executable. So the next time you go to buy a compiler, ask about the number of warnings and the level of run-time error checking. Maybe soon the vendors will improve in this area.

Source code checkers

The analysis of source code can provide many checks for common errors and is an important debugging technique. The UNIX `lint` utility is probably the best-known example of error detection by the examination of source code. Unfortunately, UNIX `lint` is also one of the least impressive source checkers available and this has probably contributed to the slow acceptance of checkers as an important tool in the software development process.

In addition to its role in debugging, the source checker can be useful to enforce coding style standards, check for common portability pitfalls, and as an automated assistant to the code inspection method of testing code. There are now a variety of free, shareware and commercial source checkers available for C, and also a handful for C++ checking.

CHECKERS IN ANSI C AND C++

It is occasionally said that UNIX `lint` and other checkers have no useful purpose in ANSI C or C++. Although it is true that the importance of `lint` is somewhat reduced, it is certainly wrong to say that UNIX `lint` has no use, and even less accurate to make this observation about the more advanced `lint`-like tools that are now available commercially and also in the public domain. In my opinion, the UNIX `lint` utility has given source checkers a bad name because it only checked for a very small number of errors.

The main area where UNIX `lint`'s importance is reduced is in the area of function argument type checking. Pre-ANSI C compilers performed no type checking of argument types and parameter types, nor even of whether the correct number of arguments was passed. `lint` was very important in identifying such argument passing errors. The advent of ANSI C has meant that prototyped functions can be used (*must* be used in C++), and these have the types and number of arguments checked by the compiler. However, there are still instances in ANSI C where the argument passing errors can arise:

   a. An ANSI C compiler is used with older code containing nonprototyped functions.
   b. A function is called in a file where it has not previously been declared (i.e., no previous definition or prototype declaration has been supplied).

The UNIX `lint` utility also has importance in that it checks for a number of other common errors that can occur as often in ANSI C or C++ as in pre-ANSI C. Such errors include null effect statements, precedence errors, and type mismatch of global variable definitions with their `extern` declarations. However, UNIX `lint` does only check for a few such errors, whereas some of the newer `lint`-like tools check for hundreds of common coding errors.

CHECKERS VERSUS RUN-TIME ERROR DETECTION

An important issue to address is how source checking tools compare with the many run-time error checking tools that are now available (see Chapter 5). In many ways, the two classes of tools complement one another and it is recommended that both be used if the budget can afford it (even if it can't, there are various free versions with a reasonable level of functionality in both tool classes!). But if it comes down to a choice between one or the other, my opinion is that run-time checking tools are more valuable. The various advantages and disadvantages are examined below.

Errors detected: Source checkers typically offer a huge range of errors, whereas the typical run-time error checking tool offers quite a narrow range of errors caught. However, the errors caught at run-time are usually the worst kind of errors (memory stomps, `malloc`/ `free` or `new`/`delete` bugs), which are a class of errors that checkers will usually not find since they depend on dynamic flow of control, rather than on static issues. On the other hand, source checkers will often find incredibly obscure bugs or portability problems.

Code coverage: One area in which source checkers excel is that they offer 100% coverage of code. Every line of code in the project is checked for errors. This differs from run-time error detection, and even from any form of testing, which will only test the given dynamic sequence of code.

Multiplatform code: Another advantage of checkers appears if your project supports multiple platforms. If you have a checker on a given platform, you can use this platform to check the source code for any projects, even those for different platforms! If the project code depends on `#ifdef`'s, then multiplatform checking can be merely repeated "make lint" executions with different `-I` and `-D` options. Make sure you check licensing agreements to see if this usage is permissible for commercial checking tools.

GUIDELINES FOR CHECKER USAGE

When running a checker on the source code for an application, there is a natural tendency to assume most warnings are harmless. However, even apparently harmless warnings such as "code not reached" or "variable defined but not used" can identify very serious bugs in the code. All warnings should be treated as bugs until proven otherwise.

Make your code warning free. When a warning message is produced, the source code should be examined for a possible bug. Even if it is correct, it is good practice to rewrite it so as to no longer provoke the warning, as is the case for any warning from a checker. For example, consider a warning about an assignment in a conditional test such as:

```
if (fp = fopen(fname, "r"))
```

A coding style that resolves this warning on the GNU C/C++ compiler adds an extra set of parentheses around the offending subexpression:

```
if ((fp = fopen(fname, "r")))
```

However, I consider the above solution to be inelegant and personally I think such statements should be recoded more cleanly so that the assignment is not even in the `if` expression:

```
fp = fopen(fname, "r");
if (fp != NULL)
```

In some cases it is impractical to modify the code to prevent the warning. It may also be inadvisable for maintenance of legacy code because of the risk of adding new bugs (i.e., the old "if it ain't broke, don't fix it!" rule). In this case, the particular warning can often be suppressed by a compiler option. This should be the last resort, not the first!

USING YOUR COMPILER AS A SOURCE CHECKER

Using all the compile-time warnings supported by a compiler can be a highly effective (and inexpensive!) form of source checking — it is like running a source checker every time you compile. Modern C and C++ compilers often have a wide variety of warnings, and these should be enabled rather than suppressed.

A particularly good example of using a compiler as a source checker is the free GNU C/C++ compiler from the Free Software Foundation (FSF). This tool is examined in detail in the section "GNU C/C++ from Free Software Foundation" on page 21, but one feature that

that stands out is the high quality of the warnings available. This makes `gcc`/`g++` a good candidate for a de facto source checking tool.

Most warnings about common coding bugs are enabled using the `-Wall` option but a few other warning options that are not implied by `-Wall` may be worth considering; the command line I use in development is:

```
gcc -Wall -Wpointer-arith -Wtraditional
```

The `-Wpointer-arith` option turns on warnings about `void*` pointers used in arithmetic (since `gcc` has an extension that treats `sizeof(void*)` as 1 rather than illegal), and the `-Wtraditional` option warns about code which may differ on older machines with "traditional" C. For example, macro expansion within a string constant is permitted by some older preprocessors.

The `-O` option, which enables the optimizer, also allows a number of other error checks, because the optimization phase creates more flow of control information allowing further error checks. For example, `-O` will catch many uses of an uninitialized variable — when combined with the `-Wuninitialized` option.

The options `-ansi` and `-pedantic` can also be used to check strict conformance of programs to the ANSI C standard.

Even if you don't use `gcc` for the actual compilation, it can still be beneficial to use `gcc` as if it were a standalone source checker. You just have to remember to throw away the object files it creates. The `-o` option can be used to make `gcc` put the object file in an unused file such as "`dummy.tmp`"; this should work even with the `-c` option.

C++ COMPILERS FOR CHECKING C CODE

The C++ language has a more restrictive type system, and thus applying a C++ compiler to C code can find some common type errors. In addition, there are a few obscure coding features that are permitted in C, but not in C++, and thus your C++ compiler has to check for them, whereas the C compiler does not. Some of the areas where a C++ compiler can improve matters include:

- non-prototyped function calls disallowed
- `enum` usage type checking
- global variables (multiple definitions)
- `switch`/`goto` bypassing an initialization
- declarations squeezing out the null byte: `char s[3]="abc";`

However, there are some irritations in using a C++ compiler to check C code due to incompatibilities between the languages. One problem is the extra keywords in C++ — you can't call a variable "`new`", or a function "`delete`". Fortunately, these problems are reasonably rare and can be converted easily.

The most annoying feature is that the `void*` type is treated differently — converting `void*` to another pointer type requires a type cast in C++, but it doesn't in ANSI C. The main problem is the `malloc` and `calloc` functions, which return `void*`, and so every call to these functions requires a type cast on the return value in C++ programs:

```
str = (char*) malloc(10);   // Type cast in C++
```

In fact, we have the rather foolish situation where the `malloc` return value was type cast in pre-ANSI C, then not required in ANSI C, and now again required for C++. If you are lucky, your C++ compiler will have the extension of making complaints about converting `void*` without a type cast into a warning that can be disabled rather than an error.

THE UNIX LINT CHECKER

The `lint` checker is a standard UNIX tool usually bundled with the operating system and the distinction of being the first C checker. Unfortunately although it was once state-of-the-art, it pales in comparison to newer checkers because of the limited set of errors detected. A number of slightly different versions are available on different UNIX variants, but the errors reported by these versions are comparable. A few UNIX platforms offer only a pre-ANSI C version of `lint`. If so, you may be able to use the `unprototize` filter to remove this limitation; see page 180. However, the majority of vendors have upgraded `lint` to handle ANSI C syntax. Unfortunately, I am not aware of a standard UNIX `lint` version for C++.

Some of the errors commonly identified by `lint` are shown in Table 3–1; the exact format of the error messages will depend on which version of `lint` you are running.

Table 3–1 Errors detected by lint

Error	Example
Function arguments have wrong types	`sqrt(2)`
Variable used before set	`char*s; strcpy(s,t);`
Null effect statement	`x<<1;`
Nonportable character comparison	`char c; if (c == EOF)`
Redefinition hides earlier definition	`{ int ; ... { int i; }}`
Function `return(e);` and `return;`	
Evaluation order is undefined	`a[i]=i++;`
Variable defined but not used	
Possible pointer alignment problem	
Function return value always ignored	
Function return value sometimes ignored	
Long assignment may lose accuracy	`int x; x = 100000;`
Type cast of integer to pointer	`char *p = (char*)100`

Generally speaking, `lint` finds very few of the large number of possible coding mistakes. Its major use in the past has been to find errors in type checking, particularly of function parameters and arguments. The introduction of ANSI C compilers with function prototyping has reduced the importance of lint, but lint can still find type errors when using multiple files and independent compilation, whereas compilers may fail to detect such errors (good environments using smart compilers and linkers can detect these type errors at link-time, but few currently do).

The lint utility also finds such errors as variables not initialized before use, functions failing to return a value (i.e., falling through to the right brace), and functions used inconsistently. In addition to potential bugs, lint examines the source for wasteful code including statements not reached and variables declared but not used.

Problems with lint

Some implementations of lint are not particularly useful. This is not because the messages produced are incorrect, but because of the deluge of distracting messages that appear, concealing any important messages. It becomes necessary to search through every single message for relevant problems, or to painstakingly modify your code to resolve each message (e.g., delete unused variable declarations). A particular case in point is the "possible pointer alignment problem" warning message, which is often produced by lint when it sees any use of malloc. Other versions of lint are not aware of the generic pointers to void (i.e., malloc's return type in ANSI C is void*) and therefore warn about casting the value returned by malloc to some other type.

More recent implementations have largely solved this problem of too much error message output. A good implementation I have seen prints out only the important messages on a line-by-line basis, saving less dangerous warnings for a summary at the end (e.g., variables not used). The problem with malloc has also been alleviated, presumably by making lint aware of the type void*. This makes lint a very powerful tool without the annoyances. When a program doesn't run as expected, it is worthwhile to test it with lint before using other debugging methods.

lint options

There are a large number of command-line options for lint. A number of the options control whether a particular warning is enabled or disabled. Unfortunately, there is inconsistency between various implementations of lint because various options are on/off by default and the option toggles the options; on some systems it will enable the warning, and on other systems it will disable it. Such options are shown in Table 3–2 using both modes of "enable" and "disable"; consult your local documentation to determine the effect on your system.

Table 3–2 Important lint options

Option	Meaning
-a	Enable/disable warnings about long assignments
-b	Enable/disable warnings about unreachable break statements
-c	Enable/disable warnings about type casts

Table 3-2 **Important lint options** *(Continued)*

Option	Meaning
-Dmacro	Define macro name (as for cc)
-h	Enable/disable heuristic error checks (e.g., null effect)
-Idir	Directory to search during #include (as for cc)
-n	Disable checking against standard lint library
-olib	Create lint library
-p	Enable checking against portable lint library
-Umacro	Undefine macro name (as for cc)
-u	Enable/disable warnings about unused functions and variables
-v	Enable/disable warnings about unused function parameters
-x	Enable/disable warnings about unused external variables

Conditional compilation using lint

lint defines a preprocessor identifier "lint". This can be used to hide dubious lines of code from lint to stop it complaining:

```
#ifndef lint
    ...        /* not checked by lint */
#endif
```

For example, one use of this macro is to prevent lint from complaining about "constants in conditional context" when using fancy macro tricks. The "do-while(0)" trick for multi-statement macros and the "if(1){}else" removal method are good examples. Consider the following macros:

```
#define SWAP(x,y) \
    do{ int tmp = x; x = y; y = tmp; }while(0)
  #define DPRINTF \
    if(1){}else   /* remove debug statements */
```

Whenever SWAP or DPRINTF is used, lint will complain about the tests of the constants 0 and 1. A simple method of suppressing these annoying warnings is to use conditional compilation based on the lint macro:

```
#ifdef lint
#    define ZERO  strcmp("a","a")
#    define ONE  (!strcmp("a","a"))
#else /* not lint */
#    define ZERO  0
#    define ONE   1
#endif
  ...
#define SWAP(x,y)   \
```

```
        do{ int tmp = x; x = y; y = tmp; }while(ZERO)
#define DPRINTF  \
        if(ONE){}else    /* remove debug statements */
```

This works because `lint` is not clever enough to identify the `strcmp` function calls as constants. Note that there is no loss in efficiency because the function calls are never compiled into object code. The compiler never sees them and only `lint` sees the `strcmp` calls.

lint comment directives

Directives can be given to `lint` from within the program. `lint` recognizes special comments, such as `/*NOTREACHED*/` and `/*NOSTRICT*/`.

The `/*NOTREACHED*/` comment specifies that the current position cannot be reached by flow of control. The most common necessity for this comment directive is because `lint` does not understand functions that do not return, such as `exit` or `longjmp`. For more information on these directives, refer to your manual entry for `lint`.

Incremental linting using make

When used with a large project, the command:

```
lint *.c
```

starts to become very slow. Not only does it take a long time for `lint` to produce the final results, but there is also the disadvantage that all files are checked, even if only one has changed. A better method is to use the `-c` option to `lint`.

The `-c` option causes `lint` to produce its own version of an object file for each source file. This is not the same sort of object file as produced by the compiler, but the idea is similar. These object files contain information for the global analysis phase of `lint`; that is, the last messages from `lint` indicating things such as which functions have inconsistent argument types, or return values that are always ignored. The filename extension of `lint` object files is ".ln"; for example, the command:

```
lint -c file.c
```

will produce the object file "file.ln" with the ".ln" filename suffix. In the process it will also identify any "local" anomalies such as a "null effect" statement.

One method of using `lint` in a `makefile` is examined below:

```
.c.ln:
    lint -c $*.c

LINTOBJS=file1.ln file2.ln file3.ln    # lint object files
lint: $(LINTOBJS)
    lint $(LINTOBJS)
```

The method is fundamentally the same as that used for incremental production of the executable version with the compiler. The command to use is:

```
make lint
```

The make utility will identify which lint object files are out of date with respect to the source files, and will apply "lint -c" to these files to produce the lint object files (and also find any local errors). Once all the lint object files have been updated, lint is applied to all of them to produce the global error listing. In this way, only source files that have changed are "relinted," which saves time (since processing all the object files is much faster) and also avoids reexamining warning messages about unchanged files.

The above makefile can be slightly improved by using the UNIX touch utility. The problem is that even if all source files are unchanged, the global analysis phase will still occur. The solution is to use a dummy file called "lint" that indicates whether all the object files have been examined before. The modified makefile lines are:

```
lint: $(LINTOBJS)
     lint $(LINTOBJS)
     touch lint    # update dummy file
```

When this modification is made, the make utility will respond with "lint is up to date" when all source files are unchanged since the last "make lint" command.

PC-LINT/FLEXELINT FROM GIMPEL SOFTWARE

Product Name:	PC-lint/FlexeLint
Purpose:	Source code checker for C and C++
Platforms:	PC-lint — DOS, Windows NT, Windows 95, OS/2 FlexeLint — UNIX (lots), VMS, MVS, Amiga, Mac (any platforms with K&R or ANSI C compiler)
Languages:	ANSI C, C++, K&R C
Status:	Commercial Product
Price:	PC-lint C/C++ — $239; FlexeLint — $998 and up
Company:	Gimpel Software
Address:	3207 Hogarth Lane, Collegeville, PA, 19426, USA
Phone:	610-584-4261
Fax:	610-584-4266
Email:	info@gimpel.com
Key Points:	• C++ common error checking • C common error checking • Very strong type checking • Highly configurable

Gimpel Software has produced a highly advanced source code checking analysis tool for C and C++, based on the same principle as lint — detection of erroneous or non-portable code constructs. There is little difference between PC-lint and FlexeLint other than pricing and platforms. They both check for coding errors in C and C++, and a C-only version is available for FlexeLint. I reviewed PC-lint 5.0 for DOS in the past, and more recently pushed a purchase order for FlexeLint through my company's bureaucracy, which is a grand feat that should indicate my high regard for this product. I am now a frequent, although not frequent enough, user of FlexeLint for Solaris.

PC-lint/FlexeLint is one of the few checkers that handles C++ code. Some of the common C++ errors detected are initializer ordering, non-`virtual` destructors and missing copy constructor or assignment operator in a class where the constructor uses `new`. This is just a sample and there are many C++ warnings.

Even if we restrict the discussion to C error checking and ignore C++ features, PC-lint/ FlexeLint is far better than the UNIX lint in numerous ways. It has a much larger set of error checks and convenient suppression of individual warnings that the programmer considers unimportant. The level of error checking is very impressive with hundreds of distinct messages which you can receive from PC-lint/FlexeLint. The tradition of UNIX `lint` continues in that a large number of the checks relate to types and their use across multiple files. The type checking is as strict as a good ANSI compiler by default, but can be made even stricter by using "strong types", which allow `typedef`'d types to be treated as separate types and mismatches to be caught (e.g., misusing your own `Boolean` type). Naturally, type checking can also be made "looser" by setting the appropriate options.

In addition to type-related errors, there are a multitude of common programming errors that are detected. The very long list includes evaluation order, `printf` formats, dubious indentation, returning an auto variable address, missing `break` in `switch` (causes fall-through) and suspicious semicolons.

The configuration options available are also impressive. Options can be passed at the command-line, in option files, and even within program comments (much more general than UNIX `lint`'s `/*NOTREACHED*/` facilities, which incidentally are also supported by PC-lint). Messages can be suppressed individually by number, by ranges of numbers, within system headers only, within individual files only, for specific identifiers, and the list goes on. In addition to message suppression, there are many more options, too numerous to mention fully; notable are the "size" options allowing specification of the byte size of integral types, and the many "flag" options which specify various aspects of PC-lint behavior (e.g., whether `char` is `signed` or `unsigned`).

The latest version PC-lint 7.0 offers an advanced technique called "value tracking" which refers to analysis of the possible values a variable can hold at any usage. Values are tracked across statements to detect cases where an error is likely. Additionally, PC-lint 7.0 has improved checking of C++ classes and various new warnings related to preprocessor macros with potential operator precedence or side-effect errors.

Overall, I am very impressed by PC-lint/FlexeLint — it is an excellent source checker and its regular usage should greatly reduce the time spent debugging.

CODECHECK FROM ABRAXAS SOFTWARE

CodeCheck is a very powerful and versatile static analysis tool that applies to both C and C++. Its programmable interface makes it useful for a variety of tasks including error detection, porting, style analysis, software metrics and standards adherence. CodeCheck is a com-

Product Name:	CodeCheck
Purpose:	Source code checker for C and C++
Platforms:	DOS, Windows 3.1, Windows 95, Windows NT, OS/2, Macintosh, Amiga, Atari, PowerPC, VMS, MVS, UNIX (Solaris, Solaris-x86, SunOS, HP-UX, AIX, OSF/1, Ultrix, DG, NCR/ AT&T, ICL, Sequent, Unisys, Pyramid, Bull and others)
Languages:	ANSI C, C++, K&R C
Status:	Commercial Product
Price:	$495 DOS/Win; $995 OS/2, Win NT; $1995 UNIX
Company:	Abraxas Software, Inc.
Address:	5530 SW Kelly Ave., Portland, OR 97201, USA
Phone:	1-800-347-5214, 503-244-5253
Fax:	503-244-8375
Email:	sales@abxsoft.com
FTP	ftp://ftp.abxsoft.com
Web:	http://www.abxsoft.com

mercial tool with a variety of supported platforms including DOS, Windows, OS/2, VMS and UNIX.

CodeCheck can be used as a source code checker for debugging and testing, but can also be used to enforce coding style guidelines and compute code metrics. The main difference between CodeCheck and other lint-like checking tools is that every execution requires a "rule file" in addition to the source files being checked. This specialized design to support multiple rule files is what gives CodeCheck its high level of flexibility. For example, you can automate compliance checking of your corporate or project coding standards.

There are a variety of example rule files shipped with CodeCheck, including files for error checking, portability checking, style checking and computing code metrics (e.g., Halstead's size metric and McCabe's complexity metric). There are even a few neat rule files such as "wrapper.cc" to detect header files that aren't "wrapped" using #ifdef, and "indent.cc" to check for correct indentation.

You can also write your own rule files. Rule files are set out in a similar manner to C code using if statements, variables and function calls. The if statements test a variety of built-in variables which are set during the parsing performed by CodeCheck. The following excerpt from an example rule file checks for macro parameter misuse by testing the built-in variable pp_arg_paren:

```
if (pp_arg_paren)
    warn(102, "Enclose macro parameters in parentheses.");
```

The parser upon which this checking is built can be configured in many ways. For example, you can choose between K&R, ANSI C, and a variety of C++ dialects. There are also minor options, such as a flag to enable nested comments, and the -T option to generate prototypes in a file.

Overall, CodeCheck is a very professional source code analysis tool that is more than an error-detecting tool. CodeCheck has application in many areas of software development including debugging, portability, maintainability, and corporate coding style enforcement.

MKS CODE INTEGRITY

Product Name:	Code Integrity
Purpose:	Source Code Analyzer
Platforms:	HP-UX, Solaris, Solaris-x86, SunOS, AIX, (MVS late 95, Windows 95 and Windows NT early 96)
Languages:	ANSI C, (C++ early 1996)
Status:	Commercial Product
Price:	$1995
Company	Mortice Kern Systems, Inc. (MKS)
Address:	185 Columbia Street W., Waterloo, Ontario N2L5Z5, Canada
Phone:	1-800-265-2797; 519-883-4346
Fax:	519-884-8861
Email:	sales@mks.com
FTP:	ftp.mks.com
Web:	http://www.mks.com

Code Integrity is a source code analysis tool for C code with C++ support planned shortly. It detects common errors, portability problems, and standards conformance violations.

The GUI makes Code Integrity very easy to use quickly. The event browser window lists all the problems detected by the analysis. The window can show detail on each problem including access to the relevant source code and suggestions for resolution. The report window shows various summaries of problems and warnings. The GUI also offers various textual reports or line and bar graphs covering issues such as API usage and simple code metrics such as lines of code.   The GUI also allows examination of all known information about a particular API call, and online help for more general issues.

An alternative to use of the Code Integrity GUI is combining command-line processing with the usual "make" sequence. By augmenting your makefile in a similar manner to the use of incremental "linting" on page 48 you can have the Code Integrity "cicc" analyzer perform its analysis in a batch mode, and view the results later via the GUI.

The source analysis involves both localized and inter-module checking with a variety of strictness levels regarding traditional versus ANSI C features. The areas of problems identification include type checking, function returns, control flow and various portability concerns. One of the central features of the analysis is detection of interface errors in calls to APIs, and checking compliance to the various standards. Code Integrity comes with a large database of common API calls with support for various standards including ANSI C, POSIX, XPG4, Motif, X11, and more. Users can add to this list with specifications for new functions using the "tspec" command to generate new API checks. The specification language is powerful and supports most checking needs.

Overall, the GUI makes the use of Code Integrity appealing. The error detection levels are good and the out-of-the-box support for checking existing standards is attractive.

PRINTFCK — FREE PRINTF ARGUMENT CHECKER

Tool Name:	`printfck`
Purpose:	Check `printf` formats against argument types
Platforms:	UNIX
Languages:	C only
Status:	Free
Author:	Andries Brouwer, Ian Darwin
Availability:	FTP *ftp.uu.net:published/oreilly/nutshell/lint/printfck.tar.Z* FTP *comp.sources.unix/volume6/printfck2.Z* (improved)
Features:	Preprocesses code to be sent to `lint`. Error checks arguments of all `printf`-like functions.

The `printfck` tool preprocesses C source files in such a way that UNIX `lint` will report type errors about mismatches between format specifications and argument types of `printf`-like functions. The improved version will also error check the `scanf` family of functions. The output of "`printfck file.c`" is redirected to a file, and `lint` is applied to that file. Naturally, this tool is no longer especially useful as many modern C/C++ compilers perform this error check automatically.

CLASH — FREE IDENTIFIER CLASH CHECKER

Tool Name:	`clash`
Purpose:	Find identifier clashes in C
Platforms:	UNIX mainly
Languages:	C only

Status:	Free
Author:	D. Hugh Redelmeier
Availability:	FTP *ftp.uu.net:published/oreilly/nutshell/lint/clash.tar.Z*
Limitations:	Ignores scopes and checks local variables

Some C linkers (and also very old C compilers) allow as few as seven monocase characters per identifier and map longer distinct identifiers with a common prefix to the same identifier, creating potential run-time errors. `clash` aims to find cases where identifiers will clash in the linkage phase by reporting distinct identifiers with common prefixes. The `-m` (monocase) option can be used for error checking of problems with case-insensitive linkers. The `-n` option sets the number of unique characters in an identifier. Unfortunately, the problem that `clash` does not understand scopes means that it issues annoying complaints about local identifiers, making its use less attractive.

SHORTC — FREE NAME CLASH RESOLUTION TOOL

Tool Name:	`shortc`
Purpose:	Creates #define directives mapping long names
Platforms:	UNIX mainly
Languages:	C only
Status:	Free
Author:	jim@ism780.UUCP, Ian Darwin
Availability:	FTP *ftp.uu.net:published/oreilly/nutshell/lint/shortc.tar.Z* FTP *comp.sources.unix/volume4/shortc.Z* and *shortc2.Z*
Limitations:	Ignores scopes and checks local variables

As with the `clash` tool, the `shortc` tool is relevant to C compilers and linkers that map names based on their first few characters. `shortc` examines C source and generates #define macros which can be used to port the code (since old preprocessors typically accept longer names than old compilers or linkers). Unfortunately, `shortc` does not understand scopes and processes local names, which is not a problem in modern compilers.

CCHECK — MINOR ERROR CHECKER FOR C

Tool Name:	`ccheck`
Purpose:	Static error checker for C

Platforms:	UNIX mainly
Languages:	C only
Status:	Free
Author:	Nick Crossley
Availability:	FTP *ftp.uu.net:published/oreilly/nutshell/lint/check.tar.Z* (UNIX), *comp.sources.unix/volume13/check.Z*
Limitations:	Only five common non-syntax errors found

This tool is a source checker for C, but checks for a very small set of common errors. The only errors found are assignment in conditional context, `if` with empty statement, dangling `else`, nested comments and unterminated comments. The small number of error checks makes this less useful than most modern compilers. The implementation uses `lex` and `yacc` and contains a small C grammar that may be of minor interest.

CCHK — SYNTAX CHECKER FOR C

Tool Name:	`cchk`
Purpose:	Syntax checker for C
Platforms:	DOS, UNIX
Languages:	C only
Status:	Free
Author:	Steve Draper, Ian Darwin, Jeffrey Mogul, Tom Anderson, Spencer Thomas
Availability:	FTP SimTel distributions as *c/c_check.zip* (DOS version) FTP *ftp.uu.net:published/oreilly/nutshell/cchk.tar.Z* (UNIX version)
Key Points:	Pre-check C programs for common syntax errors
Limitations:	Only three common non-syntax errors found

The documentation describes this tool as mainly a "pre-check on C programs before calling the compiler" and hence, `cchk` aims to produce better errors messages than many compilers. However, with modern compilers such usage appears unnecessary, except perhaps for students learning the language. `cchk` also produces warnings about three common coding errors: dangling `else` errors, nested comments and assignment confused with an equality test. This tool was raised from obscurity by Ian Darwin in his book *Checking C Programs with lint* published by O'Reilly & Associates.

STW/ADVISOR — SOURCE CODE ANALYSIS AND MEASUREMENT

Product Name:	STW/Advisor
Purpose:	Source code analysis toolset
Platforms:	Solaris, Solaris-x86, SunOS, HP-UX, OSF/1, AIX
Company:	Software Research
Address:	625 Third Street, San Francisco, CA 94107-1997, USA
Phone:	1-800-942-SOFT, 415-957-1441
Fax:	415-957-0730
Email:	info@soft.com
Web:	http://www.soft.com

STW/Advisor is one of the three major components in the Software TestWorks testing toolset from Software Research. STW/Advisor provides source code metric computation and source code analysis for errors, portability and coding style analysis.

Metrics are an important method of measuring code quality and identifying problem areas. The available metrics include Halstead metrics, cyclomatic complexity, and basic size metrics such as lines of code. Results can be presented graphically in Kiviat diagrams and as various reports identifying modules that exceeded chosen thresholds.

The source code analysis component detects erroneous and non-portable code in C programs. The list of error checks is quite impressive covering expression errors, control flow errors, preprocessor anomalies, type errors, initialization errors, and inter-module mismatches. Some of the most notable error checks are strong type checking based on typedef names, indentation-based error checking, and reporting of ANSI "quiet changes".

There are various options to control the presentation of messages. Messages can be suppressed individually, in groups, by symbol name, and based on types.

There is also a TDGEN test data generation component of STW/Advisor. This tool takes a template file of how test data values are to be chosen, a list of values, and automatically generates new test cases for the program.

CMT++ — COMPLEXITY METRICS FOR C/C++

Product Name:	Complexity Measures Tool for C/C++
Purpose:	Complexity metrics tool for C/C++
Platforms:	DOS, OS/2, Windows NT, Solaris, HP-UX
Price:	$750-$6,000
Company:	Testwell

Address:	Kanslerinkatu 8, FIN-33720 Tampere, Finland
Phone:	+358-31-316-5464 from 12 Oct. 96
Fax:	+358-31-318-3311 from 12 Oct. 96
Email:	olavip@cs.tut.fi

CMT++ is a source code analysis tool that computes various complexity metrics directly from the source code. Metrics aid the testing and maintenance processes by identifying areas of code that seem overly complex and will require extra testing. The available metrics include the McCabe cyclomatic complexity metric, Halstead metrics, and simpler practical metrics such as lines-of-code metrics. The cyclomatic complexity metric is an indication of how many test cases will be required to test a module.

CMT++ offers thresholds on the measurements and alarms when modules exceed the acceptable range. Thresholds are customizable so the user can choose a level appropriate to their organization. CMT++ produces a printed listing of all modules and the values for the metrics, and markings for those that exceed thresholds.

CLINT — Shareware C Checker

Product Name:	CLINT
Purpose:	Static error checker for C
Platforms:	DOS
Languages:	ANSI C, K&R C (not C++)
Status:	Shareware
Availability:	FTP SimTel distributions as `c/clt167.zip`
Company:	R&D Associates
Address:	16 High Street Rainham, Kent ME8 7JE England
Phone:	+(0634)361668
Email:	100013.1042@compuserve.com;
CompuServe:	100013,1042
Key Points:	— over thirty common errors checked — type checking

CLINT is a good shareware checking tool that is superior to most of the standard UNIX tools in that not only does it offer good type checking, but it also checks for a large number of common errors. Admittedly, the level of error checking is lower than some of the commercial checkers discussed here, but the low registration price makes CLINT attractive. Some of the common errors detected are nested comments, accidental empty loops, unreachable code, and all manner of type misuse. There are a large number of options to configure CLINT, and some are listed in Table 3–3; options can appear in the command-line or in a CLINT.CFG configuration file.

Table 3–3   Important CLINT options

Option	Meaning
-o	Output file
-e*num*	Limit on errors before stopping
-w*num*	Limit on warnings before stopping
-w*name*	Enable warning message *name*
−w−*name*	Disable warning message *name*
-L*library*	Create a CLINT library
-l*library*	Read a CLINT library

CLINT is available only for DOS, and is distributed as an executable file. It includes a full ANSI C preprocessor and library files for standardizing the checking for Turbo C++, Microsoft C, and Zortech C++. However, it is not limited to checking code from these particular compilers.

SEDCHECK — USING GREP AND SED

This section examines a source checker I recently wrote that detects common C and C++ programming errors by specifying regular expressions for sed in a UNIX script file. The full implementation is given on the CDROM in the sedcheck directory. The number of errors that can be caught by searching for regular expressions is very large and even grep can be a powerful debugging tool if used well. The advantage of sed over grep is that it allows messages to be added to the erroneous program lines in the diagnostic output.

The data file containing the regular expressions (in a special form) along with their corresponding error messages is called "regexps". This data file of pseudo-regular expressions is converted into real regular expressions for sed using the "makesed" script file. The full source for the resulting tool produced by this process is the script file "sedcheck". It can be applied to C and C++ source files and will report the erroneous lines with an appropriate diagnostic message.

AWKCHECK — A CHECKER USING AWK

Note that a public domain awk-like utility called *gawk* is available via FTP from GNU distribution sites. I created an *awk* version of sedcheck. The regular expressions are basically identical, but are a little less complicated because it is easier to track line numbers, filenames and the offending line of text itself. `awkcheck` is available on the CDROM in the `sedcheck` directory.

LOCK_LINT — SOLARIS THREADS SOURCE CHECKER

lock_lint is a special purpose source code checker from SunSoft for SPARC-Solaris. It checks Solaris thread programs for common errors in the use of mutexes and locks. For example, it detects deadlocks or failure to hold a lock or mutex when accessing a variable. This is a very lofty aim for a source code checker since these errors are highly run-time dependent and involve concurrency issues.

      lock_lint uses a separate set of specifications provided by the user that indicate relationships between functions, mutexes and locks. These specifications are combined with information generated in ".ll" data files by the SunSoft ANSI C compiler using the `-Zll` option. This allows an analysis of the specifications and the code to show violations of the specifications and particular conditions indicative of common thread coding anomalies. lock_lint does not detect any coding errors other than those related to locks and mutexes, as found by other checkers. However, the errors that lock_lint does detect are very difficult to detect and fix in other ways, especially those such as "race" conditions with timing dependence.

LINT-C-FRONT — DRIVER FOR UNIX LINT

The usual UNIX version of `lint` is actually a shell script, which may be slower than an executable on some platforms, although this is probably no longer true. Richard Salz has written a C version of the main driver shell script so that an executable version of UNIX `lint` can be created. The code is UNIX-specific because of its use of `fork` and `execv`, and since the code was written in 1988, it might no longer be as effective. However, this information may be useful to UNIX system administrators, and the FTP details are as follows:

```
comp.sources.misc/volume2/lint-c-front.Z
```

MEMLINTOK — PREVENT LINT MALLOC COMPLAINTS

This package by Bob Lewis is basically a header file to suppress warnings from older UNIX `lint` versions which complain about `malloc`, preventing the well-known "possible pointer alignment" error message. Unfortunately, the method is intrusive and relies on your code using special macro calls such as:

```
MALLOC_LINTOK(ptr, num, type);
```

instead of:

```
ptr = malloc(num * sizeof(type));
```

These special macros have two versions in the header file "`memlintok.h`", which are distinguished using an "`#ifdef lint`" test. The FTP details of the package are:

```
comp.sources.unix/volume20/memlintok.Z
```

QUALGEN — C METRICS AND REPORTING TOOL

Product Name:	QualGen
Platforms:	UNIX (Solaris, OSF/1, HP-UX, AIX, SGI, Ultrix and others), VAX/VMS
Company:	Software Systems Design
Address:	3267 Padua Ave., Claremont CA 91711, USA
Phone:	909-625-6417
Fax:	909-626-9667
Email:	tradi@hmc.edu

QualGen is a quality analysis tool that determines various metrics and produces graphical and textual reports for both C and Ada. It is primarily for use with the CDADL design tool also produced by Software Systems Design. C source files are processed by CDADL into a Qual-Gen DataBase (QDB) format which is analyzed based on metrics in a QualGen Metrics Language (QML) specification. This produces metrics and reports, and can also use a source code error checking feature called "PinPointer" to detect various coding anomalies and display the related source code.

The output formats for metrics and reports include graphical views (e.g., line graphs, multi-line graphs, bar charts, multibar charts, Kiviat diagrams) for viewing or PostScript output, textual reports, and WK1 formats for Lotus 1-2-3 and other spreadsheets. There are over 120 metrics available including lines of code, Halstead metrics and McCabe cyclomatic complexity metrics. Custom metrics and reports can be generated by writing QML specifications using its programming language features.

LCLINT — FREE SOURCE CODE CHECKER FOR ANSI C

Tool Name:	LCLint
Purpose:	Source code checker for ANSI C
Platforms:	OSF/1, Ultrix, SunOS, Solaris, Linux, SGI, RS/6000, UnixWare, HP-UX, Linux.

Author:	David Evans, MIT, evs@larch.lcs.mit.edu
Availability:	FTP larch.lcs.mit.edu:/pub/Larch/lclint/ Linux sites: sunsite.unc.edu:/pub/Linux/devel/lang/c/lclint*
Web:	http://larch-www.lcs.mit.edu:8001/larch/ http://larch-www.lcs.mit.edu:8001/larch/lclint.html
Mailing List:	Send signup request to lclint-request@larch.lcs.mit.edu

LCLint is an advanced source code checker for ANSI C that can also be used for more advanced validation of specifications. LCLint is an extension of the Larch project that covers specification languages, and there are a variety of academic papers on Larch and LCLint available at the main FTP site. In addition to its position at the forefront of academic research, LCLint is a useful tool in itself as a high powered source code checker for ANSI C.

When used without specifications, LCLint operates as a `lint`-like source code checker that reports anomalies including type errors, expression errors such as order of evaluation anomalies, flow of control errors such as case fall through, return value inconsistencies, and used-before-set variables. The level of error checking is high compared to UNIX `lint` implementations. An advanced option allows more restrictive type checking by treating `char` and boolean types as distinct from `int`. Specialized options allow specification of the name of the boolean type and the true and false equivalents.

The second use of LCLint is with additional specifications written in the Larch interface language. With these specifications enabled, LCLint performs stricter error checking and detects inconsistencies between interfaces and their implementation. Some of the more advanced error reports are encapsulation violation and inconsistent use of global variables.

LCLint is an advanced software program with many convenient features. Various options allow suppression of error checks and a configuration file ".`lclintrc`" is read during program startup. There is plenty of documentation at a user level and also academic research on error checking.

My Own C Checker

Finally, here is the release of my own C checker, completed many years ago. I have held off releasing it, hoping for free time to make it much better, because it was written at a time when I was weak in C coding. I am still waiting for that free time, but at least I have debugged it a little so that it usually leaks instead of crashing.

It checks C only with no C++ support, uses lex and yacc, and is based on the yacc grammar in the appendix of K&R II. There is precious little documentation, but there is useful information in the thesis and technical reports by me that are cited at the end of this chapter. The checker detects quite a few useful C programming errors, and I hope it is of use to someone as a real tool, or of interest to researchers. The distribution is in the `checker` directory of the CDROM. The LCLint checker discussed above is much better.

SIM — C SOURCE CODE SIMILARITY ANALYZER

Tool Name:	sim
Purpose:	Analyze similarity of C source files
Author:	Dick Grune
Availability:	comp.sources.unix/volume3/sim.Z

sim is a tool for analyzing two sets of source code and reporting sequences of code that appear to be "similar" based on certain rules. This tool is useful for validating software ownership, and course instructors might have a use for it. Two sequences of source code are considered similar if they have the same token structure, with differences only in comments, whitespace, identifier names, and the contents of character, numeric or string constants. The *sim* tool can find similarities within a single file or across multiple files depending on the options chosen.

FURTHER READING

The `lint` utility is widely used and is discussed in many books covering UNIX and C. Ian Darwin has written a neat book which gives fully detailed coverage of how to best use `lint`, and mentions a number of other "small" checker tools. The first publication about `lint` is the technical report written by the original author, S. Johnson. An interesting research paper showing a very advanced checker, but which detects only a limited range of errors, is the paper by Wilson and Osterweil discussing the Omega checker. Another good research paper on C++ checker design is that by Meyers and Lejter. Lastly there is my own research on a C checker which is discussed on page 61.

DARWIN, Ian F., *Checking C Programs with lint*, O'Reilly & Associates, Newton, MA., 1988.

JOHNSON, S.C., *Lint: a C Program Checker*, Computer Science Technical Report No. 65, Bell Laboratories, 1978.

MEYERS, Scott, and LEJTER, Moses, *Automatic Detection of C++ Programming Errors: Initial Thoughts on a lint++*, Technical Report CS-91-51, Department of Computer Science, Brown University, Providence, Rhode Island, August 1991 (also published *USENIX C++ Conference Proceedings*, April 1991, p29-40); available via FTP to *wilma.cs.brown.edu/techreports/91/cs91-51.ps.Z*.

SPULER, D.A., *Check: A Better Checker for C, Honors Thesis*, Dept. of Computer Science, James Cook University, Townsville, Australia, 1991. (FTP to *coral.cs.jcu.edu.au/pub/techreports/spuler-hons.ps.Z*).

SPULER, D., and SAJEEV, A.S.M., *Static Detection of Preprocessor Macro Errors in C*, Tech Report 92/7, Dept. of Computer Science, James Cook University, Townsville, Australia, July 1992/7. (FTP to *coral.cs.jcu.edu.au/pub/techreports/92-7.ps.Z*).

WILSON, C., and OSTERWEIL, L.J., *Omega — A Data Flow Analysis Tool for the C Programming Language*, IEEE Transactions on Software Engineering, Vol. 11, No. 9, pp. 832-838, 1985.

Memory allocation debugging tools

*T*here are a variety of free and commercial debugging tools that detect memory-related errors at run-time. This type of tool is probably the single most important type for achieving code quality in C or C++ programming.

The types of program errors detected by these tools are typically related to heap memory allocation and memory accesses, including array bounds violations, dangling pointer reads and writes, freeing unallocated memory, double de-allocation, using already-freed memory, NULL dereferences and many others. Although it might seem that the number of types of errors found by these tools is small in comparison to the total number of different types of errors that programmers can make, this does not take into account the relative importance of detecting these types of errors. The majority of error types will lead to some fixed and tangible failure of the program and should therefore be found and corrected during normal testing. However, memory-access errors will often be intermittent and very hard to trace because the symptoms of memory corruption may bear no resemblance to the actual cause. In fact, many such errors are not detected at all, and remain hidden as potentially harmful problems. Therefore, immediate detection of memory corruption errors leads to a significant improvement in the debugging and testing process because these errors are actually detected, and the cause is identified rather than just the symptom.

Unfortunately, the implementation of run-time error checking has a few disadvantages. Space and time efficiency suffer somewhat because of the extra code required to perform the checking. Another problem is that programs performing low-level memory manipulations (e.g., redefining `malloc` and `free`, or use of `sbrk`) may require special effort to add the checking, although it depends on the particular tool. Nevertheless, I consider these tools to be a crucial part of any professional programmer's toolkit.

COMMON MEMORY ERRORS

There are a number of common errors in the use of program memory that these memory allocation debugging tools attempt to diagnose. Almost all of these errors are likely to cause an abnormal failure of your program. Not all of the following errors will be found by all of the tools, but the majority are found by all such tools:

Deallocation of a non-allocated memory block: Attempting to use the `free` or `delete` primitives to deallocate a block of memory that was never allocated, such as a static or stack variable, is a fatal program failure. Although the experienced programmer will rarely make a mistake as basic as attempting to deallocate a local or static variable, this kind of error can arise if a data structure mixes pointers to allocated and static objects.

Deallocation of a previously deallocated memory block: Attempting to deallocate a block of memory twice is a common error, usually causing a program crash. The problem is usually that the program had two pointers to the same object, such as within some complicated data structure, and tried to deallocate them both.

Deallocation of NULL: Using `free` or `delete` with `NULL` is not actually an error in ANSI C or C++. However, this is an odd use of deallocation and many tools report an informational message for this anomalous usage. Using `free` with `NULL` was not supported in all pre-ANSI C compilers.

Read/write of previously deallocated memory block: This is a common cause of a crash or undefined program behavior. It occurs when a block of memory was deallocated, but a pointer to that object was not reset and was subsequently used. A simple example of a read of deallocated memory occurs in linked-list destruction. Consider the following buggy code:

```
for (p = head; p != NULL; p = p->next) {
   free(p);
}
```

This code references `p->next` immediately after the block `p` points to has been freed. The corrected code is:

```
for (p = head; p != NULL; p = next_ptr) {
   next_ptr = p->next;
   free(p);
}
```

This particular example is often harmless in practice; more dangerous examples occur when complicated data structures have many pointers to blocks of memory. When the block is freed, care must be taken to find all the pointers to that object to ensure they are never accessed again.

realloc moving the block: A special case of accessing freed memory is when the `realloc` function moves the memory block. When this occurs can depend on many things such as the heap algorithm used, and the error can easily lay dormant in the code. Some tools provide the ability to specify that all `realloc` calls move the block, thereby detecting all such dormant use-after-`realloc` errors.

Uninitialized read of stack memory: Local non-static variables are not initialized to zero by default (whereas global or static variables are zeroed), and contain undefined values when a function is entered. Hence, if a variable is accessed before it has been assigned a value, this can be unpredictable. In particular, if the variable is a pointer, the result is usually a crash. Naturally this only applies to *reading* a value since *writing* a value to an uninitialized block is how it gets a value.

Uninitialized read of allocated memory: The allocation of memory via `malloc`, `realloc` or `new` does not initialize the memory block. Hence, accessing the memory block before it is assigned a value is undefined and potentially fatal.

Copy of uninitialized memory: Although this is not usually an error, some of the tools report when uninitialized data is copied. This is distinguished from a "use" of the data. For example, copying a structure may have some fields that are uninitialized so far, but might be initialized later in both structures. In addition, this event is often ignored as it can be caused by harmless copying of structure padding bytes.

Overlapping blocks of memory: Some functions such as `strcmp`, `memcpy`, and `sprintf` will fail if the source of the string overlaps the destination address. ANSI C and C++ provide the safer `memmove` function as an alternative to `memcpy`; it does what `memcpy` does but also works for overlapping blocks. The solution for other functions is just to avoid overlapping arguments. Note that in my experience, overlapping uses are relatively unlikely to cause program failures, but are portability pitfalls for a few platforms.

Out of bounds reference: This error is a dangerous overwrite of the bounds on a memory block, and can apply to allocated memory blocks, stack variables or static/global variables. This problem is often indicative of going beyond the bounds of an array, or of getting two pointers confused. Many of the existing tools will only detect this error for allocated blocks; detection for stack or static objects is rare.

Mismatched allocation and deallocation: It is an error to allocate a block using one type of primitive (i.e., `malloc`, `calloc` or `realloc`, `new`, `new[]`, `XtMalloc`, etc.) and not deallocate the block with the corresponding primitive (i.e., `free`, `delete`, `delete[]`, `XtFree`, etc.). In practice, most of these primitives end up as `malloc` or `free` calls, so there is little danger of a crash for most platforms. However, there are certain combinations with crucial differences: allocation with `new` calls the constructor but deallocation with `free` or `XtFree` will not call the destructor.

In addition to these errors, memory debugging tools will typically provide information to track events such as signals received, allocation failure and bad arguments to various system functions.

MEMORY LEAKS

A memory leak is a block of allocated memory which has not been deallocated and cannot be used by the program. Another term for these blocks of memory is "garbage". Memory leaks are usually discovered by run-time memory debugging tools. Memory leaks are not an error that leads to immediate failure, but rather they increase the space requirements of the program. A program that has a few blocks of memory leaked at startup will not show any symptoms of failure. However, if leaks occur continually, the size of the process grows continually and may run out of space, leading to allocation failure.

Some of the tools will detect a memory leak immediately on the pointer assignment or deallocation where the block finally becomes inaccessible. Other tools report memory leaks only at program exit or when explicitly requested by the user, typically by calling an API function from within a symbolic debugger.

The algorithms used to detect memory leaks vary from simple to highly complex. The simplest method is to report all memory blocks that have not been deallocated. This method of reporting all allocated blocks can be useful at program exit, but does not provide very useful information during execution. It will also report blocks of memory such as global hash tables that have been used by your program all the time, and that you just couldn't be bothered to free on program exit.

The more complicated algorithms scour the data space examining every pointer object, and thereby determine which memory blocks have no pointers still pointing at them. If a memory block has no pointers to it, then you can not be using it — it must be leaked. Hence these tools using complicated algorithms can report blocks that are "obvious" leaks, as well as reporting lists of blocks that are currently allocated.

Even more sophisticated methods are needed to detect leakage of cyclic data structures because these blocks all have pointers to them, but have no pointers other than those that are part of the data structure. For example, if your program leaks an entire doubly linked list by setting the head pointer to `NULL`, each list block will have a pointer to it, but in reality you would consider it leaked as there are no external pointers to it.

Another issue with these complicated algorithms is whether to report memory blocks which have no pointers to the start of the block, but do have a pointer into somewhere in the middle. These are probably memory leaks since you usually need a pointer to the start of a block to free it. However, it is vaguely possible that you are still using the block, in which case maybe it shouldn't be considered "leaked". A realistic example is a derived object where you have a pointer to the derived object but not the base object. Some of the tools resolve this issue by reporting a different form of memory leak message; for example, Purify reports a "potential" memory leak message.

TIP: Deallocate data structures on program exit

It can be helpful for memory leak detection to explicitly seek out and destroy all data structures on program exit. There are two reasons that this can help detect memory leaks. Firstly, if all objects are destroyed, the list of allocated but never freed blocks begins to contain only memory leaks.

Secondly, tools with sophisticated memory leak detection algorithms will find more "obvious" memory leaks. Consider the following common scenario: You are allocating records of some description, and have them stored in various complicated data structures. In addition, you maintain a separate index into the records, implemented as a hash table. This index might be for fast access into the records, or it might even be to maintain a table of all valid records. Now consider what happens if you "leak" one of the records. The complicated memory leak detection algorithms will not find the record to be an "obvious" leak because there is still a pointer to the record inside the hash table; and the hash table isn't considered a leak because there's probably a global pointer to the hash table. So to get the full power of the advanced memory leak detecting tools, you should always try to destroy global data structures on exit.

As far as improving detection of such records *during* program execution, there isn't a lot that can be done. If you are really keen, you can write a function that saves the hash table to disk, destroys it, calls the memory leak API function to detect leaks, and recreates the hash table from the disk file. And, yes, I do know someone keen enough to do this! You can then call this function from within your debugger to do regular leak detection.

For the rest of us mortals, destroying the data structures on exit is adequate. The simplest method is to always destroy them in your exit cleanup routine (you do have one, don't you?). The downside is that this is inefficient since why should you bother wasting the time to reclaim memory that all operating systems (except one or two obscure ones) will clean up anyway? Hence the more efficient version is to only do this cleanup whenever running in a debugging mode. How you achieve this will depend on your application and on the memory checking tool you are using. It might be an environment variable, an API call, or some other means that you call to determine whether it is worth cleaning up the data structures. If you really hate wasted code space, you might be able to use an `#ifdef` directive, based on whether the tool is active or not.

DANGLING REFERENCES

The opposite of memory leaks is the dangling reference. A memory leak is a block without a pointer; a dangling reference is a pointer without a block. These typically arise through pointers that point at blocks of memory that have already been deallocated. Most memory debugging tools will detect uses of dangling references and report warnings about reading or writing deallocated memory addresses. The top level tools will report the stack traces for where the access is occurring, and for where the previously deallocated block was both allocated and deallocated. Unfortunately, even if the error message is this detailed with three stack traces, it isn't always easy to find and fix the cause of the bug.

The problem is that in a complicated data structure there are usually many pointers to a given object. Knowing that you didn't clear all of them when you deallocated the object is one thing; modifying the code so that you fix it is quite another! What you really need in the error report is the stack trace of where that pointer was set to point to this memory block. This isn't the same place as where the block was allocated; instead it would typically be where you copied a pointer, or added a pointer value to an index or hash table. In fact, you'd ideally like to automatically detect where there are still dangling references to a pointer when you deallocate it; actually this would give you too many false errors, but the basic idea is that you'd like to be able to easily find all the places in your complicated data structures that point at the block.

MEMORY DEBUGGING TOOL FEATURES

There are a number of memory debugging tools available commercially and freely using a variety of error detection techniques. An evaluation of these tools based only on the classes of memory errors detected ignores some important usability issues such as how quickly such an error will be detected. In general, there are two classes of memory allocation debugging tool based on when errors are detected:

- **Access-level checking**: every memory access is examined for errors including pointer dereferences and array variable operations.
- **Function-level checking**: only certain function calls provoke error checking.

Access-level implementations are very advanced tools and mainly appear in a handful of commercial offerings.

Function-level implementations are the simplest to implement and typically use link-time or macro call interception of a set of functions (e.g., all heap functions), or even a combination of link-time and macro interception. Most free tools and a number of commercial tools rely on this principle.

The techniques for error detection are well-established based on interception of function calls such as `malloc`, `free`, `new` and `delete`. Typically, allocated blocks are surrounded by blocks of memory filled with "magic" values. These blocks are periodically checked by the debugging tool (e.g., on every *nth* call to a memory allocation function), and if the magic values have been changed, this indicates that an array bounds write error has occurred. Similar magic value techniques apply for other common errors: filling `malloc` blocks with magic values allows detection of reading uninitialized `malloc` memory, and filling freed blocks can detect reading/writing freed memory. However, there is a fundamental limitation — the lack of immediate error detection. Errors involving array or pointer operations are not detected immediately and might never be detected (especially read errors which do not change magic values). Errors arising from library function calls such as `strcmp` or `strcpy` are detected immediately only if the tool happens to intercept these standard string functions. The limitation is slightly eased by the technique that the magic values filling invalid blocks can be chosen such that they are invalid pointer values, increasing the likelihood that an error will lead to an obvious failure such as a GPF or core dump. These tools often also counteract the limitation by providing options controlling the frequency of magic value checking, including API functions to perform it. Although the weakness of these techniques is undeniably etched in the memory of anyone who has used more powerful access-level tools, any function-level memory debugging tool is many times better than the absence of any tool.

Source versus object instrumentation: There are two main methods of achieving access level checking of memory accesses: object/executable instrumentation and source code instrumentation. Both of these methods annotate the program with debugging code that checks every memory access. Object or executable instrumentation refers to modifying the code after it has been created by the compiler. This type of technology is used, for example, by Purify and SENTINEL II. Source code instrumentation refers to intercepting the source code before it gets to the compiler, and to placing debugging source code to perform the error checking. Tools that use source code instrumentation include Insure++ and Bounds Checker Professional Edition. Both of these methods offer powerful access-level error checking, but they have some different advantages and disadvantages. Source code instrumentation is generally a more powerful error checking technology because more information is available before compilation, whereas only limited information is available in the created object file. Hence, source code instrumentation usually offers greater opportunities for advanced detection of common errors.

The disadvantages of source code instrumentation appear in two issues. Firstly, checking of third-party libraries for which there is no source code is difficult, and the full power is lost. Such tools usually offer some form of error checking based on function-level interception for libraries without source, and the limitation is often not too severe since you usually have the source for all the libraries that you actually need to debug.

The second major advantage of object code technology over source code instrumentation is the pragmatic issue that instrumentation requires only a single link-time operation for object instrumentation, but can require a full re-compile for source code instrumentation. Features in source code instrumentation tools that allow mixed modes with only some files instrumented are some help, but doing this loses the main advantages of the extra error checking from the source code instrumentation. Usually it is better just to accept that you need to instrument all files, and put up with the recompile any time you want to switch between an instrumented and a production build of your application.

Stack and static data: Another area of comparison of different tools arises in the area of error checking of stack and static data. Almost all the tools have their background in heap allocation checking, but stack and static data is more difficult. The types of errors that I refer to include array bounds underwrites, overwrites, and uninitialized uses of stack or static data. As a general rule, function-level tools will not detect any errors related to stack or static data, but there are a few surprising exceptions to this case. Surprisingly, many of the more advanced access-oriented tools also fail to detect some or all of the error classes for stack and/or static data.

Error reporting: Another important usability issue is the reporting of filenames, line numbers or full stack traces when an error is detected. The more advanced access-level tools will usually report full stack traces for both the cause of the error and the call stack when the related memory block was allocated. The typical function-level tool will only report the file-name and line number (i.e., a one-level stack trace) for the error and the block. Futhermore, many function-level tools do not have the technology to work backwards from code addresses to source code, and will often rely on macro interception of `malloc` and/or `new` operations through the inclusion of a debugging header file. These macros are usually portable, if some-what tricky, uses of the __FILE__ and __LINE__ macros. It becomes a trade-off, where the need to show filename and line numbers negates the convenience of a debugging version only requiring a change to the link phase.

The recycling of deallocated memory by the tool is another area where it is important to have features. Memory debugging tools will typically try to keep deallocated blocks under error checking as long as possible, but eventually it must return the block to the application or else risk memory allocation failure. Hence, these tools typically provide options specifying when, if ever, deallocated memory blocks are to be recycled.

Dвмалло: A Free Unix Debugging Library

Tool Name:	dbmalloc
Purpose:	linkable malloc debugging library
Platforms:	UNIX (many platforms)
Languages:	ANSI C, K&R C (partial C++ support)
Status:	Free (noncommercial use)
Author:	Conor Cahill
Availability:	comp.sources.misc/volume32/dbmalloc/part[00-10]
	comp.sources.reviewed/volume02/malloclib/part[00-06] (early)
	comp.sources.unix/volume22/debug_malloc/part0[12] (early)
Key points:	— linkable error checking
	— include header file to get better error messages

`dbmalloc` is a function-level UNIX debugging library built by Conor Cahill. The basic tech-nique used is the link-time interception of standard library calls related to dynamic memory allocation and their re-implementation in terms of the `sbrk` system call (which is similar to how the "real" UNIX version of `malloc` operates). This limits portability to non-UNIX plat-forms but is portable enough to support a number of UNIX platforms. In addition to link-time interception, `dbmalloc` also allows source files to include the header file `malloc.h` for reporting of the filename and line number of the statement causing the error.

As with most such libraries, the primary focus is on memory allocation debugging, including detection of errors such as block overwrites and bad `free` calls, and also memory leak reports. In addition to intercepting the standard memory allocation functions, a number of memory-related functions such as `strcpy` and `memset` are also intercepted, as well as the X Windows allocation functions. There is no explicit C++ support for debugging `new` and `delete`, but it can be added by linking overloaded versions of the global `new` and `delete` operators that call `malloc` and `free`. Unfortunately, although very good, `dbmalloc` is not quite a commercial quality library because of disadvantages such as the requirement of in-code support for function call stack tracing, a lack of run-time configurability (e.g., `dbmalloc` cannot be left in production code) and its somewhat cryptic error messages.

MEMORY ADVISOR (SENTINEL I & II)

Product Name:	Memory Advisor (SENTINEL I and SENTINEL II)
Purpose:	memory allocation debugging tool
Platforms:	UNIX (many platforms including SunOS, Solaris, Solaris- x86, HP-UX, AIX, ULTRIX, DG/UX,SGI Irix, DEC, OSF/1,NCR/AT&T, PowerPC, etc.)
Languages:	ANSI C, C++, K&R C
Status:	Commercial Product
Price:	$995-$2,895
Company:	Platinum Technology (formerly/AiB Software Corporation)
Address:	1815 South Meyers Road, Oakbrook Terrace, IL 60181-5241, USA
Phone:	1-800-526-9096, 708-620-5000
Fax:	708-241-8205
Email:	info@platinum.com
FTP:	ftp.aib.com (username: anon)
Web:	http://www.platinum.com
Key Points:	• `malloc` and `free` error checking • `new` and `delete` error checking • memory leak (garbage) detection • run-time configurable debugging output library

Memory Advisor (formerly SENTINEL) is a well-established and high-quality commercial debugging library for C and C++ aimed primarily at memory-related program errors. The main designer of Memory Advisor is Conor Cahill who also wrote `dbmalloc`, the success of which inspired him to build a commercial quality version.

The recent release of Memory Advisor 3.2 offers a product that is technically superior to its predecessor with immediate detection of memory errors. Whereas earlier versions offer only function-level interception, the new release offers complete access-level coverage, with the advantages of immediate reporting of errors, and complete coverage of memory accesses, including those in third-party libraries. With this new release, Platinum now has an impressive offering of the more advanced checking of Memory Advisor 3.2 on some platforms (including SunOS, Solaris and HP) and function checking on many other platforms. Whereas many other products offer either high technology or broad platform coverage, Memory Advisor offers the best of both worlds.

Memory Advisor 3.2 uses an interception technique called object module transformation which combines object files into a final executable that checks every memory access. This allows very advanced error checking including bounds errors for global or static memory. Both versions of Memory Advisor offer a high level of error checking, including all the "usual" errors related to heap memory allocation (e.g., bad `free`, double `free`, etc.) and a variety of portability warnings (e.g., `free` of a `NULL` pointer, or `memcpy` arguments that overlap). The older version performs a number of other error checks at every intercepted call for `malloc` chain corruption and stack corruption, and a "magic value" technique is also used to detect reads of already-freed memory blocks or uses of uninitialized `malloc` blocks. The main limitation of this version arises from its use of function call interception, which means that memory errors not arising directly from a function call (e.g., bad array index) are not caught immediately. However, Memory Advisor 3.2 is specifically designed to overcome this limitation with its lower-level memory access checking.

Memory leaks are another major form of error identified by Memory Advisor. A variety of reports are available about "garbage" blocks, and these can be customized in many ways. Reports can be made to appear at the end of execution or can be achieved through calls to various API functions.

Error reporting is quite verbose making the causes of errors simple to trace. Typically, the report includes a long human-readable description of the type of error, and stack traces of both the point at which the error is detected and also the point when the allocation of the relevant memory block occurred.

Memory Advisor is easy to use, with no changes to source code required.   All that is needed is to invoke the "sentinel" command, which has a similar usage format to most compilers. This allows a `makefile` change to require only addition of this single word in many cases.

The level of configurability is also very high including aspects such as various forms of error report suppression and the ability to prevent certain expensive error checks if performance degradation is too high. Options are set by using configuration files and environment variables which are examined at program startup and can be re-examined via API calls.

An aspect of Memory Advisor not related to its run-time error checking is its support for a run-time configurable debugging output library. There is a `printf`-like SEDBG macro which uses a double bracket method, and another macro named SEDBG_CODE which is a "large" macro allowing an entire code block as its second argument. This output can be configured based on a "level" of debugging output.

A notable feature of Memory Advisor is its explicit support for using Memory Advisor to help in beta testing a product. The manual encourages Memory Advisor to be left linked into the executable during beta testing, and error reports can be mailed electronically to the person supervising the beta test. Note that beta testers do not need a license to run the executable.

In summary, Memory Advisor is an excellent C/C++ debugging tool for UNIX platforms allowing convenient detection of the majority of memory-related errors. Memory

Advisor 3.2 allows complete checking of all memory accesses immediately, and a previous release offers a slightly lower level of checking on a much broader range of platforms.

PURIFY FROM PURE SOFTWARE

Product Name:	Purify
Purpose:	memory allocation debugging tool
Platforms:	UNIX-based — Sun SPARC with SunOS 4 or Solaris 2; also HP 9000 running HP-UX; Windows NT newly released.
Languages:	ANSI C, C++, K&R C
Status:	Commercial Product
Company:	Pure Software, Inc.
Address:	1309 S. Mary Avenue, Sunnyvale, CA 94087, USA
Phone:	408-720-1600, 1-800-353-7873
Fax:	408-720-9200
Email:	info@pure.com, support@pure.com
Web:	http://www.pure.com/
Key Points:	• low-level memory access checking • `malloc` and `free` error checking • `new` and `delete` error checking • memory leak (garbage) detection

Purify is a well-established commercial run-time debugging tool for both C and C++ that detects many memory-related programming errors. Purify 3.0 distinguishes itself by adding a new Motif GUI which offers usability improvements for the presentation, analysis and suppression of error reports. There is also a recently completed integration into HP's SoftBench development environment.

The Purify GUI also offers integration with other Pure Software products including PureCoverage for code coverage. The GUI pops up automatically when an instrumented executable begins execution. Status information about each execution is maintained, and when an error is reported, the stack traces appear and can be examined to show the source code. The GUI also automates a lot of the customization features that were only available via configuration files in previous versions. Errors can be suppressed easily, and many run-time options can be specified in GUI dialogs. Multiple executions can be displayed sequentially on the display, and each display can be suppressed to a single line summary display, or can be drilled down into a fully expanded report. The GUI also supports some editing, building and debugging features.

Naturally, Purify maintains its low level of error checking with errors detected by "object code insertion" during the linking phase. Rather than just intercepting function calls, all memory accesses are checked, conceptually by adding instrumentation code around every low-level read or write instruction. This level of checking offers the advantages that:

a. any detected memory errors are reported immediately rather than only at the next call to an intercepted library function, and

b. all memory accesses are checked, even those in third-party libraries.

Error checks include the usual heap memory related errors (e.g., bad `free`, double `free`, etc.), but the low level of memory access interception also makes it possible to find a slightly broader range of errors including uses of uninitialized memory on the stack. Unfortunately, Purify does not currently detect bounds-overwrite errors related to global or static data, but such errors are comparatively rare.

Memory leaks are another major form of error that is identified by Purify. A report of any memory leaks appears by default at the end of execution in the GUI report. The report provides a stack trace for every block, showing what sequence of functions caused the leak. More detailed memory leak reporting can be achieved by calling various API functions from within the program or from a debugger.

The error messages produced by Purify are detailed enough to trace the cause of an error. A stack trace is presented of function calls currently active when the error occurred, and also a stack trace of function calls which created the memory block involved in the error (if there is a related block). The GUI presents these stack traces and also presents the code snippets for each call.

Error suppression is available via the GUI or a ".`purify`" configuration file. There are a variety of modes for suppressing a given error type including: all instances, all instances in a given function, all instances in functions called by a given function, and all instances in a given library. Purify allows C++ names to be used in full, and "unmangles" names in error reports.

Purify is very easy to use. All that is required is a re-link of the object files using Purify's linker. Typically, all that is needed to build a Purify'd executable is an extra word, "`purify`", in the `makefile`.

Purify has a large number of other features to make it more useful in various contexts. For example, it has a large number of Purify-specific API functions to call from within a program or a symbolic debugger. These functions can be used to present various reports on memory usage and memory leaks, change the handling of errors, and for many other tasks.

Another feature is called "watchpoints" where the programmer can call a function at run-time to specify that accesses to a particular address or block of memory be reported by Purify. This can be used to detect changes to particular addresses. For example, Purify's manual suggests a watchpoint on `errno` to detect the next time `errno` is changed by a system call. Anyone familiar with watchpoints of standard UNIX debuggers, such as `dbx`, should be pleasantly surprised by the performance of these watchpoints.

An impressive aspect of Purify's documentation is the discussion of how to overcome a limitation that is typical of this sort of tool — programs that do not use `malloc` and `free` in the usual way will need some modification. The styles discussed include simple memory pools down to `sbrk` usage.

In summary, Purify is an excellent tool for detecting a variety of otherwise difficult to detect memory errors, making it very valuable in the software development cycle. The new GUI makes it very easy to use, and it retains its technical power from the low-level interception of *all* memory accesses, rather than only those arising from library function calls.

TIP: Purify ABR/ABW can be FMR/FMW

Whenever Purify reports an array bounds read or write (ABR or ABW) the report is not necessarily accurate. These reports can actually hide a `free` memory read or write (FMR or FMW) error if your free queue length is not long enough. The problem can occur if a FMR or FMW occurs a great many `free`'s later in the execution, when the previously `free`'d block has been re-allocated to satisfy one or possibly many other allocation requests. Purify puts red zones around each of these newly allocated blocks, so that when the very old dangling reference pointer that thinks it is pointing to that really old structure that was actually `free`'d a long time ago, it actually accesses the red zone of a newer block, which is reported as an ABR or ABW. Unfortunately, if you happen to access the middle of a newer valid block, you "got lucky with a wild pointer" and no error is issued. So if you get these errors and can't find an obvious cause, bump up your free queue length, and try again.

MEMLIGHT — MEMORY ERROR DETECTION

Product Name:	Memlight
Purpose:	Runtime memory error detection
Platforms:	SunOS, Solaris, NEC UNIX
Company:	Sumitomo Metal Industries, Ltd.
Address:	Japan (address unknown)
Status:	Unclear. Previously distributed as part of a commercial C/C++ testing tool suite.

Memlight detects memory errors at runtime using a patented Page Memory Management Unit (PMMU) technique. Batch mode execution is available for Memlight such as for overnight execution of unit tests with error detection.

The errors detected include the usual memory failures such as accessing freed memory, array bound violations, bad `free`'s, and memory leaks. There is also a novel feature for checking that all strings have the correct null terminator character. Error reports show the full call stack of the location and any associated memory blocks.

Memory leak reports are listings of blocks that are not freed. The leak reports are available on request or on program exit.

INSURE++ FROM PARASOFT

Product Name:	Insure++ (including Insight)
Purpose:	Memory error checking, test coverage, visualization
Platforms:	SunOs 4.x, Solaris 2.x, HP9000/7xx, 9000/8xx, IBM RS/6000, DEC Alpha (OSF/1), SGI (Irix 4.x, 5.2), SCO, Lynx, Linux, Pyramid, Sequent.
Company:	Parasoft Corporation
Address:	2031 S. Myrtle Avenue, Monrovia, CA 91016, USA
Phone:	818-305-0041
Email:	insure@parasoft.com
Fax:	818-305-9048
Web:	http://www.parasoft.com

Insure++ is an impressive memory allocation debugging tool from Parasoft. The strengths of the offering include a Motif GUI for ease of use, the source code instrumentation technology for error detection, and a number of integrated components: Inuse for memory use analysis, and TCA for test coverage analysis.

Insure++ uses source code instrumentation (SCI) technology to detect a wide variety of run-time errors including the usual memory access failures. The instrumentation of the program at the source code level offers greater possibilities for accurate error detection than the link-time interception or object code transformation used by most other tools. Insure++ takes full advantage of this freedom and detects a wide variety of run-time errors. Notably, it detects bounds overwrites for stack, static and global data which has consistently been the stumbling block of other run-time memory checking tools. Other errors detected include comparing pointers in different blocks, bad function pointer usage, and common library function errors in parameters and/or return codes.

Threads are supported by reporting the thread id with errors and detecting cross-thread allocation errors. Run-time error reports appear on `stderr` or in a log file or GUI, and give full stack traces for the error location and for any allocated block. Errors can be suppressed globally or per-function using a configuration file.

One particularly striking feature that I haven't seen in any other tool is the *immediate* detection of memory leaks. Insure++ reports an error immediately when a pointer assignment, deallocation or end-of-scope causes a block to have no pointers to it. This is far better than other tools which display leaks at the end of execution or whenever the user requests a leak analysis via an API call.

Insure++ has an impressive ability to perform complicated validation of calls to system libraries. A number of interface specifications are provided for a variety of standard libraries. There is also powerful C-like programming capability with which to add interfaces to any of your own functions.

There are also some useful compile-time error detection features for errors such as printf/scanf formats, dead code, uninitialized uses (also detected at run-time), conversion losing precision, and mismatches in global variable declarations and definitions (which `lint` is known for detecting).

The downside of source instrumentation is the convenience issue of the need to apply Insure++ as part of the compilation process for each file and not just the final link stage. This requires a more extensive effort to achieve full error checking power throughout the entire program. To resolve this dilemma, Insure++ offers good function-level error checking even if only used at the link phase, and also supports incremental error checking modes where only some files are instrumented from source code. However, if you are willing to instrument all source files, you get very powerful error checking.

Another minor limitation is related to third-party libraries where the source code is not available. Third-party libraries are checked by Insure++ for memory errors and interface failures, but the full power of source code analysis is lost. This is not too bad since the remaining error checking is of a similar level to other link-time tools that rely on function call interception, and can be improved by adding your own interface specifications to detect incorrect parameters or return codes.

Another part of the package is the Total Coverage Analysis (TCA) tool for analyzing the level of code coverage. The source code instrumentation technology records the code coverage information during execution. The coverage analysis is down below the function level to the basic block level. TCA will report in its GUI, a coverage summary and show an annotated printout of the source code showing which blocks were executed. Multiple executions can be combined into aggregated results for the total coverage over a test suite.

Another visualization component is the Inuse GUI-based tool for displaying a variety of views of heap memory. There is a high water mark for memory allocation, a historical graph display of allocated memory usage, a count of calls to various allocation functions, a block frequency bar graph showing how many blocks of each size were allocated, and a view of current heap layout to help show fragmentation

TESTCENTER FROM CENTERLINE

Product Name:	TestCenter
Purpose:	Memory error detection, test coverage, error simulation
Platforms:	SunOS, Solaris, HP-UX, AIX
Company:	Centerline
Address:	10 Fawcett Street, Cambridge, MA 02138;
Phone:	1-800-NOW-CNTR (800-669-2687), 617-498-3000
Fax:	617-868-6655
Email:	info@centerline.com

TestCenter is a memory allocation debugging tool from Centerline Software. In addition to the memory allocation debugging features, TestCenter offers built-in test coverage and error simulation features. The philosophy is that run-time error checking is more effective when code coverage and error simulation ensure the code is thoroughly exercised. There is both batch mode reporting and a convenient Motif GUI for customizing the tool and reviewing online documentation.

TestCenter is easy to use requiring only the addition of the "`proof`" command to the final link phase, which is usually a trivial change to your `Makefile`. This produces an instrumented program that automatically launches the TestCenter GUI when it begins execution.

The errors detected cover all the usual memory access failures including bounds overwrites, unaligned pointers, memory leaks, and error checking of standard C functions. Error reports present the stack trace for the error and any related allocated blocks, from which the source code can be examined.

TestCenter offers code coverage analysis facilities at the level of function calls. The coverage browser reports on the percentage of calls to a function. Both the calls to the function and the calls from that function to other functions are measured. Functions that are never called can be found as 0% in the "calls to" coverage mode. TestCenter offers a weak form of "line" coverage where the lines of code containing function calls that were not called are shown.

The error simulation features are effective and offer a broad range of customizations for simulating hard-to-reproduce problems. TestCenter offers some common failure scenarios, such as the obvious issue of `malloc` failure, all of which can be chosen and applied to the program's execution. There is also a more general feature allowing the user to specify that a function returns a particular value at a given call, or to "drop in" a replacement definition for a function so as to simulate more complex application-specific failures. These options are set and the results examined all via the GUI.

Overall, TestCenter has a broad range of features comparable to multiple product offerings of some other vendors. The memory error checking is good quality, the test coverage of function calls is adequate, and the error simulation features round off a good product.

MEMCHECK FROM STRATOSWARE CORPORATION

Product Name:	MemCheck
Purpose:	memory allocation debugging tool
Platforms:	DOS, Windows, UNIX and others with K&R or ANSI C compiler
Languages:	ANSI C, C++, K&R C
Status:	Commercial Product
Company:	StratosWare Corporation

Address:	1756 Plymouth Road, Suite 1500, Ann Arbor, MI 48105-1890, USA
Phone:	1-800-WE-DEBUG (1-800-933-3284) or 313-996-2944
Fax:	313-996-2955 (preferred) or 313-747-8519
Email:	70244.1372@compuserve.com
BBS:	313-996-2993 (24 hour)
Web:	http://www.stratosware.com/swc/
Key Points:	— uses both preprocessor macros and link-time interception — malloc/free, new/delete error checking — clever macro definitions of new and delete

MemCheck is a commercial function-level memory debugging tool from StratosWare Corporation. MemCheck works on the principle of interception of library calls by preprocessor macros and also at link-time. This technique gives the product a high level of portability and MemCheck is available on many platforms including DOS, Windows and Macintosh. It is also available for any other platforms with ANSI or K&R compliant C compilers in source code form.

When adding MemCheck to a project, the main alteration is the addition of #include <memcheck.h> to each source file. This change can be performed manually, or automatically using a supplied tool. The environment variable called MEMCHECK must also be set to enable checking.

MemCheck is a supported commercial product and the difference shines through, with many more features than the typical free malloc debugging package. The errors detected include heap-related memory errors, memory leaks, memory allocation failure, and bad arguments to various library functions. The performance is good with only 7-15K code overhead, and good run-time efficiency because MemCheck uses a binary tree to track addresses. In fact, I was particularly impressed by the facility to track addresses either in memory or using a disk data structure in a temporary file should the space used by the in-memory binary tree become prohibitive.

MemCheck offers a high level of run-time configurability, including a new Windows Control Panel configuration utility. MemCheck code never needs to be removed from a project's source code; it can be either:

1. left in the production version,
2. "linked out" by linking with a particular library, or
3. "compiled out" by defining the macro name NOMEMCHECK.

A variety of API functions are also available which I won't examine in detail. A useful feature for DOS programmers is that MemCheck performs frequent tests for NULL pointer overwrites. This can be useful for narrowing down the cause of a "null pointer assignment" error message.

Debugging of C++ memory allocation with `new` and `delete` is supported in a few different ways. The default method is link-time interception of the calls to `malloc` and `free` performed by the compiler's default new and delete operators. This means that all `new` and `delete` operations are checked, but any error messages about them are slightly misleading — referring to `malloc` rather than `new`, and without an accurate associated filename and line number. More accurate messages about `new` and `delete` can be achieved by adding definitions of the overloaded `new` and `delete` operators as a C++ source file in your project (usable sample definitions are provided with MemCheck), and also defining the macro "`NEW_OVERLOADED`" before each inclusion of `<memcheck.h>` to enable macro definitions of `new` and `delete`.

MemCheck also offers a number of extra features. Stack usage is monitored to offer statistical information and detect stack overflow at runtime. Statistics on allocation are also available, such as the high water mark of allocated memory. A stack trace on GPFs is also available to remove the need for postmortem debugging.

The main limitations of MemCheck arise from its use of library function interception. This means that memory errors arising in other ways (e.g., a bad index in an array access) are not necessarily detected immediately.

In summary, MemCheck represents a high-quality function-level memory debugging library with numerous convenience features. MemCheck will improve code quality and make a useful impact on any programmer's debugging tasks.

HEAPAGENT FROM MICROQUILL

Product Name:	HeapAgent
Platforms:	Windows 3.1, Windows 95, Windows NT
Price:	$465
Company:	MicroQuill Software Publishing, Inc.
Address:	4900 25th Ave. NE, Ste 206, Seattle WA, 98105 USA
Phone:	1-800-441-7822, 206-525-8218
Fax:	206-525-8309
Email:	info@microquill.com
Compuserve:	70751,2443

HeapAgent is a function-level link-time memory allocation debugging tool for Windows platforms from MicroQuill, who are also the makers of SmartHeap. HeapAgent is a powerful product with numerous convenience features. Errors found by HeapAgent are reported in an elegant GUI allowing access to the corresponding source code, analysis of the heap memory block, or hooks into many compiler-supplied or third-party debuggers.

HeapAgent detects errors by function-level link-time interception of heap-related operations by linking in a replacement for the standard heap allocation functions. This leads to detection of all the "usual" memory access errors, and to the well-known limitations of this technique: errors are not necessarily detected immediately, but only at the next intercepted function call; and some errors such as reading from a freed location or an uninitialized stack read are not always detected. HeapAgent does not detect memory errors related to stack, static or global data. File and line number reporting requires source modification to include the header file "`heapagnt.h`" in any files calling `malloc` or `new`. Full use of HeapAgent will require this header included in all files.

The HeapAgent GUI offers a number of useful browser features for analyzing results or correcting errors. The Allocation Browser offers easy analysis of allocated blocks, including selected views, which is useful when there are many such blocks. The Dump Browser allows viewing of the memory block that caused the error in ASCII and many other formats. The Source Browser allows viewing of the source code causing the error. The Statistics Browser reports information useful for space profiling, including total memory and total heap memory used by your application.

HeapAgent has some neat features such as good free queue control including deferred freeing, and an option to force `realloc` to always move the block, therefore catching any reliance on `realloc` leaving blocks in place. It is possible to mark blocks as "no `free`" or "no `realloc`" so as to get immediate reports if this should occur. HeapAgent also supports an idea called "agents" which are similar to conditional breakpoints but more powerful. These "agents" can specify a variety of actions that can be initiated when matching events occur.

In summary, HeapAgent offers function-level memory allocation debugging and detects a wide range of memory-related coding errors. HeapAgent will find many errors and the various browsers in the GUI make correction of detected errors an enjoyable process.

BOUNDS CHECKER FROM NU-MEGA

Product Name:	Bounds Checker Professional Edition
Platforms:	DOS, Windows, Windows NT, Windows 95
Price:	$199
Company:	Nu-Mega Technologies
Address:	P.O. Box 7780, Nashua, NH 03060-7780 USA
Phone:	603-889-2386
Fax:	603-889-1135
BBS:	603-595-0386 24 hours

Bounds Checker Professional Edition is a commercial memory debugging tool for DOS and Windows platforms. To detect errors it uses the source code instrumentation (SCI) technology from Parasoft Corporation (makers of Insure++) to detect errors via a combined effort between the two software companies. Note that previous versions of Bounds Checker have used different technology, from a combination of function interception and the use of 386 hardware interrupts to detect wild pointers. This level of error checking was quite good, but Bounds Checker Professional Edition is a step up to take full advantage of the power of source code instrumentation.

Bounds Checker Professional Edition inherits all the best features from the SCI technology of Parasoft Corporation. Bounds Checker offers a very high level of error checking for memory errors and anomalous pointer operations including those involving stack and static memory locations. Memory leak reporting is of exceptional quality because of the *immediate* reporting of memory leaks at the point where the block was actually leaked due to assignment, free, or loss of scope. Error reports are displayed in a Windows GUI and show the full call stack of the error and also any corresponding allocated block. Windows resource leak detection is a powerful feature allowing the detection of the condition where the program might never return resources to the Windows operating system.

One of Bounds Checker's strengths in this and past versions is its API checking. All calls to Windows APIs are tested for parameter errors and for error return codes. This feature will find any coding errors where invalid parameters, including bad pointers or incorrect bitmasks, are inadvertently passed to the WIN32 API due to a coding error. The WIN32 API calls are also monitored for returning error codes, which could indicate either a coding error or a valid failure code. Bounds Checker provides easy suppression of error reports so that you can weed out those that are not bugs.

Bounds Checker also provides very good runtime tracing facilities which can give insight into your program's operation. The events that can be logged include API calls, API returns, Windows messages and hooks, debugging messages and, of course, any errors detected by Bounds Checker. The trace log can be viewed in a Windows GUI which shows hierarchical views of the information, and can view source code.

Checking for WIN32 API compliance is another useful feature when writing functions for multiple Windows platforms. There are two types of API compliance checking provided by Bounds Checker: run-time and executable. Run-time checking will summarize the calls made during run-time to the various APIs into groups, indicating which Windows platforms your program is compatible with. Executable checking is a form of static checking that scans the executable for calls to nonportable API functions. Executable checking finds all function calls and does not depend on run-time sequences, but even if it finds a nonportable API call, it may not be useful if your application has nonportable API calls embedded that are not actually called at run-time (i.e., the program checks at startup which version of the program is running and calls the appropriate API functions). Also, executable checking does not work for API calls made from within DLLs whereas run-time checking does. Using both executable and run-time compliance checking is probably the best solution.

Bounds Checker has a number of run-time options to control error reporting and performance. The various error classes can be suppressed globally, or on a per-API or per-location level. There are options to suppress stack walking and only report the current file and line number for memory or resource allocations, thereby trading off performance with reported detail.

BORLAND CODEGUARD

Product Name:	Borland CodeGuard
Purpose:	Memory error checker for Borland C++
Platforms:	Windows 3.1, Windows 95, Windows NT
Price:	$99.95 (introductory price)
Company:	Borland International
Address:	100 Borland Way, Scotts Valley, CA 95066, USA
Phone:	1-800-233-2444, 510-354-3828
Web:	http://www.borland.com/

Borland's recent introduction of CodeGuard shows that it is not only the third-party tool vendors who are pressing the envelope in error checking tools. Borland is the first of the "big four" vendors to offer a companion memory error checking tool.

CodeGuard offers detection of the usual set of memory errors including bounds errors, uninitialized uses, double deallaction, and reads of deallocated memory. CodeGuard also tracks resource errors such as leaking file handles, and has validation of Windows API parameters and return values.

The implementation method is function-level interception of calls to the C run-time library or the Windows API. Hence, Borland CodeGuard is not fully leveraging the compiler technology to offer access-level checking. However, it does make some use of the technology to provide two features not common in function-level tools:

1. Interception of all calls to C++ member functions to validate the "`this`" pointer.
2. Stack and data segment knowledge to detect automatic or global variable overwrites.

Although it is obviously strongest with Borland's compiler and integrated debugger, Code-Guard can also be used with other standalone debugger products, or as a command-line tool. When used as another integrated tool in Borland's IDE, CodeGuard can break in the debugger on the line causing an error, and write error reports to the IDE message window. Double clicking on the messages allows navigation to source code from within the IDE. There is also a configuration tool for suppressing message reports based on various criteria, and to customize the message format.

VMON AND VMEMCHECK FROM BROWN UNIVERSITY

Tool Name:	vmon, vmemcheck
Purpose:	memory allocation debugging

Platforms:	UNIX
Languages:	ANSI C, C++,
Status:	free
Author:	Steve Reiss
Availability:	FTP *wilma.cs.brown.edu* as file *pub/aard.tar.Z*

The Computer Science Department at Brown University offers a free package for memory debugging under UNIX. The package detects memory errors such as freeing bad memory or using uninitialized memory. The tool works at a low level by intercepting memory accesses and also calls to `malloc` and `free`. `vmon` produces trace output about memory accesses and `vmemcheck` can be used to analyze the traces either at run-time or postmortem.

The `vmon` and `vmemcheck` tools are available as part of Brown University's AARD toolset via FTP from `wilma.cs.brown.edu` as the file `pub/aard.tar.Z`. There is also a variety of other interesting software engineering projects at that site.

IDCLIB: A FREE MINOR DEBUGGING LIBRARY

Tool Name:	*idClib*
Purpose:	standard library run-time checker
Platforms:	UNIX-based
Languages:	ANSI C, C++, K&R C
Status:	free
Author:	Ian Cottam and Jon Taylor (University of Manchester, UK)
Availability:	FTP *ftp.cs.man.ac.uk:pub/idclib_1.4.shar* Companion CDROM in directory *idclib*
Key Points:	• checks arguments to many standard functions • uses pre-compilation tool, not preprocessor macros
Limitations:	• no memory block error checking • no memory leak tracking

The *idClib* library by Ian Cottam is a debugging library with similar aims to most debugging libraries discussed here. However, rather than using macro or link-time interception, it uses a compiler-like tool for pre-compilation of C files which converts standard C library function calls to `idC` library calls. The *idClib* functions perform argument checking and then call the corresponding standard functions. At present, version 1.4 does not perform any detailed checking of `malloc`/`free` blocks, but this would not be difficult to add.

One notable feature is that the pre-compilation tool also enforces a particular programming style, called *idC* for "Ian's disciplined C", and warns about infringements of this style. The style restrictions are discussed in Ian Cottam's interesting technical report:

COTTAM, Ian D., *idC: A Subset of Standard C for Initial Teaching*, Tech Report UMCS-92-12-3, Dept. Computer Science, University of Manchester, England, 1992. (available via FTP from *ftp.cs.man.ac.uk* in directory *pub/TR* as file UMCS-92-12-3.ps.Z)

A distribution of the *idClib* library is currently available via anonymous FTP from *ftp.cs.man.ac.uk/pub/idclib_1.4.shar* (filename may change with upgrades).

MALLOC-TRACE: A SUN MALLOC DEBUGGING LIBRARY

Tool Name:	malloc-trace
Purpose:	malloc debugging library for Sun
Platform/s:	SunOS 3.2
Status:	Free
Author:	Mark Brader
Availability:	*comp.sources.unix/volume18/malloc-trace.Z* Companion CDROM in directory *malloc-trace*
Key Points:	— linkable memory debugging using sbrk

Yet another malloc/free debugging library is available for Sun called malloc-trace. It is a linkable library with implementations of malloc in terms of sbrk. Running the program with malloc-trace enabled causes a log file "malloc.out" to be created. This can be later examined by a shell script called prleak, which reports memory usage statistics and diagnoses memory leaks. Unfortunately, this library is not highly portable, and the (limited) documentation refers only to the Sun platform.

MNEMOSYNE — FREE C MEMORY DEBUGGING LIBRARY

Tool Name:	mnemosyne
Purpose:	memory leak tracing
Platforms:	UNIX-based
Languages:	K&R C
Status:	free
Author:	Marcus J. Ranum

| Availability: | FTP comp.sources.misc/volume16/mnemosyne/part01.Z |
| Key Points: | — macro interception of malloc family
— memory leaks traced only after execution |

The mnemosyne package uses macro interception of the malloc family of library functions. All C files must include "mnemosyne.h" after all #include <...> directives. At run-time, mnemosyne tracks all memory allocation operations in memory, and also writes them to disk files. Common errors such as a bad free, double free, or malloc failure are written to a log file or to stderr.

For detection of memory leaks, the mnemalyse program is called after execution to interpret the data files produced by a program run with mnemosyne enabled. This produces a report of memory blocks that were not deallocated. Although this is a reasonable package, it is a little dated, and does not offer some features common in larger packages such as run-time configuration and run-time leak reports.

MALLOC DEBUG LIBRARY — FREE UNIX LIBRARY

Tool Name:	malloc-1.2.0
Purpose:	memory debugging and leak tracing
Platforms:	UNIX (requires sbrk)
Languages:	ANSI C, not K&R C, not C++
Status:	free (Gnu Library Public License)
Author:	Gray Watson
Availability:	FTP *comp.sources.unix/volume26/malloc-1.2.0/** Companion CDROM in directory *malloc*

This malloc debugging library is a linkable version that offers numerous debugging features. The package creates a UNIX library libmalloc.a which is linked in to perform error checking. Also available is a "malloc.h" header file that can be included to enable macro interception of library functions to allow error diagnostics with line and filename informa-tion. The errors detected include bad deallocations, fence-post memory block overwrites and uses of already-freed memory. There is also a variety of features supporting logging of mem-ory leaks and memory allocation statistics. In addition to intercepting the malloc family, a large number of other standard functions, such as many string functions, are intercepted and checked for errors.

This is a high quality package with good documentation and neat features such as GNU-like self configurations for a variety of UNIX platforms. The distribution also includes a malloc_dbg program that can be used to help configure the environment variables needed to enable memory debugging. There is no explicit C++ support, but it could be added quite simply by supplying overloaded versions of new and delete that call malloc and free.

LEAK — FREE UNIX MEMORY LEAK LIBRARY

Tool Name:	leak
Purpose:	memory leak tracing library
Languages:	ANSI C, no C++ support
Status:	free (non-commercial use)
Author:	Christopher Phillips
Availability:	FTP *comp.sources.unix/volume27/leak/**
Key Point:	— macro interception; post-run leak detection
Limitation:	— very limited error detection

The "leak" library is a memory allocation debugging library based on macro interception of library calls. All C files must include a "leak.h" header file; running the program then creates log files. Memory leaks are found by running a "leakdump" utility after the program has completed. A minor feature of the implementation is its use of the ndbm UNIX database library to maintain its internal data structures.

As the author says, leak is a "quick and dirty" method of finding memory leaks. It has many limitations such as very limited error checking (the only error found is freeing an unallocated pointer), no support for debugging any functions other than malloc, free and realloc, and no run-time memory leak reports.

DR DOBB'S JOURNAL MALLOC DEBUGGING LIBRARIES

Tool Name:	various malloc debugging libraries
Status:	free
Authors:	Lawrence D. Spencer; Jim Schimandle; Alan Holub
Availability:	SimTel sites: *ddjmag/ddj9008.zip* (*spencer.lst* and *schimand.lst*)
Simtel sites:	*ddjmag/ddj8806.zip* (*dmallocc.zip* and *malloch.zip*)

The August 1990 issue of Dr Dobb's Journal contains two different memory allocation debugging libraries. All Dr Dobb's source files are available via FTP through SimTel sites in the ddjmay directory. The article references are:

SPENCER, Lawrence D., *Debugging memory allocation errors*, Dr Dobbs Journal, August 1990.

SCHIMANDLE, Jim, *Encapsulating C memory allocation*, Dr Dobbs Journal, August 1990.

Lawrence Spencer's method doesn't use macro interception (although it could easily be added), but instead requires programmers to explicitly call special functions such as `mem-Malloc` and `memFree` instead of `malloc` and `free`. Jim Schimandle's library uses macro interception of `malloc`, `free`, and `realloc` and supports limited error detection (i.e., freeing invalid pointer) and memory leak reports.

Finally, a limited debugging library by Allen Holub appears in the June 1988 distribution. It provides `dmalloc`, `dcalloc` and `dfree` functions and a header file "`malloc.h`" that redefines `malloc`, `calloc` and `free` to these debugging functions (though it doesn't pass line or filename information). Error diagnostics are limited to an invalid pointer passed to `free` and allocation failure.

MORE FREE MEMORY ALLOCATION DEBUGGING TOOLS

This section examines a few more free tools that came to my attention too close to the writing deadline. Hence they are not evaluated to the depth of others in this chapter.

ElectricFence — free memory allocation debugging tool

Tool Name:	ElectricFence
Purpose:	Memory debugger using virtual memory hardware interception
Author:	Bruce Perens
Availability:	Linux sites: e.g. *sunsite.unc.edu:/pub/Linux/devel/lang/c/ElectricFence**

ElectricFence is a memory allocation debugger that uses a unique method to detect memory errors. The underlying hardware support for virtual memory handling is used to efficiently detect illegal references. ElectricFence detects the usual set of errors such as referencing uninitialized memory, bad `frees`, and memory overruns.

Checker — free Linux memory allocation debugging tool

Tool Name:	Checker
Purpose:	Memory allocation debugging for C and C++
Author:	Tristan Gingold
Availability:	Linux sites: e.g. *sunsite.unc.edu:/pub/Linux/devel/lang/c/Check** and */lang/c++/Check**

Checker is a memory error detection tool and garbage collector. The underlying technology is code insertion. The usual set of errors are detected including invalid pointers, uninitialized read, and so on. Checker requires the use of `gcc` or `g++`.

WISH — COMPILER MEMORY ALLOCATION DEBUGGING

Has it ever occurred to you that every feature of these software tools could just as easily be provided by your compiler? This lucrative market niche for run-time memory access validation tools exists mostly because no compilers offer such features. Compilers could probably do a much better job! The interception of memory accesses required for this type of run-time checking requires only a modification of the compiler backend code generation routines. Every memory read or write access could be intercepted immediately. Even if the compiler only offered callbacks for reads and writes (i.e., even if no libraries using these intercepts to track memory usage were provided), it would then be possible for users without low-level knowledge to write very sophisticated memory validation routines offering immediate detection of violations.

Alternatively, a few modifications to compiler code generation techniques would ease some of the limitations of even the best third-party tools. For example, current tools typically cannot detect boundary reads and writes (i.e., array bounds overflow) on static or stack allocated variables. The problem is that these variables are packed very tightly and so a bounds violation looks like a valid read of the next variable. The compiler could overcome this limitation by offering an option to place padding areas between the variables, and supplying an API to determine whether an address is valid. There are plenty of other improvements that compiler-supported error checking could offer. For example, one very fancy feature would be knowing the type of variable being accessed by a read or write.

WISH — VENDOR APIS FOR DEBUGGING LIBRARIES

All of these home-grown memory allocation debugging libraries suffer from a common set of limitations (e.g., stack address overwrites are hard to detect, and stack backtraces are difficult to produce portably). Most of these limitations would disappear if compiler vendors would utilize their low-level intimate knowledge of their particular platform to provide an API including functions for tasks such as to:

- determine what type of memory an address is: stack, heap, string literal, static or global variable.
- determine the size of an allocated memory block from its address.
- determine what primitive was used to allocate a block (i.e., `malloc`, `calloc`, `realloc` or C++ `new` operator).
- produce a stack trace at a given point, and save it for later use (i.e., provide a "stack context" abstract data type with various facilities).

For example, a function call "`mem_address_type(addr)`" could return 0 for unknown (i.e., not enough information or "unimplemented for this platform") or otherwise a bitwise-or of all the possible types of address: 1 for stack, 2 for heap, 4 for static variable, 8 for global variable, 16 for floating-point constant, etc. Hopefully, vendors or readers with platform-specific knowledge will be able to implement functions such as this and make them available.

Debuggers

*A*lmost all implementations of the C or C++ language come with at least one tool for debugging of programs: an interactive debugger. This class of tool is an incredible software innovation but we accept it as a matter of fact these days. The debugger is a highly versatile debugging tool that works at both ends of the compilation process — it coordinates debugging effort between the final machine code and the original source code by translating machine addresses into symbolic names. It allows you to get under the hood and see exactly what is going on with the program's execution.

Debuggers go by various names. They are also called "symbolic debuggers" or sometimes there is an even more pedantic distinction of calling them "source code debuggers" if they operate directly from the source code files as opposed to the assembly-based debuggers. Thus, we could separate debuggers into "symbolic debuggers" which work only with the executable (and a postmortem dump), and "source code debuggers," which also work directly with the source code files. However, we won't consider this classification any further, and will refer to all forms as just debuggers. Enough said.

DEBUGGER FEATURES

There is an immense variety of existing debugger tools and naturally there is great variation between products. However, the basic features provided by debuggers are very similar and typically include:

- stack traces
- breakpoints
- conditional breakpoints
- "watching" data locations
- single-step execution
- repeatable single-step execution
- attaching to a running process
- modifying variables during execution
- reverse execution or back tracing
- multi-screen debugging
- inspection and display of complex data structures

All these features can be used to start, stop, and restart execution, while examining program data values and the call stack. The usual manner of usage is to set breakpoints at various execution points (typically on entry to particular functions, or at particular line numbers of files). The program is then run and execution then continues till a breakpoint is triggered, whereupon control is returned to the user at the debugger to use commands to print values, see the stack trace, etc. Then execution is usually continued to another breakpoint and the process repeated.

Breakpoints: Breakpoints are a truly fundamental feature of modern debuggers. Typically they offer features to set breakpoints on entry to a function, at a given line in a file, and on certain other events such as message arrival. Breakpoints mainly serve to break execution of the program but some debuggers offer fancy actions that can occur instead of stopping such as enabling or disabling another breakpoint.

Conditional breakpoints: Conditional breakpoints add a condition to ordinary breakpoints that must evaluate to true before the breakpoint will stop the program's execution. This feature is not as frequently used as unconditional breakpoints but it can really save you. One real-life example that comes to mind was the need to step through to the 104th iteration of a loop: few debuggers have any good support of loops, and so you can visualize clicking "Step" many times. However, setting a conditional breakpoint on the expression "i==104" inside the loop makes it easy!

Debugger watchpoints: Facilities to "watch" a location are particularly useful, because the programmer is notified of any reads and/or writes to that location. Poor debuggers will require the user to step through the code and manually examine the watch window for any changes to the variables. A good debugger will automatically stop execution when a location changes. However, be warned that not all debuggers implement watchpoints particularly well. In my experience any use of watchpoints provided by UNIX debuggers (especially dbx) shows such poor performance that all major vendors will have standardized their platform APIs long before your program completes.

Single-step execution: Most debuggers offer some form of single-step execution mode where statements are executed one at a time. This is a particularly useful mode for debugging or even just for code browsing. There are a few types of "stepping" that are typically available:

- step into function calls;
- step past a function call;
- continue until function returns.

One feature I'd like to see but haven't is stepping until a loop completes. The obvious workaround is to set a breakpoint just after the loop and then continue execution. This is a reasonable solution for the better point-and-click debuggers, particularly those with a "run to cursor" command. However, a special loop skipping command would be a welcome addition to UNIX command-line debuggers.

Repeatable single-step execution: The main difference between using stepping a number of times and choosing to continue execution is whether the source code window is updated with the current location (and data windows with current values, etc.). Another level of stepping features is an automated repeated- step mode which updates the source code window at regular intervals. This gives the appearance of slow-motion execution and goes by various names such as repeated-step, step-step execution or animation facilities.

Attaching debuggers to processes: Attaching to a running UNIX process is another powerful feature now available on most UNIX debuggers such as dbx and gdb. The debugger can "attach" to a running process as needed, rather than always running the program from within the debugger. This attach feature can be crucial when attempting to debug multi-process applications. For example, trying to debug a daemon program is typically difficult because the usual method of implementing a daemon is for it to set up a child process (so as to lose the dependence on the terminal and for other reasons), and then have the parent process actually die. Running the daemon application within the debugger won't last long; instead you have to attach to the child process to continue debugging the important code. dbx provides the -a command line option for attaching; gdb allows a PID to be passed as an argument, and also offers an "attach" command for within the session. The "detach" command complements the attach features allowing you to give the process back to the operating system after a long and arduous debugging stint.

Modifying variables during debugging: Setting the value of a variable from a debugger can be a useful technique, although it is a feature that should not be overused. It is bad policy to get into the habit of changing the executable to see if you can fix a bug, since you can easily forget to propagate the changes back to source code.

Reverse execution or back tracing: An amazing feature that is starting to be available in more debugger tools is reverse execution. This allows you to step backwards in time and see what happened earlier in the program's execution. This feature requires the debugger to store information about the execution of the program (e.g., old values of variables that were overwritten). Typically reverse execution is limited to tracking back to the last operating system request since these are much harder to reverse (e.g., how do you reverse a file operation? In theory it's possible to do, but efficiently?).

Multi-screen debugging: Debugging problems on some machines and operating systems can be hampered by the need to see the program on the entire screen and also the debugger windows. For example, trying to debug a graphical program is difficult when the debugger always needs to take back the screen. This can be a problem for DOS or Windows programs, or even for X/Motif programming with the annoying "grabbed screen" problems. The facility to debug on one monitor and run the program on another is a neat feature supported by some debuggers.

Inspection and display of complex data structures: Most debuggers have some method of viewing the current value of variables. UNIX debuggers have a "print" command; Windows debuggers typically offer a "watch" window. The best type of feature to look for is one that can display complex data structures such as arrays easily. Ideally an entire linked list should be able to be displayed, but typically the user has to manually follow links either by clicking on the pointer or typing commands.

Integration with the editor and build environment: When you detect a bug, it's convenient to switch back to the text editor, make the source code change, and rebuild ready for the next debugging session. Whether the debugger is integrated with the editor and build environment to facilitate this swapping will greatly affect your productivity.

DEBUGGER USAGE STRATEGIES

My personal experience with the use of debuggers has gone from an initial reluctance to using debuggers for anything other than postmortem debugging, to the current state of affairs where I rarely run a program outside of a debugger! No matter what platform, a debugger is a fantastic tool once you learn how to use it to its fullest.

The most rudimentary use of a debugger is to invoke it only once the program has failed abnormally. Using a debugger is the easiest way to find out what line of code caused the segmentation fault or bus error under UNIX.

But postmortem debugging is nowhere near stretching the limits. Running your program within a debugger is a far more valuable use of the tool. For starters, if there is a GPF, segmentation fault, bus error or other fatal error, the debugger will trap it immediately without generating a dump file. Hence there is no wasted disk space for the dump file and no wasted time starting up the debugger. So are you convinced yet? If you aren't, try using breakpoints and single-stepping through some code.

One of the best pieces of advice for programmers is: **single-step all new code.** Single-stepping through your code in the debugger is a valuable technique for debugging and code maintenance. Although programmers are well-known to be the worst people to debug and test their own code, single-stepping through your own code can be quite valuable in looking for any "surprises" in the flow of control. In addition, single-stepping through code offers a useful maintenance technique for familiarizing yourself with the dynamic flow of control in legacy code, analogous to the way a browser can give you an overview of the source code issues. In short, a useful rule of source code maintenance is: **single-step old code too!**

In addition to all the various uses in your own individual programming repertoire, the debugger can assert its presence in a team environment. The ideas of code inspections and walkthroughs have gradually come into vogue recently as techniques for delivering error-free software. Typically, both are formal meetings where a group examines the source code written by one individual. The difference is that a code inspection is a static examination of the source code, whereas a walkthrough involves "executing" the code on a particular set of inputs. Where a source checker can aid code inspections, the debugger can be an important tool for more professional code walkthroughs. Rather than the "whiteboard method" of manually tracing through the code with variable values on the whiteboard, why not use the debugger to do all the work? Executing the code within the debugger in single-step mode offers all the dynamic features that a walkthrough is all about. Instead of using a whiteboard, the important variable values can be displayed in the watch window. Why do it the old way when you have a good *tool*?

DR WATSON — WINDOWS POSTMORTEM DEBUGGER

The technique of postmortem debugging applies to any operating system capable of providing some form of stack dump. Unfortunately, programs running in unprotected MS-DOS do not have the capability of producing a dump, and therefore postmortem debugging is not possible. However, because Windows can run in protected mode, it offers a feature whereby such failures (e.g., UAEs and GPFs) are detected and produce a dump of program state. Dr Watson is one of the tools using this facility to provide postmortem debugging.

Dr Watson is produced by Microsoft and shipped with the production version of Windows 3.1 so all installations should have it. To start Dr Watson choose File->Run from the Program Manager menus and find "drwatson.exe" in the windows directory.

Dr Watson is a debugging tool that runs in the background until a fatal error is detected. When a GPF occurs, Dr Watson will pop up a warning dialog indicating the problem and write a description to a log file. The executable name is drwatson.exè and the log file is drwatson.log in the \windows directory. The log file contains a great deal of information such as the cause of the error, hardware register contents, and a stack trace. Unfortunately the stack trace is in hexadecimal and mapping the address to the source code requires examination of a map file to determine the function, and then an object file listing with line number comments to determine the exact statement causing the fault. But despite this long process, Dr Watson is a valuable method of extracting information about a crash and you can leave it run in the background with minimal overhead for the system.

WINSPECTOR — BORLAND'S POSTMORTEM DEBUGGER

WinSpector is a postmortem debugging tool similar to Dr Watson that is available with Turbo C++ or Borland C++. WinSpector runs in the background and only pops up a warning dialog when it detects a UAE (e.g., divide by zero or stray pointer). A log file is generated in "\windows\winspctr.log" and if the postmortem dump option to WinSpector is enabled (and this is recommended) a binary dump file is also stored in "\windows\winspctr.bin".

WinSpector is a lot easier to use than Dr Watson in Windows in various areas. Firstly WinSpector can be started as a windows application whereas Dr Watson has to be run from the Program Manager's Run menu option. WinSpector also has a Windows GUI whereby you can set options and view error logs, whereas Dr Watson is a DOS executable that only pops up a simple dialog message whenever you double click on its icon.

The log file reports on the states of various aspects of program execution such as the cause of the error, the list of executing tasks and a stack trace. By default the stack trace involves hexadecimal addresses but can be mapped to symbolic function names if a ".sym" file is available to WinSpector at the time of the exception. This ".sym" file can be generated from a ".map" file that can be generated by enabling the map options in the Turbo C++ or Borland C++ IDE, with the bcc -M option or the Tlink /m option. This ".map" file can be converted to a ".sym" file using the tmapsym utility that is part of the distribution. The buildsym utility is another alternative method for creating a ".sym" file via the exemap and tmapsym utilities.

The dfa standalone utility is also available for post-processing of the dump file "\windows\winspctr.bin" with the executable file. The output trace file is generated in "dfa.out" or another file specified by the /O option to the dfa utility.

MULTISCOPE CRASH ANALYZER — POSTMORTEM DEBUGGER

The MultiScope debugger package includes a postmortem debugging feature that is not common in Windows debuggers. The MED feature detects runtime exceptions and dumps the state of your program's memory and data structures to a disk file. Naturally MultiScope has limited features when invoked in a postmortem debugging mode, since you cannot continue execution. However, the usual postmortem information is available such as the all-important stack trace.

The detection of UAEs is done by the MEDWP executable which must be running in the background just as Dr Watson and WinSpector do. When an error is detected, a postmortem dump ".PMD" file is created. The MultiScope Crash Analyzer is used to examine the postmortem dump file at a later stage. For example, a customer at a remote site could send you the PMD file for you to debug locally.

There are also a couple of API functions to force MED to produce a postmortem dump should the application detect an internal failure. For example, this would be used if your project has its own *assert* macro defined, and this allows MultiScope to debug assertion failures at customer sites. To use these APIs, your program must link with the MED library and call the MEDInit function.

TURBO DEBUGGER FOR WINDOWS

Turbo Debugger for Windows (TDW) comes with Borland's compiler suites Turbo C++ and Borland C++. TDW has a very impressive suite of debugging and tracing features that makes it one of the most powerful debuggers I have seen yet. Postmortem debugging is not supported directly by TDW but is available via the WinSpector utility from Borland.

The one minor nuisance with TDW is the DOS-based full screen interface rather than a native Windows interface. TDW is a Windows application that runs a DOS GUI. However, other advantages more than compensate, and it is easy to adjust to the different GUI style which is easy to use as far as DOS GUIs go. The debugger swaps between the DOS screen for the debugger and the application's screen view which can become annoying despite the "smart" swapping algorithm. One solution is to use a second monitor for debugging if your hardware supports it.

However, the debugging and tracing features are impressive. Program execution can be controlled via options to trace into, step over or continue until function return. The "Animate" feature is a powerful repeated-stepping option with a specifiable time delay at each step. There is also the fancy "Back Trace" option for reverse execution; this allows the user to undo the previous statement. Admittedly the reverse execution feature has the limitations that: (a) history recording must be on while executing, and (b) back tracing will only work until the previous statement was some API call for which the previous state is hard to compute. However, I can't see any technical method whereby these limitations could be avoided either.

There are also many features for examining data. Various view windows allow watching of the stack (including function arguments), local variables, and global variables. There is a hierarchical view of C++ classes and an alphabetical listing of them. The "Evaluate/Modify" feature allows expression evaluation and modification of variables. The "Inspection" window also allows watching of chosen variables in more detail. Lower-level views of the CPU registers, assembly code instructions and numeric processor are also available.

Breakpoints and watchpoints can be set in a variety of modes. In addition to basic breakpoints, they can be programmed to perform actions including logging, execution of an expression, enabling and disabling another breakpoint. Conditional breakpoints allow the user to break only when a condition is true. Breakpoints are also possible on modification of a global variable. Hardware breakpoints are also supported.

Windows-specific debugging issues are also addressed in a number of ways. Messages can be traced a la Spy and WinSight. The global and local heap can also be inspected. Debugging of DLLs is also supported by TDW.

In summary TDW has many features for controlling program execution, setting breakpoints and data inspection and this brief review really does not do the product justice in that area. These neat features more than compensate for the slight annoyance of a DOS-based GUI, and TDW is one of the best Windows debuggers around.

QUICKC FOR WINDOWS DEBUGGER

QuickC for Windows is available from Microsoft as an integrated development environment and this includes a debugger. This tight integration makes it easy to flip back and forth between editor and debugger while making changes and rebuilding. This saves a lot of time over other less integrated environments where rebuilding is less automatic.

The usual contingent of run-time execution controls are available from the Run menu, and some on the toolbar. The list includes go, continue to cursor (effectively a temporary breakpoint at the current cursor position), trace into, step over, and restart. There is also an

"Animation" facility for repeated trace-into operations, where the source code window is updated with each trace, and there are three speed choices. Breakpoints can be set for specific statements and thereby entry to a function, and also on receipt of a Windows message. Conditional breakpoints with an expression that must be true are also available.

Data viewing is available through a number of windows. There is a watch window for expressions and variables, a locals window for local variables of the current function, a stack trace and lower-level views such as a CPU registers window. The "Modify Variable" option allows changing a variable, but there is no way to call a function from the debugger.

The QuickC GUI is a true Windows GUI and the debugger is no exception. There is no screen swapping and there are also some nice features of the GUI. For example, breakpoints can be set at the cursor position via the toolbar, and variables can be watched by clicking on the name and choosing the QuickWatch option. Overall the QuickC for Windows debugger is a little light on features but offers a convenient integrated debugger and inherent productivity advantages therein.

CodeView for Windows

CodeView for Windows (CVW) is Microsoft's debugger for the Microsoft C/C++ compiler suite. CVW does not support other compilers — not even QuickC which is also from Microsoft. CVW is not fully integrated with Microsoft C/C++ and runs in its own window.

The feature set offered by CVW is good in the areas of execution control and data examination. The features are similar to QuickC including go, trace into, step over, continue to cursor, and animation (repeated tracing with source code updating). Breakpoints can be unconditional or conditional and can be activated by Windows messages. The local window shows local variables and the watch window can show variables or expressions. Low-level aspects such as memory and registers can also be viewed, and even modified by just typing a new value. In fact, all variables can be changed this way, and there is also the ability to call functions from within the debugger. There is also support for displaying the global and local heaps.

With the release of CVW version 4.0 the debugger tolerates the Windows system although it is still a character-based application in a Windows window. This alleviates the screen swapping issues in earlier CVW releases but the GUI is still not a true Windows GUI and this is a sticking point. Another issue with the GUI is that a lot of the features are not available through GUI elements such as menus, dialogs or toolbar buttons. Instead they are available as typed commands, which is a style that is more like UNIX than Windows.

Periscope — Hardware-assisted Debugger

Product Name:	Periscope Model IV
Platforms:	DOS, Windows 3.1, Windows 95, OS/2, embedded
Price:	$3,000-$5,000

Company:	The Periscope Company
Address:	1475 Peachtree St., Suite 100, ATLANTA, GA 30309, USA
Phone:	1-800-722-7006; 404-888-5335
Fax:	404-888-5520
Email:	102370.1026@compuserve.com

Periscope is a low-level hardware-assisted debugger rather than a software debugger. Although it does not truly match the criteria of a debugger for C/C++ application programming, Periscope does deserve an honorable mention for its more specialized uses. It is particularly useful for debugging real-time and time-sensitive software such as games, communications and embedded software. Periscope comes with a hardware card that sits on the hardware bus and a CPU interface card, which give Periscope similar power to an in-circuit emulator (ICE). This low-level power enables you to trace hardware events for later mapping back to source and to use hardware breakpoints.

UNIX POSTMORTEM DEBUGGING

Some of the more common debuggers under UNIX are `sdb`, `gdb` and `dbx`. UNIX debuggers are reasonably good but tend not to be as useful as the multi-window debugging often allowed on smaller machines. However, one thing they all have in common is the availability of postmortem debugging of a UNIX core dump.

Postmortem debugging is a particular method of using a debugger to examine a "dump" of the program's state, which was produced by the operating system upon detection of some abnormal condition. This is a well-known technique under UNIX, where a "`core`" file is produced for errors such as a segmentation fault or bus error. The effect of a core dump is that the entire program memory contents (including stack, heap, and global variables) are dumped to a file.

Although the method of examining the `core` file depends on the UNIX debugger used, the basic idea remains the same. The debugger is used to examine the `core` file in conjunction with the executable program, to determine the state of the program when it failed. A stack trace of all functions called is usually available, and the values of variables can be examined.

Note that for useful debugging it is often necessary to compile the program using the "`-g`" option to the compiler, so that symbolic information is left in the executable for use by the debugger. If this symbolic information is not available, the debugger will not be able to get as much information out of the dump. It should still be able to produce a listing of the function names of the call stack, but will probably not have line number information or parameter values available.

The most common use of postmortem debugging is in the detection of the cause of some abnormal termination such as a "segmentation fault" or "bus error." However, the method can be invoked upon the detection of a number of other errors, either by the user or within the program itself. If the programmer, while testing the program, encounters an error and wishes to perform postmortem debugging, it is a simple matter of pressing the two-key sequence <ctrl-\> to send the SIGQUIT signal to the program and thereby provoke a core dump (assuming this signal is not trapped by the program).

If the program itself detects an error of some sort (e.g., control reaches a point where it should not), the program can terminate abnormally and produce a "core" file. The simplest method is to use the standard assert macro that accepts an expression that must be true:

```
assert (i >= 0 && i < n);   /* Check the index is valid */
```

The assert macro is supported by ANSI C and C++ in the header file <assert.h>. The assertion expression is checked at run-time, and the program will terminate with a core dump if it is false. A special case is control flow sequences that should not occur which are often protected via a simple assertion:

```
assert(0);   /* Should never get here! */
```

If the condition cannot be easily coded as an assertion expression, an effective method in ANSI C or C++ is to call the abort standard library function. The abort function will provoke a core dump under UNIX and is actually the primitive called by the assert macro:

```
abort();        /* suicide with core dump */
```

Another method in ANSI C or C++ under UNIX is to use the raise library function, which sends signals to the program itself:

```
raise(SIGQUIT);    /* suicide with core dump */
```

If this function is not available, as is the case in some pre-ANSI implementations, it is also possible to use the UNIX library functions kill and getpid, as follows:

```
kill(getpid(), SIGQUIT);   /* core dump */
```

TIP: postmortem debugging stripped UNIX executables

Postmortem debugging on an executable that has been "stripped" by the UNIX strip command can be difficult due to the absence of naming information. The same problem arises in debugging an executable that has not been built with the compiler "-g" option. A solution to such problems is available if your organization has good build management schemes in place. You can use the non-stripped version of the executable combined with the core file to achieve better trace information. This way, you get all the details you would have gotten from a non-stripped crash.

TIP — coding functions for debuggers to call

An important technique in the usage of debuggers is writing functions specifically to be called from within the debugger. These can usually be functions with and without parameter lists, as debuggers provide methods of passing arguments to called functions.

For example, such functions might perform self-tests or produce reports on the status of some large data structure. Note that any variables that are modified by these functions should be qualified as `volatile` to make the compiler aware that these variables may be modified in unpredictable ways.

Functions for debugger usage need not be from the particular application. A useful example of calling functions from a debugger would be a function to print the current memory leak list, as in some of the memory allocation debugging packages. Furthermore, many commercial tools also provide functions for this purpose; for example, Purify offers many API functions that can be called from a debugger, such as to print the current heap status.

ADB — A UNIX DEBUGGER

Tool Name:	`adb`
Purpose:	UNIX low-level debugger
Platforms:	UNIX
Languages:	works at assembly level
Status:	UNIX tool
Key Points:	very low-level debugging
Limitations:	not a source-level debugger

The `adb` debugger is a low-level debugger for many UNIX platforms. It offers a cryptic but powerful set of commands that can be used for interactive or postmortem debugging. There is some symbolic support such as a simple backtracing facility. There isn't really much more to be said about this old debugger. You use it only if you have to, such as for debugging the kernel using the `-k` option to `adb`. As a general purpose debugger, the absence of source code debugging makes it very cumbersome and not of particular use to the average programmer. I've never used it and have no future plans to do so!

DBX — A UNIX DEBUGGER

Tool Name:	`dbx`
Purpose:	UNIX debugger
Platforms:	UNIX
Languages:	C and C++, others too
Status:	UNIX tool

dbx is a debugger supported on most UNIX-based systems. It was originally available on Berkeley UNIX versions, but its usage has now spread to most UNIX platforms. A typical invocation is as follows:

```
dbx a.out
```

A summary of commands is given in Table 5–1. For full symbolic support it is necessary to compile the program using the -g option to the compiler. This causes the executable to contain symbolic information which is used by the debugger. If the program has not been compiled this way, dbx will still continue, but it will not recognize program names and most of its information will be in the form of hexadecimal addresses.

Table 5–1 dbx commands

Command	Meaning
quit (q)	Quit dbx
run (r)	Run the executable
help (h)	Help (online)
where	Stack trace
print	Print variable values
call	Call function
assign	Change value

There are far too many dbx commands to fully cover here. Some of the important ones are the "-a" command line option to attach to a running process, the "call" online command to call a function and the "assign" command to change the value of a variable during a session.

POSTMORTEM DEBUGGING WITH DBX

The dbx debugger can be used as a postmortem debugger to locate the cause of a program failure after a "core dump" (e.g., as caused by a segmentation fault or bus error). The command to achieve this is usually:

```
dbx a.out core
```

The where command can be applied at the dbx prompt to give a stack trace, which indicates the function, source file and line number of the failure. Most of the dbx debugger features are invoked as if the program had just been executed by dbx up to the failure. For example, the values of variables can be printed using the print command.

GDB — A FREE UNIX DEBUGGER

Tool Name:	gdb
Purpose:	X Windows debugger
Platforms:	UNIX
Languages:	C and C++, others too
Status:	Free
Availability:	GNU distributions, filename: gdb* Companion CDROM in directory gdb
Key Point:	— debugging C++ from gcc/g++

gdb is a free debugger produced by the Free Software Foundation. It is similar to other line-based UNIX debuggers such as dbx in terms of features and user interface. A typical invocation would be:

```
gdb a.out
```

When using gdb for postmortem debugging after a core dump, the command becomes:

```
gdb a.out core
```

Some of the most important commands are shown in Table 5–2. All commands can be abbreviated if the prefix is unique. For full symbolic support, the program must be compiled with debugging information included; typically, this is achieved by the -g compiler option.

Table 5–2 Commonly used gdb commands

Command	Meaning
attach	Attach to a running process
set	Change value of a variable in the program
where	Stack trace of the function call sequence
run	Start or restart the executable with optional arguments
step	Step over statement or into a function call
next	Step over statement (including function calls)
print	Print expressions including function calls
continue	Continue execution after a breakpoint

As with all GNU software, it can be copied via FTP from the sites discussed in the section "**Free tools — GNU software**" on page 9. The filenames usually have a "gdb" prefix but are subject to change.

TIP — Debugging with emacs and gdb

The popular free UNIX-based emacs editor has a very useful mode where it interacts with the GNU gdb debugger. It provides source code tracking automatically knowing where the program is currently executing. A buffer pops up where all breakpoint stops, and all "step" and "next" commands are mirrored by changes in the source window. Admittedly, this on-screen source code tracking is nothing new to debuggers on personal computers, but it's quite a revelation for UNIX debuggers! Within emacs, the mode is entered using ESC then 'x' then gdb and RETURN (i.e., the standard method of starting an emacs command called gdb).

TIP — UNIX debuggers and bad function pointers

A quite confusing cause of a segmentation fault on some UNIX platforms is a NULL or bad function pointer value. An invalid or uninitialized callback in X windows programming is a typical example. This fault causes problems on a few of the common UNIX debuggers, with a strange function call stack report from the "where" command. If you ever see the following report for a stack trace, you can bet it's an invalid callback:

```
noname()
```

And the same error causes a strange stack trace report from gdb. In fact, gdb even diagnoses that you may have uncovered a gdb internal bug (which you haven't). However, gdb is a little better in that at least it gives the function where the bad callback call occurs.

DUEL — AN EXTENSION TO GDB

Tool Name:	Duel
Purpose:	extension to GNU's gdb for advanced flow control
Platforms:	UNIX
Languages:	C and C++, others too
Status:	Free
Availability:	FTP *ftp.cs.princeton.edu:duel/duel.tar.Z* Linux: *sunsite.unc.edu:/pub/Linux/devel/debuggers/gdb** Companion CDROM in directory duel
Key Points:	— fancy expression operators — control flow constructs (if, while)

Duel is intended as an extension to existing debuggers, but currently only supports C debugging using gdb. All Duel commands are prefixed with the command dl, thus making the new features easy to add to existing debuggers. The many extensions offered by Duel include a large number of compact operators for more effective examination of data, and C-like `if` statements and loops. There are far too many extensions to examine in detail, but the power of Duel shows up clearly in the following use of the `-->` extended operator (two minus signs) to traverse an entire linked list and print the `data` field of each list node.

```
gdb> dl head-->next->data
```

Duel is free software available via FTP from `ftp.cs.princeton.edu` in the directory `duel` which contains many files including *duel.tar.Z* which is a complete distribution, and copies of a technical report as files *usenix.paper.ps.Z* and *usenix.paper.dvi*; the same report is also available separately in the file *reports/1992/399.ps.Z* from the top-level FTP directory.

Duel is now offered as part of some `gdb` distributions, notably the Linux distribution. Unfortunately, the main GNU archives do not currently integrate Duel into `gdb`.

XXGDB — X WINDOWS EXTENSION TO GDB

Tool Name:	`xxgdb`
Purpose:	X Windows extension to GNU gdb debugger
Platforms:	UNIX (SunOS, Solaris, Ultrix, Linux, SCO, Bull)
Languages:	C and C++, others too
Status:	Free
Authors:	Po Cheung, Pierre Willard, Dean Michaels
Availability:	X11 contrib distribution: *ftp.x.org:/R5contrib/xxgdb.108.tar.gz* *sunsite.unc.edu:/pub/Linux/devel/debuggers/xxgdb** Early version: *comp.sources.x/volume1[12346]/xxgdb* Companion CDROM in directory *xxgdb*
Key Points:	— debugging C++ from gcc/g++ — X Windows graphical debugging

`xxgdb` is an X Windows front end to `gdb`. However, `xxgdb` is not maintained by the Free Software Foundation, and instead is part of the X11 contributions. Note that the `xxgdb` distribution also includes the `xdbx` front end for the `dbx` debugger. `xxgdb` and `xdbx` share much code and have a very similar architecture with the launching of `gdb` or `dbx` as a child process.

The GUI interface consists of a variety of windows including a source code window, a message window for `gdb` error messages, a command window with buttons for many common `gdb` commands, and a dialogue for typing `gdb` commands (i.e., any not supported by buttons). The simplest command buttons include *run*, *cont*, *next*, *step*, *finish*, and *quit*. Breakpoints can be set and removed via the source code window and are marked by little stop signs. The stack trace is seen via the *stack* button. Variables and expressions can be evaluated by selecting them and choosing the *print* button. Values are displayed in popup windows and pointer expressions can be navigated by clicking on the pointer to pop up a new data window. A useful set of buttons are *Yes* and *No* that respond to any gdb questions.

Overall, this interface empowers gdb with an easier to use full screen interface. However, it is still obvious that you're using a command-line debugger behind the scenes, and the experience is not as good as a fully native debugger.

XDBX — X WINDOWS EXTENSION TO DBX

Tool Name:	xdbx
Purpose:	X Windows debugger
Platforms:	UNIX (X Windows) including SunOS, Solaris, Ultrix, Linux
Languages:	C and C++, others too
Status:	Free
Availability:	FTP with *xxgdb* (see above) with some separate xdbx versions: X11 contrib distribution: *ftp.x.org:/R5contrib/xdbx** *sunsite.unc.edu:/pub/Linux/devel/debuggers/xdbx** Companion CDROM in directory *xdbx*
Authors:	Po Cheung, Pierre Willard
Key Points:	— graphical front end to dbx

An X windows front end for dbx called xdbx is available as part of the xxgdb distribution. Refer to "xxgdb— X Windows extension to gdb" on page 107 for acquisition details. However, some maintenance releases for xdbx have been separated out into xdbx files. The similarity to xxgdb is very great.

The windows include source code viewing, call stack, interacitve command-line window, and various command buttons. Supported dbx commands include *run*, *step*, *next*, *cont*, and *return*. Breakpoint support includes *stop at* for line number breakpoints and *stop in* for function breakpoints. The *where* button shows the stack trace and *up* and *down* control the current function context.

Data structures can be interrogated via point-and-click on Sun dbx version. By clicking on a pointer value in a data window you can pop up a new window with the data that is being pointed to.

DBXTOOL — SunOS GRAPHICAL DBX INTERFACE

Sun offers a tool called "dbxtool" which enhances dbx by providing a SunView graphical interface. dbxtool has all the functionality and commands of dbx, but with the addition of a more convenient graphical user interface. The GUI allows point-and-click control over breakpoints and program execution. As with dbx, it can be used for post-mortem analysis or interactive debugging.

DDD — GUI Front-end to GDB and DBX

Tool Name:	Data Display Debugger (ddd)
Purpose:	X Windows/Motif GUI front-end for gdb and dbx
Platforms:	SunOS, Solaris, AIX, HP-UX, SGI, Linux, OSF/1, Ultrix
Authors:	Dorothea Luetkehaus and Andreas Zeller
Availability:	X11: ftp.x.org/contrib/devel_tools/ddd* or contrib/utilities
Web:	http://www.cs.tu-bs.de/softech/ddd/ (example screens)
Mailing List	Requests to: ddd-users-request@ips.cs.tu-bs.de
Survey Paper:	ftp://ftp.ips.cs.tu-bs.de/pub/local/softech/ddd/ddd-paper.ps.gz

The ddd debugger offers a GUI interface over the command-line UNIX gdb and dbx debuggers. This allows the developer to drive the debugging session with mouse clicks. There is naturally support for flow of control, source code viewing, and breakpoint features.

The main differentiating feature of this debugger over other GUI front-ends is its data viewing capabilities, from which it gets its name. ddd allows complicated data structures to be viewed as graphs with nodes for blocks and lines for pointers. This offers an intuitive display of the program's data, and complements the usual debugger features for analysis of program runtime execution.

Although similar to xxgdb/xdbx in launching in its use of an existing debugger process, ddd offers many more advanced features. The already mentioned data display improves on the manual interactive point-and-click navigation through data structures with automated viewing of the entire structure. Further evidence is the list of enhancements in the latest revision including argument histories, reloading of changed source files, C++ name disambiguation dialogs, breakpoints marked as stop signs, and support for gdb's low-level assembler and register information.

TGDB — Free TCL Front-end for GDB

Tool Name:	tgdb
Purpose:	GUI front-end for the GNU gdb debugger based on TCL
Author:	Jonathan Swartz
Availability:	TCL archives: ftp://ftp.aud.alcatel.com/tcl/code/tgdb* sunsite.unc.edu:/pub/Linux/devel/debuggers/tgdb-1.0.src.tgz (Source)

tgdb is a GUI front-end for the GNU gdb debugger implemented using the TCL script language. It offers the advantage of translation of mouse actions into the typed commands that gdb requires.

MXGDB — FREE MOTIF GUI FRONT-END TO GDB

Tool Name:	mxgdb
Purpose:	GUI front-end to the GNU gdb debugger
Platforms:	UNIX (SunOS, Solaris, Linux, SCO, Bull, SVR4, SGI, HP-UX, MIPS, Ultrix)
Author:	James Tsillas
Availability:	X11 contrib: e.g. ftp.x.org:/R5contrib/mxgdb* or /contrib Linux: sunsite.unc.edu:/pub/Linux/devel/debuggers/mxgdb*

mxgdb is a Motif-based GUI front-end for the free GNU gdb debugger that is based on the xxgdb front-end for xxgdb. As for xxgdb, mxgdb allows gdb to be driven by the mouse via various buttons and menus to launch commands to gdb. There is a dynamically updated source code window display, buttons for common commands, and a window for interactive typed commands. mxgdb is available via FTP from the X11 *contrib* archives and there is a Linux port available.

UPS — A FREE X WINDOWS DEBUGGER

Tool Name:	ups
Main Purpose:	stand-alone X windows debugger
Platforms:	UNIX (SunOS, Ultrix, Linux)
Languages:	C and C++
Status:	Free
Author:	Mark Russell (originator), Rick Sladkey, Rod Armstrong
Availability:	X11 archives: e.g., ftp.x.org:/contrib/ups* and /R5contrib/ups* Linux: sunsite.unc.edu:/pub/Linux/devel/debuggers/ups*
Key Points:	— GUI-based debugger not based on any other debugger — includes a source code interpreter

ups is a free debugger for C that runs under X11 or SunView. Newer releases offer C++ features including support for the g++ and cfront compilers. The basic concept is to have a GUI-based debugger rather than a text-based debugger. ups is part of the X11 contributions, is maintained, and has been ported to a variety of UNIX architectures. Note that ups is a debugger built fully by Mark Russell and *not* a modification or front-end to GNU's gdb debugger. Hence, the feature set is unique and definitely worth a test run.

ups has two main windows, one with program source code, and one with the current program state information including a stack trace window. Clicking on a variable in the source display brings up a watch window, which is also editable to change values. Clicking on a pointer, union or structure member expands out to the value, and you can even traverse linked data structures this way.

One notable feature is that ups contains an interpreter for C that allows the addition of code fragments to your program simply by editing them in the source window. For example, this allows adding a debugging printf without recompilation. However, such a facility should not be overused — it is far better to modify the original source and rerun, than to over-use this feature and forget what code was added.

EPC EDB MOTIF-BASED DEBUGGER

Product Name:	edb
Purpose:	Debugger for EPC ANSI C and EPC C++
Platforms:	Solaris, Solaris-x86, Sequent, SGI, ICL, DG, Unisys, SVR4, NCR/AT&T, Pyramid, NEC, Tandem
Status:	Commercial Product
Price:	Bundled with EPC ANSI C and EPC C++ compilers
Company:	Edinburgh Portable Compilers
Address:	1906 Fox Drive, Champaign, IL 61820-7334, USA
Phone:	1-800-372-1110, 217-398-5787
Fax:	217-398-6386
Email:	info@epc.com

edb is an advanced Motif-based debugger for use with EPC's compiler products rather than a general debugger for UNIX. edb has both a command-line and a Motif GUI interface. The GUI displays source code, machine code, the call stack and data watchpoints. Naturally, edb has control flow support for step into, step over, and return. Various types of breakpoints can be set and they are remembered across debugging sessions.

The GUI also includes a development environment called Code-It that provides integration with editor and make. This gives control over the edit-compile-debug cycle from within the debugger for improved development productivity.

SOFT-ICE FOR WINDOWS DEBUGGER FROM NU-MEGA

Soft-ICE is a low-level debugger that provides many of the features of an In-Circuit Emulator (ICE) debugging tool. However, as the name suggests, Soft-ICE provides these ICE features

Product Name:	Soft-ICE
Platforms:	DOS, Windows 3.1, Windows NT, Windows 95
Company:	Nu-Mega Technologies
Address:	P.O. Box 7780, Nashua, NH 03060-7780, USA
Phone:	603-889-2386
Fax:	603-889-1135
BBS:	603-595-0386 24 hours
Email:	softice@numega.com

in software without any additional hardware. It does so by loading Windows on top of itself and intercepting all the low-level requests via the 386/486 hardware interrupts. Because of this special technology, Soft-ICE can not only debug ordinary DOS or Windows applications, but can also offer source level debugging of Windows device drivers, Windows virtual device drivers, TSRs, and VxDs. Soft-ICE can even debug more than one application at a time to trouble-shoot complicated systems.

The display screen for Soft-ICE is a full-screen character-based display using the keyboard for commands. Nothing else is happening on your computer when this display is up. This screen can be popped up at any time via a <Ctrl-D> hot key. Alternatively there is support for debugging on a second monitor, or via the serial port such as using a second PC with a null modem.

The display offers a number of windows for display of useful information. The Register Window shows hardware register values and permits editing. The Watch Window shows data locations or variables. The Data Window displays memory location and permits editing of stored values. The Code Window shows C source code, disassembled code or a mixed mode with source and assembly. The Command Window allows input of Soft-ICE commands.

There are numerous breakpoint options available at the application and system level. There are breakpoints on Windows messages and realtime breakpoints on memory read/write (via the hardware detection), I/O port read/write, and interrupts. Soft-ICE can also show internal Windows information including the VxD map, global and local heaps, task list, page table information, and exports from Windows USER, GDI and KERNEL. Flow of control during execution can be altered with various stepping options. When debugging an application with debug information available, Soft-ICE can single-step into or over functions, and step to the next line of source code. Assembly level control is also available, and Soft-ICE can even create a back trace of all executed instructions for problem diagnosis.

Overall, although Soft-ICE's application debugging features may not compare well against a good application-level debugger, Soft-ICE is particularly strong on debugging low-level code and real-time applications. Soft-ICE can even debug the Windows kernel.

MULTISCOPE DEBUGGER

Product Name:	MultiScope Debugger
Platforms:	DOS, Windows, OS/2
Price:	DOS: $179; Windows: $379
Company:	Symantec Corporation
Address:	10201 Toree Avenue, Cupertino, CA 95014-2132, USA
Phone:	1-800-441-7234, 408-253-9600; autofax — 1-800-554-4403
Fax:	408-252-4694
Web:	http://www.symantec.com

MultiScope is a powerful application-level interactive debugger for Windows. MultiScope supports a variety of C++ compilers including those from Microsoft, Borland, and, of course, Symantec. Some of the major features offered include a Windows GUI, C++ support, graphical data structure display, and message spying features. Also available is Windows UAE/GPF postmortem debugging support via the MultiScope Crash Analyzer as discussed in a separate section of this chapter.

The MultiScope for Windows GUI is a native Windows GUI rather than a DOS-like character interface, and has all the conveniences that Windows GUIs offer. An interesting approach to the window-swapping annoyances of sharing screen real-estate is the MultiScope "remote control" window. This is a small window with buttons for the common run-time controls such as stepping, stop and animation. There is also a character-based interface to support a second monitor. CodeView devotees also have available a command-line that supports CodeView commands to reduce the learning curve.

There is an impressive set of controls over run-time execution including the common ones (e.g., step into, step over, and continue until function returns), and some interesting additions including "continue until the next function call". Breakpoints can be set on statements, assembly instructions, function entry or C++ member function entry. Conditional breakpoints are also supported where a condition must be true. Hardware memory breakpoints using the 386/486 interrupts allow detection of reads and writes without performance degradation.

There are a great many windows in the GUI for examining data. The Class window allows browsing of C++ classes and there is also browsing of C++ objects. The Module window shows all files used in the project. The Calls window shows a stack trace of function calls and double- clicking on the function shows you the parameters and local variables. Data browsing is also easy to do by clicking on objects in the displays. For example, clicking on a pointer will follow it and objects can be viewed as different types using a "sticky type transfer" command. Low-level views are supported by views of hardware registers and the Memory window for examining memory locations.

Message spying is fully integrated with other MultiScope debugging features. The Spy window shows all Windows messages for one or many windows. Breakpoints can be set on a message and the source window updated to show the function handling the message. Users can also post or queue messages to windows from within the debugger.

Finally, the most impressive aspect of MultiScope is the Graphic Data window that shows a state-of-the-art graphical representation of dynamic data structures. Structures are represented as nodes (with the fields shown) and pointers represent the arcs between the structures. The value gained from viewing the overall structure of a dynamic data structure cannot be understated. This feature is certainly state-of-the-art for visual debugging features.

WISH — GRAPHICAL DEBUGGER

When I started this book, one of my biggest wishes was for a "graphical debugger" that showed data structures as directed graphs with nodes and arcs. Now there are a few debuggers with this form of graphical display, including *MultiScope* and ddd. So now I'm going to wish for more of them! There are also lots of enhancements that are possible to present various graphical views of your program during execution.

## CHAPTER 6

Run-time tracing tools

*D*ebuggers are typically interactive tools that give the user full control over the execution of the program. Although debuggers are powerful tools, they are sometimes too powerful for a specific task. There are a number of other debugging tools that operate at run-time including tracing tools and tools to analyze the window hierarchy in Microsoft Windows or Motif and X Windows.

Run-time tracing tools report on the execution of a program at given points. They usually do so without giving much control over its progress. The tracing output typically goes to a window, standard output/error, or to a log file. Tracing tools are a valuable debugging tool as they have minimal impact on program execution. An instrumented version of the program can often be shipped and the trace information conditionally enabled. A typical example of a tracing tool or library is the variety of debugging printout styles that are available. However, the following sections will show this to be far from the extent of the possibilities.

MICROSOFT WINDOWS DEBUGGING VERSION

Microsoft has shown great initiative in releasing a version of Windows with extra debugging checks enabled. This helps programmers to detect bugs in their programs by performing error checking at the lowest possible level — in the operating system. The debugging version of Windows is simply the basic operating system EXE and DLL files with extra error checking. It is available as part of the Windows SDK for application developers.

SPY AND DDE SPY: MESSAGE TRACING IN WINDOWS

The Spy tool is part of the Microsoft Windows SDK that is used for tracing messages in the Microsoft Windows environment. Messages form a major part of the Windows architecture, and are passed between windows, and between the application and the operating system. For example, an application receives messages from the operating system regarding mouse or keyboard input. Spy intercepts these messages and thereby offers a useful tracing tool for debugging.

Because Spy intercepts messages from the operating system, Spy does not need any extra code hooks in the application, and can operate on any application and not only those developed by you. It can be an interesting exercise to apply Spy to any of your Windows applications. The application to trace is chosen by clicking on a window and then Spy will record all the messages to that window, and display information about some of the properties of the window itself. Spy can be used to monitor one window or all windows. The information gathered about messages includes the type of message and the associated parameters. Messages can be filtered based on message type, and can be displayed to a window or logged to a file.

In addition to Spy, the Windows SDK offers the DDE Spy application for monitoring Dynamic Data Exchange (DDE) messages. This applies to applications using the DDE facility to communicate with other Windows applications. DDE Spy traces the messages and can track a variety of DDE-related information such as which applications are DDE servers and what DDE conversations are currently active.

WINSIGHT: MESSAGE TRACING FROM BORLAND

WinSight is a message tracing tool with features that are largely a superset of those offered by Spy. WinSight is available as part of the Borland C++ compiler environment product from Borland. Messages can be traced to a window or to a log file.

In addition to the tracing features, WinSight has an elegant tree-structure view of the window hierarchy. This can yield valuable insight into the structure of your GUI and demonstrate visually any problems with the interface. It also offers an alternative to the click-on-the-window method for choosing the window that you want to trace or examine properties. Hidden windows are also available in this hierarchy. Double clicking on a window in the tree will show its properties.

DBWIN — WINDOWS ERROR TRACING TOOL

DBWIN is a useful tool that is actually an example application that comes with the Windows 3.1 SDK and hence has full source supplied. DBWIN is also available independently of the SDK from the Microsoft Developer's Forum on CompuServe. Any errors detected by the Windows API are logged to the DBWIN window. Even better error detection is afforded by combining DBWIN with the debugging version of Windows that has more validation of its API calls. DBWIN offers a variety of fancy features including support for a second monitor and the ability to break to the CodeView for Windows debugger when a problem is detected.

WINSCOPE — WINDOWS EVENT TRACING

Product Name:	WinScope
Platforms:	Windows 3.1, Windows 95, Windows NT
Price:	$149
Company:	The Periscope Company
Address:	1475 Peachtree St, Suite 100, ATLANTA, GA 30309, USA
Phone:	1-800-722-7006; 404-888-5335
Fax:	404-888-5520
Email:	102370.1026@compuserve.com

WinScope is a tracing tool for 16-bit Windows applications from the makers of the Periscope debugger. The traced events include Windows messages, API calls, hooks, Toolhelp notifications and Debug kernel messages, making WinScope's tracing more powerful than the various Spy tools.

Events can be viewed in real time or saved for later. There is great flexibility in the choice of tracing features with selection based on windows, API classes, message classes, and more. The WinScope GUI offers various views of the messages, reporting details of parameters and return values by decoding them to a meaningful form (e.g., boolean returns translated to true or false). Exception interrupts are also caught and stack traces are available, offering some of the functionality of Dr Watson and WinSpector for postmortem debugging.

WinScope offers integrations with various other debuggers such as CodeView, Turbo Debugger, Multiscope, Soft-ICE and the Visual C++ debugger. In combination the programmer gets good interactive debugging with added tracing features. WinScope also integrates with StratosWare's memory allocation debugging tool called MemCheck to show memory leaks or errors in the trace.

FOOTPRINTS — RUN-TIME TRACING TOOL

Product Name:	Footprints
Platforms:	OS/2, Windows 3.1, Windows NT , AIX
Price:	$59-$99 for Windows 3.1 and OS/2 (no royalties)
Company:	Hardy Software Systems, Inc.
Address:	Two Riverway, Fifth Floor, Houston, TX 77056, USA
Phone:	713-871-1448
Fax:	713-871-1449
Email:	DPH@HSOFT.COM

Footprints is a run-time tracing tool for C/C++ designed for real-time and multithreaded programs. The main advantage is efficient tracing via internal buffering of 32K blocks to reduce the I/O cost that can occur in debugging-`fprintf` libraries. Footprints offers a tracing API with 64 separate "ids" for trace messages so as to group relevant messages together. Debugging code can also be added to execute when a trace id is enabled.

The components are a DLL, and an OS/2 Presentation Manager GUI or a Windows GUI. Footprints works by adding tracing calls to your code, linking with the DLL, and then running your program causing trace data storage to a file. After execution the GUI is used to examine the trace results. Analysis and trace output formatting is done offline in the GUI to further reduce the overhead of tracing at run-time. Shipping tracing support in production code is supported and trace output data files can be returned by the customer for later examination in the GUI.

XAMINER — TRACING X WINDOWS

Product Name:	Xaminer
Purpose:	Tracing/recording X Windows events
Platforms:	Solaris, Solaris-x86, SunOS, HP-UX, OSF/1, SGI, AIX, Ultrix, DG, Pyramid, ICL.
Status:	Commercial Product
Company:	Performance Awareness
Address:	8521 Six Forks Rd., Raleigh, NC 27615, USA
Phone:	919-870-8800
Fax:	919-870-7416

Email:	info@PACorp.com
Web:	http://www.PACorp.com

Xaminer records user activity for X Windows applications for later playback. All X protocol requests are recorded and archived without any noticeable degradation in performance. Xaminer can record one or multiple X client applications connected to a display. Recorded sessions can be played back offline using the Xaminer Presentation Player which offers various features such as normal speed, pausing and variable speed playback. Xaminer tracing can be used for disaster analysis, auditing, transaction analysis and even employee productivity analysis.

PUREVISION FROM PURE SOFTWARE

Product Name:	PureVision
Purpose:	remote testing administration tool
Platforms:	Solaris
Languages:	ANSI C, C++, K&R C
Status:	Commercial Product
Company:	Pure Software, Inc.
Address:	1309 S. Mary Avenue, Sunnyvale, CA 94087, USA
Phone:	408 720 1600
Fax:	408-729-9200
Email:	info@pure.com, support@pure.com
Web:	http://www.pure.com/

Although it has a specialized focus, the PureVision product from Pure Software can be categorized as a tracing tool for C and C++. It offers a form of lightweight instrumentation of the process so that your product is shipped in an instrumented form and execution information can be collected from remote sites. This is ideal for distribution of a Beta version of software in that it automates the collection of user feedback.

PureVision performs instrumentation at the final link-stage using Pure Software's Object Code Insertion technology, and does not require source code changes. Instrumentation is light and the performance hit is nowhere near that of full-blown checking.

The information collected by PureVision is in two broad categories. Progress data is collected including the number of executions, durations, environment, and version information. The second type is crash information. PureVision detects when a program crashes and will report the full stack trace and other related information. Feature-based information can be collected by the programmer specifying a function name to indicate that a particular product feature has been exercised.

The remote executable returns information to the software producers through Internet email, or by disk/tape if email is impossible or undesirable for security concerns. Remote test customers have control over the transmission of email results. The PureVision Motif GUI stores information in a database and presents a number of standard charts and reports, and has the facility to create SQL-based custom reports.

TRACKDECK FROM DASHBOARD SOFTWARE

Product Name:	TrackDeck
Purpose:	Visual debugging tool
Platforms:	Windows
Languages:	C and C++
Status:	Commercial Product
Company:	DashBoard Software
Address:	4 Louis Avenue, Monsey, New York 10952, USA
Phone:	914-352-8071
Fax:	914-352-8071 (same as phone number)
Email:	76620.750@compuserve.com
Key Point:	— Graphical viewing of variable's values

TrackDeck is a new type of graphical debugging and performance analysis tool for C and C++ under Windows. TrackDeck allows the programmer to "look into" the program and examine data values during execution. This makes it sound like a symbolic debugger, but it isn't, and TrackDeck has two main advantages over symbolic debuggers:

1. A symbolic debugger must "step" through execution, but TrackDeck execution continues automatically; and
2. TrackDeck offers graphical viewing of data values.

This graphical viewing is the most important feature of TrackDeck. As their manual says, "a graph is worth a thousand print statements". Variables can be presented graphically as dials or history graphs. Naturally the dials and graphs can be customized in various ways: size, color, etc. Data values can also be viewed as ordinary values (i.e., like a symbolic debugger watch window) and a message logging facility is also provided. There is also the flexibility to specify simple functions such as average, minimum or maximum for a given value, or to supply a callback function for more complicated functions.

TrackDeck has two separate parts: a DLL that detects changes to monitored variables and a separate viewing program that extracts this information about variable values and presents it graphically to the user. Thus the debugging information is automatically updated as the program executes, but the performance degradation this causes is only a few percent.

Although it is definitely an interesting new tool, TrackDeck has some important limitations. A minor issue is that rather than grabbing variable names and their addresses from the executable or object files, using TrackDeck requires source code modification: one function call per address to be monitored. Presumably this limitation arises because TrackDeck supports multiple C/C++ compilers. Another minor problem is that the monitoring of variables on the stack suffers if the function returns, because the address becomes invalid. However, there are API functions provided to handle stack addresses. A more major issue is that only a few simple forms of expression can be monitored: single variables, and variables indirectly referred to by one or more pointers. TrackDeck does not present a graphical view into larger linked data structures which is the logical extension of this idea.

In summary, TrackDeck is an interesting foray into the future world of graphical debugging tools, and is certainly a level above looking through reams of output from print statements.

CTRACE — UNIX RUN-TIME TRACING UTILITY

An older debugging tool is the `ctrace` utility which is available in most versions of UNIX. The purpose of `ctrace` is to automatically produce debugging output without the programmer adding any debugging statements to the code. `ctrace` is a filter that accepts as input a C source file, and outputs a modified version of the C source file with output statements added. Thus the use of `ctrace` requires an extra stage during compilation.

Unfortunately, the `ctrace` utility has so many limitations that it is not of great practical use for professional programmers. The version of `ctrace` that I examined was so old that it would not accept ANSI C code, refusing to recognize function prototypes. I am not aware of an ANSI C version of the `ctrace` utility. If such a version exists `ctrace` could become a useful debugging tool.

TRACE — UNIX SYSTEM V UTILITY

The trace utility is a standard UNIX tool available on most System V variants of UNIX. The basic syntax is:

```
trace program arguments
```

This traces the program at runtime, and produces a trace listing on standard output with one line per event. The trace listing records system calls and signals raised. The system call information includes function name, arguments passed, the return code, and even error message information if applicable.

There are a handful of options available with `trace`. The -p option is interesting, enabling `trace` to attach to a running process, and then detach using the keyboard interrupt

<ctrl-c>. Child processes of a traced process are not traced, and setuid privileges are lost during tracing.

TRUSS — UNIX SYSTEM V UTILITY

The truss utility is similar to the trace utility and is also available on most System V variants of UNIX. The basic operation of truss is identical to trace with reporting of system calls (including function arguments, return codes and error message information) and signals. The main differences are some extra features not supported by trace: following child processes, reporting of machine faults.

truss supports all the command line options of trace, and quite a few others as shown in Table 6–1. The -p option attaches to a process as with trace, but is generalized to accept more than one process pid, and the tracing can be stopped via hangup, interrupt or quit signals. The most powerful options are the -t, -v and -x options that apply to individual system calls, and can be negated by using a prefix ! character before the system call name. The -r and -w options can be useful for tracing file handling.

Table 6–1   truss options

Option	Meaning
-p list-of-pids	Attach to running processes
-f	Follow child processes
-c	Count system calls and signals
-a	Arguments to exec system calls displayed
-e	Environment for exec system calls displayed
-i	Ignore sleeping/blocked system calls till completion
-l	Lightweight process id shown in trace output
-t[!]list-of-calls	Trace or ignore system calls by name
-v[!]list-of-calls	Verbose reporting of structures enabled by name
-x[!]list-of-calls	Hexadecimal display of tracing information
-s[!]list-of-signals	Signals traced/excluded by name or number
-m[!]list-of-faults	Machine faults to trac/exclude by name or number
-r[!]list-of-fds	Display input buffer for read calls
-w[!]list-of-fds	Display output buffer for write calls
-o filename	Output file for the trace

EDITRES — X WINDOWS WIDGET ANALYZER

`editres` is a widget hierarchy analysis tool that is part of the standard X11 distribution. There are a few different versions of `editres` but they basically operate the same. They all allow the inspection and modification of the application's widget hierarchy. Some of the features are similar to Spy and WinSight for Microsoft Windows message tracing.

The application to be examined is chosen by clicking on the main window. The main `editres` display is a graphical tree view of the widget hierarchy for an application. Individual widgets in this tree can be selected, and their resource settings examined and modified. Changes to a window's resource appear immediately after modification. This is particularly useful for playing with color schemes for dialogs, without the need to rerun the application each time. When you're finished, `editres` can save changes in an X defaults format; however I usually edit them before adding them to the main X resource file because I try to use more generic widget descriptions that are less fragile to GUI layout or naming changes.

Support for `editres` must be hard-coded into the application (usually protected by an `#ifdef` to prevent its appearance in production code) using the code:

```
XtAddEventHandler (top,0,TRUE,_XEditResCheckMessages, NULL);
```

In this code "`top`" is the top level shell widget and the callback function is defined in the "`libXmu.a`" library; hence the link stage must use "`-lXmu`".

WIDGETLINT — DOUGLAS YOUNG'S X TOOL

WidgetLint is a "home-grown" runtime debugging tool which takes the name "lint" because it performs error checking not because it analyzes source code. The basic idea is a function whereby the widget hierarchy is recursively scanned at run-time, with some checks for common errors added. The details for this excellent book are:

> YOUNG, Douglas A., *Motif Debugging and Performance Tuning*, Prentice Hall, New Jersey, 1995.

The source code for WidgetLint and other code from the book is available via FTP to *ftp.prenhall.com* in *pub/software/doug_young* as file *young.debug.tar.Z.*

DBUG: A FREE DEBUGGING OUTPUT LIBRARY

The `dbug` library is a free package that provides a number of standard macros which the programmer can insert into the program. A typical example is the use of a DBUG_ENTER macro at the start of the function and replacing the `return` statement with a DBUG_RETURN macro. These macros will produce tracing output to the screen or a log file, which can be analyzed at run-time or postmortem. The overall configurability of the package is quite good, and the macros can be compiled-out easily. `dbug` is available via FTP and I found it at `ftp.germany.eu.net` in the `pub/programming/lib/dbug` directory, but it is a good idea to do an "archie" search to find a site close to you.

MORE FREE TRACING TOOL REFERENCES

This section examines a few more tools that came to my attention too close to the writing deadline. Hence they are not evaluated to the depth of others in this chapter and are included mainly for completeness.

strace — free UNIX system call tracing tool

Tool Name:	strace
Purpose:	Trace system calls
Platforms:	Solaris, SunOS, SVR4, Linux
Authors:	Paul Kranenburg, Branko Lankester, Rick Sladkey
Availability:	Linux sites: e.g. sunsite.unc.edu:/pub/Linux/devel/strace/

`strace` is a tracing tool for UNIX system calls similar to the `trace` and `truss` tracing tools. It traces and decodes system calls to show the behavior of the program under test.

Mec — free Linux tracing and replay tool

Tool Name:	Mec
Purpose:	Trace execution and allow replay within debugger
Author:	Michael Elizabeth Chastain
Availability:	Linux sites: e.g. sunsite.unc.edu:/pub/Linux/devel/debuggers/ mec*

Mec allows the tracing of program execution into a disk file. The session can be played back within a debugger at a later date or on another machine. The current release is mainly a proof of concept, but future releases may be available by the time you read this.

Profilers

The first rule of performance improvement is: *don't*. We all know the dangers of the over-enthusiastic micro-optimizations and the inevitable errors they introduce. But performance improvement is a necessary part of program development. It's also one of the most fun!

My favorite buzzword for performance improvement is "deslugging". Unfortunately I no longer have the reference to the journal article where this term was coined.

When improving a program's performance, it is vital to know where the speed bottlenecks are. There is a saying that 90% of the time is spent in 10% of the code. Hence, common sense dictates that when making a performance improvement you should aim to speed up the code that is most frequently used, rather than wasting your time tweaking infrequently used code. The programmer can often guess where the program is spending most of its time, but that's exactly what it is — a guess! The modern method of determining what code to change is to take advantage of the many sophisticated "profiler" tools available in the public domain and commercially.

PROFILER FEATURES TO LOOK FOR

The basic aim of a profiler is to help you to optimize your program and it is on this basis that a profiler should be evaluated. Features of a profiler that you should examine include:

- **Granularity of measurement:** The most basic level of measurement is the total time taken up by the program. This is trivially available via the UNIX `time` function and similar commands on other platforms. Profiler tools always go at least down to the next level, which is the time spent by each function. The next level down is the time spent by "basic blocks" — these are sequences of code without any branches or loops, and are a well-known artifact in the construction of the flow graph for a function. The next level down is breaking each block into its individual statements. Even lower than that would be measurement of the cost of each operation in an expression or statement, such as the analysis of the time in the expression `y=a+b*c` into the time spent by `*`, `+` and `=` operators. Expression level analysis might be of occasional value in squeezing the most speed out of inner loops or other heavily visited expressions. However, none of the existing profilers I am aware of go into that level of fine-grain detail for expressions.

- **Measurement metrics:** when a profiler displays the functions (or blocks or statements) using the most time this is implicitly reporting the most common metric: execution time. Another simple metric is the number of calls to a function or executions of a statement. Sometimes this count can be more meaningful than time spent. There are a number of other metrics but I haven't seen any existing profilers that use them; see the later "Wish" section for discussion.

- **Aggregated call graph results:** An important aspect of the metric is the reporting of aggregate results for modules of code. Profilers will usually have the feature of adding time spent in descendant functions in the call graph to the current function, such that the result for the "main" function is 100% (well, actually that's not completely true, because of system startup code and initialization of global objects and calling their constructors). The aggregate results can give more insight into the general area of a program that requires performance improvement. An aggregate value of call counts is not as immediately meaningful and is not commonly available (which I personally think is a pity since this aggregate call count metric can give useful information, such as for determining which parts of the code have too many function calls and need the use of C macros or C++ inline functions).

- **Reporting and display of results:** A good profiler should have as flexible reporting of results as possible. Results should be displayed as absolute values or as percentages. Results should be able to be aggregated for descendants or shown without any aggregation. Sorting of results is important to show the most frequent occurrences, and the least frequent occurrences (e.g., to find never-called functions!). Graphical display of results, such as bar graphs or pie graphs, is a neat feature that can give more rapid insight into where the mountains of CPU usage are located. Reporting features for export to common spreadsheet formats can also make managers more comfortable that you're doing real work even though you're enjoying it.

• **Support for multiple executions:** Just like debugging, performance enhancement is often implemented as a three-phase process of find it, fix it, and forget it. The third phase should really be "check it". This means testing the program in the debugging process, and means re-profiling for performance enhancement (well, maybe you should test it after performance enhancement too!). Profilers often have features that allow you to verify that your newly optimized program did run faster than the older version. Another feature involving multiple executions is summation or averaging or results over a number of executions, to give a more accurate picture of a program's performance when executed against a broad test suite.

Profiler Implementations

There are a number of methods used to produce execution profiles of a program's execution. The standard UNIX profilers such as `prof`, `pixie` and `gprof` use a method of "sampling" where the program counter's location is detected and analyzed regularly; usually every clock tick. This method requires kernel support such as that from the `profil` and `monitor` system calls. The use of sampling is inherently inaccurate for timing measures, because of the times when the program counter is not analyzed; however, the granularity is usually adequate for meaningful results. On the other hand the regular sequencing of analysis at each clock tick does have pathological cases where results are grossly out of scale. Call counts using this method are usually more accurate and often 100% guaranteed because function calls are more easily detected.

Another method of implementing a profiler is the instrumentation of the object or executable files with code that gathers performance statistics. Thus the executable increases in size and loses some performance, but whether this is better or worse than kernel-supported sampling is not clear (although I know on which side I'd place my bets until proven otherwise). However, the information gathered by instrumentation is more accurate than sampling. An example of a profiler using this method is the Quantify profiler from Pure Software. The method of instrumentation also offers the flexibility to compute performance metrics other than just function calls and time used, such as memory allocated, but unfortunately I haven't seen a tool that actually offers other metrics yet.

Timing Programs Without Tools

If the full execution time for a program is all that is needed (which is almost never the case), there are a few simple options. Your highly sophisticated wristwatch tool can be used. The UNIX `time` utility can also be used, and there are two versions of the `time` command — a stand-alone utility in /bin, and a command built into csh. In either case, the command line to run is:

```
time myprog myargs
```

There is also the UNIX timex command that prints process time on standard error. timex offers a few more detailed options such as accounting of child process times and size.

For more detailed information, it is possible to hard-code calls to a number of time-related system calls and compute simple profiles using code. The clock system call measures processor time at very low granularity, and is portable to many platforms. To get the time in seconds rather than ticks, divide by CLOCKS_PER_SEC, the ANSI C macro, or CLK_TCK, a nonstandard macro that is common to many UNIX variants. In addition, UNIX has the time system call which reports the current time in seconds, and the gettimeofday call with microsecond accuracy.

Another system call supported by many UNIX platforms, but not part of ANSI, is the getrusage call that returns resource usage for the current process. This allows measurement of very low-level aspects such as process size, page faults, context switches and signals.

However, you really don't want to mess around with adding lots of extra instrumentation code to your application. You'd rather use a *tool* to do the work for you.

PROF — UNIX PROFILER

Under UNIX the standard C profiling utility is called "prof". This utility calculates the percentage time consumed by each function. This is valuable information when considering which functions to make more efficient.

To use prof, compile the program with the -p and -g options to cc (strictly speaking, the -p and -g options are needed only at the link stage of compilation) and then execute the program. Provided the program terminates normally, via exit or returning from main, a data file called "mon.out" will be generated. This file contains the data to be used by prof in preparing an execution profile for the program. To examine this profile, assuming your executable is named "myprog", type the command:

```
prof myprog
```

This command will generate a profile of your program's execution from which the functions that use the most time can be identified. Note that the percentages calculated are only approximate because the profiler uses sampling techniques during interrupts and these samples might not provide a fully accurate picture. For example, if the program has a very small and fast function, this function might be completely missed. Dynamically loaded libraries might also not be correctly profiled, resulting in misleading results.

There is an odd method of handling the times attributed to static (non-global) functions. The default is to add times to the global function preceding the static function, which can result in misleading results. The -g option is hence recommended for timing profiles. Note that function call counts are not added to the global function and hence the choice of -l or -g does not affect call count results.

Table 7–1 Options to prof

Option	Meaning
-a	Address used for sorting of symbols in displayed output (increasing order)
-c	Calls used for sorting of symbols in displayed output (decreasing order)
-n	Name used for alphabetic sorting of symbols in displayed output (decreasing order)
-o	Octal addresses printed
-x	Hexadecimal addresses printed
-l	Static functions not included (this is the default and not recommended!)
-g	Static functions included (recommended)
-C	Demangle C++ names
-h	Header suppression on the printed output (for processing output)
-m file	Use file instead of "mon.out" as input data
-s	Summary printed on standard error
-V	Print version of prof on standard error
-z	Zero-value functions (calls or time) included in the output

PIXIE — UNIX PROFILER

The `prof` utility only produces estimates based on statistical sampling of the program counter at regular intervals throughout the execution of the program. The `pixie` utility can be used under UNIX to get more accurate counts on the number of times each statement in a function is executed. It measures the number of times each *basic block* is executed. A basic block is a sequence of code containing no branches.

The `pixie` utility is applied to the already generated executable file. There is no need to recompile the executable with the `-p` option. The command:

```
pixie a.out
```

will generate a new executable file, "`a.out.pixie`". When executed this will generate a data file called "`a.out.Counts`" containing coverage data. A data file of function addresses called "`a.out.Addrs`" is also generated. The next step is to run the new executable:

```
a.out.pixie
```

and then the count file can be examined using either `prof` or `pixstats`. Two possible commands are:

```
pixstats a.out
```

or the use of `prof` with the `-pixie` option:

```
prof -pixie a.out
```

Both of these commands will generate a variety of information. `prof  -pixie` will generate an ordering of functions based on instruction cycle counts, another based on invocations,
and a list of instruction counts for each basic block. `pixstats` generates a whole wealth of
useful information including summaries of opcode distributions and register usage. For more
information, examine the UNIX manual entries for `pixie`, `pixstats` and `prof`.

GPROF — UNIX PROFILER

The `gprof` tool is a profiler available on many UNIX platforms that is similar in many
respects to `prof` but a little more detailed in its analysis. Profiling data is generated by sampling methods, and `gprof` requires compilation with the `-pg` option or the `-xpg` option,
depending on the compiler. Information computed about program execution includes number
of calls to functions and the time spent in functions (and their descendants).   There are a variety of options for altering the presentation the profiling data as listed in Table 7–2. An example usage of `gprof` is:

```
gprof a.out gmon.out -z   # Find unused functions
```

The output produced by `gprof` is a number of reports. The first report is similar to that from
`prof` and displays number of calls to functions, and the amount of time spent in each function as a value and as a percentage of the whole. In addition, there is a report on the time distribution when descendants of functions are considered, and a report displaying instruction
and call counts for all functions that form a recursive cycle in the call graph.

Table 7–2   gprof Options

Option	Meaning
-a	Suppress statically declared functions
-b	Brief descriptions for each field
-C	Demangle C++ names
-c	Call-graph building
-D	Store difference information of multiple profiles in "gmon.sum"
-E function	Exclude function (and descendants) from printing and time cal-culations
-e function	Exclude function (and descendants) from printing
-F function	Use function (and descendants) as the only functions for printing and calculations

Table 7-2 gprof Options *(Continued)*

Option	Meaning
-f function	Use function (and descendants) as the only functions for printing
-n number	Number of functions to display in profiles
-s	Store sum of multiple profiles in "gmon.sum"
-z	Zero usage display (useful for finding unused functions)

QUANTIFY FROM PURE SOFTWARE

Product Name:	Quantify
Purpose:	Profiling tool
Platforms:	SunOS, Solaris, HP-UX
Languages:	ANSI C, C++, K&R C
Status:	Commercial Product
Company:	Pure Software, Inc.
Address:	1309 S. Mary Avenue, Sunnyvale, CA 94087, USA
Phone:	408-720-1600, 1-800-353-7873
Fax:	408-720-9200
Email:	info@pure.com support@pure.com
Web:	http://www.pure.com/

Quantify is an execution profiler from the makers of the well-known Purify run-time error detection tool (see "Purify from Pure Software" on page 75). Quantify makes use of the same object code insertion technology and hence does not suffer from the inherent inaccuracy of the sampling techniques used by the standard UNIX profilers prof and pixie. Profiling code is inserted at link-time to perform the measurement tasks during program execution.

One of the main distinguishing features of Quantify over the common UNIX profilers is its Motif GUI browser for examining profiling results. There are two main views of the results: textual and graphical. The textual view shows each function and the percentage time taken. There are a variety of options for altering the presentation of this information including suppressing various classes of functions and sorting the output by different metrics (e.g., current function only or including all descendents). Quantify allows the use of call count metrics and CPU cycles, which is computed by counting the cycles used along the execution paths as part of the instrumentation process. In addition to function-level profiling, counts and cycles are examined at the basic block level, and Quantify offers another textual view: instrumented source code showing the most used code statements.

The graphical view offered by Quantify is a function call graph showing all paths starting from main down to the leaves. This call graph is a useful code browsing features in itself even without the profiling information that is shown graphically. Heavily traveled paths are shown by thicker lines in the graph allowing quick visual identification of bottlenecks (i.e., functions with thick lines going in but thin lines going out, or a thick line path that goes all the way to the leaves). There are a variety of options for this call graph view, including the ability to focus on a sub-graph for more detailed profiling of a portion of the program.

There is also an extensive API to allow control of the profiling process from within the execution of the program itself. For example, this allows the specification of which portions of the program's execution are to be profiled. The API is also useful when working within a debugger where calling these functions can allow you to alter profiling interactively from within a debugger session.

Multiple executions are also supported by Quantify in two ways. Two runs can be compared as a before and after test to make sure an optimization has fixed a performance problem. In addition, multiple runs can be aggregated to give a full picture of where an application is spending its time when all features are fully exercised.

Overall, Quantify is an impressive profiling tool. The GUI makes it easy to examine results from one or many executions in text or graphical form. The accuracy gained from the use of instrumentation rather than sampling is valuable, and this information is kept at the statement level for very detailed measurement.

XSPERT — PROFILING X WINDOWS

Product Name:	XSpert
Purpose:	Profiling and benchmarking tool
Platforms:	Solaris, Solaris-x86, SunOS, HP-UX, OSF/1, SGI, AIX, Ultrix, DG, Pyramid, ICL.
Status:	Commercial Product
Company:	Performance Awareness
Address:	8521 Six Forks Rd., Raleigh, NC 27615, USA
Phone:	1-800-849-4562, 919-870-8800
Fax:	919-870-7416
Email:	info@PACorp.com
Web:	http://www.PACorp.com

XSpert is a tool for benchmarking X terminals by capturing the X protocol stream and replaying it to the X server without delays. This can give a realistic indication of the performance of an X terminal when running your application. It also gives you the ability to see what X requests your application is making, and thereby assist in tuning your X Windows application. The main features for profiling are reports of the X server requests. These can be sorted by type, frequency or byte count, and various summaries including histogram displays are available. These can all help to tune the performance of your X Windows GUI application.

XMON — FREE X WINDOWS TRACING TOOL

Tool Name:	xmon
Purpose:	Tracing the X Windows protocol
Availability:	X11 contrib: FTP ftp.x.org/contrib/dev_tools/

xmon is a free X Windows tracing tool that displays all the requests to the X server from an X client application. X events are collected and printed on standard output in character form. xmon can be used to monitor the events from one or more X clients. The classes of events and level of detail are customizable, allowing the programmer to focus on areas of interest.

Examining the events sent between an X client and server can be useful for a number of programming tasks including debugging and performance tuning. Tracing the X events is a particularly good way of detecting common X performance pitfalls such as unnecessary objects created or compound objects managed too early.

TURBO PROFILER FROM BORLAND

Turbo Profiler is a very impressive offering from Borland for DOS and Windows profiling. It is bundled with Borland C++ and is an interactive tool similar to Turbo Debugger. In fact, the GUI is a character-based DOS-like interface that uses screen swapping to profile Windows applications. This is a minor annoyance but far better than the total lack of GUI of some similar DOS tools, and in fact the GUI has some neat graphical facets, such as character-based bar graphs of profiles.

Turbo Profiler uses instrumentation of object code to gather 100% accurate information, rather than using inaccurate program counter sampling techniques. The metrics that are available include execution counts and processor time, available at both the function and line level.

There really is no comparison between Turbo Profiler and Microsoft Source Profiler. Turbo Profiler has far better presentation features and is easier to use. The GUI used by Turbo Profiler wins easily over the complex batch commands of Microsoft Source Profiler.

PROF.MSC — FREE PROFILER FOR MICROSOFT C

Purpose:	Profiler for Microsoft C or Microsoft Quick C
Platforms:	DOS: Microsoft C v5.00, Microsoft QuickC

| Availability: | comp.sources.misc/volume8/prof.msc |
| Author: | Diomidis D. Spinellis |

This profiler tool works by sampling the program counter at each clock tick via interrupts. The program counter is mapped to a function via object ".MAP" files and this produces approximate percentages of the time spent in each function. Although sampling is not as accurate as instrumentation of object files, the results are usually reasonably accurate and very useful.

To use this profiler you need to compile your program with a linker map file available (e.g., use the /MAP option to the linker), link in the profiling object file appropriate to the memory model, and insert a call to the profiler prof_start API function. Unfortunately static functions are not present in map files, and the documentation recommends "-Dstatic=" to avoid using static functions when profiling, thereby improving the accuracy. When the program terminates normally it will produce an execution profile at a function level in the text file "prof.out". This file can be read directly and there is also a "profprt" utility supplied to print results, including a "-h" option to produce a textual histogram of the results.

CPROF — FREE PROFILER FOR TURBO C

Purpose:	Profiler for Turbo C
Platforms:	Turbo C v2.0
Availability:	comp.sources.misc/volume8/cprof_tc
Author:	Peter J. Holzer

cprof uses interrupts to perform regular sampling of the program counter, maps this to a function name using linker map files, and thereby computes the time spent in each C function. This tool is basically a port of the "prof.msc" profiler for Microsoft C to Turbo C. The usage and technical details are identical to those covered in that section.

PROFILE — FREE MICROSOFT C AND TURBO C PROFILER

Tool Name:	profile
Platforms:	DOS: Microsoft C v5.1, Turbo C v2.0
Status:	Free (public domain)
Available:	comp.sources.misc:volume9/proft.ms
Author:	Bjorn Larsson

profile is an impressive profiler for DOS compilers that overcomes some of the limitations of the free DOS profilers already mentioned. In particular, it does not require modifying the program code to link with a profiling library or call an API function, and also handles <ctrl-c> elegantly. However it is still limited to function call profiling and does not track basic blocks. This package also offers a good variety of options and features for configuring the output.

The idea behind profile is sampling of the program counter via hardware interrupts, mapping that to function names via linker map files, and thereby computing percentages of time spent in functions. Sampling has an inherent inaccuracy but usually still offers very useful results. Using profile requires that you create a linker map file via LINK /MAP or the TLINK '/l/c' option. No *static* functions are represented in the map file so that the only way to gather information on these functions is to #define static to nothing in interesting files. The command to use is:

```
profile [options] program arguments
```

The results are generated in a human readable description of the times spent in each function as a percentage and a number of hits. The presentation takes into account intrinsic system functions and a variety of options are available, as shown in Table 7–3.

Table 7–3 Options to profile

Option	Meaning
-a	Address used to sort functions in output report.
-d	DOS and BIOS memory included in the profile.
-i	Intrinsic functions included in the output.
-n	Names used to sort functions in output report.
-0	Zero-hit functions included in output report.
-#<n>	Multiple executions *n* times aggregated.
-m<mapfile>	Map file instead of default from program name.
-o<outfile>	Output file instead of default from program name.

LCOMP, LPRINT — FREE SUN/VAX PROFILER TOOL

Status:	Free (Public domain)
Platforms:	Sun 3, VAX
Available:	comp.sources.unix/volume20/lcomp Companion CDROM in directory lcomp
Author:	Paul Haahr

This profiler is an interesting tool although the distribution is a little old, the ports few, and I'm not sure if it has been maintained. lcomp works as a profiler tool by using instrumentation of assembly code rather than the less accurate sampling methods of UNIX prof. The lcomp tool is used to perform the instrumentation by assembly code post-processing, and execution will produce a data file "prof.out" provided that the program terminates via exit. The lprint utility is then used to print the results in a variety of formats including summaries by file and by function, and source code printouts with associated counts.

lcomp works with both C and Fortran code but is limited to use with the Portable C Compiler. The profing metrics computed are execution counts rather than times, but are available at the basic block and statement level. The documentation includes some interesting discussion of technical details, hints on how to port to other assembly languages, and a reference to an article on which the technique is based:

WEINBERGER, Peter, *Cheap Dynamic Instruction Counting*, AT&T Bell Labs Tech Journal Vol. 63, No. 8, Oct 1984, pp. 1815-1826.

SWAPTUNER — PAGE FAULT REDUCTION TOOL FROM MICROQUILL

Product Name:	SwapTuner
Platforms:	Windows 95, Windows NT
Price:	$1,495
Company:	MicroQuill Software Publishing, Inc
Address:	4900 25th Ave NE, Suite 206, Seattle WA, 98105
Phone:	1-800-441-7822, 206-525-8218
Fax:	206-525-8309
Email:	info@microquill.com
CompuServe:	70751,2443
BBS:	206-488-5575

SwapTuner is a performance improvement tool for Windows 95 and Windows NT that reorders functions so as to reduce the number of cross-page function calls. Because Windows 95 and Windows NT break memory into pages used for swapping memory to disk, an application can spend a great deal of its time in page faults, which refers to the situation where you require data or call a function in a page that is not currently in memory. A severe case of frequent page faulting is usually called "thrashing" because the application spends more time with disk I/O than it does doing useful work. SwapTuner reduces these problems by computing a new ordering of functions for a relink of the application.

The first step that SwapTuner requires is an execution of your application using the Microsoft Call/Attributive Profiler (CAP) to record the number of calls and build a call tree. You can do so multiple times in order to get a large picture of your application's performance over a wide test suite. SwapTuner uses this information to compute an initial measure of the number of cross-page calls, and uses this metric repeatedly to find a more efficient ordering of functions. The algorithms used by SwapTuner are quite interesting since the solution space of possible orderings is exponential. SwapTuner uses a combination of iterative "hill climbing" and simulated annealing to find better solutions by descending valleys to find cheaper orderings and climbing hills to avoid getting trapped in a local minima. The GUI displays a historical graph of the cost metric over all possible orderings as the computation progresses. Because SwapTuner is really crunching away with these algorithms, the analysis takes hours and is best left to run overnight to try to find the best ordering it can.

Once you are satisfied with the progress of the analysis, you can stop SwapTuner and uses its best ordering so far. SwapTuner will then create a ".ord" ordering file specifying the better link ordering. Relink your application with this ".ord" file and performance degradation due to page faulting should be history.

SPACE MEASUREMENT

The measurement of the space-efficiency of a program has received less attention in the area of profiling tools. Technologically speaking there is no reason space cannot be measured, but it appears that programmers in general are less interested in space efficiency. This may seem justified since space is "free" but extra space leads to extra time spent in paging memory.

UNIX has a couple of commands that can be used to determine the size of static data segments: `size` and `nm`. The `size` command can be used on object files, libraries and executables. It reports the static space used by various parts of the program including program code, static data, and uninitialized data (bss). The `nm` command can also be useful as it reports statistics about identifiers in an object file and can, with some difficulty, be used to report the size of functions or global variables. Consult the manual pages for details on `nm` and `size`.

As far as measuring dynamic space requirements, there isn't much to say. The current generation of profilers and debuggers do not seem to offer this functionality. Memory allocation debugging tools can usually report the total heap usage, but this does not account for overhead or heap fragmentation. Even if they did account for overhead, a measure of the heap size would be of limited value anyway for an instrumented executable with different heap allocation primitives.

The best UNIX solution so far is abysmal: use the "ps" command. The `ps` command reports on many process issues and one of them is process size. Hence the solution is to run `ps`, look for your process, and find the number in the size column (usually the number of 512 or 1024 byte blocks). This technique is non-portable even to other UNIX variants since `ps` has different formats on all operating systems (`ps -elf` on System V and `ps -auxww` on BSD variants) and often differs between versions of the same operating system. However, I have seen a piece of C code specifically aimed at spawning "ps" with the output collected, finding the line for the current pid, and finding the size.

Wish — Space Usage and Other Metrics

None of the run-time profiling tools I've seen seem to offer much in the way of features for measurement of the various uses of memory by a program. Memory consumption by a program has a very direct effect on a program's run-time performance due to paging algorithms and should be measured. A good profiler tool should report the size of static memory areas, and have options for reporting the size of run-time areas such as the stack and heap.

There is no technical reason why run-time tools such as profilers, memory checkers or debuggers cannot keep track of the usage of the stack. Even compilers could track this information either as an option, or perhaps only when run-time stack overflow checking is enabled when the penalty would be very low for the extra arithmetic. This feature could track the current stack depth, a high-water mark, and even a historical profile of stack usage.

Heap space measurement is surprisingly lacking in many tools. Existing run-time memory checker tools often provide a method of determining the heap memory allocated at the given moment, but don't seem to keep a high-water mark or a historical profile of the heap usage. In addition, features for statistical analysis of the various sizes and numbers of each allocated block seems missing. For example, it would be nice to be able to determine how many of a given object were allocated or deallocated, such as to decide whether more cached memory blocks are needed.

A more advanced feature for heap measurement would be to use heap allocation as the metric in profiling reports. Profilers routinely measure time used by functions or basic blocks. It isn't much of a leap to measuring memory allocated or deallocated as a performance metric. In theory, a profiler could report any number of other metrics, but the state-of-the-art in profilers don't seem to have reached reporting of more advanced metrics such as: heap space allocated, stack space used, number of floating-point operations, number of calls to particular functions, number of I/O operations, number of memory reads/writes, and, in general, any other aspect of a program's execution at run-time for which you'd like to know how often it occurs and where it occurs with the highest frequency. A really good profiler should be able to help the programmer solve some uncommon performance improvement tasks such as optimizing I/O-bound programs, reducing the working set size, or resolving process size growth problems due to heap fragmentation by providing a memory allocation "turmoil" metric.

Another alternative for stack measurement is that a source code analysis tool could build a call graph from the source code and estimate the maximum stack depth (assuming no recursion) via a depth first search of the call graph and counting the functions called on the longest path. The depth of function call nesting is an interesting statistic in itself, but combined with estimates of how much stack space each function would consume, this algorithm would yield a maximum stack space estimate. If the compiler did this itself, its estimate of each function's stack space usage could be totally accurate.

Pretty printers

There are a number of tools available to produce nicely formatted C or C++ code from your source files. These tools are commonly called "pretty printers" or "code reformatters". Pretty printers are useful tools for cleaning up your own code (e.g., saving you time in not needing to correctly format your code while creating it) and also for examining other programmer's code during program maintenance.

Another different type of tool is one producing fancy hardcopy printouts of program source code, and these tools are also often called "pretty printers" which can lead to some confusion. This chapter examines both types of pretty printer tools.

CB — UNIX C CODE REFORMATTER

Tool Name:	cb
Purpose:	Code reformatter for C
Platforms:	UNIX

Languages:	C only, not C++
Status:	UNIX tool (commercial)
Key Points:	• Reformats C code to K&R brace style • Indentation levels are corrected
Limitations:	• No C++ support; fails on C++ comments • Not configurable: only one bracing style (K&R)

There is a standard UNIX tool distributed on most UNIX platforms which reformats C code, although it does not handle C++ code. The name "cb" stands for "C beautifier".

The usage method of cb is as a simple filter from standard input to standard output. Hence to reformat your file "myfile.c" to a better style, use:

```
cb < myfile.c >newfile.c
```

The main effect of cb is to realign braces in the "K&R" style of the opening left brace on the end of the statement line, and the closing right brace aligned with the keyword, such as:

```
if ( ...) {
    ....
}
else {
    ....
}
```

Unfortunately, the usual implementation of cb has many limitations. It cannot be used on C++ code because it separates the division signs in a // comment (among other problems). Even for C reformatting, cb is limited by its total lack of configurability. For example, if you don't want the K&R brace alignment style, well, that's just too bad.

CB AND SED FOR C++ REFORMATTING

A neat trick is to create a UNIX shell script that uses the sed utility to trick cb into correctly handling the C++ tokens on which it usually chokes, including :: and //. Because the algorithm used by cb is quite simple, relying on counting braces rather than on fully parsing the code, this approach is quite successful and the following script gives a reasonable C++ reformatter which we might call "cb++" or "cbplus":

```
#!/bin/sh
# cbplus:  use cb and sed to beautify C++ code
#
symbol=MAGIC_C_PLUS_PLUS_COLON_COLON_TOKEN
sed -e 's,\(//.*\),/*C++ \1 C++*/,' \
    -e "s,::,$symbol,g" $* |
cb |
sed -e 's,/\*C++ \(.*\) C++\*/,\1,' \
    -e "s,$symbol,::,g"
```

The usage method of this script is somewhat different to cb. Whereas cb accepts only standard input, a filename can be supplied to cbplus:

```
cbplus myfile.cpp > newfile.cpp
```

This script is available on the book's companion CDROM in the cbplus directory. Unfortunately this script is still not perfect. It is left as an exercise to the reader to extend the solution to handle other C++ tokens such as the newer ->* token.

INDENT — C/C++ CODE REFORMATTER

Tool Name:	indent
Main Purpose:	Code reformatter for C and C++
Platforms:	DOS, UNIX and most ANSI C compilers
Languages:	C and C++
Status:	Free
Authors:	Peter Hadfield, Jon Saxton, James Gosling, David Willcox, Joseph Arceneaux, Jim Kingdon
Availability:	Hadfield's SimTel C/C++ version: c/indents.zip Hadfield's SimTel C/C++ version: c/indentx.zip (DOS) GNU C/C++ indent from GNU: indent-1.8.tar.gz (UNIX, DOS) BSD-like C/C++ indent comp.sources.misc/volume21/indent/* Saxton's improvements; DOS and OS/2 port: comp.sources.misc/volume30/indent/* Yet another version: comp.sources.unix/volume18/indent/* Companion CDROM in directory indent
Key Points:	• C++ reformatting supported (in many versions) • Many configuration options for reformatting style • Brace style can be changed (not always K&R) • Default options in an "indent.pro" file
Limitations:	Many different conflicting versions of "indent" exist

It is difficult to discuss indent, since there are lots of different versions around. Some but not all of these versions are:

1. GNU indent for C and C++ (free);
2. SimTel versions for C and C++ (free; based on GNU's); and
3. BSD UNIX version for C (not free).

Unfortunately each version has slightly different features. For example, a version installed on your UNIX system will likely have different features to those versions available for FTP. The most major difference to watch out for is that some versions do not support C++ and might make a mess out of : : and / / tokens. Another major problem is that some versions take the second source filename to be an *output* file, thus causing the following command to erase one of the unwitting user's source files:

```
indent *.c     # Whoops! (some UNIX versions)
```

Some of the minor differences between versions you might come across include:

- options specified as -c:70 versus -c70 (i.e., with and without a colon)
- default options in ".indent.pro" (UNIX hidden file) versus "indent.pro"
- backup file suffix ".Bfile" (some UNIX versions) versus ".bak"

Naturally, the only solution is to carefully read the documentation for your version of indent. The SimTel and GNU free versions have their own documentation files, and the documentation for an installed UNIX version is available, as usual, via "man indent".

Let us now examine the typical behavior of the indent reformatter. The source file is reformatted "in place" and a backup file with a filename extension of ".bak" (or sometimes ".Bfile") is created.

The most notable feature of indent is its massive number of command-line options to configure the reformatting mode. Unfortunately, the actual options differ across versions so they are difficult to discuss in detail. Some important options to look into are shown in Table 8–1. These can be specified at the command-line or via a default file "indent.pro".

Table 8–1 Common indent options

Option	Purpose
-br, -bl	brace layout method (K&R and others)
-c	column where comments start
-i	indentation level (number of spaces)
-l	length of line (maximum allowed)
-bc, -nbc	newline after commas in declarations (enable/disable)
-+	enable C++ support (it exists if this option exists)

PPC — FREE CODE REFORMATTER FOR C

Tool Name:	ppc (Pretty Printer for C)
Purpose:	Code reformatter for C (and C++)
Platforms:	DOS, UNIX and most others with K&R C compiler

Languages:	ANSI C, K&R C (also C++ fixes by myself)
Status:	Free
Availability:	FTP from SimTel collection as c/ppc.zip
Author:	Richard Conn
Key Points:	• Reformats brace style and indentation in C code
Limitations:	• Badly coded and not robust (e.g., crash on 400 character lines) • Quite a few bugs in the reformatting • Poor reformatting of comments, not a fancy algorithm • There is no documentation

ppc is a code reformatter for C written by Richard Conn and based on the cb utility. ppc is available on SimTel (see "Free tools — SimTel archives" on page 10) as file "ppc.zip" in the "c" directory.

The reformatting actions performed by ppc are similar to those of cb, but the usage is quite different. Files are taken from the list of options and are reformatted "in place" with a backup file containing the old version. An example usage is:

```
ppc myfile.c
```

ppc is available on both UNIX and DOS, and should not be difficult to port to other platforms. Note that ppc cannot be used for C++ reformatting as it handles // and : : poorly.

VGRIND FOR TROFF OUTPUT

Tool Name:	vgrind
Purpose:	Pretty printing C/C++ into troff
Platforms:	UNIX only (and not all variants)
Languages:	ANSI C, K&R C, C++, others too
Status:	UNIX tool
Key Points:	• Creates troff file from C or C++ source code. • Bolds keywords, italicizes comments, numbers lines, etc.

The vgrind utility is a UNIX pretty printer for producing nicely typeset code examples using the troff UNIX typesetting program (or alternatively, GNU's groff typesetter which is a much improved version of troff).

There are a variety of options to alter the behavior, with the options differing slightly across UNIX variants. Some typical options are shown in Table 8–2. Note that C++ format-

Table 8–2 Common vgrind options

Option	Purpose
-f	Filter mode (e.g., for "tbl file ǀ vgrind -f ǀ troff")
-n	No bolding of keywords
-d	Different language (e.g., "-d cc" for C++).

ting may be supported by an appropriate entry in the file `/usr/lib/vgrindefs`, even if C++ is not mentioned by the manual pages.

TGRIND FOR TEX OUTPUT

Tool Name:	`tgrind`
Purpose:	Pretty printing C/C++ into TeX
Platforms:	UNIX, DOS
Languages:	ANSI C, K&R C, C++, others too
Status:	Free
Availability:	with TeX and LaTeX distribution typically in directory:.../contrib/van/tgrind up-to-date version by Jerry Leichter via FTP venus.ycc.yale.edu
Key Points:	• Creates TeX file from C or C++ source code. • Bolds keywords, italicizes comments, numbers lines, etc.

The `tgrind` utility is similar to `vgrind` except that it produces TeX output rather than `troff` output. The main format actions are bolding keywords, italicizing comments and placing line numbers and function names at regular intervals in the right margin. The usage is simply:

```
tgrind myfile.c
```

This produces a file "`myfile.c.tex`" which can then be used in any manner consistent with ordinary TeX documents.

    `tgrind` is not limited to formatting the C language but C is the default. The `-l` option can be used to specify a different language from one of a number of supported languages. The main effect of using this option is the bolding of the correct keywords. The usage for C++ is one of `-lC++`, `-lc++`, `-lCplusplus` or `-lcc`, such as:

```
tgrind -lcc myfile.cpp
```

Note that these `-l` options for C++ usage might not be documented (e.g., my system supports them, but they're not in the manual page).

LGRIND FOR LATEX PRETTY PRINTING

Tool Name:	`lgrind`
Purpose:	Pretty printing C/C++ for LaTeX
Platforms:	UNIX
Languages:	C and C++
Status:	Free
Availability:	`alt.sources` distributions: `volume92/lgrind*` e.g. `lth.se:/pub/netnews/alt.sources/volume92/sep/lgrind*`
Authors:	Van Jacobson, Jerry Leichter, George V. Reilly
Key Point:	— Font changes for keywords, comments, strings etc.

The `lgrind` utility for LaTeX formatting is largely based on the `tgrind` utility for TeX formatting. Hence, `lgrind` offers similar formatting features including page headers, bold keywords and preprocessor directives, comments in italics, and placing line numbers and function names at regular intervals in the right margin. The manner of usage is simply:

```
lgrind file.c > file.tex
```

Similarly as for `tgrind`, there are also quite a few command-line options for `lgrind` as shown in Table 8–3. The most important is probably the `-l` option which changes the language; use `-lc++` or `-lCC` for C++. Also interesting are the `-i` and `-e` options. The `-i` option specifies that `lgrind` should produce a partial LaTeX document, which can be later included as part of a larger document. The `-e` option allows `lgrind` to act on LaTeX files for its input, only formatting the portions identified as source code; refer to the manual for details. If neither `-i` nor `-e` are specified, the default is to produce a full LaTeX document.

Table 8–3 Common lgrind options

Option	Purpose
-l	language: -lc++, -lCC for C++ (default: -lc)
-n	no bold keywords
-h	header for pages
-i	included text; produce partial LaTeX file from program
-	read standard input
-d	definitions file (default: lgrindefs)
-e	embedded text processing of a LaTeX file

Unpacking the UNIX `shar` archive version of `lgrind` turned out to be tricky since the archive file "`lgrind`" extracts the manual file called "`lgrind.1`" which overwrites the `shar` file of the same name; hence expand "`lgrind.1`" before expanding "`lgrind.2`" and "`lgrind`". Installation of `lgrind` requires editing of the `Makefile` to change directory names, and may require source code changes (especially if you want to use `gcc` to compile). As suggested in the file "`lgrind.Re`", I changed the "inline" variable to "`Inline`" (4 instances). Furthermore, line 345 in "`lgrind.c`" has too few arguments for the `fprintf` causing a core dump when `lgrind` is run without arguments. I'm not sure what the argument should be, but I used `fname` (because it looks like the next `fprintf` call has been given the argument by accident), and it seemed to work.

SAPP POSTSCRIPT OUTPUT OF C AND C++

Tool Name:	`sapp` (still another pretty printer)
Purpose:	Pretty printing C/C++ into PostScript
Platforms:	UNIX only
Languages:	ANSI C, K&R C, C++, others too
Status:	Unclear (Free?)
Availability:	FTP `amadeus.stanford.edu`; file: `pub/SAPP.TAR`.
Author:	Arturo Salz
Key Points:	• Creates PostScript file from C or C++ source code. • Page headers, and nice fonts for keywords and comments.

`sapp` is a UNIX pretty printer capable of formatting many different programming languages into a postscript file with nice formatting. The effects produced include font changes for keywords and comments, page headers and a title page. `sapp` can also put two source code logical pages onto a page (using the `-2` option), and draw an outline around every page (the `-o` option).

By default the PostScript file is sent immediately to the printer (via `lpr`), but this can be overridden by using the `-p` option to put the result in a file. Different languages can be specified using the `-f` option: `-f  .c` for C (default), and `-f  .C` for C++. Hence, to format a C++ file "test.cc" to a postscript file "`test.ps`", we use:

```
sapp -f .C -p test.ps test.cc
```

`sapp` produces very nice output, but unfortunately, it supports only UNIX platforms. Also, if you are not the system administrator, and are just building `sapp` in your own directory, you'll need to change the DEFAULTDIR macro in "`main.c`" to be the directory in which you are building `sapp`, so that `sapp` can find its keyword file.

PSGRIND — POSTSCRIPT PRETTY PRINTER FOR C

Tool Name:	`psgrind`
Purpose:	Pretty printing C into PostScript
Platforms:	UNIX
Languages:	C but not C++, other languages too
Status:	Unclear (free ?)
Availability:	FTP to sun.soe.clarkson.edu:pub/src/psgrind/*
Key Points:	— Creates PostScript file from C source code. — Bolds keywords, italicizes comments, numbers lines, etc.
Limitations:	— No C++ support in default version.

There are a few options to `psgrind` as shown in Table 8–4. Note that the `-l` option supports a large number of languages — look through the `vgrindef` file to see how many. The default version has no C++ support but the `-l` option can be used to provide this if you add a C++ definition to the `vgrindef` data file, or if your system administrator already has.

Table 8–4 psgrind options

Option	Purpose
-n	no bolding of keywords
-l	language
-h	header for each page
-wide	wide format for 132 columns
-2	two logical pages per physical page
-	read standard input instead of filenames

I had a few minor difficulties porting `psgrind` to my UNIX platform. The problem was some non-ANSI C coding in one file: `perror` was incorrectly declared as returning `char*`, so I commented out this declaration, and also the subsequent use of the return value of `perror` in an `fprintf` call. I also had to change the directories in the `makefile`, but this would not be a problem for a system administrator installing the tool.

CGRIND — POSTSCRIPT PRETTY PRINTER FOR C

`cgrind` is a very interesting pretty printing tool in that it works differently to other similar tools like `psgrind` and `sapp`. Instead of being a program that modifies the C source, it con-

Tool Name:	`cgrind`
Purpose:	Pretty printing C into PostScript
Platforms:	UNIX, DOS, should be usable all platforms
Languages:	C but not C++, other languages too
Status:	Unclear (free?)
Availability:	FTP to sun.soe.clarkson.edu:pub/src/cgrind/*
Author:	Joe Larson (`joe@dayton.dhdsc.mn.org`)
Key Points:	— Creates PostScript file from C source code. — Works by prepending PostScript "programs" to the C source
Limitations:	— No C++ support

sists of a number of PostScript "program" files which are prepended to the C source file so as to generate a pretty output formatting. How easy it is to forget that PostScript is actually a programming language! The following command creates a PostScript version in landscape mode:

```
cat showline.ps land.ps test.c > test.ps
```

Unfortunately, I could not get the commands `land2/land4` and `port2/port4` to work correctly, and kept receiving an error from the `ghostview` previewer, and the printer not recognizing the result as a PostScript document.

The `cgrind` directory also includes a second tool in the file "`cgrind.c`", which is a more conventional pretty printing tool. This filters C source files to the standard output in such a way that the other PostScript programs are then able to make keywords bold and comments italicized. A typical sequence would be:

```
cgrind file.c > tempfile.c
cat showline.ps land.ps tempfile.c > test.ps
```

There also a few minor options; see the documentation in the "`Read.Me`" file and also in the comments in "`cgrind.c`" for more information.

This tool was slightly difficult to compile on my UNIX platform. `cgrind.c` was modified to include "stdtyp.h" rather than <dayton/`stdtype.h`>, and "`stdtyp.h`" was modified so that it did not include any other header files (the ones it includes are non-ANSI), and also defined a "`bool`" type as an alias for `int`.

CPR — C PRETTY PRINTER

Tool Name:	`cpr`
Main Purpose:	Pretty printing C for line printers

Platforms:	UNIX, MS-DOS
Languages:	C only
Status:	Free
Author:	Dave Tutelman
Availability:	comp.sources.misc/volume9/cpr_dt.Z(improved) comp.sources.misc/volume5/cpr (original version) Companion CDROM in directory `cpr`
Key Points:	• Paginates large files intelligently • Table of contents for files and functions
Limitations:	• No C++ support

`cpr` is the only pretty printer we have examined that is used mainly for line printer output. The main features of `cpr` are pagination to the correct page length with page headers. The pagination algorithm is also intelligent enough not to start a new function too close to the bottom of the page — exactly how close is satisfactory is controlled by the -p option. Naturally, `cpr` also performs the local font changes necessary to make keywords bold and comments italic. There are also quite a few command-line options as shown in Table 8–5.

Table 8–5   cpr options

Option	Purpose
-c	Look for functions only if file is a ".c" file.
-C	Produce *only* table of contents, no listing.
-n	Number lines in the listing.
-N	Start each file listing on page 1.
-s	Sort table of contents by function name (in each file).
-S	Case-insensitive version of -s.
-x, -X	Like -s/-S, but sort across files.
-l *n*	Page length (default is 66 lines)
-w *n*	Page width at which to fold lines. (Default = don't fold lines)
-p *n*	How many 16ths of a page can be used, and still start a new function on this page (-p0 puts a new function on each page; default is 12)
-r *n*	How many blank lines to leave after a '}' (default is 5)
-t *n*	Tab stop width in characters (default is 8)

Table 8–5 cpr options *(Continued)*

Option	Purpose
-T *file*	Print contents of *file* before table of contents.
-f *argfile*	Read arguments from *argfile*.
-	Read input from standard input.

Note that to install cpr, you will need to first edit the makefile to comment out the undesirable system definitions. To see the options, simply run cpr without any arguments, and you should see something similar to Table 8–5. To see the options without a UNIX core dump afterwards :-), change line 161 of "cpr.c" (i.e., the last entry for the synopsis array of strings variable) from ' \ 0 ' to " " (the empty string).

cPost — C to PostScript Pretty Printer

Tool Name:	*cPost*
Purpose:	Pretty printing C to PostScript
Platforms:	OS/2 (executable file only)
Languages:	C and C++
Status:	Free, but with limited rights; see the license file
Availability:	FTP software.watson.ibm.com:/pub/os2/ews/cpost.* FTP archive.latrobe.edu.au:archive-disk2/os2/ibm/ews/cpost.* FTP ftp-os2.cdrom.com:pub/os2/ibm/ews/cpost.* FTP ftp-os2.nmsu.edu:os2/ibm/ews/cpost.*
Author:	Patrick Mueller
Key Points:	• converts source or header files to PostScript • supports C++ comments
Limitations:	• Few platforms supported

cPost takes one or more C source or header files and builds a single PostScript file containing nicely formatted versions of the C files. A typical use of *cPost* in a project is:

```
cpost *.c *.h > doc.ps
```

There are a great many options for modifying the formatting behavior. Rather than examining them all, the most important are listed in Table 8–6; refer to the *cPost* documentation for full explanation of all the options. Default options can also be set in a CPOST environment variable.

Table 8–6 cPost common options

Option	Purpose
-c*ext1,ext2*	filename extensions *ext1* and *ext2* are C source files
-h*ext1,ext2*	filename extensions *ext1* and *ext2* are header files
-k*key1,key2*	*key1* and *key2* are keywords
-k@file	uses a file of keywords
-o*file*	output file(default: standard output)
-p[+-]	enable/disable function per page pagination
-t*num*	tab stops every *num* characters
-?	help — display online help

C++2LATEX/C2LATEX — FREE LaTeX PRETTY PRINTER

Tool Name:	c++2latex, c2latex
Purpose:	Pretty printing C/C++ for LaTeX
Platforms:	UNIX, MS-DOS
Languages:	C and C++
Status:	Free (GNU "copyleft" license)
Availability:	comp.sources.misc distributions: volume26/ c++2latex/*(also try an archie search for c++2latex)
Authors:	Norbert Kiesel, Joerg Heitkoetter
Key Points:	— Font changes for keywords, comments, strings etc.

c++2latex can be used to build entire LaTeX documents, or to build parts of them for inclusion in other documents. The main features are the use of different fonts for keywords, comments, string literals and preprocessor directives. The default fonts for all these types of text can also be overridden by command-line options, as shown in Table 8–7

Table 8–7 c++2latex options

Option	Purpose
-a	ANSI C mode (default is C++ mode)
-b	brace tab size (default 4 blanks)
-c	complete LaTeX file
-h	header on each page enabled

Table 8–7 c++2latex options *(Continued)*

Option	Purpose
-i	indentation width of blank (default 0.5em)
-n	no alignment of comments to right side of page
-o	output file (default is filename with ".tex" suffix)
-p	pipe output to stdout, not an output file
-s	size of font (default 10)
-C *font*	comment font (default italics)
-H *font*	header font (default 'sl')
-K *font*	keyword font (default bold)
-P *font*	preprocessor directive font (default typewriter)
-S *font*	string literal font (default typewriter)
-T *number*	tab stop width (default is 8)
-V	version number printed on standard error

I had minor difficulties making version 2.0 from *comp.sources.misc/volume26* compile on Ultrix, due to little things such as inconsistent use of "`const`" in the code. I also received a linker error that `yywrap` was undefined so I defined it at the end of "`main.c`" as "`int yywrap() { return 1 }`" after which everything went well.

C_PRETTY FOR WORD FOR WINDOWS

Tool Name:	`c_pretty`
Purpose:	WordBasic Macro for Microsoft Word for Windows for formatting C code nicely
Platforms:	MS-DOS, Windows
Languages:	C but not C++
Status:	Free
Author:	Philip Ryan
Availability:	FTP via SimTel in file windows3/c_pretty.zip
Key Points:	• bolds keywords, italicizes some important functions • bold-italic for preprocessor directives, comments in italics

Unlike the other pretty printers in this chapter, this tool is used with the popular word processor, Microsoft Word for Windows. `c_pretty` makes it easy to create nice looking documents out of C source code. The main changes in appearance of the document are the use of better fonts for keywords, standard library functions, preprocessor directives and comments.

PPS — POSTSCRIPT PRETTY PRINTER

Tool Name:	pps
Purpose:	PostScript pretty printing of lots of languages
Platforms:	UNIX (Sun, Vax, Gould, CCI, RT, other BSD)
Languages:	C (C++ extension possible)
Status:	Free
Availability:	comp.sources.unix/volume17/pps.Z
Key Points:	• creates Postscript output • runs very quickly

pps creates PostScript output files from a variety of different languages including C, awk, lisp, sh, and more. The resulting Postscript file shows the source code with nice fonts, line numbers in the right margin every 10 lines, function names in the right margin where they begin, and a header file on each page.

There are a variety of useful command-line options. The −C, −K, −S and −I options change the fonts for comments, keywords, strings and other text, respectively. The −n option specifies how frequently line numbers appear (defaults to 10), the -h option sets the header text, and the −t option sets tab stop widths.

The tool does not have explicit support for C++, but this can be added reasonably easily. Copy the `lex` input file "c.l" to "cplus.l" and add the appropriate definitions to the Makefile — add cplus to the LANG macro list, and copy the line creating c from c.o and modify it to refer to cplus:

```
cplus: cplus.o lind.o
    $(CC) $(CFLAGS) -o $@ $@.o lind.o -ll
```

Then modify the `lex` input file "cplus.l" to add extra C++ keywords to the keywords array, and also add the following rules:

```
<INITIAL>\/\/   { begin(CPCOMMENT); ECHO; }
<CPCOMMENT>[\n] { space(yytext); begin(INITIAL); }
[\n] { space(yytext); }
[\t\f]+ { /* NOTE: \n removed */ space(yytext); }
```

Add CPCOMMENT to the end of the %Start declaration, then run the command "make cplus", and you should then be able to pretty print C++ using:

```
pps -1 cplus file.cc > file.ps
```

CPG — FREE C FORMATTER FOR LINE PRINTERS

Tool Name:	cpg
Purpose:	Source code formatter/pretty printer
Platforms:	UNIX; any K&R C compiler
Languages:	C (and C++ to a limited extent)
Status:	Free
Author:	Steven List
Availability:	comp.sources.unix/volume2/cpg+mdep3.Z(Revised) comp.sources.unix/volume1/cpg+mdep3.Z (Original)
Key Points:	• modifies listings for line printer output • table of contents produced of files and functions

cpg is a pretty printer for standard line printer output that is similar to the standard UNIX pr tool, but has more C specific features. Its main features are pagination (assuming 60 lines per page), page headers, and the production of a table of contents at the end of the listing. Thus cpg can also be a useful documentation generation tool. Although cpg is intended only for C, its algorithm is so simple that it works quite well for pagination of C++ programs as well, although it does not properly recognize some C++ function definitions (e.g., class member functions don't appear in the table of contents).

The only command-line options are -t to set tab stops, and -b to specify that the basename of the filename be used in headers. However, cpg does respond to a number of "triggers" inside C comments, all of which have a capital letter immediately after the * character. Some examples are /*P*/ for page ejection, and /*F filename*/ to set the filename for subsequent page headers.

C PRINTER IN DR DOBB'S JOURNAL

Tool Name:	C printer
Purpose:	Source code formatter for line printers
Platforms:	UNIX, DOS, any K&R C compiler
Languages:	C

Status:	Free
Availability:	SimTel sites ddjmag/ddjcspec.zip; filename `winter.1st`; (UNIX/VMS patches in file `poole.1st`)
Author:	Stewart Nutter, Ron Winter, Kevin Poole
Key Points:	• modifies listings for line printer output

Apparently this is a tool that prints neatly paginated source code listings. However, although there are some patches by Kevin Poole that create a version of the tool portable to MSDOS, UNIX and VMS version, there was inadequate documentation for me to get these patches to work. I tried a quick UNIX port by defining `near`, `far` and `huge` as nothing macros, supplying my own `strdup` function, and commenting out uses of the DOS functions `_strdate` and `_strtime`. There was a `NULL` dereference at a `strcmp` call in `binary_search_sorted_data_base` requiring a safety test, and also some tests `length>65535` which had to be replaced with 0 to force it to fail. However, the code appears full of portability bugs for UNIX use, and I couldn't get it to work adequately.

C-Vision — Listing, Documentation and Reformatting

Product Name:	C-Vision
Purpose:	Documentation and reformatting for C and C++
Platforms:	DOS, OS/2
Languages:	ANSI C, C++, K&R C
Status:	Commercial Product
Price:	$239
Company:	Gimpel Software
Address:	3207 Hogarth Lane, Collegeville, PA, 19426, USA
Phone:	610-584-4261
Fax:	610-584-4266
Email:	info@gimpel.com

C-Vision is presented by Gimpel Software as a solution to the write-only C problem — once written, it cannot be read. There are a number of distinct components in the package for code reformatting, pretty printing and analysis including:

- C-LINES: produce source code listings
- C-FORMAT: reformat source code
- C-COMMENT: reformat source code with special comment formats

- C-XREF: cross-referencing analysis
- C-TREE: textual tree diagrams based on the cross-reference analysis
- C-TDUMP: dump cross-references to ASCII for database import

C-LINES produces pretty source code listings for a printer or in a PostScript file. The translations include prefix line numbers, font changes for keywords and comments, titles and subtitles, footers, and outlines of logical blocks. There is support for a number of common printers with special control codes used.

C-FORMAT is a code reformatter with a reasonable number of options to control the format. The main features are re-indentation of source, repositioning of braces and expression spacing. Indentation is the main feature and can be controlled for case/default labels with a special option, and there are options to control where lines are broken. Braces can be positioned in a number of ways including K&R-style or Pascal-like condensed format. The spacing of the operators in an expression can be controlled by a configuration file. Preprocessor directives such as `#define` can be indented according to their nesting. There are options to indent the entire `#define` or leave the # character flush left and indent the `define` keyword.

C-COMMENT is a minor addition to C-FORMAT that formats comments with better alignment. It has various options to control the positioning of comments that are alone on lines, or next to code. Comments across multiple lines can be aligned to a given column. There is also some support for multi-line comment blocks.

C-XREF produces cross-references of all symbols in the project and also stores information in a database for C-TREE to use. C-XREF can call C-TREE directly as part of its operation. The output report from C-XREF is a combined alphabetized cross-reference of symbols in all files with information about all their references. An encoding scheme displays information compactly about declarations, definitions, address-of & operations, `#undef` directives, functions declared by use, and functions defined. There are numerous options to limit the files or symbol names considered based on location or their category (e.g., macros, locals, etc.).

C-TREE uses cross-reference information to produce a number of lists and textual tree reports. The lists of symbols can show a summary of all symbols or all unused symbols. The tree diagrams are not fancy graphical displays with circles and arcs, but are ASCII reports like those from the UNIX `cflow` command. The hierarchy tree is a function call graph showing function uses and optionally global or extern variable uses. The inverse hierarchy tree is called the "access tree" to show what functions call or use a function or variable. C++ class inheritance can be shown by the class hierarchy tree or the inverse tree. Symbols in each tree can be restricted based on various options, and trees can be rooted on a chosen symbol.

The textual methods of displaying the graphs as ASCII "trees" are interesting. A fully displayed function call graph would usually show nested levels, but will also have arcs "up" the tree from low-level functions calling higher level functions, and also from recursive cycles. The one line per function method used by C-TREE has to account for these up arcs, and a few displays methods are possible. The "hierarchy tree" shows each function once only, shows all downward arcs, and places any upward arcs in brackets after the identifier. Another view is the "indented outline tree" where there is one line per arc and each function can appear more than once. In this tree the functions are expanded at each level and all called functions shown even if expanded above in the tree. In this view all upward arcs are shown in the listing and the only arcs in square brackets after the line are recursive calls. Both of these tree forms can give useful structural feedback about the function call graph or C++ class hierarchy.

PRETTY PRINTING USING MINOR UNIX TOOLS

There are a number of ordinary UNIX tools that can be used effectively in pretty printing code for neater hardcopies. Some of the tools include:

Table 8–8 UNIX tools for pretty printing

Command	Purpose
pr	Paginate text file for line printer
expand	Replace tabs with spaces
unexpand	Replace spaces with tabs
cat -n	Prefix line numbers
sed	Change patterns
awk	Change patterns
perl	Change patterns

The first tool to mention is pr, which formats text files for line printers, 60 lines to a page. It can be useful for printing C or C++ source files to a line printer.

The UNIX tools expand and unexpand can be useful in reformatting C/C++ source code that has too many tab characters. The expand command replaces all tab characters with the correct number of spaces. The command accepts any number of filenames and puts the modified text to the standard output stream. A typical usage of expand for a single file is:

```
expand myfile.c >newfile.c
```

Tab settings can be adjusted via the -number option where a number prefixed with a minus sign is assumed to set the next tab. Thus a usage such as "expand -10 -20" will set two tab stops at columns 10 and 20. If there is only one tab stop specified, such as "expand -4", then this sets infinitely many tab stops every 4 characters.

The companion tool, unexpand, replaces any significant sequences of space characters with tab characters. The usage method is identical to expand, without output going to standard output. Naturally, this tool is used less often than expand.

The cat utility has a useful option for putting line numbers before each line of a source code file — the -n option. Hence "cat -n" can be used in a pipeline for typesetting source code.

The sed utility can be used to replace patterns in your source code with other patterns. For example, the following simple shell script will bold all if and while keywords and italicize all C++-style comments for the `troff` typesetting command (or GNU's `groff`). It also converts all backslashes to double backslashes so that they appear correctly in `troff` output (otherwise all the `\n` sequences in strings and elsewhere will cause havoc with `troff`).

```
#!/bin/sh
# Pretty print C/C++ for troff using sed
# by D.Spuler, 1994.
sed \
-e 's/\\/\\\\/g'      \
-e 's/\([^a-zA-Z_]\)if\([^a-zA-Z_]\)/\1\\fBif\\fP\2/'\
-e 's/\([^a-zA-Z_]\)while\([^a-zA-Z_]\)/\1\\fBwhile\\fP\2/'\
-e 's/\/\/\(.*\)$/\/\/\\fI\1\\fP/'      \
$*
```

Note that because `sed` operates on each line separately, it has problems with any multiple line constructs such as long C-style comments.

The `awk` utility can be used to create a pretty printing sequence, and is more effective than `sed` because it is not restricted to single line patterns. Another more recent tool similar to `awk` is the `perl` language. It is left as an exercise to the reader to make a fully functional pretty printer using `sed`, `awk` or `perl`.

Language conversion tools

*B*elieve it or not, C and C++ are not the only pro-gramming languages in existence. However, one can easily argue they are becoming the pro-gramming languages of choice, given that most requests for language translation tools are for conversion to C or C++ from another language, rather than in the other direction. The typical scenario is needing to convert an existing legacy application program written in another lan-guage into C or C++ code. However, before we launch into a discussion of converting legacy code written in dozens of languages, let's first discuss how to convert between our two favor-ite coding dialects.

C TO C++ CONVERSION

Many software shops are upgrading from C to C++ coding, and in addition to all the organi-zational problems of the transition, such as reeducating the developers, there's the niggling annoyance that C is a subset of C++. *Almost*. The reality is that C code will not make it through a C++ compiler without a fair amount of effort. The subset of C that will compile via both C and C++ compilers is sometimes called "typesafe C". Here's a summary of some of the things that will stop a C program compiling as C++:

- identifiers with names that are C++ keywords: `new` seems to be the most common culprit, but many of them contribute occasionally.
- conversion from `void*` generic pointers to other pointers require type casts: calls to `malloc` are the main example
- non-prototyped function calls are impossible

The general rule which is simplistic but surprisingly accurate is: "*C warnings are C++ errors.*" No longer can you blithely cast away any troubles between different pointer types, and this is especially true of pointers to functions. Callbacks have to be exactly the right type in C++, right down to the very last `const`. Function prototype declarations must always be available to every call. And existing prototypes are a danger in themselves, especially if they are sporadically placed throughout the code, rather than in a header file close to the function definition. A wrong argument type such as a `const` difference, or an `int` instead of an `enum`, will lead the C++ compiler to treat them as overloaded declarations of the same function name, leading to linkage failures due to functions where the definitions appear to be "missing" to the C++ compiler.

So the natural question is: What tools are available? It should be obvious that conversion from procedural C to C++ code using all of the object-oriented features isn't realistic. But what about a tool to massage C into "typesafe C"? It could automatically change those keywords, add those type casts, and alert you to any occurrences of the more obscure pitfalls. Alas, I haven't seen one yet, and the best solution so far is the brute-force approach of compile using C++ and resolve all error messages. On the upside, having done this you'll have cleaner code and most likely will have identified one or two obscure bugs in your program along the way!

C++ TO C CONVERSION

Converting a C++ program "down" to C is most commonly needed because of multiplatform portability woes — not all platforms have good C++ compilers! In this situation it isn't strictly necessary for the output to be human readable, but only that a C compiler will grok it. So the problem is to find a C++ compiler that produces C source code as its intermediate representation. Unfortunately, I can't offer much in the way of assistance for this problem, as I haven't come across a good solution. Early versions of the commercially available *cfront* C++ translator created C code as the intermediate language, but this is no longer the case. The GNU g++ compiler also goes directly to lower-level assembly/machine languages and is no help for this particular problem.

CONVERSION OF OTHER LANGUAGES

With the popularity of C and C++, most of the conversion requests are from another language to either C or C++. This is fortunate since it is far easier to convert into C or C++ than it is to convert from C or C++ to another language. The systems programming background of C makes it one of the lowest level languages in existence, and most other languages do not offer such low level primitives in which to mimic C/C++ operations. But this very fact makes the conversion from another language into C or C++ possible. In fact, some compilers of other languages have used C as their compiled form because of its universal availability.

The details of conversion obviously differ with each programming language. The aim is to map features of other languages as closely as possible into C/C++ constructs. For example, Pascal conversion is relatively easy because most of the features map one-to-one between the languages (e.g., Pascal's records and C's structs). Conversion to C++ can be even easier because of the wider range of features available — for example, conversion of Fortran is easier in C++ because C++ classes can be used to mimic the Fortran *complex* data type, whereas conversion to C requires the addition of more complicated code sequences to mimic complex arithmetic expressions.

PTOC/PTC — FREE PASCAL TO K&R C TRANSLATOR

Tool Name:	`ptoc/ptc`
Platforms:	Pascal or C compiler required
Status:	Free
Available:	FTP comp.sources.unix/volume10/ptoc in Pascal; also patches in comp.sources.unix/volume13/pas2c.pch.Z
Author:	Per Bergsten

There is some confusion since the tool is "`ptc`" but the distribution calls it "`ptoc`". Unfortunately, the `ptc` translator is a little dated for use as a practical tool because it lacks ANSI C support, but it still represents an important piece of work with some interesting conversion methods. The translator itself is written in Pascal with a C version available that was translated by `ptc`.

`ptc` supports conversion of ISO Pascal with two common extensions ("`otherwise`" and "`external`") but no support for the numerous Pascal variants available. Typically an entire Pascal program is converted but there is some support for converting code fragments.

The details of the Pascal to C conversion are quite interesting since Pascal and C are superficially similar but differ on many details. `ptc` ensures almost total semantic equivalence with only a few potential pitfalls such as complicated flow of control related to nested functions, and issues such as the assumption that "`x mod y`" translates to "`x%y`" which may be incorrect for negative values. Let's look at some of the hoops through which `ptc` must jump to ensure equivalence:

- constants: integers are converted to `#define`, but strings are converted to static variables to avoid duplication (an optimization many C compilers perform automatically these days).

- booleans are converted readably to C using `#define`'s for `true`, `false`, and `boolean`.
- variables with C keywords such as "`struct`" are prefixed to avoid C syntax errors.
- uppercase letters in identifiers are converted to lower case to avoid mixed case pitfalls, but this loses some readability along the way.
- subranges map to an appropriate integer type.
- Pascal arrays are converted to C structures with an array member for pass-by-value semantics
- Pascal variant records use dummy member names in C (not anonymous unions).
- Pascal sets are converted to structure containing an array of shorts, and set operators are converted to C function calls using the bitwise operators.
- To convert Pascal file operations, `ptc` extends the C `FILE` type because Pascal file operations do not map directly to C standard I/O operations. For example, there is the well-known pitfall that "`while(!feof(fp))`" in C is not the same as "`while not eof(fp) do`" for reading until end of file.
- A difficult method with global pointers is used to convert Pascal nested functions and procedural parameters to a C equivalent. Some obscure cases are not accurately converted.
- non-local Pascal `goto` statements map to `longjmp` and `setjmp` calls in C.
- Pascal blocks, `if`, `case`, repeat-until, all map directly to C with trivial changes.
- Pascal "`with`" statements map to C with similar efficiency by storing a pointer to the structure.
- `for` loops do not map directly because of different semantics such as the upper bound evaluated only once in Pascal. Hence `ptc` uses some temporary variables to ensure correct Pascal meaning, but this behavior can be configured in favor of readability rather than rigid equivalence.
- pass-by-reference of Pascal "`var`" parameters is handled by pointer operations, especially since Pascal arrays are wrapped in C structures to give Pascal-like pass-by-value semantics.
- Pascal "div "and "/" division operators map to C's "/" operator with casts where needed.
- operations on enumeration types are cast to `int` in C to avoid compilation warnings or errors.
- Pascal record comparison operators are converted to function calls in C.
- The "`^`" operator followed by "`.`" is converted to C's "`->`" operator.

The behavior of the `ptc` translator can be configured, not by command-line options, but by editing constants in the Pascal source code. Among other things, the "`otherwise`" and "`external`" extensions can be prevented and `for` loops can be translated to code with less rigorous semantic equivalence but greater readability.

P2C — FREE PASCAL TO C TRANSLATOR

Tool Name:	p2c
Main Purpose:	Pascal to C conversion
Platforms:	UNIX (HP, Sun 3)
Languages:	Pascal, C, Modula-2, Turbo Pascal
Status:	GNU license agreement (except for generated code)
Author:	Dave Gillespie
Address:	256-80 Caltech, Pasadena CA 91125
Availability:	FTP comp.sources.unix/volume21/p2c
	FTP comp.sources.unix/volume22/p2cpatches
	Companion CDROM in directory p2c

p2c is a full featured professional tool with good documentation. In addition to basic language features, p2c converts Pascal language extensions from Turbo Pascal, Vax Pascal, Modula-2 and Oregon Software Pascal. The generated C code works in both 16-bit and 32-bit C compilers although this is less important in modern times.

Note that the *comp.sources.unix* distribution is shar'd and I had problems extracting it. In the end I had to create the directories HP/include, HP/import, src and examples in the directory where I was extracting it before the 'sh' commands would extract it all correctly.

CFORTRAN.H — FREE LIBRARY FOR MIXING FORTRAN AND C

Name:	cfortran.h
Platforms:	AIX, SGI, DEC, VAX VMS, VAX Ultrix, Sun, CRAY, Apollo, HP, LynxOS
Available:	comp.sources.misc/volume20/cfortran/part[01-02]
	Updated version: cfortran/* from zebra.desy.de
Author:	Burkhard Burow

Although this tool is not a language conversion tool per se, it belongs in this chapter as it provides a bridge between languages. The "cfortran.h" tool is a header file that makes it easy to mix Fortran and C code without paying attention to machine dependencies such as calling sequences of particular platforms or compilers. It provides hooks for converting calls in both directions: calling Fortran from C and calling C from Fortran. The basic implementation is a set of macros for C code. Calling Fortran from C is supported by macros to provide prototypes of Fortran functions so they can be called from C. Conversely, the calling of C functions from Fortran is supported by wrapper C functions that encapsulate the conversion between different calling conventions. Hence the calling of C functions from Fortran is less efficient due to the wrapper function, but calling Fortran from C does not suffer this way. In addition to functions, there is support for modifying Fortran common blocks from C code.

FOR_C AND FOR_C++ — FORTRAN CONVERSION

Product Name:	FOR_C and FOR_C++
Platforms:	DOS, HP-UX, Solaris, SunOS, RS/6000 (AIX), SGI (Irix), VAX VMS
Price:	Starting at $675 ($195 evaluation copy)
Company:	Cobalt Blue, Inc.
Address:	555 Sun Valley Drive, Suite K-4, Roswell, GA 30076, USA
Phone:	+1(770)518-1116
Fax:	+1(770)640-1182
Email:	sales@cobalt-blue.com
Web:	http://www.cobalt-blue.com

FOR_C converts Fortran to readable and maintainable C. There is support for both standard Fortran-77 and many VAX, MILSPEC, PRIME, IBM-VS, DG, HP, Microsoft and Fortran-90 extensions. FOR_C includes basic static analysis and error checking capability and a related tool called FOR_STUDY is available for more in-depth analysis.

 The conversion to C matches Fortran semantics while retaining its readability. FOR_C offers the choice between exact duplication of Fortran I/O routines or optional conversion of READ and WRITE to fscanf and fprintf and OPEN/CLOSE to fopen/fclose. Fortran-77 character arrays are translated to null-terminated C strings. There is also a de-include facility for optimizing commons in parameters in Fortran include files, and options for optimizations of assignments, intrinsics, and single dimension arrays during the conversion. C source is available for run-time libraries implementing missing Fortran-77 functions.

 FOR_C++ is similar to FOR_C but takes advantage of C++ features for even more readable code. Parameters are mapped to C++ constants. Fortran intrinsics are converted to overloaded C++ functions where possible. There is direct conversion of the Fortran complex type to a C++ complex class. Fortran character arrays can use a C++ string class, or C-like null-terminated strings. C++ reference parameters are used to reproduce Fortran calling semantics. inline functions are used for performance where appropriate.

F2C — FREE FORTRAN TO C OR C++

f2c is a freely distributed tool for conversion of Fortran to C or C++ code, developed by AT&T and Bellcore. All arguments with a ".f" or ".F" suffix are considered Fortran files,

Platforms	UNIX (RS/6000, Sun, any it will compile for!)
Availability:	GNU distribution as file f2c*, bug fixes via FTP to netlib.att.com or by email from netlib@research.att.com Companion CDROM in directory f2c
Author:	AT&T Bell Labs, Bellcore, and Carnegie Mellon

and a corresponding C file is created with a ".c" suffix. The C file includes the header file "f2c.h". The resulting C program may require the linking options "-lF77 -lf77 -lm" which may require additional -L options to locate the libraries. Some of the options to f2c are listed in Table 9–1.

Table 9–1 f2c options

-C	array subscript checking
-c++	C++ code generated instead of C
-ec	Uninitialized COMMON in separate files
-ext	Warn about Fortran extensions
-r8	promote REAL to DOUBLE
-A	ANSI C output (default is K&R)
-R	Do not make REAL into DOUBLE PRECISION
-P	Prototype file "file.P" created
-E	uninitialized COMMON become extern
-U	case of variables and external names kept
-a	Local variables automatic
-c	Fortran source included as comments
-g	Fortran line numbers included as comments
-u	Default type is undefined
-w	Suppress all warnings
-z	Do not implicitly recognize DOUBLE COMPLEX

PASCAL AND BASIC TO C FROM TECHNOSOFT

Company:	Technosoft
Address:	PO Box 8210, Rockford IL 61126-8210, USA Enterprise House, Cherry Orchard Lane, Salisbury SP2 7LD, UK

Phone:	815-397-3214 (USA), +44-722-414201 (UK)
Fax:	815-397-0619 (USA), +44-794-884087 (UK)

Technosoft offers a number of language tools for converting Pascal or Basic to readable and maintainable C code. The language dialects supported for conversion to C include Vax Pascal, Turbo Pascal, Microsoft Pascal, Microsoft GW-Basic, Microsoft Quick Basic, and Microsoft Professional Basic. Additionally, Turbo Pascal with Objects can be converted to C++ code.

BAS_C — BASIC TO C FROM GOTOLESS CONVERSION

Product:	BAS_C
Platforms:	DOS
Price:	$275-$425 (eval copy: $45)
Company:	Gotoless Conversion
Address:	7105 Dee Cole Drive, The Colony, TX 75056, USA
Phone:	214-370-8200
Fax:	214-370-2612
Email:	gotoless@pic.net

BAS_C automatically translates spaghetti BASIC code into structured, readable C source code. The resulting C code is indented correctly, and structured by replacing GOTO statements with *while*, *switch* and *for* C statements. The scope of BASIC variables is analyzed and BAS_C makes them local or global in the resulting C code. The output C code is also optimized by removing unused variables and dead code from the BASIC program.

The converted C code is more portable than the BASIC program because BAS_C converts a BASIC statement into equivalent C statement or a call to the standard C library. Inherently non-portable MSDOS-specific issues such as *peek* and *poke* are handled through the BAS_C run-time library. Graphics and screen oriented BASIC code is converted to the equivalent C calls for your compiler. There are a number of options that allow you to control the dialect of C that is produced, including Microsoft C and Borland C.

ASSEMBLER TO C FROM GOTOLESS CONVERSION

Product Name:	A2C (assembler to C)
Platforms:	DOS (translates 68K or Z80 assembly)

Company:	Gotoless Conversion
Address:	7105 Dee Cole Drive, The Colony, TX 75056, USA
Phone:	214-370-8200
Fax:	214-370-2612
Email:	gotoless@pic.net

A2C translates Motorola 68K and Zialog Z80 assembly source code into readable and maintainable C source code. The advantages of C code over assembly are well-known: readability, portability, reliability, and many more available libraries and tools.

Multi-file translation is used to read all source files before generating the resulting output. Spaghetti code is translated into structured code with high level constructs such as `if-then-else`, `while`, `do-while` and `for`, and the code is also indented for readability. Low-level assembly features such as passing information to subroutines via registers are converted to C parameters. Array usage such as indirect reference is also detected and translated into arrays. Unnecessary register operations in assembly code are also eliminated, such as the intermediate registers used to calculate expressions in assembly code.

Prototype extraction tools

*T*ools that automatically generate header files are amongst the most useful tools you can have. Personally I've made use of a simple UNIX shell script for years, but now that I've found the extraction tools discussed in this chapter, that script is history.

Extraction of function prototypes is the most common requirement. Prototypes are typically placed in header files, with various schemes in existence for choosing how many header files a module should use. Prototypes of functions that are used only in a single source file can be placed at the top of the source file to ensure safe usage of functions throughout the source file. This latter comment is mainly applicable to prototypes of `static` functions.

Prototypes are not the only things to go in C header files. There are `extern` declarations of global variables, `#define` preprocessor macros, `typedef` declarations, `struct`, `union`, and `enum` declarations. For C++ there can also be `inline` function definitions, `const` variables, and, of course, let's not forget `class` declarations! However, for the majority of these constructs, they are usually placed in header files immediately, so a tool to extract them from source code isn't very important. The only header file constructs for which automatic generation is useful are function prototypes and `extern` variable declarations.

REFRESHER COURSE ON FUNCTION PROTOTYPES

Functions should be declared before they are used and the "prototype" is used for this purpose, especially when making function calls across multiple files. Function prototypes have a simple syntax that is very similar to an ordinary function definition. The difference is that the body of the function (i.e., {...}) is left out and a semicolon is placed after the function header (i.e., after the right bracket of the parameter list). A function prototype always ends with a semicolon. Hence, a simplistic version of the syntax of a function prototype is:

```
return_type  function_name ( parameter_list ) ;
```

The parameter list for an ANSI C or C++ prototype can be an ordinary list of parameter declarations with full types and parameter names:

```
int  max(int x, int y); /* parameter names in */
```

Alternatively, it can be a list of abstract type declarators (i.e., the name of the parameter is left out, only the type is put in the list):

```
int max(int, int);  /* parameter names out */
```

Both forms are syntactically correct in C or C++ and the choice is a matter of style. You can even use a hybrid method of naming some parameters and not naming others. Leaving the parameter names in the prototype may be preferable because of the documentation benefits it provides, but in some cases they should be omitted for name space reasons (e.g., a common name space violation of the ANSI C standard in many commercial compilers was for the standard header files to be vulnerable to a #define that happened to hit one of the parameter names). The compromise method is to put the parameter names in comments in the middle of the prototype:

```
int max(int /*x*/, int /*y*/); /* parameter name comments */
```

When ANSI C is not available, old-style function declarations are also possible. They are identical to ANSI prototypes, except that the parameter list is empty. Some examples of K&R C function declarations are:

```
int max();
char *strcpy();
```

Naturally, ANSI prototypes should be used wherever possible because of the benefits of compile-time argument type checking. The above K&R prototypes do not specify how many parameters there are or what the parameter types are.

A special case is that the prototype for a function without any parameters differs between K&R C, ANSI C and C++. The three forms are shown below:

```
void no_params();        /* K&R style */
void no_params(void);    /* ANSI C style */
void no_params();        /* C++ style */
```

Although the K&R style looks the same as C++, it has a different meaning. The above K&R declaration is actually stating that there are an unknown number of parameters, whereas the C++ style (and also the ANSI C style) are stating that no parameters are allowed. The ANSI C style is also supported with identical meaning in C++, although the third form is "pure" C++ coding style. However, I recommend using the ANSI C style for both ANSI C and C++ compilers, since it is unlikely that C++ vendors will stop supporting the ANSI C syntax.

extern with function prototypes

Function prototypes in any of the above styles (K&R, ANSI or C++) can also use the `extern` keyword such as in the example below:

```
extern int max(int, int);
```

Using `extern` is unnecessary, as the meaning is identical for function prototypes, since the semicolon rather than the {..} function body indicates that it is a prototype. However, using `extern` does have the documentation benefit of making it even more obvious that it is a prototype declaration rather than a definition.

HEADER FILE ORGANIZATION

There are a variety of organization schemes for maintaining header files in a large project. The worst is to place all declarations in a single header file that is included by all source files. The best method (probably) in C is to have header files per source file: One header file contains prototypes needed by other source files to call the functions defined in that file; the other contains all internal declarations, such as types, macros and `static` function prototypes. The naming of header files for such a scheme is tricky; one possibility is different file extensions such as ".h" for the public header file and ".ih", say, for the internal header file.

However, the arrangement of two header files per source file leads to a blowout in the number of files for a project, which may make it unacceptable. The majority of projects thus involve some sort of compromise, often leading to interdependence problems such as needing to include one header file to declare a type, so that you can include another header file with a prototype that happens to use that type. This sort of dependence can be removed by careful arrangement of the header files so that they are self-sufficient. It may be necessary (or convenient) to have some header files include a few major header files containing important type declarations.

Although the above discussion hasn't adequately covered the area of header file organization, which is even more involved when you start having C++ classes, this book isn't really the right place for a full discussion, so let's move on. I will make one final point that is often not fully understood by reasonably new programmers: *The header file of function prototypes should be included in the source file where they are defined.* Although there is no strict need to do so, this is very useful for checking that the declarations in the header file match the actual function definitions.

MERGING ANSI AND PRE-ANSI PROTOTYPES

For portability it can be very useful to have prototypes that are valid for both pre-ANSI C and ANSI C compilers. The simplest method is to use two lists of prototypes which are distinguished by a macro test on __STDC__ and also __cplusplus if it is possible that a C++ compiler will be used (in fact, you might even want to also test the old C++ macro, c_plusplus, just in case you get an older C++ compiler). An example of this treatment of function prototypes in header files is:

```
#if defined(__STDC__) || defined(__cplusplus)
void my_function(int x, int y);
    /* .. more ANSI C or C++ prototypes */
#else
void my_function();
    /* .. more pre-ANSI prototypes */
#endif
```

A common technique is to use a preprocessor macro to avoid the duplication, which may be error-prone. The above code becomes:

```
#if defined(__STDC__) || defined(__cplusplus)
#define PROTOARGS(x) x
#else
#define PROTOARGS(x) ()   /* empty list */
#endif
```

This makes use of the double-bracket macro technique and the function prototypes become:

```
void my_function PROTOARGS((int x, int y));
```

When compiled with an ANSI compiler the parameter types are left in. When a pre-ANSI compiler is used, only an empty parameter list is seen by the compiler.

REFRESHER COURSE ON EXTERN VARIABLE DECLARATIONS

Suppose we wish to define an external variable max_len in one file and use it in another. The definition of max_len in the first file is just a definition of a global variable (outside of any function definition):

```
int max_len;
```

However, the second file cannot use max_len without declaring the variable as external to that file. This is achieved using the extern specifier. The declaration below must be placed at the top of the second file (i.e., it must appear before the first use of the variable):

```
extern int max_len;
```

It is incorrect to define max_len without the extern specifier in the second file, because this will lead to compilation errors (actually linkage errors) because of the multiple declarations of `max_len`. Thus, the general method of using external variables is that the variable must be

a. *defined* in exactly one file, and
b. *declared* using `extern` in any other files using it.

Note that initialization of the variable is allowed in the *definition*, but not in any of the `extern` declarations. Only the non-`extern` *definition* should have an initialization.

(This is not actually the full story on `extern` variables in ANSI C, although it is mostly accurate with respect to C++. The ANSI C standard allows a concept of "tentative definitions" in which it is possible to have more than one definition. However, the principle of one non-`extern` definition and many `extern` declarations is the most portable and least error-prone assumption. Note that tentative definitions are disallowed in the C++ standard so they're really not worth worrying about.)

Header files with extern declarations are the easiest way to satisfy the "one definition, many declarations" rule. The header file of `extern` declarations must be included in all files that do not contain the variable definitions. The header file should also be included where the global variables are *defined* (i.e., even in the source file, say, "`main.c`"). Though it is not strictly necessary because the definition also declares the variables, including the header file ensures that the definition and `extern` declaration have the same type. A compilation error is produced if the types differ. If the header file is not included, there is no way for the compiler to check for the correct types (although some form of *lint* code checking tool can do so).

PREPROCESSOR TECHNIQUES FOR EXTERN

It is possible to avoid the need for maintaining both a definition and declaration of a global variable by using a preprocessor technique to cause the header file with declarations, say "`extern.h`", to both *declare* and *define* global variables. To achieve this, a file of `extern` declarations is maintained, containing declarations similar to that below:

```
extern int x;
```

The variables are not *defined* in the C/C++ source file (or any file). Instead, the lines of code shown below are placed in the source file (i.e., in one source file only):

```
#define extern /* Replace "extern" with nothing */
#include "extern.h"
#undef extern  /* revert to no change for safety */
```

The first line defines the word "`extern`" to be changed to whitespace. In effect, every occurrence of `extern` in the header file is deleted. An `extern` declaration without the `extern` keyword is a definition. In all files except "`main.c`" the variable `x` is qualified by `extern`. However, if `extern` is replaced with nothing in "`main.c`" (using the code fragment above) the global variables are defined exactly once, as required.

Problems with initialization

The disadvantage of this method is that global variables cannot be easily initialized using the `var=exp` syntax. Initializations in the header file usually cause compilation errors when `extern` is not deleted, because `extern` declarations cannot initialize variables (though some compilers may be lenient). Initializations can be included with more fancy preprocessor usage, but the trouble tends to outweigh the gain. For example, the header file can check if `extern` is defined and include the initialization only if `extern` is defined (i.e., if `extern` is being removed).

```
extern int x     /* no semicolon */
#ifdef extern
   = 2                /* initialization */
#endif
   ;        /* semicolon at the end of the declaration */
```

Unfortunately, this mess is needed for each initialized variable. An alternative is to keep two alternate copies of the variable declarations in the one header file:

```
#ifdef extern
   int x = 2;
   ... /* other variable definitions with initializations */
#else
   extern int x;
   ... /* other extern declarations for these variables */
#endif
   ... /* other extern declarations without initialization */
```

This method leads to the inconvenience of duplication (though non-initialized variables need not be duplicated). This duplication makes it more difficult to check the consistency of the two versions. To do so, you must include "extern.h" twice in "main.c": once with `extern` defined as nothing; once without.

```
#define extern    /* Replace "extern" with nothing */
#include "extern.h"  /* Define global variables */
#undef extern
#include "extern.h"  /* Check consistency */
```

Another more reasonable alternative is to use a special macro, say INIT, which takes the initialization expression as a macro argument. This macro hides the expression when `extern` declarations are being created, and adds it in when definitions are required.

```
#ifdef extern
#define INIT(exp) = exp /* initialization */
#else
#define INIT(exp)    /* declaration */
#endif
/* use of the macro in header file ... */
extern int x INIT(2);
```

There are still problems with any initializations containing commas that aren't nested inside brackets. The main offenders are initialization lists for array, `struct` or `class` initializations. For example, the following use of the `INIT` macro won't work because ANSI C and C++ do not permit variable-argument macros.

```
extern int arr[] INIT( { 1, 2, 3, 4, 5 } );
extern struct op y INIT( { 1, 2, 3 } );
```

If you're using GNU's `gcc` compiler, you can use the very handy GNU extension for variable-argument macros. This non-standard syntax uses the . . . (elipsis) token in macro definitions:

```
#ifdef __GNUC__ /* GNU C extension */
#ifdef extern
#define INIT(args...)  = args   /* initialized definition */
#else
#define INIT(args...)   /* declaration */
#endif /* extern */
#endif /* __GNUC__ */
```

One possible workaround for standard C is the neat hack to force commas to be processed later in the macro expansion process, after arguments have been processed:

```
#define COMMA ,
extern int arr[] INIT( { 1 COMMA 2 } );
extern struct op y INIT({ 0 COMMA "abc" });
```

However, although it is effective, readability suffers a good deal and this method may not be satisfactory.

PROTOTYPE EXTRACTION USING GREP AND SED

The tool below is a shell script that uses `grep` to extract lines that match the pattern of a function definition, and uses `sed` to add the semicolon on the end of the line (and some other tasks). The script file is shown below and is also available on the book's companion CDROM in the `sedproto` directory. The first line is a comment, but the rest of the script file is actually one very long pipeline. For simplicity, it has been split into a number of lines.

```
#!/bin/sh
# Script file: extract function prototypes
# from C/C++ source code files.
# by David Spuler
grep '^[a-zA-Z][a-zA-Z0-9\* _]*(.*)[^\;]*$' $* | \
sed -e 's/^[^:]*://'                           \
    -e 's/\/\*.*$//'                           \
    -e 's/[ \t]*$//'                           \
    -e '/^switch[ ]*(/d'                       \
    -e '/^return[ ]*(/d'                       \
    -e '/^static[ ]/d'                         \
    -e '/^main[ ]*(/d'                         \
    -e '/^if[ ]*(/d'                           \
    -e '/^while[ ]*(/d'                        \
    -e '/^for[ ]*(/d'                          \
```

```
-e '/^else[ ]*if[ ]*(/d'                              \
-e 's/$/;/'
```

This script assumes that function definitions always start on the first character of a line and that the entire list of function parameters must be placed on one line. It is assumed that there are no comments in the middle of the parameter list (although comments are allowed after the closing right bracket). Furthermore, it is assumed that local declarations are indented (although if this is not true, some checks remove the most common falsely matching lines). If these restrictions are not adhered to, some functions may be missed or the output of the tool may become incorrect.

The script file can be explained in terms of each step. The grep utility is used to search for the pattern: a line starting with a letter, then containing only letters, digits, underscores, spaces and * (for pointer types) until a left bracket is found. The line must also contain a right bracket and have no semicolons.

Lines matching this pattern are then piped through sed to perform a number of changes. sed is used to delete the filename and colon added to the lines by grep (some versions of grep may not have this problem), then to remove comments and spaces after the right bracket and to add a semicolon to the end of the line. Finally, sed is used to delete lines which matched the pattern, but are not function definitions or would not be appropriate as function prototypes. For example, if an if statement begins at the first character, it will match the pattern. However, many of these checks could be omitted if you indent statements inside a function. There are two special cases which match the pattern but may not be appropriate as a function prototype — static functions and the main function. A header file that will be included in more than one source file should not contain prototypes of static functions — this will cause a compilation error because the function is not *defined* in every file. The main function also matches the pattern, but it is rather pointless to declare it in a header file, so it is removed from the output.

Equivalent C program

Although the regular expressions used by grep and sed look complicated, the actual working of the script file is quite simple. Hence, if grep and sed are unavailable it is not difficult to write a C program that does the same job. The equivalent C program is available on the CDROM in the sedproto directory.

EXTERN EXTRACTION USING SED

The automatic generation of extern declarations using sed is more difficult than for function prototypes. The solution chosen here is using indentation, by assuming that local declarations are indented whereas global declarations start at the first column. A script file to find many global variable declarations is given below (and available on the companion CDROM in the sedproto directory):

```
#!/bin/sh
# Script file: extract variable declarations
# from C/C++ source code files
```

```
grep '^[a-zA-Z][a-zA-Z0-9_]*\
[\* &][\* &]*[a-zA-Z][^()]*;'  $*   |\
sed -e 's/\/\*.*$//'          \
-e 's/[ ]*$//'                \
-e 's/^[^:]*://'              \
-e 's/{[^}]*}//g'             \
-e 's/[ ]*=[^,;]*//g'         \
-e '/^extern /d'              \
-e '/^return /d'              \
-e '/^typedef /d'             \
-e '/^static /d'              \
-e '/^register /d'            \
-e 's/^/extern /'
```

The first two `sed` commands remove comments and trailing whitespace from the lines. The main feature of this script file is the `grep` command which looks for an identifier followed by at least one space or star followed by a letter, and having no brackets on the line (to avoid function definitions) and ending with a semicolon. The next `sed` command fixes the output from `grep` (not needed in all versions). The next `sed` removes pairs of braces that would appear in array initializations (because the next step would fail on the commas in the initializer lists), and then the initialization is removed by deleting the = up to the first comma or semicolon. A number of inappropriate declarations are removed, such as `static` variables and `typedef` declarations. Finally, the keyword `extern` is added to the front of the line.

extern extraction using sed with cb

Since the above script relies on indentation of local variables, we should preprocess the source code to ensure that local variables are actually indented. The UNIX `cb` code beautifier fits the bill perfectly. The modified script becomes:

```
#!/bin/sh
# Extract variables from C/C++ files using
# the UNIX tools grep, sed and cb
cat $* | cb | \
grep '^[a-zA-Z][a-zA-Z0-9_]*\
[\* &][\* &]*[a-zA-Z][^()]*;'  |\
sed -e 's/\/\*.*$//'          \
-e 's/[ ]*$//'                \
-e 's/^[^:]*://'              \
-e 's/{[^}]*}//g'             \
-e 's/[ ]*=[^,;]*//g'         \
-e '/^extern /d'              \
-e '/^return /d'              \
-e '/^typedef /d'             \
-e '/^static /d'              \
-e '/^register /d'            \
-e 's/^/extern /'
```

Unfortunately, there are problems with applying this method to code with K&R function prototypes, since the definitions of the function parameters also appear on the left. In addition, using `cb` in this manner causes initialized array and structure variables to no longer be extracted, even if they are on the one line in the original source. Note that this script is available on the book's companion CDROM in the `sedproto` directory.

Multiline scripts using awk or perl

These scripts work reasonably correctly for ordinary declarations and even for array or `struct` initializations on a single line, but there is a problem with removing multi-line initializations and extracting `struct` variable declarations because `grep` and `sed` work a line at a time. A possible solution is to use the `awk` utility or a C program to extract lines up to the closing semicolons. This is left as an exercise to the reader.

EXTERN EXTRACTION USING SPECIAL LABELS

Another solution to extraction of `extern` declarations using `grep` and `sed` is to adopt the style of declaring all global variables as "PUBLIC" (or some other word), where PUBLIC is `#define`'d to be nothing in all C source files. This allows a `grep` for the word PUBLIC, the output of which is then processed to remove the word PUBLIC, comments and initializations and add the keyword `extern`. This is available on the CDROM's `sedproto` directory.

```
#!/bin/sh
# Script file: extract variable declarations
# from C/C++ source code files.
# Requires all global declarations
# to use the special word "PUBLIC"

grep '^[ ]*PUBLIC[ ]' $*    |    \
sed -e 's/\/\*.*$//'               \
-e  's/^[^:]*://'                  \
-e  's/[ ]*$//'                    \
-e  's/{[^}]*}//g'                 \
-e  's/[ ]*=[^,;]*//g'             \
-e  's/PUBLIC//'                   \
-e  's/^[ ]*/extern /'
```

An even simpler solution suggested to me by Tim Chambers is to use a standard C comment such as `/*PUBLIC*/` somewhere on the line defining the function. This avoids the need to define PUBLIC as a nothing macro, or to remove the word PUBLIC from the extracted line.

EXPORT TOOL IN PRETTY PRINTER

Tool Name:	export
Main Purpose:	extract prototypes, variables, macros and typedefs
Platforms:	UNIX
Languages:	ANSI C, K&R C (not C++)

Status:	Free
Availability:	FTP *sapp* from `amadeus.stanford.edu:pub/` `SAPP.TAR` (file "`export.c`")
Author:	Arturo Salz
Key Points:	• looks for special keyword to begin extraction
Limitations:	• assumes one variable per declaration

An interesting little tool to extract function prototypes appears as part of the `sapp` pretty printer by Arturo Salz (see section "sapp PostScript output of C and C++" on page 146). The file "`export.c`" is a stand-alone tool to perform this task. The tool looks for the keyword "`public`" in C files and exports any global variables or `typedef` declarations so declared.

This tool operates on C code and will export `extern` declarations, function prototypes, `typedef` declarations and preprocessor macros to a header file. Although it requires "`public`" at the first character of the line, it will look across multiple lines to find full declarations. For variable declarations, it adds the "`extern`" keyword, strips initializations and also removes array sizes. It will also copy macros if they have the word "`public`" on the previous line with no other characters, not even whitespace.

One minor limitation is that it assumes only one variable declared per "`public`" statement and so does not correctly handle "`public int x,y`" although I view this coding style as undesirable, so this limitation is a feature! Also, the function prototypes created are in the pre-ANSI C form, without parameters or types (the parameters appear as commented out), but modifying the code to fix this limitation is trivial (modify the two `fputs` likes at line 141 and 149 to not output the start and end of the comment). For use with C++, it would be necessary to change the word it seeks (`public`) to another that is not a C++ keyword, like PUBLIC or EXPORT, and also change the processing to handle symbols such as ':' in declarations.

The code itself is in pre-ANSI C although to clean it up to ANSI C or C++ code does not require much effort. There are a few minor problems such as `mktemp` modifying a string constant (they aren't guaranteed to be writable by ANSI C), and a variable-argument function, `Crash`, which should be rewritten to use `<stdarg.h>`. Full function prototype declarations with argument types are also required at the top of the file, and the file should include various standard header files.

UNPROTO — FREE FILTER TO REMOVE ANSI C

Tool Name:	`unproto`
Main Purpose:	Filter to remove ANSI C syntax
Status:	Free
Author:	Wietse Venema

Availability:	FTP to ftp.win.tue.nl:/pub/unix/unproto4.shar.Z comp.sources.misc/volume27/unproto/part0[1-2] (Patches in volumes 28 and 38, and early versions in volumes 23 and 26)
Languages:	C only (not C++)
Platforms:	UNIX (SunOS, Ultrix, Microport System V)
Key Points:	• filter between standard preprocessor and compiler
Limitations:	• won't fix all ANSI syntax (e.g., `const`, `void*`) • not very useful as stand-alone filter

The `unproto` tool works as a filter between a UNIX C preprocessor and the parsing stage. It transforms ANSI C syntax to pre-ANSI syntax. For example, function prototypes are converted so that they do not have parameter types in the output. This tool can be used to turn an old C compiler into an ANSI C compiler, and may also be used to upgrade an old `lint` shell script.

`unproto` is a preprocessor that first calls the C preprocessor (e.g., `/lib/cpp`) and then performs its own modifications on the output from that preprocessor. The `unproto` preprocessor can be used with the standard C compiler by forcing the compiler to use `unproto` as an alternative preprocessor. Most UNIX C compilers have an option to permit this, and the various methods are covered in the documentation provided.

The `unproto` tool can be used as a stand-alone filter, reading from standard input and outputting to standard output. However, doing so causes the code to be preprocessed by the standard preprocessor, thereby including header files, expanding macros and removing comments, and also introducing all manner of items specific to the platform. Thus modifying code this way is not appropriate for removing ANSI C prototypes from code that must be ported to other platforms.

This is a well written tool that does not have fundamental limitations like requiring a particular source code layout style. The C code is parsed properly and very complicated declarations can be handled by the parser.

PROTOIZE AND UNPROTOIZE — GNU CONVERSION TOOLS

Tool Name:	`protoize, unprotoize`
Main Purpose:	Filters to remove or add ANSI C prototypes
Platforms:	UNIX
Languages:	ANSI C, K&R C
Status:	Free (GNU Public License)
Availability:	GNU distributions as part of `gcc` (file: protoize*) Companion CDROM in directory `protoize`

Author:	Ronald F. Guilmette
Key Points:	• `protoize` adds ANSI C prototypes • unprotoize removes ANSI C prototypes
Limitations:	• won't fix all ANSI syntax (e.g. `const`, `void*`)

The `protoize` and `unprotoize` pair of tools are distributed as part of the GNU `gcc` compiler. They allow the conversion between the ANSI C and K&R C style of function prototypes, but do not support a full-scale conversion between ANSI C and traditional C. These tools are very high quality because they are based on the `gcc` compiler, and thus employ full parsing techniques, rather than relying on source code format.

These filters operate "in place" by modifying the source file and replacing them with the converted output. A backup copy of the original file is kept in a ".save" file.

Let's discuss `protoize` first: `protoize` will convert all non-prototyped function definitions to use ANSI C prototypes and is therefore useful for converting a project from K&R C to ANSI C. In addition, by specifying the -1 and -g options, it will also insert prototype declarations of functions when it finds a function that is used without a prior declaration.

`protoize` operates globally across all files supplied and thus can fix up calls between files. Understandably, variable argument functions using `<varargs.h>` are not converted to use `<stdarg.h>`; you have to do this manually. `protoize` also doesn't account for needing `typedef` names or structure declarations; if it inserts a declaration you may need to move certain type declarations around to ensure that declaration can be parsed.

The `unprotoize` tool operates as an inverse to `protoize`. It converts ANSI C prototypes into K&R C prototypes and is useful for porting ANSI C code to K&R C compilers. However, the resulting K&R C code will not necessarily be in a form that can be compiled by a K&R compiler, nor is it necessarily correct code! The removal of prototypes causes function calls to no longer have implicit argument type conversions, and in cases where these conversions are crucial, the use of `unprotoize` can introduce bugs into the code. `unprotoize` does *not* insert the needed type casts automatically. The suggested solution is to add explicit type casts to these arguments in the original ANSI C source code, using the -Wconversion option to `gcc` to determine where these casts should be placed. Only when no warnings appear from -Wconversion should `unprotoize` be used.

CPROTO — FREE PROTOTYPE AND VARIABLE EXTRACTOR

Tool Name:	`cproto`
Main Purpose:	prototype and variable declaration extractor for header files
Status:	Free
Author:	Chin Huang

Availability:	comp.sources.misc/volume29/cproto/*(Revised)
	comp.sources.misc/volume28/cproto/*(Patches
	comp.sources.misc volumes 29, 30, 34, and 37)
	comp.sources.misc/volume17/cproto/part[01-02] (older version)
	(Patchescomp.sources.misc volumes 17 and 18)
	comp.sources.unix/volume20/cproto (early version)
	Companion CDROM in directory `cproto`
Languages:	ANSI C, K&R C
Platforms:	UNIX, DOS (Borland C and Microsoft C at least)
Key Points:	• `-v` option extracts variables
	• Four prototype formats including macro technique

The `cproto` prototype extraction tool operates by parsing the C program as its input and thus does not have any reliance on source code format. This ensures high-quality results, but unfortunately prevents its use for C++ prototype extraction, since C++ is not fully parsed. Conversion between ANSI C and K&R prototypes is supported in both directions. Thus this tool is useful for creating prototypes for both dialects of C.

There are a variety of useful options. The `-s` option adds static functions to the output. The `-f` option chooses between four output formats: K&R prototypes with commented parameter lists, ANSI prototypes, ANSI prototypes with commented parameter names, and the double-bracket macro technique for merging ANSI and K&R prototypes in one header file. The double-bracket macro technique is further supported by the `-m` option which specifies the macro name, and the `-d` option which suppresses the definition of the macro, so that you can supply your own. Even more formats are available by combining `-c`, which specifies the removal of comments, with the `-f` settings.

A good feature that is available is the promotion of parameter types when dealing with K&R prototypes. The types `char`, `short` and `float` can cause problems when mixing prototyped and non-prototyped functions. Hence `cproto` converts `char` and `short` to `int`, and `float` to `double`. This behavior can also be suppressed using the `-p` option.

Finally, the `-v` option (combined with `-e`) adds `extern` declarations of global variables to the output. Initialization expressions and initializer lists are thrown away. Thus `cproto` can be used to generate header files for functions and also for global variables.

ANSI2KNR — FREE CONVERSION PROGRAM

Tool Name:	`ansi2knr`
Purpose:	convert ANSI C prototypes to K&R style
Platforms:	UNIX (DOS port)
Languages:	ANSI C, K&R C
Status:	Free (GNU public license)

Availability:	GNU sites as part of `ghostscript` package (files `ansi2knr.1` and `ansi2knr.c`)
Key Points:	converts ANSI prototypes to K&R
Limitations:	depends entirely on source code format

The `ansi2knr` conversion tool is available as part of the GNU *GhostScript* package. It is not a particularly elegant package and relies completely on the program having a particular format for function definitions, namely that of having the function name starting at the left margin and the entire parameter list on one line, such as:

```
int
my_function(int x)
{   ...   }
```

The tool is useful to the *GhostScript* package which does use this style. If you don't use this style, `ansi2knr` is not particularly useful as a stand-alone tool, although that is not what it is intended to be.

CEXTRACT — FREE C PROTOTYPE EXTRACTOR

Tool Name:	`cextract`
Purpose:	prototype extractor for header file
Platforms:	UNIX (DOS port)
Languages:	ANSI C, K&R C, C++
Availability:	comp.sources.reviewed/volume02/cextract/* comp.sources.reviewed/volume01/cextract/* (older version)
Status:	Free
Author:	Adam Bryant
Key Points:	• extracts function prototypes • simple documentation features included

The main purpose of `cextract` is to automatically create header files of function prototype declarations from C code. A neat feature of the tool is that it produces both ANSI C and K&R C prototypes in the same header file, but separated by a conditional test based on `__STDC__`.

This is a good package that should be highly portable and is well documented. There are a whole range of command-line options. The `+s/-s` option is important for specifying whether static functions are to be extracted.

Also nice is the `+Z` option which merges the ANSI C and K&R prototypes using the well-known double bracket pair macro technique. Another notable feature is support for extracting comments related to each function and/or file to be placed at an appropriate place in the header file (+C, +c and +F options), and also to sort the prototypes generated globally or by file (+a and +A options).

Although the tool was not originally meant for C++ analysis, it now has some C++ support such as handling // comments and :: tokens, and I found it could be used reasonably well for gathering prototypes from C++ code. However, there were a few documented minor C++ problems (e.g., the handling of default arguments clashes with the +r option) and no doubt more pitfalls in the handling of newer C++ tokens such as the ->* operator,

Also part of the cextract features is its use as a simple documentation tool. The -n option generates documentation as ordinary text; the -N option supports the generation of nroff and troff output with properly formatted fonts.

LINT-PROTO — PROTOTYPE EXTRACTION FROM K&R C CODE

Tool Name:	lint-proto
Purpose:	extract prototypes from K&R C source
Platforms:	UNIX, Atari, DOS (any K&R C compiler)
Languages:	K&R C (not ANSI C)
Availability:	comp.sources.misc/volume3/proto.Z
Status:	Free
Author:	Duncan White
Key Points:	prototype extractor for K&R C code
Limitations:	prototypes can't be extracted from ANSI C code relies on source format: function header on one line

The proto tool examines K&R C source files for function definitions formatted in a particular way: the entire function header must appear on the one source code line including the function return type, the parameter list, and the declarations of the parameter types. This makes it very fragile, and will produce incorrect prototypes if the function return type and/or parameter declarations are not on one line (it will emit a warning for the latter).

A reasonable feature of the prototype extraction is that two forms are generated, ANSI C and K&R prototypes, separated by a macro test on the name HASPROTOS. The user must define HASPROTOS for ANSI C; for example, a test of __STDC__ could be used to set it, although this test is not explicitly generated by proto. This tool doesn't support any other formats such as combined ANSI and K&R prototypes using macro techniques.

The -f option causes proto to extract the K&R function definitions as written in the file. The documentation calls these "pretty printed" versions but I can't see any practical use for this option since it doesn't generate valid K&R prototypes (the parameter type declarations are still there).

PROTO — PROTOTYPE AND VARIABLE EXTRACTOR

Tool Name:	`proto`
Purpose:	prototype and variable extractor for header files
Platforms:	UNIX only (BSD)
Languages:	ANSI C, K&R C
Availability:	comp.sources.unix/volume16/lint-proto.pch.Z
Status:	Free (difference files only)
Author:	Jon Leech
Key Points:	prototype extractor based on BSD `lint` access to `lint` source required to build `proto -V` option extracts variable declarations

This tool, called `proto`, is a modification of BSD `lint` to produce a prototype extractor tool. Unfortunately, the `lint` source is proprietary and there are only difference files in the distribution. Thus the `proto` tool can't be built without access to `lint` source code.

The `proto` tool produces prototype declarations in a few different styles: K&R style with comment parameter lists, ANSI C style, and a macro style:

```
DECL(void fn_name, (int arg1, int arg2));
```

The tool is quite old and it shows in a few minor ways. For example, the macro technique relies on the old C++ macro `c_plusplus` instead of the ANSI C++ macro `__cplusplus`. Even using `__STDC__` would be better than the old C++ macro.

The `-V` option can be used to output `extern` declarations of global variables. Thus `proto` can be used for most header file needs.

FDECS — GENERATE ANSI PROTOTYPES FROM K&R C

Tool Name:	`fdecs`
Purpose:	generate ANSI C prototypes from K&R C
Platforms:	UNIX only
Languages:	K&R C only
Status:	Free
Availability:	comp.sources.misc/volume6/fdecs.Z
Key Points:	shell script based on `sed`
Limitations:	cannot extract prototypes from ANSI C

Note that this archive doesn't un-*shar* very well — the input file to sh cannot be called fdecs since the archive contains a file with that name.

The fdecs tool is a shell script that searches K&R C source files for non-prototyped function declarations, and outputs the corresponding ANSI C prototypes to the standard output. Thus it can be used to put ANSI C prototypes in header files for projects using K&R C code, which is a useful part of moving from K&R to ANSI C. The implementation is a surprisingly clever shell script that searches across multiple lines for the required items (such as the parameter declarations after the right bracket), and also correctly defaults undeclared parameters to int type. Unfortunately, fdecs cannot be used to extract prototypes from ANSI C source code, and will generate nonsense prototypes if it is so used. It also does not perform any conversion of parameter types that should be promoted, such as char, short and float. The only option is -Idir which specifies that source code be run through the preprocessor using "cc -E" before prototype extraction is performed.

Editors

An editor is a fundamental part of any C or C++ programming. Since they are both undeniably languages based on text sequences, the form of "text editor" you use can have a big impact on your productivity.

The trend these days is toward advanced features specifically aimed toward programming tasks, rather than just the generic text editor of yesteryear. Even the free UNIX `emacs` editor has begun to offer an impressive array of features for programming.

FEATURES OF A GOOD PROGRAMMING EDITOR

There are a lot of different features that can aid you in your programming. Let's take a look at the features of a programmer's editor you might want. However, don't take it as a given that you'll find one editor with all these features quite yet, or if you do, let me know!

Function definition/use location: this feature is also known as "tags" to UNIX users teethed on `vi` or `emacs`. The ability to move around the source code through different files to find the definitions or uses of functions, variables, macros, or any other identifier, is a very powerful ability. In this area the features of editors and browsers begin to overlap.

Syntax-based auto-indentation: automatic indentation of the program text following a particular style (ideally this style is configurable), without the need for your fingers to tap the space or tab keys repeatedly. Typically this applies to large-scale indentation issues such as function definitions and flow of control statements such as `if` statements and loops. Automatic spacing of arithmetic expressions is another convenient feature but is rare.

Syntax highlighting: the use of font style or color to indicate particular lexical elements in the program text such as reserved words, identifiers, comments, constants, etc. This can greatly increase the readability of code on your screen. For example, unclosed comments show up easily!

Syntax correction: this feature involves the editor correcting any minor errors in your code. Typical examples of features that are available are automatic correction of mismatched parentheses or brackets. One day an editor might detect you forgot to initialize your variable, warn you, and even add it in for you. I'm still waiting for an editor that will automatically change my bubble sort into quicksort....

VI — THE OLD FAVORITE UNIX EDITOR

You're not a true UNIX programmer until you've argued the virtues of `vi` and `emacs`. And yes, I certainly have, and if you guessed that I backed `vi` you'd be spot on. Unfortunately I seem to be on the losing end of the battle and most of my co-developers are `emacs` converts. In fact one of the concessions I had to make to this book (although not to my group, of course!) is to learn `emacs` so as to avoid the biased one-eyed pro-`vi` discussion that is about to follow.

The `vi` editor and its ugly duckling "`ed`", have been around for almost as long as UNIX existed. The name "`vi`" comes from the fact that it's a "visual" editor rather than the text-based style of `ed`. UNIX purists know that the one true pronunciation is like "vee-eye" rather than "vy". Just like UNIX, the `vi` editor is cryptic, difficult to learn, and amazingly cool.

The downside, which I hesitate to report, is the lack of a number of nice features that `emacs` has to offer. For example, `vi` has no syntax highlighting, syntax correction, nor `gdb` debugger support. Only `emacs` can really be said to compete with the more advanced editors available as part of integrated development environments.

Basic vi features

While I do not want to launch into a long tutorial on all of `vi`'s features, in my experience many novice users do not use `vi` anywhere to its full capability. The features are not explained in detail here, but mentioned so as to focus your search through the documentation for `vi`. For more information, read the UNIX manual entries for `vi` and `ex`. Every time I read these manuals I still learn something new.

There is more to the familiar cut-n-paste "yank" and "put" commands than is immediately apparent. Markers can be set at a particular place using the m*x* command where *x* is any lowercase letter. These markers can be used to yank blocks of code more easily; a marker is specified using the single quote character and the lowercase letter: '*x*.

Buffers are useful for storing text, especially for moving blocks across multiple files. Buffers are indicated by double quotes followed by a lowercase letter. For example, "a10dd cuts 10 lines into buffer *a*.

The special numbered buffers "1 to "9 are used by vi to keep the last 9 blocks of deleted text. Hence, if you delete something, and it is too late to undo it, the text can sometimes be found in these buffers; so try "1p.

Basic vi features for C/C++ programming

Now that we've dealt with some basic cut-n-paste commands, let's look at some advanced features of vi that are useful for C and C++ programming.

The % command is very useful for C programming. When positioned over a left parenthesis, brace or bracket, pressing % moves to the corresponding right parenthesis, brace or bracket, and vice-versa. If the bracket is unmatched, the terminal will beep. This makes % very useful for checking the extent of code blocks and matching parentheses.

The section movement commands [[and]] are useful to C or C++ editing, more by accident than design. These commands will usually move to the top or bottom of a function, or if already there, will move to the next function above or below.

The { and } paragraph movement commands also have their uses. I find them a useful method of skipping over long comment blocks (e.g. file change histories).

Editing multiple files with vi

Novice users of vi have a very bad habit — they keep trying to quit vi. This loses your place within the file, and if you follow the cycle of "edit, exit, make, edit again" for resolving program syntax errors, you'll find it getting tiresome pretty quickly. One alternative is simply to have a couple of windows open at a time, one for the editor and one for commands. However, proficient vi users can do most things from within the editor itself using some of the following methods.

Never quit vi just to edit another file; instead use *:e filename* to edit another file. There is also the abbreviation *#* for the previous filename, and so you can use *:e#* to edit the previous file. Even this shortcut has a shortcut! The key sequence *<ctrl>-6* is equivalent and will swap to the previous file.

If you get tired of typing long filenames to go between directories, use the chdir command to change vi's current working directory:

```
:chdir ../..
```

To include another file in the middle of the current file use *:r filename* such as for including your own specially defined templates.

Shelling out of `vi` is a very useful feature. This refers to the use of *:!command* from within `vi` to execute UNIX commands without leaving the editor. A very common use of this is compiling your program with:

```
:!make
```

As another example, to `grep` the current file use the `%` macro for the current filename:

```
:!grep static %
```

A friend of the `%` macro is the previously mentioned # macro for the previous filename, which is useful such as for:

```
:!diff % #
```

vi key macros

Typing `:!make` frequently gets tiresome after a while. A better alternative is to create a `vi` key macro that maps one keystroke to that command. There are a number of keys unused by `vi` including Q, q, v, and also many control characters.

```
:map Q :!make<ctrl>-v<RETURN>
```

This complicated command is necessary to include the `<RETURN>` key in the macro expansion. Normally the `<RETURN>` key would end the map command, and to get the `<RETURN>` key into the replacement text the `<ctrl>-v` sequence must precede it.   Another use of the `<ctrl>-v` trick is to allow a control key instead of the Q key, by preceding the control key sequence with `<ctrl>-v`.

Designing key macros requires good use of the basic `vi` key commands. The most commonly used commands are presented in Table 11–1 for revision:

Table 11–1   Common vi commands

x	Delete current letter
X	Delete previous letter
i	Insert before letter
a	Append after letter
I	Insert at beginning of line
A	Append to end of line
$	Move to end of line
0	Move to beginning of line
^	Move to first non-space character on line
rx	Replace current character with character x
R	Enter overwrite mode

Table 11–1 Common vi commands *(Continued)*

G	Go to end of file
~	Change case of a letter

You should also know which ones put vi into insert mode (i, I, a, A, c, C, R), requiring use of the <ctrl>-v trick to embed an <ESC> in the macro text to return to command mode. For example, consider the macro for commenting out a line in C:

```
:map g I/*<ctrl-v><ESC>A*/<ctrl-v><ESC>
```

To reverse the commenting-out process it is necessary to delete two characters at the start and end of the line. The macro is;

```
:map v ^xx$xx
```

Macros are not very convenient if they must be typed in each time vi is invoked. Fortunately, key macros can be stored in a definition of the environment variable EXINIT or more commonly in ".exrc" files. Complicated macros can be placed, one per line, in a file called ".exrc" in the home or current directory. When vi is started, vi executes these commands. Note also that the home directory .exrc file is not used if the shell variable EXINIT is set, so it is usual to remove any such definition.

CTAGS — IDENTIFIER TAGS FOR VI

The vi editor supports a form of definition location called "tags". To use tags a special data file full of tag information about identifiers must be built by a separate executable called "ctags". The options available for ctags are shown in Table 11–2:

Table 11–2 ctags options

-a	Append to existing tags file
-t	Typedef tags are included
-f file	Filename to store tags information (default is "tags")
-x	Print functions, filenames and definitions to standard output
-w	Warning suppression (e.g., suppress "Duplicate found")
-v	Print functions, filename and "page" to standard output

The simplest command to build a tags file for a project is:

```
ctags -w -t *.[ch] */*.[ch] */*/*.[ch]
```

A more mature method is to use the append mode and build tags for each subdirectory using a "make tags" target, such as:

```
ctags -w -t -a $(SRCS)
```

Once the tags file is available, the command to find the definition of a variable, function or macro is the :ta command:

```
:ta identifier
```

If the identifier is found, this causes vi to open the file and move the current editing session into it. It's easy to return to the old file with :e# or <ctrl>-6.

By default, the vi editor only looks for "tags" in the current directory (and a system directory), but this can be changed by setting the "tags" vi variable within vi, or preferably within your ".exrc" file in your home directory. An example for .exrc to specify the particular tags file is:

```
set tags=/usr/users/spuler/tags
```

Unfortunately, if you switch between projects a lot, you'll have to remember to change your tags setting in the .exrc file. Alternatively, make the "tags" file a link, and in your script to switch between projects, simply change the link setting to the appropriate tags file. Doing it this way you can pick up the new tags settings without needing to exit your vi window!

ctags is usually available as part of the standard UNIX tools. A free version is available from *comp.sources.misc/volume31/tags++/* that supports ctags and etags (emacs tags) for both C and C++. ctags is also freely available with emacs sources as part of etags.

EMACS — RISEN STAR OF UNIX EDITORS

The emacs editor is a freely available editor developed originally by Richard Stallman, founder of the Free Software Foundation. emacs is now supported by the Free Software Foundation and offers the high quality that has become expected of this software. In fact, emacs is so fully featured that perhaps this section more rightly belongs in another chapter alongside discussion of the various IDEs available on the market.

Watching a power emacs user perform simple programming tasks is an eye-opener to what can be accomplished within a good editor. The advanced software development features supported by emacs include make support (including easy location or any compilation errors), syntax correction, syntax highlighting, identifier definition and use location, support for the gdb debugger (that converts gdb into a full screen debugger), and much more.

All of these fancy features can be performed within an emacs buffer. If you thought you could accomplish a lot without leaving your vi window, then emacs is an impressive surprise. Some of my colleagues once tried to play a practical joke on our boss by taping a message to the underside of his mouse to disable it. Unfortunately the joke backfired as they waited in vain for hours for his discovery and eventually gave the game away in frustration. He was a power emacs user and, even in an X Windows environment, had no need to move his mouse at all!

As this anecdote shows, the primary interface for emacs is keystroke based, although there are now a number of X-based versions extending emacs with pull-down menus and mouse point-and-click support. While the basic keystroke commands are not any easier to learn than `vi`, the overall feature set is more complete for programming tasks. In fact, the only complaint I have heard of `emacs` by `emacs` devotees is that its commands require too many two-finger commands. This is perhaps the cause of the humorous rumor that the name "emacs" stands for "Escape Meta Alt Control Shift"! The name actually comes from the more prosaic phrase "editing macros".

Describing `emacs` commands in text requires a few conventions. `C-x` is the usual representation of the two-key combined keypress of the control key and the `x` key. `ESC-x` refers to the escape key and then the `x` key in sequence (not combined). Although any key can follow the escape key, the `x` key is special, and leads to a command prompt at the bottom of the window allowing a continuation of the command. For example, we will use `ESC-x help` to refer to the escape key, then the `x` key, then the `help` command and then the `RETURN` key.

General emacs features

There are so many neat features in `emacs` that there are whole books on the subject. `emacs` offers a range of major features such as multiple edit buffers, unlimited undo, regular expression search and replace, and auto-indentation. The "dired" directory editor is a great tool for browsing files and directories.

Help is available via the `C-h` key or `ESC-x help`. The tab key also attempts to auto-complete any partially written `ESC-x` command, which is useful when you forget the exact command. The `ESC-x apropos` command can be used to search for relevant commands.

`emacs` can be customized dynamically by ad-hoc commands and loading LISP command files with `ESC-x load-lib`. Key sequences can be remapped to suit your preferences, and the list of commands available from `ESC-x` is dynamic. There are various named parameters used by the commands, and these can be altered. The `edit-options` command is a powerful method of editing various `emacs` settings.

FTP can be performed conveniently within `emacs` by loading the "ange-ftp" library with the `ESC-x load-lib` command. Once loaded, `ESC-x find-file` allows the specification of an FTP site and remote directory name, after which the regular "dired" command works as if the remote files were stored locally.

There are many other important tasks that you can do within the `emacs` editor that you may have been using other external commands to achieve. For example, you can read mail, browse Internet news groups, spell check and print documents. Anything that you cannot do directly can naturally be done using an interactive UNIX shell in an `emacs` edit buffer.

Editing C/C++ source code in emacs

A number of modes are supported via `emacs`' LISP-based language, and you can even write them yourself. In fact, there are a number of freely available customizations of `emacs` for common programming languages, naturally including C and C++, and many of them now ship with the various `emacs` distributions. `emacs` will automatically place you in the appropriate editing mode for a file based on its extension so that loading a C file will start you in the C editing mode.

These C and C++ modes offer a variety of neat features. There is automatic reformatting of code blocks via selecting a region and choosing ESC-x indent-region. The tab key is usually mapped to indent-line for reformatting one line at a time.

The ESC-; sequence is the usual mapping for indent-for-comment that indents the comment on the line to the comment column. In the simplest case it adds an empty /**/ comment and places the cursor in the middle.

Moving around C/C++ source code is simplified by a few commands. C-u a is mapped to beginning-of-defun and moves to the beginning of the current function or the previous function. Similarly, C-u b moves to the end of the current function or the next one. Numeric repetition arguments can be used to move many functions.

Software development tools in emacs

Binary files are fully supported by emacs and patching of executable files is another neat trick to do with emacs. Not that I encourage anybody to do debugging this way, but finding and changing strings within an executable does have its occasional use.

emacs supports the GNU gdb debugger with a special mode available via ESC-x gdb. This launches the command-line execution of gdb within one buffer and displays program source code files in another buffer. The current source code file is updated every time the debugger regains control over the program, and this makes gdb commands like step and next as good as on any full-screen debugger!

Compilation using build is supported by emacs with error message location provided your compiler uses a standard format for the error message. The main command to start compilation is ESC-x compile to launch the building command (usually make). The location of the next error message can be located using the ESC-x next-error command, which is also usually bound to the C-x ` key sequence.

An interesting feature is that there is an emacs front-end for the GNU cvs version control system called pcl-cvs. This is available from various cvs distributions including the distribution from Linux archives: e.g., *sunsite.unc.edu:/pub/Linux/devel/ver_cont/cvs**.

emacs also has built-in support for locking of files, which can be useful on multi-developer projects. Among other things, emacs will warn you if a file changes "under you" from someone else's modification and thereby helps to avoid lost updates. However, in reality this feature is only valuable if you are in a project not using any other method of version control.

ETAGS — IDENTIFIER TAGS FOR EMACS

emacs has an identifier tag facility just as vi does, but emacs tags are rather easier to use. The basic operation is that a file called TAGS is built using the standalone etags utility that is available with any emacs distribution. Typically, you add etags support to your makefile to do this. If you just want to build the tags for the entire project occasionally, the command sequence in my project for the top-level makefile is effectively:

```
rm -f TAGS
find . -name '*.[ch]' -exec etags -atTSd '{}' ';'
```

This uses the -a option to add to the TAGS file and -t to also tag typedef names. Schemes with automatic incremental rebuilding of tag files every time a file is changed are possible to do, but I think the extra build time reduces productivity and occasional builds are adequate.

Once the `TAGS` file is available, there are some simple to use commands for locating uses. `ESC-.` finds the identifier you are currently located on and `ESC-.name` finds a particular tag. `ESC-,` finds the next occurrence of a tag which is useful for large projects with multiple copies of functions from stubs (and incidentally something you cannot do with `vi` tags!). There are a large number of additional tag commands shown by "`apropos tags`" such as `visit-tags-table` to specify the tags file and `tags-apropos` for regular expression searching of the tag list, but I won't examine them in detail.

`etags` is part of the `emacs` distributions and is a separately built executable. Another version of `etags` is available from *comp.sources.misc/volume31/tags++/* for C and C++, but it is no doubt out of date compared to the `etags` versions shipped with `emacs` today.

XEMACS — FREE X-BASED EMACS

`xemacs` is a free extension of `emacs` for X Windows. The traditional character-based `emacs` editing buffers are wrapped inside a window. There is a menu bar with a variety of common `emacs` commands that can be performed without keystrokes. The cursor can be moved by clicking on a location within the buffer using the mouse pointer.

`xemacs` is available in the usual GNU software mirror archives. One example is *ftp.uu.net/package/gnu/xemacs/*.

LEMACS — FREE X-BASED EMACS

`lemacs` stands for Lucid `emacs` and is a free version developed by Jamie Zawinski formerly with Lucid. `lemacs` offers an X-based GUI around the `emacs` buffers. Almost everyone in my project group uses `lemacs` rather than `xemacs`. Features for programmers include color syntax highlighting, easy function location via menus, `cvs` support, and much more.

XCORAL — FREE X WINDOWS EDITOR AND C/C++ BROWSER

Tool Name:	`xcoral`
Purpose:	X Windows editor and C/C++ browser
Availability:	X11 contrib: ftp.x.org/contrib/editors/xcoral*
Authors:	Lionel Fournigault, Bruno Pages and Dominique Leveque

`xcoral` is an interactive X Windows editor with special support for editing C, C++, LaTeX and HTML. The editor offers a variety of useful C/C++ features including color syntax highlighting, automatic indentation, and blinking parenthesis pairs.

The built-in C/C++ browser offers a number of useful features. The browser mode displays files, functions, classes, and methods in various subwindows. Single-clicking an object opens a "Visit Window" to view the object, and a double-click loads the chosen object into the editor for editing.

`xcoral` also has support for building via launching a command such as `make` from the editor. Each error message can be visited in turn with the files loaded into the editor at the affected line. Output from `grep` or other commands with the correct output format can also be processed in this way.

The implementation of `xcoral` is powerful with the use of an ANSI C interpreter called Smac. This allows a C-like language to be used to define editor modes, and customize many issues such as key-bindings, macros, and mode parameters. An example of the latter is that you can change parameters for the C mode to alter the indentation behavior.

FREE X WINDOWS EDITORS FROM X11 CONTRIBUTIONS

The X11 "contrib" distribution includes a number of free editors with an X Windows interface. These editors are briefly discussed below.

asedit — free X Windows editor

Tool Name:	`asedit`
Purpose:	X Windows editor
Availability:	X11 contrib: ftp.x.org/contrib/editors/
Author:	Andrzej Stochniol

`asedit` is an X Windows editor based on the Motif text widget. Some of the general editing features include multiple undo/redo, international support, bookmarks, and search and replace. Programmer editing features are not very comprehensive but include bracket matching and auto-indentation.

e93 — free X Windows editor

Tool Name:	`e93`
Purpose:	Editor for X Windows
Availability:	X11 contrib: ftp.x.org/contrib/editors/

`e93` is an X Windows editor with support for the TCL script language. Editing features include unlimited undo/redo, search and replace (including regular expressions) and double-mouse-click bracket matching.

aXe — free X Windows editor

Tool Name:	aXe
Purpose:	X Windows editor
Availability:	X11 contrib: ftp.x.org/contrib/editors/aXe*
Author:	Jim K. Wight

aXe is an editor built using the Athena text widget. Some of its interesting features include unlimited undo, parenthesis matching, regular expression searching, and TCL support.

xed — free X Windows editor

Tool Name:	xed
Platforms:	SunOS, Solaris, DG, NeXT, Mach, Linux
Purpose:	X Windows editor
Availability:	X11 contrib: ftp.x.org/contrib/editors/
Author:	Randolf Werner

nedit — free X Windows Editor

Tool Name:	nedit
Purpose:	X Windows editor
Availability:	X11 contrib: ftp.x.org/contrib/editors/nedit
Author:	Mark Edel

nedit is a Motif editor with features for general editing and also various programmer-friendly features. Programming features include auto-indent, block indentation, bracket matching (with graphical flashing), compilation error location, and ctags support.

STARPOWER — SOFTWARE DEVELOPMENT ENVIRONMENT

Product Name:	StarPower
Platforms:	UNIX: Solaris, Solaris-x86, AT&T, Sequent, Unisys, SCO, UnixWare, LynxOS, QNX, most Intel/UNIX

Status:	Commercial product
Price:	$595
Company:	Computer Innovations, Inc.
Address:	1129 Broad Street, Shrewsbury, NJ 07702-4314
Phone:	908-542-6121
Fax:	908-542-5920, 1-800-922-0169
Email:	Sales@StarPower.com
FTP:	ftp.StarPower.com (user: anonymous)
Web:	http://www.StarPower.com

StarPower is a Motif-based programming editor/IDE for UNIX platforms. *StarPower* has many features of an advanced text editor including color syntax highlighting and keyboard accelerators, and also features of an IDE with project definition, build/make features and sccs support. Project definition support involves specifying a set of source files as a project that is treated wholly for editing, searching, compile, make and sccs. Support for sccs is built into *StarPower* with automatic check out of files for editing and checking in of deltas. An advantage of *StarPower* is its one click build with automatic saving of all edited files and launching of the compiler or make. Error messages can be examined with quick access to the source code file for editing. *StarPower* has a high degree of customizability in areas such as the colors for syntax highlighting, accelerator keys, sccs commands and compile commands.

RIMSTAR PROGRAMMER'S EDITOR FOR WINDOWS AND OS/2

Product Name:	RimStar Programmer's Editor
Platforms:	Windows 3.1, Windows 95, Windows/NT, OS/2
Price:	$199: Standard Edition; $299: Professional Edition
Company:	RimStar Technology, Inc.
Address:	91 Halls Mill Road, Newfields, NH 03856, USA
Phone:	800-746-7007
Fax:	603-778-2408
Email:	rimstar@world.std.com
Web	http://www.rimstar.com

RimStar's Programmer's Editor is a visual editor with full GUI-based editing and numerous features of interest to programmers. There is support for C and C++ programming including color syntax highlighting, indentation, brace matching and block indent/outdent. Built-in browsing features allow the locations of uses and definitions of a given symbol across multiple files. Compilation of the project can be launched within the editor with editor support for jumping to the location of compilation errors.

There are also various general features that you would desire in a good editor including multiple undo/redo, timed automatic save, bookmarks, clipboard import/export, hex editing, project support, and UNIX or BRIEF style regular expression search and replace. Keyboard mappings exist to simulate the environment of a number of other popular text editors so as to lower the learning curve. Full customization is possible using the ANSI C macro language with over 300 API functions corresponding to various editor features. The C++ Professional Edition includes C++ browsing capabilities with graphical display of class hierarchies and call trees.

SLICKEDIT — MULTIPLATFORM PROGRAMMER'S EDITOR

Product Name:	Visual SlickEdit
Platforms:	Windows 3.1, Windows 95, Windows NT (80x86, Mips, Alpha, PowerPC), OS/2, UNIX (AIX, HP, Solaris, SunOS, SGI, DEC, Linux, SCO)
Price:	$295: for Windows or OS/2; UNIX: $195-$395
Product Name:	SlickEdit
Platforms:	DOS, UNIX (SunOS, Solaris, Solaris-x86, HP9000, QNX, SGI, UnixWare, AIX, DG, Sequent, OSF/1, Linux, EP/IX, Coherent)
Price:	$195-$295
Company:	MicroEdge, Inc.
Address:	Attn. Sales Department, PO Box 18038, Raleigh, NC, 27619-8038, USA
Phone:	(800) 934-EDIT, (919) 831-0600
Fax:	(919) 831-0101
Email:	sales@slickedit.com
FTP:	ftp://slickedit.com/pub/demos/microedge
Web:	http://www.slickedit.com

Visual SlickEdit and *SlickEdit* form a suite of editors for many platforms with binary compatibility of macros, templates and bitmaps. They share a rich set of common features with a number of extra features in *Visual SlickEdit*. Some of the features of interest to C and C++ programmers are interactive file comparison, syntax completion, color syntax highlighting, spell checking of comments and string literals, brace matching, and indentation support including the *SmartPaste* automatic reindentation of pasted or drag-n-dropped code to the correct indentation level. Project management features include compilation and `make` support with navigation from error messages, function tagging, and versioning check-in/check-out.

There are numerous other features you would expect of a powerful editor such as multiple undo/redo, multi-file search and replace, autosave timed backups. There are emulation modes for Brief, `emacs` and `vi` for faster learning. The Slick-C macro language allows customization of many features of the editor using a C-like macro language. Aspects that can be customized include menus, the button bar, fonts and coloring.

CodeWright — Programmer's Editor for Windows

Product Name:	CodeWright & CodeWright Fusion
Platforms:	Windows, Windows/NT
Price:	CodeWright: $229; CodeWright Fusion MSVC: $149
Company:	Premia Corporation
Address:	1075 NW Murray Blvd., Suite 268, Portland, Oregon 97229, USA
Phone:	1-800-547-9902, 503-641-6000
Fax:	503-641-6001
Email:	sales@premia.com
Web:	http://www.premia.com

CodeWright is a highly featured editor designed for use by programmers with strong support for C, C++ and many other languages. Features include *ChromaCoding* (color syntax highlighting and modification bars), smart indentation, hex editing of binary files, and spell checking of comments and string literals. A selective text display facility allows you to focus on important code such as lines with a particular identifier, or source as seen after the processing of `#ifdef` directives. Naturally there is an adequate complement of editor features such as bookmarks, auto-saving, multiple buffers, file `grep`, and fast access to Windows SDK help.

Project management is supported by various features. There is an inbuilt class browser to show code structure and report on and locate the uses of identifiers throughout the project. There is support for compilation and location of source code related to error messages for many compilers. There is strong support for multi-developer projects via version control integration and various other features. File differencing and merging is available with support for previous versions of a file. File locking or automatic detection of other users writing a file in the editor are available. Tight integration with the Microsoft Visual C++ IDE is available via a special version of *CodeWright* called *CodeWright Fusion*.

CodeWright uses an interesting method of using DLLs for customizations rather than using a proprietary macro language. Users can write their own DLLs or choose from many already available to extend *CodeWright* features.

WISH — HUNGARIAN NOTATION AUTOMATICALLY

Hungarian notation is the common name for a particular style of identifier naming where the prefix is used to convey information. There are many variations but they all involve the representation of identifier type or scope in the name. For example, to show scope you might use "g_" for global variables, "s_" for static variables and "p_" for parameters. To show type you would typically use "i" for integer, "p" for pointer, etc. leading to "gpix" or "g_pi_x" standing for a variable called "x" that is a global pointer to an integer.

This sort of scheme has many supporters and detractors. Basically, it adds a lot of value, but takes some getting used to. In my current project we are moving to a scheme showing scope, but not yet using the type prefixes.

If you think about it enough, the very popularity of Hungarian notation is an indictment of the current set of tools. There would be no value in it if better editors showed scope and type information some other way. Existing editors base color syntax highlighting only on the token type, and identifiers all look the same. So here is my wish for color highlighting of identifiers based on their scope and type. Hopefully macros, typedefs, and standard library identifiers can be differentiated too. Admittedly, addressing the issue for B&W hardcopy may be tougher, but isn't the need for printouts removed by a good browser tool?

Browsers and Documentation Tools

A small project is easy to keep in your head — you know exactly where everything is, which files and functions do what, and life is swell. Alas, most projects are not small, and the great techniques of modularity and object-oriented design are not a panacea for complexity.

Browsers are tools aimed at improving your ability to comprehend larger amounts of code. They offer textual summaries of what stuff is where doing what, and a good graphical browser offers graphical displays of important architectural structures to improve your comprehension. They aim to increase your understanding of the overall picture, as well as increase your ability to cope with the large volume of details of the actual implementation of that vista.

There are a number of tools available for C and C++ programming that fit this description of a browser. The ones we will focus upon here are those that delve directly into the C or C++ source code. The ones we'll largely leave alone are those that are part of a higher-level object-oriented design package where the actual structure of the views of the higher project's structure that are available in the "browser" are what determines the detailed form of the code, rather than the other way around. This chapter assumes you have some C or C++ source code and you want to understand it better to improve your productivity.

BROWSER FEATURES

It's a little hard to distinguish the features of a browser from the features of other components. For example, many editors have features for moving around source code to locate uses of identifiers, which is a form of browsing. In addition, many of the reporting aspects of a browser tool border on features of tools such as documentation generation tools and source code metric analysis tools, which both generate useful reports about source code structure. Some of these views are even present in apparently dissimilar tools such as profilers or coverage tools. Nevertheless we'll now try to set aside this ambiguity and discuss what the features of a browser tool are:

Code browsing features: a browser is, after all, supposed to allow you to "browse" source code, so the simplest features are those that allow you to look through the source in an ad-hoc unplanned manner. Location of identifier declarations, definitions or uses is a fundamental feature and should be supported for all the language artifacts: variables, macros, typedefs, classes, comments. Good handling of multiple files and directories is also imperative for browsing of a large project.

Structural displays: a good browser will offer a number of informational reports of the structure of the project's source code. These reports are valuable regardless of whether the output is graphical or textual — most people will choose graphical over textual without thinking about it, but the textual reports showing structure via indentation or other means are often quite powerful and such tools should not be discounted. Of course, visual presentation does offer the extra power of color, shapes, and even (maybe) limited animation. Some of the structural views that a browser should present include:

- **C++ class inheritance hierarchy:** the hierarchy of inheritance can be displayed as a directed acyclic graph, or a multiway tree in the absence of multiple inheritance (actually, to be precise, the representation for an entire project is a group of DAGs or multiway trees). A good view of this hierarchy will show in some manner (e.g., color) on the arcs of the graph, the use of `public`, `private` and `virtual` inheritance relationships. Similarly, different representations of the nodes can show information about each class such as whether they are a `virtual` base class.
- **Function call graph:** the sequence of functions called by other functions can be shown as a graph, where cycles show direct or indirect recursion.
- **Control flow graph:** graph of code control flow and basic blocks generated by branch and loop statements. Note that the term "flow graph" is often used as a term describing what I term a call graph here; presentation of a true flow graph of basic blocks is rare. Its localized nature makes it less valuable in comprehending project structure, but it can yield insight into how a given function operates.

Reporting: all these graphical views of code structure are nice, but they don't help kill trees. Putting it on paper seems to engender these displays with more value and the ability to print out these views, or alternatively to allow exporting for conversion to common spreadsheet formats, is a valuable feature of a browser.

Multiple version comparison: the ability to regularly build these views and then compare then with previous versions can be useful. Admittedly, comparing two graphs can be quite meaningless, but comparing metrics about these graphs can be interesting (at least to management).

GREP — STANDARD UNIX UTILITY

As silly as it sounds, `grep` is a source code browser that is powerful for some simple tasks. In the absence of tags, `grep` is a quick way to find all declarations and definitions of identifiers. Regular expressions carry considerable power and `grep` can still be the best way to find particular configurations of C or C++ tokens.

REFINE/C — BROWSING AND DOCUMENTATION FOR C

Product Name:	Refine/C
Platforms:	Solaris, SunOS, HP-UX, AIX
Status:	Commercial product
Price:	$5,900
Company:	Reasoning Systems
Address:	3260 Hillview Avenue, Palo Alto, CA 94304
Phone:	415-494-6201
Fax:	415-494-8053
Email:	info@reasoning.com
Web:	http://www.reasoning.com/

Refine/C is a browsing, documentation, and reengineering tool for legacy code. To this end, Refine/C provides numerous code browsing capabilities and export facilities for supporting "forward-engineering" CASE tools. Reasoning Systems also offers a separate product called Software Refinery that is a development toolkit for building custom reengineering tools.

In addition to these advanced reengineering features, there are a number of facilities of Refine/C for code browsing, documentation generation and coding standards enforcement for ANSI C and K&R C. The X Windows GUI provides a number of views/reports of project source code including graphical display of the function call graph, and cross-reference lists of functions, variables and types.   Refine/C also offers a report on violations of coding standards with over 30 predefined standards and the ability to add your own standards.

CC-RIDER — BROWSING AND DOCUMENTATION

Product Name:	CC-Rider
Platforms:	DOS, Windows, OS/2
Company:	Western Wares
Address:	P.O. Box C, Norwood, CO 81423, USA
Phone:	970-327-4898
Fax:	970-327-4479
Email:	ccrider@westernwares.com, CompuServe 72540,3270
Web:	http://www.westernwares.com/ccrider

CC-Rider is a multipurpose tool that allows programmers to analyze, browse and document their C or C++ source code. The basis of CC-Rider is an analyzer component that stores information about the project into a database file. The browser and documentation components access this information to give you various views of your project.

Browsing features start with symbol location, symbol list browsing and cross-referencing analysis including information about all the different types of "references" to a symbol with literally dozens of them (e.g., modified, read, defined, expanded, cast, used in -> operator, etc.). Then analysis phase can also generate function prototypes with various options, including separation of static and global prototypes, use of argument names, and related function comment capturing. However, the full power of CC-Rider comes out in the visual presentation of structural information about functions and classes in the project. There are many different graphical tree views of functions and classes as shown below:

- class hierarchy tree — this shows the class inheritance hierarchy with options to show `virtual` inheritance as dashed lines, show multiple inheritance, show structs as classes, and show template instances.
- class ancestry tree — inverse of the hierarchy tree showing class inheritance in reverse.
- call tree — shows the function call tree for the program with options to only show defined functions, show data references, show member or nonmember function calls. These various options allow unimportant symbols such as system library calls to be excluded to show application information.
- caller tree — inverse of the call tree to show all functions calling a given function.
- class nesting tree — show nested class relationships with options to show unnested classes, show `enums`, show `friends`, show `structs`, show `template` instances.
- file tree — show #include relationships between files.

In addition to the configurations mentioned above, the symbols displayed in graphs can be controlled via "filters" based on filenames and symbol names to include or exclude various symbols from views. All of these graphical views can be customized visually with control over aspects such as fonts, color, shapes, and even which mouse actions have what effect. Clicking on objects in the graphs allows you to navigate to more specialized information and even get to source code. In addition, each view can be previewed and printed with additional customizations for the printed result.

CC-Rider runs in visual mode under Windows and text mode with fewer features under DOS or OS/2. The various graphical and textual views are very powerful, but should you need further analysis CC-Rider can be extended via API calls. CC-Rider comes with documented API calls in prebuilt library files that allow access to the CC-Rider database to develop custom reports or analysis. The analyzer can also be run from the command-line to build the database via make or other project building methods.

GrafBrowse/C — Browsing and Documentation Tool

Product Name:	GrafBrowse/C
Platforms:	UNIX (Solaris, OSF/1, HP-UX, AIX, SGI and others)
Company:	Software Systems Design
Address:	3267 Padua Ave., Claremont CA 91711, USA
Phone:	909-625-6417
Fax:	909-626-9667
Email:	tradi@hmc.edu

GrafBrowse/C is a graphical tool for browsing C code structure and printing documentation. GrafBrowse/C works in conjunction with a C/PDL product called CDADL also available from Software Systems Design. Hence, GrafBrowse/C is useful to projects using a C/PDL (Program Design Language) which is primarily those with Mil/DoD requirements to satisfy. The CDADL processor analyzes the source files to generate structure information that is viewed using the GrafBrowse/C GUI. Some of the views that can be produced include:

- callby tree: show calls to a given function
- code file declaration diagram: show internals and externals for a source file
- file depends tree: show the file dependency hierarchy
- function declaration diagram: show internals and externals for a function
- header file declaration diagram: show internals and externals for header files
- include tree: show all files included
- includeby tree: show all files that include the given file
- invocation tree: show all calls made by a function (i.e., function call graph)

Tree views can be displayed in a crossing or non-crossing layout, and the depth level of the tree can be chosen. All views can be printed to a PostScript file for hardcopy generation with numerous print format options such as scaling to fit on one page or multi-page generation.

DocGen/C — Automatic Mil/DoD Documentation

Product Name:	DocGen/C
Platforms:	UNIX (Solaris, OSF/1, HP-UX, AIX, SGI and others), VAX/VMS
Company:	Software Systems Design
Address:	3267 Padua Ave., Claremont CA 91711, USA
Phone:	909-625-6417
Fax:	909-626-9667
Email:	tradi@hmc.edu

DocGen/C is an automatic documentation tool for C that automatically prepares Mil-Std documentation to satisfy DoD-Std-2167, DoD-Std-2167A, NASA SMAP, Mil-Std-490 and Mil-Std-1679 requirements. The produced documentation will satisfy all of the requirements for DoD-Std-2167 STLDD and SDDD or 2167A SDD documents and Mil-Std-490 C5 specifications. DocGen/C not only provides templates for the DIDs for DoD-Std-2167A, but also automatically analyzes the C source code to provide the required information in these documents. Pseudocode and design algorithms can be automatically extracted if the C source code has been annotated using a C/PDL (Program Design Language) such as the C-based Design and Documentation Language (CDADL) product also produced by Software Systems Design. The output file formats produced by DocGen/C include ASCII, RUNOFF, `troff/nroff`, LaTeX and Interleaf.

CDADL — Program Design Language for C

Product Name:	CDADL (C-based Design and Documentation Language)
Platforms:	UNIX (Solaris, OSF/1, HP-UX, AIX, SGI and others), VAX/VMS
Company:	Software Systems Design
Address:	3267 Padua Ave., Claremont CA 91711, USA
Phone:	909-625-6417

Fax:	909-626-9667
Email:	tradi@hmc.edu

CDADL is a C-based Program Design Language (PDL) that maintains detailed design information and pseudocode in C comments next to the code implementations. By maintaining the design and code information together, CDADL can detect design anomalies and coding errors automatically. CDADL can report on the completion of the project including TBD sections, create project documentation, and trace requirements to code. A particular form of pseudocode is used with keywords only for the major flow of control constructs.

CDADL is part of a suite of tools from Software Systems Design called C/CDADL Integrated Software Lifecycle Environment (CISLE). This includes GrafBrowse/C to produce graphical views, DocGen/C to generate Mil/DoD documentation, and QualGen/C for reporting and graphing various quality metrics.

C-XREF AND C-TREE IN C-VISION FROM GIMPEL SOFTWARE

C-XREF produces a cross-reference listing of identifiers in a program, and a database of information that is used by C-TREE to produce textual displays of tree structure. The trees supported include function call hierarchy, inverse call hierarchy, C++ class hierarchy, and its inverse. These tools are part of the C-Vision package from Gimpel Software and are discussed fully in the section "C-Vision — listing, documentation and reformatting" on page 155.

ID — IDENTIFIER CROSS-REFERENCES FOR C

Tool Name:	`id`
Purpose:	Identifier and cross-reference analysis
Availability:	comp.sources.unix/volume11/id/
Author:	Greg McGary

The `id` package consists of a `mkid` facility to build a database of all uses of identifiers, preprocessor names, string literals and numeric values, and a variety of query tools that present this information on request. This database is generated directly from C source code using the `mkid` program. This program accepts filenames as arguments, or a file containing a list of filenames using the `-a` option to `mkid`, which is useful for large projects with too many files to list on the command line.

There are a great many queries permitted on the identifier database. The lookup id "`lid`" program allows querying for all uses of an identifier across multiple files. The `grep` id "`gid`" program allows regular expression search on identifier names. The edit id "`eid`" program allows launching of an editor on all locations of a given identifier. The `-a` option to `lid` allows searching the database for uses of numerical values, useful to track all uses of a magic number across multiple files (heaven forbid!).

CCOUNT — COMPUTE STATISTICS ABOUT C SOURCE CODE

Tool Name:	ccount
Purpose:	Statistical analysis of C source code
Availability:	comp.sources.misc/volume42/ccount/ and also from Linux sites: e.g. sunsite.unc.edu:/pub/Linux/devel/lang/c/c_count*
Author:	Joerg Lawrenz, Universitaet Karlsruhe

The ccount measurement tool computes various simple metrics from C source files. Some of the attributes measured include the number and length of functions, blocks and various control statements, number and length of comments, and the number of operators in expressions. All of these various measurements can be analyzed statistically using the tools to present averages, medians, percentiles, sums and fractions.

The ccount tool is implemented as a number of components. The basic "ccount" component is a lex/yacc parser for C that handles many parsing issues and generates masses of data about each file it analyzes. The "ccounter" shell script simplifies applying ccount to many files. Various Perl scripts such as "stattyM" further analyze the combined measurements to present more meaningful summary reports on various aspects of the source code.

CALLS — FREE FUNCTION CALL TREE FOR C

Tool Name:	calls
Purpose:	Function call analysis from C source code
Author:	Tony Hansen, M. M. Taylor, Alexis Kwan, Kevin Szabo
Availability:	comp.sources.unix/volume3 files calls.Z and calls_4.2.Z

The calls utility presents the function call graph in a concise textual layout to show program structure. Each function occupies a single line on the output report and indentation shows the level of the calling sequence. Recursive calls are marked in the listing with a "<<<" prefix. Functions that were not detected in the source files are marked in the listing with an "[external]" suffix.

By default each function is only further expanded with its descendents the first time it appears in the flow graph. The -v option can be used to force expansion on every occurrence. The -f option can be used to specify a particular root symbol instead of the default "main" symbol. The -wN option changes the report width from 132 to N.

CXREF — FREE CROSS REFERENCE ANALYSIS FOR C

Tool Name:	`cxref`
Purpose:	Cross references for C
Availability:	comp.sources.unix/volume1/cxref.Z
Author:	Arnold Robbins

The `cxref` tool analyzes C source files and generates a cross reference listing to standard output. The `cxref` tool analyzes the C source code for all types of uses of identifiers and other tokens. The output report includes identifiers, numeric constants, string literals and character constants.

The various categories of constants in the output report can be omitted using the options `-i` (omit integer constants), `-f` (omit floating point constants), `-c` (omit character constants), `-s` (omit string constants), and `-C` (omit all types of constants). By default the report collates cross-references across all files, and the `-S` option can be used to separate reports into each file. The `-F` option can be used to ignore case in identifiers and string or character constants, and the `-w` option controls the width of the report.

IDENTLIST — IDENTIFIER LISTINGS FROM C SOURCE

Tool Name:	`identlist`
Purpose:	Identifier listings from C source
Availability:	comp.sources.unix/volume16/identlist.Z
Author:	John Rupley

The `identlist` utility examines a C source file and generates an output report with a list of all external declarations, and a list of identifiers used in the file. The `cdeclist` filter is used to generate the list of external declarations from source files. This list includes functions, arrays, variables and structures, with one line per object. The `identlist` filter generates the list of identifiers from source files. The shell scripts driving these filters make use of the standard C preprocessor to handle conditional compilation and expand macros.

GENMAN — FREE DOCUMENTATION TOOL FOR C++ CLASSES

Tool Name:	`genman`
Purpose:	Automatic generation of C++ class documentation

Availability:	comp.sources.misc/volume10/genman.awk.Z
Author:	Bob Mastors

genman is a UNIX tool that uses the awk scripting language to generate standardized C++ class documentation directly from the C++ source files. The format of the documentation has a brief description of the class first, then a list of public members, then private members, and then various other attributes including a list of defined macros, included files, structures, and source files. Finally, there is a "summary" list of every class member generated from the comments nearby. The overall output format is similar to UNIX manual pages which explains the name "genman".

Note that there are problems un-archiving the shell archive from the *comp.sources.misc* distribution since "genman.awk" is itself an extracted file. One solution is to rename genman.awk.Z to genman.sh.Z before extracting it.

FUNNELWEB — LITERATE PROGRAMMING TOOL FOR C

Tool Name:	FunnelWeb
Purpose:	Literate programming for C
Availability:	ftp.adelaide.edu.au:/pub/funnelweb/ comp.sources.unix/volume26/funnelweb/
Author:	Dr. Ross N. Williams

FunnelWeb is a literate programming tool for the C programming language. Literate programming is the term for combining source code and documentation in the same source file, pioneered by Donald Knuth's WEB system for Pascal. FunnelWeb is a full-blown literate programming tool for C with advanced features and good documentation.

C2MAN — FREE DOCUMENTATION TOOL FOR C

Tool:	c2man
Platforms:	UNIX, DOS, OS/2
Status:	free
Availability:	comp.sources.misc/volume42/c2man-2.0/
Author:	Graham Stoney

c2man is a tool for automatic documentation of C programs by extracting comments from the source code. It generates UNIX-style manual pages for functions and global variables in the program. The manual pages are available in a variety of formats including `nroff`/`troff`, TeXinfo and LaTeX. C++ documentation features are not supported in this version, but may be forthcoming in the future.

The output manuals refer to functions or global variables (with the `-v` option). Functions that are `static` are ignored unless the `-s` option is chosen. `c2man` can read either source or header files to gather the information it requires. Useful manual pages require a reasonable level of comments in the source code for `c2man` to extract. The comment preceding a function definition (or global variable) is treated as describing that function. Comments beside each function parameter are needed for `c2man` to report useful information in the PARAMETERS section of the manual page. To present the RETURNS section of the manual page, `c2man` searches for the word `"returns"` in the block comment for the function. There is special support for enumerated types where `c2man` can extract comments about each value.

MORE FREE BROWSING AND DOCUMENTATION TOOL REFERENCES

This section examines a few more tools that came to my attention too close to the writing deadline. Hence they are not evaluated to the depth of others in this chapter and are included mainly for completeness.

c-bat — C Browsing and Analysis Toolkit

Tool Name:	`c-bat`
Purpose:	Cross-reference analysis
Availability:	Linux sites: e.g., sunsite.unc.edu:/pub/Linux/devel/lang/c/c-bat*
Author:	Eckehard Stolz

`c-bat` generates cross-reference information at compile time. It can be used to locate uses or definitions of an identifier representing a variable or function. The release is not finished now and may offer much greater functionality in the next version.

mkid — free tool for cross-reference analysis

Tool Name:	`mkid`
Purpose:	Cross-referencing and identifier analysis
Availability:	Linux sites: e.g., sunsite.unc.edu:/pub/Linux/devel/mkid*
Author:	Greg McGary

`mkid` builds a database of information about identifiers and other tokens from the source code. You can then query this database to extract information about the location of uses and definitions of identifiers and tokens. This allows powerful cross-reference analysis and other code analysis tasks.

cflow — free function call graph tool

Tool Name:	`cflow`
Purpose:	Function call graph analysis
Platforms:	UNIX (includes SunOS, Linux)
Availability:	Linux sites: e.g., sunsite.unc.edu:/pub/Linux/devel/lang/c/cflow*
Authors:	Andrew Moore, Steve Kirkendall, Tony Hansen, Kevin Szabo, Alexis Szabo, Alexis Kwan, M.M.Taylor, Marty Leisner

`cflow` is a free tool that analyzes the function call sequence to generate a function call graph. This graph is displayed using a character-based indentation scheme rather than a graphical window.

cstrings — extract C strings for internationalization

Tool Name:	`cstrings`
Purpose:	Extract C strings for internationalization
Availability:	Linux sites: sunsite.unc.edu:/pub/Linux/devel/lang/c/cstrings*
Author:	Eric S. Raymond

`cstrings` is a "quick-and-dirty" tool to extract strings from C code. It converts them into `#define` directives to aid in the internationalization of all the text output messages in an application.

## CHAPTER 13

Test coverage tools

*T*est coverage tools measure the extent to which all parts of a program have been exercised by a test suite. This analysis of the coverage is performed by looking into the code and watching what parts are executed. Hence, these tools are also called code coverage tools as it is the coverage of the source code that is examined.

The aim of a regression test suite is to test all the features of a program, and a test coverage tool is to determine how much of the code has been tested. Has a given function even been called useful? If it hasn't, and that function represents a crucial feature, then the test suite should be improved.

TYPES OF COVERAGE METRICS

There are a variety of metrics used to determine what proportion of the code has been tested. Ideally, we'd like to take a requirements document and see how many of the product's features have been tested. More realistic is checking at various levels of detail what code has been executed. Some of the most common metrics are:

- function call coverage
- function call pair coverage
- line coverage
- statement coverage
- branch coverage (or decision coverage)
- path coverage
- condition coverage

Function call coverage is the most obvious measure. It determines which functions have been called. If a function is not called, maybe that's a whole feature not tested. A companion measure is function call pair coverage which measures how many calls to functions have been exercised. Whereas function call coverage measures how many functions have been called, function call pair coverage measures how many of the calls to the function are covered.

Line coverage is a simple measure of execution that determines which lines of code have been executed. It provides a good idea of which parts of a function have been executed. Statement coverage is a slight improvement that measures execution of all statements, which may differ from line coverage for multi-statement lines of code.

Branch coverage improves on line and statement coverage in that it always tests all possible branches of an `if` statement, `switch`, or loop. Branch coverage is also known as decision coverage because it measures the branches leading from decision points. This measure is an important improvement in precision over line coverage. For example, line coverage on an `if` statement without an `else` will only report whether the `if` statement was executed, and whether the statements inside the `if` clause were executed; line coverage provides no indication whether the `if` test ever failed. Branch coverage will report on whether both success and failure of the `if` condition were tested.

Path coverage is an even more general measure. A path is a sequence of branches, and path coverage detects how many of the possible paths through a function have been tested. Since loops lead to an infinite number of paths, loops are tamed in a few ways such as by treating them as a single path, or as two paths based on zero and one-or-more iterations.

Condition coverage examines the conditional expressions in more detail, and provides more valuable information about the execution of conditional tests with multiple conditions. At its best, this measure examines all the possible states of the truth table of a multi-condition expression to ensure all possible true/false conditions are tested.

ERROR SIMULATION AND CODE COVERAGE

A valuable feature that is available with some code coverage tools is the ability to simulate failures of various kinds. This makes it easier to create a test suite that exercises some of the less frequently travelled lines of code. Exception handling code is one of the hardest types of code to test, simply because of the effort to raise the conditions.

Memory allocation failure is one of the most important resource failures to handle. Since it leads to `NULL` pointers in places where this is rare, the chances of a product crash in memory failure handling are great. The simplest method of handling this in C is to provide wrappers for all allocation calls that perform some simple cleanup, possibly print a message, and exit. However, a more realistic behavior for a commercial quality program is to attempt to continue, propagating failures up through levels of modules, and testing this code is important. Even the neat C++ exception handling language support is far from easy to use in a correct manner. Exercising this code is likely to find bugs.

The same comments apply to file operations and their rare failures. Sure, your program works fine provided it has enough disk space to create its temporary work files, but how well does it handle a full disk? File failures could include write failure (simulating disk full conditions), read failure, file not found, could not create file, could not lock file, etc.

In a normal test suite the effort to test these conditions would be high, but with error simulation facilities you can request allocation failures as part of the regression test suite and improve your code coverage with relative ease.

RUN-TIME ERROR CHECKING AND CODE COVERAGE

Run-time error checking tools as discussed in Chapter 5 are a good complementary tool to code coverage tools. Memory stomps or use of deallocated memory do not always yield an obvious program failure, and in fact the program can often work correctly. Hence running your test suite with your ordinary executable may not always uncover hidden memory bugs. The solution is to execute a version with run-time error checking enabled. In this way any anomaly leads to a tangible failure and won't quietly sneak past QA.

HOW MUCH COVERAGE IS ENOUGH?

A commonly asked question about test coverage is, "How much is enough?" Should 80% be considered an adequate level of coverage? 90%? 100%? Most of the test coverage tools will provide a global metric estimating what proportion has been tested. The issue here is how significant it is.

This kind of question is very simplistic. A higher percentage of code coverage is usually better, provided we're talking about the same coverage measure. However, reaching 100% coverage is next to impossible. It seems feasible that a test suite should exercise all the features of a product, but a reasonable percentage of code in a product is purely for handling exceptional conditions. Developing a test suite to exercise rare conditions is difficult and resource intensive. Error-simulation tools are available (often as part of test coverage tools or with run-time memory debugging tools), but even with these tools it is almost impossible to reach 100% coverage.

Personally, I consider it pointless to attempt to measure the quality in a testing process by just a single number. There are so many factors in the software development process that are far more important than what percentage of code coverage is tested. For example, is a test suite with 100% coverage adequate even if none of the test results are inspected?

PROFILERS ARE CODE COVERAGE TOOLS

There is an intimate relationship between profilers and coverage analysis tools. Data generated by profilers is a superset of that required by code coverage tools. Counts of executions of functions, statements or basic blocks are usually produced by profilers, in addition to time results. It is exactly these counts that code coverage tools use in their analysis. Hence in the past, numerous UNIX scripts have been written to convert profiler data into useful code coverage analysis tools. Eventually some code coverage tools emerged as independent tools in their own right, with a different emphasis than the profiling tools.

The implementation methods used by code coverage tools are also identical to those of profilers. Some tools use sampling methods whereas others use the more accurate code instrumentation technique.

GCT: A FREE TEST COVERAGE ANALYSIS TOOL

Product Name:	gct
Purpose:	Test coverage tool
Platforms:	Many (includes SunOS, HP, AIX, SCO, Ultrix)
Languages:	ANSI C, K&R C
Status:	Free (copyleft), commercially supported
Availability:	FTP cs.uiuc.edu:pub/testing
Author:	Brian Marick
Phone:	217-351-7228
Email:	gct-request@cs.uiuc.edu

Brian Marick has produced a free tool for automated test coverage analysis under UNIX called gct for "Generic Coverage Tool". gct works by taking C files and adding source code to them. The process is transparent because gct automatically calls the system C compiler after augmenting the source code (alternatively, the modified source can be extracted). The resulting augmented executable produces a tracing log at program termination, which can be analyzed by a number of tools provided for this purpose. A variety of code coverage measures are provided including branch coverage, multi-condition coverage, loop coverage, relational operator coverage, routine coverage and call coverage, just to mention a few.

gct is available via FTP from *cs.uiuc.edu* in the *pub/testing* directory. A brief overview is in the file GCT.README and the full distribution is in the gct.files directory (actually a link to another directory). The distribution includes plenty of good documentation and testing examples and is supported commercially by Brian Marick.

BTOOL — FREE BRANCH COVERAGE TESTING TOOL

Tool Name:	btool
Purpose:	Branch coverage measurement

Platforms:	UNIX (SunOS, Motorola, probably others)
Authors:	Thomas Hoch, K. Wolfram Schafer, and Brian Marick.
Availability:	ftp.uu.net/pub/c-utils/btool.tar.Z

`btool` is a test coverage tool that measures the percentage of branches that have been exercised. It can find conditions that have not been exercised in both true and false branches. The implementation uses source-to-source instrumentation that adds measurement code. During execution, the program stores coverage data in memory, and writes a log file on termination.

This log file is analyzed offline using the `breport` tool to determine the coverage level. Multiple log files can be combined by the `bmerge` tool to produce an aggregated coverage measure over a large test suite. The `bsummary` tool produces the overall report including the total coverage percentage.

`btool` is based on the GNU C compiler sources and is therefore distributed freely under the GNU Public License. Note that `btool` is a little old and largely superceded by Brian Marick's `gct` coverage measurement tool.

CTC++ — TEST COVERAGE ANALYZER FOR C/C++

Product Name:	CTC++
Purpose:	Test coverage analysis for C/C++
Platforms:	DOS, Windows 3.1, Windows NT, Solaris, HP-UX, Linux
Price:	$1,050-$6,000
Company:	Testwell
Address:	Kanslerinkatu 8, FIN-33720 Tampere, Finland
Phone:	+358-31-316-5464 (+358-3-316-5464 from 12 Oct 96)
Fax:	+358-31-318-3311 (+358-3-318-3311 from 12 Oct 96)
Email:	olavip@cs.tut.fi

CTC++ is a test coverage analyzer for C/C++ programs that determines how effectively a test suite has exercised a program. There are a number of coverage modes that are available including function call coverage, decision coverage, statement coverage, and interface coverage. The interface coverage measure is an effective measure of how thoroughly the members of the interface for a C++ class have been tested.

CTC++ produces an instrumented version of the program using a special preprocessor. Instrumentation can be performed incrementally during development when files are changing. Each file can have a different type of coverage enabled. Executing the instrumented program generates a history trace file. Results are examined using the CTC++ postprocessor utility that produces a variety of reports about the coverage from one or many executions.

The execution profile listing shows the source code annotated with indications of how well exercised the code was. The untested code listing is a more restricted source listing of lines not tested. The interface coverage report shows how many times each class member was called. The coverage summary listing shows the level of coverage for each function in a histogram format and marks all those below the user-specified threshold.

CTC++ can also function as a performance measurement tool for program tuning. There is a special timing instrumentation mode that uses the ANSI `clock` function or a user-defined cost function to measure how much time is used by each function. The execution time listing shows the number of calls and the time taken for each function.

STW/COVERAGE — TEST COVERAGE ANALYSIS TOOLSET

Product Name:	STW/Coverage
Purpose:	Test coverage analysis
Platforms:	DOS, Windows 3.1, Windows 95, Windows NT, Solaris, Solaris-x86, SunOS, HP-UX, OSF/1, AIX
Company:	Software Research
Address:	625 Third Street, San Francisco, CA 94107-1997, USA
Phone:	1-800-942-SOFT, 415-957-1441
Fax:	415-957-0730
Email:	info@soft.com
Web:	http://www.soft.com

As part of the integrated Software TestWorks toolset, STW/Coverage provides a number of tools for test coverage analysis. The coverage measures include branch coverage, call coverage, call-pair coverage, and path coverage. The implementation is based on the addition of instrumentation to source code. Tests can be executed through the GUI or in batch mode.

Coverage results are presented in a number of intuitive graphical displays that can be exported as PostScript. There is a directed graph view of the control flow of a function showing all paths, and a call graph view of all the functions in the system. These graphs can be annotated with color to highlight untested or heavily executed paths. Source code views indicate lines of code that are not executed. Subtrees of the call graph can be analyzed for more focused analysis.

Multiple test executions can be aggregated to give results from a test suite. Selective instrumentation is available to focus on or omit particular modules. Source code for the run-time module is available for embedded testing in C, C++, Ada or Fortran.

TCOV — SUN LINE COVERAGE ANALYSIS

The `tcov` coverage analysis tool offers a primitive level of line coverage analysis for Sun-3 and Sun-4 systems. `tcov` requires that a program be compiled with the `-a` option to the `cc` compiler. Statistics are generated during execution of the program and placed in files with a ".d" suffix where the prefix corresponds to the name of the ".c" files. Program execution must terminate normally via `exit` or a `return` from `main` (the same restriction applies to `prof` and `gprof` profilers).

As an example, after execution, the command:

```
tcov f.c
```

will look for a "f.d" data file and produce a new file "f.tcov" containing an annotated source code listing based on the source code from "f.c" and the coverage data from "f.d".

By default, the execution counts generated by `tcov` are for each basic block. This can be changed to statement level counts using the `-a` option to `tcov` as shown in Table 14–1.

Table 14–1 Options to tcov

| -a | Statement level coverage analysis (better than basic block) |
| -n | Display line numbers of n most frequently executed statements |

PURECOVERAGE

Product Name:	PureCoverage
Purpose:	Test coverage tool
Platforms:	SunOS, Solaris, HP-UX
Languages:	ANSI C, C++, K&R C
Status:	Commercial Product
Company:	Pure Software, Inc.
Address:	1309 S. Mary Avenue, Sunnyvale, CA 94087, USA
Phone:	408-720-1600, 1-800-353-7873
Fax:	408-720-9200
Email:	info@pure.com support@pure.com
Web:	http://www.pure.com/

PureCoverage is a code coverage tool from Pure Software that is tightly integrated with their Purify memory allocation debugging tool (see section "Purify from Pure Software" on page

75). In addition to the convenient Motif GUI, both PureCoverage and Purify can now be easily integrated into HP's SoftBench development environment.

To measure coverage, object code instrumentation is used to augment the executable with code that counts the frequency with which a path is taken. This gives a much greater accuracy than sampling methods. PureCoverage uses the same instrumentation technology as Purify and their compatibility allows coverage to be examined while testing for memory errors. This also allows the coverage analysis to go down to the basic block level to find branches and individual statements not adequately tested.

The Motif GUI is also shared by Purify and PureCoverage with support for PureCoverage appearing as an umbrella button. In this way the PureCoverage parts of the GUI can be launched to review information about function and line coverage. Functions are shown with the number of calls with a graphical tick or cross as a pass/fail status based on customizable thresholds. Coverage of individual branches or statements is shown by presentation of the source code annotated with execution counts, and showing unexecuted lines with inverse highlighting. These various features give good visual feedback as to what proportion of the code has been exercised in testing.

In addition, there is support for warnings based on the failure to meet test coverage thresholds. Coverage results can also be exported in a spreadsheet-friendly format to allow further analysis using pretty graphs by anyone who has an MBA.

C-COVER FROM BULLSEYE TESTING TECHNOLOGY

Product Name:	C-Cover
Purpose:	Test coverage tool
Platforms:	DOS, Windows 3.1, Windows 95, Windows NT, OS/2, PowerPC, UNIX: SunOS, Solaris, Solaris- x86, Ultrix, Linux, HP-UX, AIX, AT&T, Unisys, DG, OSF/1, Pyramid, SGI, SCO
Languages:	C++, ANSI C, K&R C
Status:	Commercial Product
Price:	$800 ($700 for each additional copy)
Company:	Bullseye Testing Technology
Address:	5129 24th Ave NE, Suite 9, Seattle, WA 98105
Phone:	1-800-278-4268
Fax:	206-524-3575
Email:	info@bullseye.com
Web:	http://www.bullseye.com

C-Cover uses source code augmentation to add test coverage measurement to C or C++ code. Coverage metrics include function coverage and extends to branch coverage with support for single and multiple condition measurement. This means C-Cover will report coverage of the branches arising out of `if`, `switch` and loop statements, and also the `?:` ternary operator and C++ `catch` clauses.

To use C-Cover you add "`covc`" to your compile command and link with a run-time library. Coverage data is collected during execution and saved at termination. A reporting tool is used to examine the coverage results to show percentages of functions called and branches covered, and an annotated source code view is also offered.

BBA — BASIC BRANCH ANALYZER FROM HP

Product Name:	bba (Basic Branch Analyzer)
Purpose:	Test coverage tool
Platforms:	HP-UX
Languages:	C++, ANSI C, K&R C
Status:	Commercial Product
Company:	Hewlett-Packard
Phone:	1-800-752-0900
Web:	http://www.hp.com

`bba` is a test coverage tool for C and C++ that is part of HP's SoftBench tool suite. The coverage level is the branch or equivalently basic block level, where coverage of each logical branch is measured. Instrumentation is added to the execution using the `bbacpp` preprocessor. The data file containing the coverage information is written on normal program termination or under a few other circumstances including a debugger command.

`bba` can be used as a command-line tool or launched from the SoftBench Tool Manager. The `bba` interface consists of three windows: summary window, source window and a list of active files and functions. The summary window shows the various summary coverage reports including file coverage levels, function coverage levels, and histogram representations of the results. The source window shows the source code for a file or function that you selected, with annotations of the branches. The active files/functions window shows all the files and functions that were instrumented for the coverage analysis.

An interesting feature is the method of dealing with branches with the option to "ignore" it. This is relevant to branches unlikely to ever be executed, such as exception handling code, and effectively removes them from consideration in the coverage calculations. You can ignore files, functions, or individual branches.

## CHAPTER 14

Testing tools

*T*here are quite a few tools available for automating the testing process, especially the repetitive commands required for regression tests. This section presents a survey of a number of tools in this area. Many of the tools consist of a number of distinct features used for different aspects of the testing and QA process. Some of the testing and QA techniques to be seen in these tools include:

- Static analysis — the analysis of source code for error checking, portability checking and coding style enforcement as performed by some specialized tools in Chapter 4. This feature is also available in many of the testing tools covered in this chapter.
- Metrics — a special case of source code analysis is the computation of metrics about the source code to provide a quantitative measure about its complexity and maintainability. A number of metrics have been popularized including McCabe's cyclomatic complexity metric which gives indications about the number of paths requiring testing, and Halstead's metrics examining size and maintainability issues.

- Coverage analysis — the dynamic analysis of what execution paths have been exercised by the test suite. A number of tools with this specific feature are covered in Chapter 14, and various tools combining coverage analysis with other testing features are examined in this chapter.
- Unit testing — this refers to self-tests performed by a driver for a module or small group of modules. This has traditionally been achieved by programmers adding extra test driver `main` functions to files or directories. Automation of this process is now possible through tools that generate the test drivers directly by analysis of the source code to discover the parameter types, and path analysis to choose good test cases.
- Test case generation — the choice of cases under which to test the program has long been a manual process based on intuition, experience, and general rules such as that of testing "boundary conditions". Tools now exist that automatically generate test cases either from requirements, or via the generation of data files based on templates. A common feature of these tools is *minimization* of test cases to reduce the number of test cases required to cover the requirements or execution paths.
- Performance testing — this feature is similar to that of execution profilers, but is more general in that results can be incorporated into the overall testing process. Poor performance becomes just another type of defect found during testing.

CAPTURE-PLAYBACK REGRESSION TESTING TOOLS

Automating the actual execution of tests and the assessment of their correctness is one of the most major advances in testing tool capabilities. With automated regression testing you can set up a test suite once, and then have the computer run the tests in batch mode, reporting any test cases that fail. This is not really a new concept in testing since batch mode testing of command-line programs has been common, such as running unit tests overnight. However, the latest tools can automate GUI program execution.

GUI testing tools embody the true spirit of capture-playback regression testing tools. These tools have a "capture" mode where the keystrokes, mouse movements, and mouse clicks from an interactive session are captured by the testing tool during execution. This session becomes a test case for the "playback" mode where the sequence is automatically replayed. This playback is achieved by sending the events to the windowing system which is possible on most GUI platforms including Microsoft Windows and Motif/X Windows.

Validation of Test Correctness

An important part of executing a test is validating the results. It is also a costly task to perform manually. Capture-playback tools offer various methods to automate the validation of test results. The simplest method is to store bitmaps for the screen during capture mode, and to perform an image comparison during playback. However, this can be sensitive to issues such as the window manager. More intelligent validation can include comparison of screens at the object level by analysis of windows and other widgets. For example, widgets can be interrogated for the text they are displaying, and this can be validated. Alternatively, some tools offer Optical Character Recognition (OCR) to determine what characters are displayed in a bitmap image, regardless of the type of GUI objects.

Validation of non-GUI command-line utilities is also available, although it usually receives less attention. This is achieved through validation of aspects such as printed output, exit statuses and contents of resulting data files.

Scripted Testing

The capture mode of a testing tool is valuable in that it allows novice users to generate test cases just by "playing" with the product. Many tools offer scripted tests as an alternative to the capture mode for more sophisticated testers. This allows more complicated tests to be performed by QA engineers. There is also tighter control over correctness validation since scripts usually offer various primitives for validation.

Script languages in modern test tools usually offer an "object-oriented" method of specifying actions. For example, this means the script can state the equivalent of "click on the dialog OK button" instead of "click at position x,y".

Client/Server Testing

The testing of a client/server application throws another level of complexity into the process of regression testing. Automation of test cases for client/server applications requires driving the execution of both sides of the client/server application. Testing of the client typically involves the techniques of GUI capture-playback, whereas the server is usually a non-GUI application and more traditional testing techniques. Script languages for client/server testing usually offer advanced features for synchronizing the distributed applications.

Programming Language Independence

One of the important issues in the market for test tools is the generality of the products for automated regression testing. Whereas most of the tools in other chapters have been specific to C or C++ programming, automated regression testing tools are often generic and usable for any programming language. Although some testing tools use internal C/C++ facilities, many of them use operating system or windowing system facilities to perform the needed capture and playback of external events for testing. This independence from the programming language means that the market for testing tools is not limited to C and C++ software developers, but extends into the general market for application development tools.

One particularly important segment of the market is the IS departments of large companies and their development of in-house applications. Programming language independence of many of the testing tools has allowed them to be available to test in-house applications developed with 4GLs or other rapid prototyping tools. Hence, unlike many of the other chapters in this book, many of the tools covered here apply not only to C and C++, but to any application development environment or programming language.

DEJAGNU: FREE AUTOMATED TESTING TOOL

DejaGnu is a free tool from GNU for automated testing on many platforms, and is currently used to test other major tools produced in the GNU toolset. DejaGnu tests are written in *expect* which uses Tool Command Language (Tcl). Regression testing is an obvious application of DejaGnu's automated testing, but not the only one. DejaGnu is designed to allow consistent testing of a program across multiple platforms, with support for both batch and interactive programs (e.g., it has been used to test both `gcc` and `gdb`). Unfortunately, it does not currently support GUI-based testing, although this is an intended area of future work (and may well have been achieved by the time you read these words!).

DejaGnu is available at any of the usual GNU sites as discussed in section "Free Tools –GNU Software" on page 9. At the time of writing, the filename is `dejagnu-1.0.1.tar.gz`. The distribution also includes implementations of `tcl` and `expect`, and numerous test suites.

DejaGnu was originally developed by staff at Cygnus Support (see page 22) who provide commercial support for GNU software. Online information about DejaGnu is available on the Web via *http://www.cygnus.com/doc/dejagnu/dejagnu_toc.html*.

PREVUE-X — AUTOMATED X WINDOWS TESTING

Product Name:	preVue-X
Purpose:	Performance/regression testing for X Windows
Platforms:	Solaris, Solaris-x86, SunOS, HP-UX, OSF/1, SGI, AIX, Ultrix, DG, Pyramid, ICL.
Status:	Commercial Product
Company	Performance Awareness
Address:	8521 Six Forks Rd., Raleigh, NC 27615, USA
Phone:	1-800-849-4562,919-870-8800
Fax:	919-870-7416
Email:	info@PACorp.com
Web	http://www.PACorp.com

preVue-X is an advanced tool for automated regression testing, load testing and performance measurement for all X Windows applications. It uses a non-intrusive method to record and playback user actions for the application. User actions are recorded into a script format called VU and these scripts reproduce the events from a particular session. This leads to the programmable and repeatable testing needed for regression testing.

The scripted approach makes it easy to generate loads without needing real hardware and users. The VU script language is an advanced programmable C-like language with major facilities including timestamping and synchronization. VU also provides tolerance for minor

GUI changes by using an object-oriented syntax for specifying events applying to objects (e.g., stating that the user clicked an OK button rather than a particular screen coordinate). This makes regression testing independent of changes in geometry.

There are a number of validation options for regression testing. preVue-X can check bit images, text strings and the X protocols for indications that the application has behavior that is not expected and possibly incorrect. Response time can also be measured to gain insight into performance problems.

PREVUE-C/S — SERVER LOAD TESTING

Product Name:	preVue-C/S
Purpose:	Server load testing
Platforms:	Solaris, Solaris-x86, SunOS, HP-UX, OSF/1, SGI, AIX, Ultrix, DG, Pyramid, ICL, AT&T.
Status:	Commercial Product
Company	Performance Awareness
Address:	8521 Six Forks Rd., Raleigh, NC 27615, USA
Phone:	1-800-849-4562, 919-870-8800
Fax:	919-870-7416
Email:	info@PACorp.com
Web	http://www.PACorp.com

preVue-C/S provides automated testing facilities for client-server applications by emulating the client actions to test server performance and reliability. Client actions from remote PCs are not needed to test the server under realistic conditions and in a repeatable manner. Scripts in a C-like language are used to emulate client actions with full programming capability and realistic features such as simulation of user reaction times. This automated testing is used to record network traffic, measure server performance, and provide repeatable tests. This allows both performance tuning and regression testing of the server piece of a client-server application.

WINSATELLITE — CLIENT LOAD TESTING

Product Name:	WinSatellite
Purpose:	Client load testing
Platforms:	Windows 3.1, Windows 95, Windows NT, Solaris, Solaris-x86, HP-UX, OSF/1, SGI, AIX, Ultrix, DG, ICL, AT&T.

Status:	Commercial Product
Company:	Performance Awareness
Address:	8521 Six Forks Rd., Raleigh, NC 27615, USA
Phone:	1-800-849-4562, 919-870-8800
Fax:	919-870-7416
Email:	info@PACorp.com
Web:	http://www.PACorp.com

WinSatellite is a companion piece for preVue-C/S for testing both sides of a client-server architecture. Where preVue-C/S emulates client activity on the server machine, WinSatellite works on the client machine to drive the client application for testing and performance measurement of the client piece. WinSatellite will record user sessions and these can be converted to a script for repeated execution in a test plan.

QA PARTNER FROM SEGUE SOFTWARE

Product Name:	QA Partner
Purpose:	Automated testing
Platforms:	Windows, NT, 95, OS/2, Macintosh, UNIX (many)
Status:	Commercial Product
Company:	Segue Software
Address:	1320 Centre Street, Newton Centre, MA, 02159, USA
Phone:	617-796-1000
Fax:	617-796-1610
Email:	info@segue.com
Web:	http://www.segue.com

QA Partner is an advanced object-oriented tool for automated testing of GUI applications. It offers the same fundamental idea as capture/playback testing systems, but with a GUI twist. Some of its notable features include cross-platform testing, distributed testing and performance testing.

The single-most significant feature of *QA Partner* is its inherent support for GUI testing. Test scripts operate on a higher abstraction level than older testing tools. Objects in an application's GUI are treated as just that — *objects*. For example, input events are not tied to a particular screen location. Clicking on a window can be specified as an action on a window object and *QA Partner* will find the current location of that window at run-time. Similarly, the examination of test results goes beyond the old-style method of bitmap recording, which isn't really adequate for testing modern GUI applications.

The high abstraction level of test scripts offers an important advantage in cross-platform testing. The same scripts can be used to test an application on a variety of platforms, provided the *logical* organization of GUI objects is similar. Another interesting advantage is that testing international versions of the same product will not require major script changes.

All testing scripts are written in a 4GL language specifically designed for testing called Visual *4Test*. *4Test* offers low level constructs such as variables and flow of control alongside the higher level treatment of GUI objects. Notably, *4Test* is compiled rather than interpreted, so that scripts are not a performance burden. Scripts are created using the *Script Development Environment* which is a similar concept to a graphical environment for programming, or users can record/playback techniques.

CANTATA FROM IPL

Product Name:	Cantata
Purpose:	Dynamic testing, coverage analysis and static analysis
Platforms:	DOS, Windows 3.1, Windows 95, Windows NT, OS/2, VMS, PowerPC, UNIX (Solaris, Solaris-x86, SunOS, HP-UX, OSF/1, Ultrix, DG, AIX, Linux)
Languages:	C++, ANSI C, K&R C
Status:	Commercial Product
Company:	IPL — Information Processing Limited
Address:	Eveleigh House, Grove Street, Bath, BA1 5LR, UK
Phone:	+44-1225-444888
Fax:	+44-1225-444400
Email:	ipl@iplbath.com
Web:	http://www.iplbath.com/

Cantata is an automated testing tool for C and C++ programs that is commercially available from IPL. Cantata is available on a variety of platforms including UNIX, VMS, DOS, Windows and OS/2. Cantata offers three major features: dynamic testing, coverage analysis and static analysis. Results from these three areas can be incorporated into a single pass/fail scheme for test scripts.

Dynamic testing refers to the overall use of test scripts to execute tests and verify the program correctness for these tests. Cantata is not a capture/playback regression testing tool capable of testing the final product as a black box, but instead Cantata performs white box testing of the program by driving it from the inside. This makes Cantata valuable for unit testing and system integration testing.

The central test driver is the Cantata Test Harness (CTH) which is a library of testing directives. A test script is actually a `main` function in C/C++ which uses a structured format. The test script can be written manually or created using the Cantata Test Script generator utility. There are facilities for setting initial conditions, CHECK directives for testing whether test results are satisfactory, and all tests can be combined into a pass/fail scheme. Unit testing is aided by various stubbing features to mimic functions that are not available. Performance measurement values can also be created to identify bottlenecks for program tuning, and these measures can also be part of the pass/fail scheme. The most important outcome of the CTH-driven test executions is the results file that details steps, highlights failures, and summarizes the success or failure of all tests.

Coverage analysis examines the extent to which the tests have exercised the program. Coverage analysis can be incorporated into a dynamic test, and does not require postprocessing of result files. The implementation method is the instrumentation of source code using a special preprocessor. The supported coverage metrics include statement coverage, decision (or branch) coverage, condition coverage, and function call coverage. An interesting coverage measure is data value coverage where a variable is analyzed to ensure it has held all values from a user-specified set. Various reports show the results of the coverage analysis including highlighting of untested code.

Static analysis can be incorporated into the testing phase via the computation of various complexity metrics. There are two types of metrics available: "academic" metrics (e.g., McCabe's, Halstead's, Harrison's and others) and "common sense" metrics such as statement count metrics and various C++ class metrics. It is also possible to define your own metrics.

Static analysis can also allow the enforcement of coding style standards. For example, the standard might disallow `goto` statements or `switch` statements without a `default` clause. The various metrics can also be incorporated into a pass/fail coding standard.

Graphical reporting of results is possible via the Flowgraph Display System. This generates a picture file in PostScript or HPGL2 that shows the control flow of a module. This graph can be annotated with results from static analysis or the coverage results.

SOFTTEST — REQUIREMENTS-BASED TEST CASE GENERATION

Product Name:	SoftTest
Purpose:	Test case generation from requirements
Platforms:	Windows, OS/2, UNIX
Price:	$2,500 per license
Company:	Bender and Associates, Inc.
Address:	P.O. Box 849, Larkspur, CA 94977, USA
Phone:	+1-415-924-9196
Fax:	+1-415-924-3020
Email:	info@softtest.com

SoftTest is an automated test case generation tool that uses rigorous analysis of requirements to identify test cases and manage the testing process. SoftTest is not a tool that automates the execution of software tests. Instead, SoftTest is a management tool that can ensure test cases are adequate to fully exercise the requirements. SoftTest can be used in conjunction with manual testing procedures or other capture-playback regression testing tools. It does not matter what environment or programming language is used for the implementation of the product. In addition to offering SoftTest as a product, Bender & Associates offers consulting and training services to guide an organization to better quality.

SoftTest accepts a formal requirements document for an application, or a subsystem forming part of an application. This requirements document uses a precise specification language that avoids the ambiguities of natural language. The very production of such a precise specification of project requirements is an important issue in itself. SoftTest can immediately identify any blatant inconsistencies in the requirements.

SoftTest uses a rigorous mathematical approach to analyze the requirements document. The algorithm is based on the cause-effect graphing method developed in the 70's at IBM by William Elmendorf. Using this method, SoftTest generates a set of functional variations and then generates a set of test cases that test all functional variations. The set of test cases is chosen to be an efficient set without the redundancy inherent in random choice of test cases.

SoftTest offers a number of features for the management of test suites based on the requirements. A coverage matrix is available to show which test cases cover which function variations. A test definition matrix summarizes the entire test suite library. SoftTest also archives test suites and helps identify new cases needed when requirements change for enhancement requests.

PANORAMA C/C++ — STATIC AND DYNAMIC ANALYSIS TOOL

Product Name:	Panorama C/C++
Purpose:	Testing and QA via static and dynamic analysis
Platforms:	Windows 95, Windows NT, Solaris, SunOS, HP-UX
Price:	$995-$8,000
Company:	International Software Automation, Inc.
Address:	7677 Oakport Street, Suite 105, Oakland, CA 94621, USA
Phone:	510-632-6688
Fax:	510-632-3388 or 510-769-6269
Email:	isa@netcom.com

Panorama C/C++ is a suite of five tools for testing and quality assurance of C and C++ projects. The main features include complexity metrics, test coverage measurement, performance profiling, code browsing and documentation based on various structural views, and test case management. The front-end is a Motif GUI that provides many useful reports and code views. Alternatively, all of the static and dynamic analysis tests can be scripted for auto-mated results. The five integrated tools are now addressed in turn below.

Panorama OO-Test provides test coverage analysis with high level measures such as template class/function, down to lower level measures such as branch, segment, condition and condition-segment coverage. All results are presented intuitively in the GUI via bar graphs or highlighted source code listings. Panorama OO-Test can also analyze test case effectiveness and choose those test cases for the most cost-effective coverage.

Execution times and frequency are also recorded as part of the coverage analysis and the GUI can present execution profiles. These allow detection of performance bottle-necks for code optimization.

Panorama OO-SQA offers both static and dynamic metric analysis. Dynamic metrics are based on code coverage results. Static metrics include measures of inheritance, methods per class, coupling, and code reuse. All the metric results can be presented in color-coded bar charts, Kiviat diagrams or histograms.

Panorama OO-Browser generates the class inheritance graph, function call graph or class-function coupling chart from the source code. By navigating through the GUI you can investigate various relationships between classes and modules to assess maintenance impacts.

Panorama OO-Diagrammer generates various system-level, class-level and segment-level diagrams from source code. There is explicit support for navigating through the source code for assisted code inspections and walkthroughs, which are an important bug reduction coding technique. Using the coverage data from OO-Test, it can show analysis of path condi-tions covered and unexecuted segments.

Panorama OO-Analyzer generates over 150 reports and charts to document a program. Reports include information on classes, global and static variables, and complexity metrics. All reports are available through the GUI in a convenient index.

AUTOMATED TEST FACILITY — CLIENT/SERVER TESTING

Product Name:	Automated Test Facility
Purpose:	Automated testing of client/server applications
Platforms:	Windows 3.1, Windows 95, Windows NT, OS/2
Price:	$18,000 (starting configuration)
Company:	Softbridge, Inc.
Address:	125 CambridgePark Drive, Cambridge MA 02140, USA
Phone:	1-800-955-9190, 617-576-2257
Fax:	617-864-7747
Email:	market@sbridge.com

Automated Test Facility (ATF) is an automated testing tool that offers features such as regres-sion testing, performance testing, and load testing. ATF can be applied to standalone or client/

server applications written in any application development language, naturally including C++.

ATF allows automation of test cases through capture/playback methods or a flexible scripted approach. This allows novice users to use the simple capture/playback method of playing recorded "tapes" of events, and more technical users to write scripts for more advanced tests. The script language is highly advanced allowing a variety of actions including sending keystrokes or mouse events, analyzing windows, menu actions, and much more.

Testing of client/server applications is enabled through ATF's distributed architecture. One PC serves as the "executive" machine that controls all tests, and it can drive the events on up to fifty other machines in order to test client/server applications under realistic conditions. This allows the modeling of concurrent access, stress loads, and any distributed features of the application. Naturally, the ATF executive can control applications on its own box for testing simpler standalone applications.

ATF can run tests unattended and report on the results. Test validation methods include text comparison, bitmap comparison, file comparisons, database validation, and resource utilization analysis.

HINDSIGHT — TESTING AND COMPREHENSION TOOLSET

Product Name:	Hindsight
Purpose:	Software comprehension, testing and QA
Platforms:	Solaris, SunOS, HP-UX, OSF/1, AIX, SGI, NEC UNIX
Price:	$8,390
Company:	IntegriSoft
Address:	44 Airport Parkway, San Jose, CA 95110, USA
Phone:	1-800-867-8912, 408-441-0200
Fax:	408-441-8751
Email:	info@integrisoft.com
Web:	http://www.integrisoft.com

Hindsight is an advanced tool offering features for software testing, comprehension, static and dynamic analysis. There is support for C, C++ and Fortran programming languages. Hindsight is an integration of a variety of components:

• Hindsight/SLA — structure and logic analysis: automatically produce structure charts, J-diagrams, control flow graphs, and over 50 reports based on source code analysis. This helps programmers gain insight into their code for better comprehension, documentation, maintenance or reengineering. Users can navigate through the GUI to analyze structural information or produce hardcopy documentation. Printer formats include PostScript, HPGL, HPGL2 and PCL5.

- Hindsight/FC — flow charting: display a graphical flow chart for each function. This is a useful graph of the function's flow of control that can be annotated with line numbers or text from source code lines.

- Hindsight/TCA — test coverage analysis: instrument the code to collect coverage information during execution. Coverage measures include function, segment, and condition coverage. Textual reports are available and graphical feedback is available as structure charts or J-diagrams can be annotated with results of the coverage analysis.

- Hindsight/SIM — error simulation: the effectiveness of coverage analysis can be improved by seeding the program with simulated errors to test error handling or exception handling code. Functions can return a simulated value (e.g., for `malloc` to fail) with built-in support for over 800 UNIX system functions and user-defined functions.

- Hindsight/METRX — SQA metrics: the available metrics include static metrics such as function size, McCabe cyclomatic complexity, Halstead metrics, and dynamic metrics based on test coverage. Metrics are reported in tables, bar graphs, or Kiviat diagrams. Thresholds can be set on metric values and failing functions highlighted.

- Hindsight/RG — report generator: allows the generation of advanced documentation based on results of other Hindsight components. User reports can be created based on the various static and dynamic metrics.

- Hindsight/TPA — test planning analysis: allows analysis of the effectiveness of test cases. A minimization feature is available to remove any redundant test cases for more efficient testing. Reports on all the test cases are available.

- Hindsight/MT — module tester: better unit testing of modules is enabled by automatic creation of the driver function source code and a `makefile`. The unit tests can be created, compiled and executed automatically.

STW/Regression — Automated Regression Testing Toolset

Product Name:	STW/Regression
Purpose:	Automated regression testing capture/playback toolset
Platforms:	DOS, Windows 3.1, Windows 95, Windows NT, Solaris, Solaris-x86, SunOS, HP-UX, OSF/1, AIX
Company:	Software Research
Address:	625 Third Street, San Francisco, CA 94107-1997, USA
Phone:	1-800-942-SOFT, 415-957-1441
Fax:	415-957-0730
Email:	info@soft.com
Web:	http://www.soft.com

STW/Regression is a suite of tools for automated testing of batch and GUI applications. In addition there are components for remote testing, automated demonstration of applications, and test management.

The CAPBAK component functions as a capture/playback testing tool by allowing both capturing of test cases, and their creation using a script language. Replay and test scripts are in the C language to avoid the need to learn a new proprietary language. Correctness verification can be done on-the-fly or in a batch mode after execution. Verification methods includes bitmap comparison, widget comparison, and OCR-based text comparison.

The SMARTS utility is a more advanced method of automating the execution of the test cases. It allows organization of tests, automation of their execution, and the generation of various reports of the results. The status report lists all outcomes, the history report lists all tests known, the regression report lists only those tests that failed, and the certification report summarizes the success/fail ratio of tests. Through the use of an Automated Test Script (ATS), the SMARTS utility allows sophisticated test execution through the GUI or in an unattended batch mode.

The EXDIFF utility offers comparison of files and images for more sophisticated difference analysis. There is support for analysis of ASCII and binary files, and also pixel differencing of images saved by CAPBAK or the *xwd* standard X windows dump utility.

CTB — Automated Unit Test Generator

Product Name:	C Test Bed System
Purpose:	Test harness generator for unit tests
Platforms:	DOS, Windows NT, OS/2, Solaris, HP-UX, SGI, Linux
Price:	$1,350-$7,000
Company:	Testwell
Address:	Kanslerinkatu 8, FIN-33720 Tampere, Finland
Phone:	+358-31-316-5464 (+358-3-316-5464 from 12 Oct 96)
Fax:	+358-31-318-3311 (+358-3-318-3311 from 12 Oct 96)
Email:	olavip@cs.tut.fi

CTB solves the problem of how to perform unit tests on a C module or C API. CTB generates a test bed that enables rapid deployment of unit tests early in the development process. Automatic generation of unit tests is significantly easier than manual development, and the tests are usually more comprehensive.

CTB analyzes C header or source files to find interfaces to test, then generates test driver code automatically, and then all is linked with the CTB run-time library to create an executable performing the tests. The test driver can be run interactively with commands from the user, or in batch mode using a script file, which is useful for automating overnight execution of unit tests. The command syntax is actually a small C interpreter with extra support for testing commands such as test script execution.

The expected results of unit tests can be specified interactively or in the test scripts. Assertions are a powerful feature supported for specifying the correct results, and CTB automates assertion checking and records all failures. There is also optional testing for system errors such as setting the C *errno* variable and heap consistency.

There is powerful support for adding stub functions. This allows unit tests for subsystems to occur even if other components are not available. The stub facility can specify return values, check assertions, and perform various measurement and tracing tasks. Stubs can be removed easily via a compiler define as the true functions become available.

McCabe ToolSet — Testing, QA and Reengineering

Product Name:	McCabe Visual ToolSet
Platforms:	Solaris, Solaris-x86, SunOS, HP-UX, AIX, OSF/1, Ultrix, SGI, DG, SCO, Windows, Windows/NT, OpenVMS
Company:	McCabe & Associates, Inc.
Address:	5501 Twin Knolls Road, Suite 111, Columbia, MD 21045, USA
Phone:	800-638-6316, 301-596-3080
Fax:	410-995-1528
Email:	info@mccabe.com
Web:	http://www.mccabe.com

McCabe offers a large suite of advanced metric analysis, test coverage and visualization tools that automate various aspects of testing and quality assurance. These tools are offered for C++ programs and a large number of other programming languages. The use of metrics allows formal analysis of areas of the source code that are error-prone and unmaintainable. This technology is combined with tools for visualization of the structure of the program using graphical displays. In addition, McCabe offers dynamic testing tools, such as the McCabe Instrumentation Tool that measures how much source code was exercised by test cases.

The cornerstone of the technology is analysis of source code to compute complexity metrics. The well-known McCabe cyclomatic complexity metric bears the name of the company founder and this expertise carries over into the analysis tools with many metrics available. Some of the available metrics include traditional metrics such as the McCabe cyclomatic complexity metric, Halstead metrics, line count metrics, and integration complexity metrics, and a number of modern object-oriented metrics that are of specific value to C++ coding including measures of public data access, polymorphism and overloading, and class inheritance depth metrics. There is also the capability to specify new customized metrics or to derive new metrics from existing metrics, in order to satisfy a particular measurement need.

Metrics are presented in a variety of formats including tabular, scatterplot and Kiviat diagrams.

The McCabe Visual Toolset includes various visualization tools including the Battlemap Analysis Tool (BAT) for graphical information presentation. BAT works in two distinct modes: static analysis mode for code metrics, and dynamic analysis mode for test coverage visualization. In static analysis mode, BAT displays graphs of modules and components showing the structural organization, and displays nodes and green, yellow or red depending on whether the module is testable, unreliable or unmaintainable according to source code metrics. In dynamic analysis mode, BAT's green, yellow and red indicate levels of test coverage completeness, to quickly show where further test cases are needed. Another important view of the code offered by BAT is the flowgraph display that shows control flow paths in the code.

McCabe's white box testing tools offer unique insight into the tests required for validating source code modules. The use of the cyclomatic complexity metric identifies test cases required for complete unit testing of a module. The McCabe Instrumentation Tool tracks all tested paths and graphically displays all untested paths in unit and integration tests. The coverage measures include simple measures such as branch and statement coverage, and more complicated measures involving the cyclomatic complexity metrics.

McCabe's Visual Testing ToolSet offers a number of features for creating documentation for the testing process. There is support for export to FrameMaker and Interleaf, in addition to PostScript, HPGL and ASCII reports. There is also support for generation of documentation supporting standards such as DoD 2167A.

The McCabe Visual ToolSet supports reengineering and maintenance of a complicated software system through various features. The effect of a change or addition to the system can be analyzed by the tools and the results visualized easily. McCabe's support for a variety of languages aids in the migration of legacy code to the newer object-oriented paradigm.

## CHAPTER 15

Parser tools

T here are a variety of tools available for implementing parsers for programming and script languages in C and C++. The traditional UNIX favorites are the `lex` and `yacc` pair for generating a lexical analyzer and a parser component, respectively. These tools are "tried-and-true" and although many academics will tell you that `lex` and `yacc` are far from the state-of-the-art, they are still the de facto industry standard for C and C++. A number of free and commercial variants have sprouted up to facilitate development using `lex` and `yacc`, and there are now a few good books on the subject.

One reasonably common request related to parser generation is the generation of a parser for the C or C++ languages themselves. There are a number of `yacc` grammars available for C and C++. There are also example compilers with source code, and other products including test suites and fully-implemented C/C++ compiler front-ends, to assist you in building an application or tool requiring a C or C++ parser.

LEX — UNIX LEXICAL ANALYZER GENERATOR

The lex utility is a standard UNIX utility for generating a lexical analyzer component from a specification file. Lexical analysis refers to examining an input stream of characters and producing a stream of tokens as output. The lex input file specifies the patterns of tokens that the lexical analyzer will recognize. The lexical analyzer is implemented as C code generated by lex, and most modern implementations produce ANSI C code. This C file can be compiled and included in your program. Some implementations of lex require the linking of a separate library "libl.a" with the program. lex is often used in conjunction with the yacc utility to form a lexer and parser pair.

Table 16–1 lex options

Option	Meaning
-f	Faster tokenization (trades space with larger scanner tables)
-n	Do not display output
-t	Print file to standard output
-v	Verbose mode

FLEX — GNU LEXICAL ANALYZER GENERATOR

The flex utility is offered by GNU as an alternative to UNIX lex. The advantages include faster code and offers some extensions to the features. flex implements most of the functionality of lex but there are some obscure exceptions that are documented in the flex distribution. Some implementations of flex require the linking of a library "libfl.a" but later versions seem to have removed this need.

Table 16–2 flex options

Option	Meaning
-F	Faster scanning (larger tables)
-I	interactive scanner
-L	suppress #line directives
-T	trace mode
-8	generate 8-bit scanner
-b	backtracking information generated
-c	No effect (compatibility only)
-d	Debug mode
-f	Fast scanner (larger table)

Table 16–2 flex options *(Continued)*

Option	Meaning
-i	Case-insensitive
-n	No effect (compatibility only)
-p	Print performance report
-t	Produce file on standard output
-v	Verbose mode
-s	Suppress unmatched
-Cx	table compression options
-Sfile	skeleton file

YACC — UNIX PARSER GENERATOR

The `yacc` utility is a parser generator tool available under UNIX, and is an acronym for "yet another compiler compiler". There are a number of versions of `yacc` arising from Berkeley and System V UNIX variants. They are basically compatible but there are rare exceptions.

`yacc` is most often used with `lex` and there is much similarity between the two tools. Just like `lex`, `yacc` takes a description file and generates a C file as output. The description file for `yacc` is a language *grammar* which is a very general representation of a language syntax. For example, many programming languages including C can be represented by a grammar, and there are a number of `yacc` grammars that describe the C programming language as discussed in section "ANSI C Grammers" on page 248.

There are a number of useful options as shown in Table 16–3. In my experience the most useful are `-d`, `-v` and `-p`. The `-d` option is almost always used, and the `-p` option can help with multiple parsers. The `-v` option is useful in determining the cause of shift-reduce and reduce-reduce conflicts: the `-v` option generates the file "`y.output`" and you can then search for the keyword "conflict" in that file (possibly this tip is specific to one `yacc` variant).

Table 16–3 yacc options

Option	Meaning
-d	Define statements put in generated "y.tab.h" file
-v	Verbose mode; creates report file "y.output"
-l	Suppress #line directives in the output C file
-t	Enable debug mode in generated parser code
-p	Prefix to use instead of "yy"

BISON — GNU Parser Generator

bison is a utility very similar to yacc offered by GNU. All yacc features are supported and bison offers a large number of improvements. The file handling of bison and yacc differ in that "bison file.y" will produce "file.tab.c" whereas yacc always produces "y.tab.c". However, bison offers the "-y" option which will force it to generate "y.tab.c" for compatibility. Some of the extra features offered by bison are multiple parsers in one program and line number support in productions.

Table 16–4   Some of bison options

Option	Meaning
-y	Generate y.tab.c for compatibility with yacc
-d	Generate header file with token definitions
-l	Suppress #line directives
-p prefix	Use prefix instead of yy
-v	Verbose mode; generate output file
-V	Version of bison.

PCYACC from Abraxas Software

Product Name:	PCYACC
Purpose:	Parser generator
Platforms:	DOS, Windows 3.1, Windows 95, Windows NT, OS/2, Macintosh, Amiga, Atari, PowerPC, VMS, MVS, UNIX (Solaris, Solaris-x86, SunOS, HP-UX, AIX, OSF/1, DG, NCR/AT&T, ICL, Sequent, Unisys, Pyramid, Bull, etc.)
Languages:	ANSI C, C++
Status:	Commercial Product
Price:	$495 DOS/Win; $995 OS/2, Win NT; $1995 UNIX
Company:	Abraxas Software, Inc.
Address:	5530 SW Kelly Ave., Portland, OR 97201, USA
Phone:	1-800-347-5214, 503-244-5253
Fax:	503-244-8375
Email:	sales@abxsoft.com
FTP:	ftp://ftp.abxsoft.com
Web:	http://www.abxsoft.com

PCYACC is a complete environment for building LALR language parsers. There is both a lexical analyzer generator and a parser generator: PCLEX and PCYACC. Both have full backward compatibility with UNIX `lex` and `yacc` and also various enhancements.

PCLEX has various features in addition to UNIX `lex` features. There is no run-time library to link to in the generated scanner. There is a `-i` option to generate case insensitive scanners. The default lexer skeleton is also visible, and can be changed if needed. Multiple scanners can be defined in one program.

PCYACC generates ANSI C or C++ parser source code from the grammars. It is compatible with UNIX `yacc` input files and offers the usual features in error reporting, recovery, conflict resolution, and reporting. The C++ code that is generated is object oriented with YACC classes used. The parser can work with lexers from PCLEX or with hand-generated lexers that define a `yylex` function. Support for multiple parsers in a single program is also available. The skeleton parser can be modified, but the default skeleton is internal to the PCYACC program for improved performance. There is a **-t** option that generates an ASCII representation of the parse tree from the grammar.

The distribution includes good documentation, various full-blown examples, and extra tools. The additional development tools provided include a Yacc cross-reference tool and a Yacc debugger. Language engines for over 25 languages, naturally including C and C++, are provided in the distribution.

Yacc++ — lex and yacc in C++

Product Name:	Yacc++ and the Language Object Library
Platforms:	DOS, Windows 3.1, Windows 95, Windows NT, OS/2, HP-UX, Solaris, SunOS, SGI, DEC
Price:	$995 commercial; $500 academic/non-commercial
Company:	Compiler Resources, Inc.
Address:	85 Main Street, Suite 310, Hopkinton, MA 01748, USA
Phone:	508 435 5016
Fax:	508-435-4847
Email:	compres@world.std.com, CompuServe 74252,1375

Yacc++ is a commercial product for LR(1) parsing that is more than a rewrite of `lex` and `yacc` in object-oriented form. Yacc++ combines the functionality of `lex` and `yacc` in that C++ lexer and parser classes are automatically generated from lexical and grammar specification files. Yacc++ improves on `yacc` by extending the grammar notation with regular expression support that allows more natural expression of various language constructs including optional items without empty productions, and lists without recursive productions.

Existing `yacc` grammars are not fully compatible with Yacc++ for reasons such as the addition of a lexer section to the syntax. However, the upgrade path is well documented, and the incompatibility is probably a blessing in disguise because it encourages the use of better features in the Yacc++ grammar syntax.

There are a number of major features that remove good old `yacc`'s limitations. Multiple parsers are permitted in one program, and even multiple instances of the same parser because of reentrant parser and lexer objects. Yacc++ parsers can have multiple points of entry into the parse tree to allow matching with selected branches of the parse tree such as to allow matching of an expression within a grammar for an entire language. Reuse of code for partial grammar implementations is supported in Yacc++ by multiple inheritance and special grammar primitives. Yacc++ also allows the reversal of the traditional control flow where the parser called the input routines, to an event-driven version where the input routines collect a token and call the parser. Automatic generation of the abstract syntax tree (AST) is supported by a CONSTRUCT primitive in the grammar.

Yacc++ comes with the Language Object Library that provides a variety of classes related to parsing. AST objects are used by the CONSTRUCT primitive. Error objects write errors or pop up windows using Borland OWL or Microsoft MFC, and can also offer syntax assistance showing legal expected values at the place of the error. Input objects can read from istreams, fstreams, istrstreams or strings. Symbol table and symbol classes simplify the creation of the symbol processing that is usually required for a non-trivial language parser.

VISUAL PARSE++ FROM SANDSTONE

Product Name:	Visual Parse++
Purpose:	Parser generator
Platforms:	Windows 3.1 and 95, Windows NT, OS/2, UNIX (AIX, SunOS, SCO, HP)
Languages:	C, C++, Visual Basic, Delphi
Status:	Commercial Product
Price:	$299
Company	SandStone Technology
Address:	950 Shore Crest Road, Carlsbad CA 92009, USA
Phone:	619-929-9778
Fax:	619-929-9848

Visual Parse++ offers a GUI-based method of developing and debugging a language parser. The output programming language for the parser can be C, C++, Visual Basic or Delphi. Visual Parse++ generates data tables and a "`reduce`" member function to provide a full parser from the input grammar specification. The C++ parser uses C++ classes, and the C version uses a set of C API functions.

The power of the visual environment is fully enabled in the debugging phase where you can visually trace execution, and interactively control progress. During execution of your parser you can view many parser objects. You can view the input data stream and watch characters get consumed. The parser stack is always visible showing tokens. Lookahead symbols are also optionally shown. Grammar rule matches are shown visually through highlighting, shifts and shown visually, and reductions are shown in two stages for easy visualization. Errors are error recovery actions can also be watched in motion. Conflicts can be resolved interactively with the choice via a mouse click.

A variety of debugger-like features are available during parsing. Within the IDE you can step through parser actions, and set breakpoints on various conditions such as grammar rules. With a button click you can step, run, and animate, just like a good C/C++ integrated programming debugger.

In addition to all the visual features, there is some power underneath. Multiple parsers can be defined in one program. The lexer can read from files, streams and strings. A special `SyncErr` token is available for advanced error recovery. Parsers for C, C++, SQL, HTML, RTF, Modula 2 and other languages are also included in the distribution.

MKS Lex & Yacc

Product Name:	MKS Lex & Yacc
Purpose:	Parser generator
Platforms:	DOS, Windows 95, Windows NT, OS/2
Languages:	ANSI C, C++, Turbo Pascal
Status:	Commercial Product
Price:	$299
Company:	Mortice Kern Systems Inc. (MKS)
Address:	185 Columbia Street W., Waterloo, Ontario N2L5Z5
Phone:	1-800-265-2797; 519-883-4346,
Fax:	519-884-8861
Email:	sales@mks.com
FTP:	ftp.mks.com
Web:	http://www.mks.com

MKS Lex & Yacc is a parser generator tool compatible with UNIX `lex` and `yacc`, that builds a parser in C, C++ or Turbo Pascal. The product includes two distinct components: MKS Lex and MKS Yacc.

MKS Lex is compatible with UNIX `lex` and also has a number of advanced features. It handles the full 8-bit character set including null in the input stream. There is support for input from strings, streams or files. Multiple scanners are allowed in each program.

MKS Yacc is compatible with UNIX `yacc` with extra features. It offers optional static or dynamic allocation of parse tables, and has advanced error detection features. There is also support for multiple parsers in a single program. Conflict resolution is simplified by a unique preferences method for choosing the action.

The distribution also includes a tracing tool for debugging grammars called YACC Tracker. This allows interactive tracing of the parser actions during debugging. There are also example grammars for ANSI C, C++, Pascal, dBase IV, SQL, HyperTalk and PIC. Parsers generated by MKS Lex & Yacc can be distributed commercially without royalty.

ANSI C GRAMMARS

There are numerous sources for `yacc` grammars for C. Some of the sources are as follows:

ANSI/ISO C standard contains a grammar for C that is very close to being `yacc` acceptable.

Jeff Lee's yacc **grammar for ANSI C** which is based on the ANSI C standard grammar is available via anonymous FTP to *ftp.uu.net/usenet/net.sources/ansi.c.grammar.Z*. This is an ANSI C grammar from the April 1985 draft ANSI C standard. It is a full program to do syntax checking on C and includes a scanner and yacc grammar with one shift/reduce error for the if/else construct.

Jim Roskind's yacc **grammar for ANSI C** is available via anonymous FTP to ics.uci.edu in pub/*grammar*.

GNU C compiler contains a yacc grammar for C; see section "GNU C/C++ from Free Software Foundation" on page 21 for a discussion of acquisition details.

Kernighan and Ritchie, 2nd edition, has a grammar in an appendix of the book.

W. M. McKeeman and S. Trager and J. L. Cohen and T. Yang, "C Grammars", Technical Report 87-02, Wang Institute, February, 1987

SCHILDT, Herbert, "Building your own C interpreter", Dr Dobbs Journal, August 1989, SimTel sites *ddjmag/ddj8908.zip*; filename *schildt.lst*.

PCYACC from Abraxas Software (see Section "PCYACC from Abraxas Software" on page 244) has a drop-in C engine and a yacc grammar for C.

Visual Parse++ from SandStone Technology (see section "Visual Parse++ from SandStone" on page 246) has a drop-in C parser.

MKS Lex & Yacc from MKS includes an example of a full scanner and parser for ANSI C; see section "MKS lex & yacc" on page 247.

C++ GRAMMARS

Although the C++ language is hard to accurately describe in a grammar, there are quite a few offerings:

Jim Roskind's yacc **grammar for C++** is available via anonymous FTP to *ics.uci.edu* (128.195.1.1) in the *ftp/gnu* directory as files *c++grammar2.0.tar.Z* and *byacc1.8.tar.Z* Also available from *mach1.npac.syr.edu* (128.230.7.14) in the *ftp/pub/C++* directory as *c++grammar2.0.tar.Z* and *byacc1.8.tar.z*

ARM appendix has a C++ grammar; the full book reference is:

ELLIS, Margaret A., and STROUSTRUP, Bjarne, The Annotated C++ Reference Manual, Addison-Wesley, 1990. (Known as the "ARM")

John Dlugosz grammar for C++:

DLUGOSZ, John M., "A Home Brew C++ Parser", Dr Dobbs Journal, December 1989, available via anonymous FTP at Simtel sites as *ddjmag/ddj8912.zip*; filename *dlugosz.lst*

PCYACC from Abraxas Software (see section "PCYACC from Abraxas Software" on page 244) has a drop-in C++ engine and a yacc grammar for C++.

Visual Parse++ from SandStone Technology (see section "Visual Parse++ from SandStone" on page 246) has a drop-in C++ parser.

MKS Lex & Yacc from MKS includes an example grammar for C++; see section "MKS lex & yacc" on page 247.

Nathan Myers C++ parser written in C++ is available from *ftp://ftp.uu.net/ net.sources/c++.scanner.Z*

Compiler Test Suites

An important part of compiler design is testing. There are a number of sources of test suites for C and C++.

Plum Hall Test Suite: Plum Hall (1 Spruce Ave., Cardiff, NJ 08232, USA)

C Torture Test: The FSF's GNU C (gcc) distribution includes a *c-torture-test.tar.Z*

Kahan's paranoia test: FTP *research.att.com:/netlib*, tests C floating-point operations.

PERENNIAL C++ Validation Suite; phone: 408-748-2900; fax:408-748-2909; email: info@peren.com; address: Perennial, Inc., 4699 Old Ironsides Drive, Ste. 210, Santa Clara, CA 95054, USA. Over 25,000 test cases, exception handling, template testing, I/O streams, etc.

Modena Software, Test++ and OPT++: C++ Validation Suites from MODENA, 1-800-MODENA-1, Tel:408-354-5616, fax: 408-354-0846, email: modena@net-com.com; address: 236 N. Santa Cruz Avenue, Suite 213, Los Gatos, CA 95030, USA.

Test++: validation of all Draft ANSI/ISO C++ language features.

OPT++: C++ optimization test suite: tests whether the compiler performances advanced C++ optimizations: virtual function call elimination, return value optimization, copy optimization.

INLINE — FREE C INLINER

Tool Name:	inline
Status:	Copyright (all rights reserved)
Available:	comp.sources.unix/volume11/inline
Author:	S. McGeady
Address:	3714 SE 26th Ave., Portland, OR 97202
Phone:	(503) 235-2462

This tool was intended to offer performance enhancements by expanding all calls to functions defined as "inline" into straight line code. Since all C++ compilers now offer this trivially, this tool has no practical use. However, it is an interesting example of a compiler-like tool working on the token level without a grammar.

PLUM FREE C TIMING BENCHMARKS

Tool Name:	Plum benchmarks
Available:	comp.sources.unix/volume20/plum-benchmarks
Author:	Dr. Thomas Plum (Vice-Chair of the ANSI C Committee)

This distribution is a set of short C programs that time common C operations including function calls and expression operators. These can be used to measure the efficiency of compilers. They are highly portable and use the ANSI C `clock` function.

CHAPTER **16**

More Tools

FILE COMPARISON TOOLS

File comparison tools are most often part of a larger suite of tools for a source code versioning system or configuration management system. However, there are some stand-alone tools that can be occasionally useful. The most common need for comparing two similar source code files occurs with different versions of the same file. In a good versioning system this is a method of displaying changes between revisions. If your site has poor revision control then differencing tools can become important in comparing the multiple copies of source that appear. But if your site isn't using revision control then you have much bigger problems than whether there is a file difference tool!

diff — UNIX utility

The "diff" utility for line-based file differencing has been available with UNIX almost since inception. This is a utility accepting two filenames as arguments and producing a listing of the differences on standard output. This list can be inspected to identify the lines that are different. The algorithm used by diff is line-based and highly effective in presenting the lines that have changed in a format identifying blocks of altered lines. Some of the options to diff that can be useful for comparing source code files are in Table 16–1.

If the filename arguments to diff are actually directory names, diff performs a comparison of all files in the directories. This can be useful for comparing entire libraries of source code for differences.

Table 16–1 diff options

Option	Meaning
-c	Shows lines of context (additional lines near the changed lines)
-b	Ignore leading blanks (spaces and tabs)
-e	Patch output format for ed
-i	Ignore case of letters
-t	Expand tabs into spaces for comparison (tabs stay in output)
-w	Ignore whitespace totally for comparison (spaces and tabs)

The list of differences produced by "`diff -e`" is actually in a patch format accepted by the UNIX "`ed`" utility. This feature of `diff` allows the second file to be re-created from the first file and the differences, but this is a feature I've never had occasion to use.

dxdiff — UNIX graphical file differences

The `dxdiff` tool is available on some UNIX platforms, notably DEC Alpha platforms. It provides a graphical view of differences in two files, by placing the two files in adjacent subwindows with highlighted areas pointing out the differences. Although the difference algorithm appears similar to the UNIX `diff` command, the graphical dimension makes all the difference! No longer is there any need to try to decode the cryptic output and line numbers of `diff`.

A more advanced version of `dxdiff` is available on some platforms, and indeed probably most by the time you read this. The main advance is a "merge" capability offering a "splat" button whereby a third file can be created interactively taking pieces of the two files that you require.

tkdiff — free TCL-based graphical file differences

The `tkdiff` tool by John Klassa is part of the free distribution of tools using the TCL scripting language. `tkdiff` is ported to a wide variety of platforms, as with all TCL tools. The display of file differences is similar to that of `dxdiff` with side-by-side display of the files, combined scrolling, and graphical highlighting of sections of code that differ. There is built-in support for `rcs/cvs` revisioning systems. There is no merging capability yet. `tkdiff` is available from the TCL archives at *ftp.aud.alcatel.com/tcl/code/tkdiff**.

bdiff — UNIX tool for differencing large files

The UNIX `bdiff` utility is almost identical to the UNIX `diff` utility except that it is capable of handling larger files. It breaks up long files and passes parts of them through `diff`. Obviously I don't write large enough programs since I've never had cause to use this tool.

sdiff — UNIX side-by-side diff with merging

The UNIX `sdiff` utility prints the two files side-by-side with each line separated from the line in the other file by a margin of spaces. If the lines differ then `sdiff` places a > or < in the margin to indicate added or deleted lines. By default allow lines are displayed, but the `-s` option shows only different lines. This output format is as close as you can get to a graphical display of differences in a text-based window.

Interactive merging is another advanced feature offered by sdiff. When launched with the `-o` option, `sdiff` stops whenever it detects a difference and waits for a user choice. This command-line choice using one character answers to choose an action is not the easiest to use, but is effective.

rcsdiff and sccsdiff — not useful as general differencing tools

`rcsdiff` is part of the GNU `rcs` versioning tool, and `sccsdiff` is part of the UNIX `sccs` versioning tool. Neither `rcsdiff` nor `sccsdiff` are usable as a general file differencing utility. Both rely on the existence of a source code repository and are used to difference versions of source files.

GNU diffutils and wdiff

GNU software archives include two sets of file differencing tools. The `"diffutils"` package includes GNU versions of `diff`, `sdiff`, `diff3`, and `cmp`. These offer the usual features of their UNIX versions with some GNU extensions including handling of character sets and binary files. The GNU `wdiff` tool is a front-end to GNU `diff` that compares two files for word differences. It is particularly useful for comparing two documents that have been edited and reformatted with words redistributed across lines. Theses tools are available from any GNU archive site.

WISH — Token-based file differences

Although file differencing tools such as `diff` and `dxditt` are very useful, it would be so much more useful to offer an intelligent differencing algorithm based on knowledge of C/C++ syntax. The `-b` and `-w` options to `diff` that ignore whitespace are a start, but it would be far more useful to apply the difference algorithm at the token level. Another partial solution is to write a script that compares two files by piping them through `cb` to format them, and then pass them to `diff` or `sdiff` to show differences.

Ideally this kind of new difference tool would be integrated into source management tools such as `rcs` and `cvs`. The advantages would be, for example, the ability to ignore changes made to comments or indentation (e.g., if another programmer reformats your code!), and this would focus your attention onto the actual important changes in the code. This would be very useful whenever you're trying to perform code maintenance.

MAKE AND RELATED TOOLS

The UNIX standard utility called "make" is a widely used tool under UNIX. However, Windows programmers won't understand what all the fuss is about, nor indeed will UNIX programmers with the budget to afford a good CASE tool or IDE. The ability to build a project from source code files is an automatic feature to most Windows compiler environments and more advanced IDE platforms. This is definitely a major weakness in UNIX as a development platform. Maybe this weakness explains the recent joke from one of my Windows colleagues' that "unfortunately we still have to support legacy platforms such as UNIX".

The UNIX make utility

In the UNIX environment, there is a utility to aid in the design and maintenance of multiple-file programs called "make". Once set up, make automates the build process for a project. The programmer need only type "make", and the files needing to be compiled are compiled automatically. The make utility examines the dates of modification of files, to see if they have changed, and recompilation occurs if needed.

The disadvantage of using make is the need to create a special file in the directory, called "Makefile" or "makefile". This file is a text file that specifies which files of your program depend on other files, and the compiler options to specify.

When a makefile controls a large number of files, some of the options to make can be useful. The important options for UNIX make are shown in Table 16–2.

Table 16–2 Common make options

Option	Meaning
-f file	Filename of the makefile
-i	Ignore return values in failed commands
-k	Continue on non-dependent files after failure
-n	No execute — only print commands
-s	Silent mode — suppress printing of commands
-t	Touch files that need updating rather than execute commands

The -f option specifies the file to be used instead of the default files "makefile" or "Makefile".

The -s option causes make to suppress the printing of the commands it executes. However, it does not suppress the output produced by the commands when they are executed.

The -n option displays the commands that make would normally execute, but does not execute them. This is useful to see which files would be recompiled.

The -t (touch) option touches those files that are out of date. In other words, it marks them as recompiled without actually recompiling them. For example, this can be useful if a source code change would lead to needless compilation, such as adding comments in a header file. However, probably preferable to using "make -t" is a safer method of "untouching" the header file only. This can be done by using the UNIX `touch` command. In fact, I have an "`untouch`" script that touches header files back to an early date. The `-l` option to the `ls` command displays file modification times and the `-t` option will list files ordered by this timestamp.

The `-i` option causes `make` to ignore the return results from the shell commands it executes. This explains how `make` knows to stop compiling when a syntax error occurs — because `cc` returns a non-zero value. However, there are cases when it is annoying to rely on these values (e.g., when a program is returning the wrong value). Note that it is also possible to prefix a particular command with a minus sign causing only that command's return value to be ignored.

After a major change to a number of the C source files, it is sometimes desirable to recompile the lot. The `make` command will do this, but has the problem that it will stop if one file has a syntax error. There is nothing more annoying than beginning a build before lunch and returning to find a syntax error message in the first file. The `-k` option specifies that `make` continue with any other compilation not dependent on a problematic file. The file with the syntax error can then be fixed, and `make` executed again, this time only recompiling the offending file and linking some libraries. Note that the `-i` option could be used to ignore the returned value, but this would lead to a dangerous link of old object files into the executable. Unfortunately, error messages are often missed in the output, so the `-k` option can lead you to run an old executable and wonder why the bug didn't get fixed. This is bad enough, but `-i` would lead to an inconsistent executable. To avoid this problem with `-k`, either check the executable file dates, or try plain "`make`" without options, to make sure all files compiled.

MKS make

MKS offers an advanced `make` utility as part of its generic suite of UNIX-like utilities for DOS and Windows platforms. MKS `make` supports extensions to ensure compatibility with `makefiles` from BSD `make` and System V `make`. The `makefile` extensions from Borland `make` and Microsoft `make` are not all fully supported due to incompatibility, but can be easily resolved.

Company:	Mortice Kern Systems Inc.
Address:	185 Columbia Street W., Waterloo, Ontario N2L5Z5, Canada
Phone:	1-800-265-2797, 519-884-2251
Fax:	519-884-8861
Email:	inquiry@mks.com, sales@mks.com
CompuServe:	73260,1043
BIX:	mks
BBS:	519-884-2861
Web:	http://www.mks.com/

GNU make

The GNU software version of the `make` utility is a high-quality tool. It supports POSIX 1003.2 and includes most BSD and System V extensions. Various GNU additional extensions include parallel compilation, long options, conditional execution, and text manipulation functions.

In my experience, GNU `make` is one of the best make tools available with its stability and support for advanced features. The building or porting of GNU `make` is usually one of the first steps in porting a UNIX project, even to a non-UNIX platform. GNU `make` is available as part of all GNU software archives.

makedepend — generate make dependency lists

The `makedepend` utility examines C source files to determine which files depend on other files. The output from `makedepend` can be used in `makefile` entries for the `make` utility. In this way, `makedepend` automates the determination of the build order for larger projects.

There are a number of implementations of `makedepend` or similar tools. Notably, `makedepend` is freely available from GNU archives as part of the GNU `make` toolset.

Most implementations of `makedepend` have the option of modifying the `makefile` in place by using a line something akin to *"don't delete this line — makedepend depends on it!"*. I don't really recommend this usage because it plays havoc with the deltas on the `makefile` in versioning systems, with large changes each time you check it in. I prefer to create a separate dependency file that is included by the `makefile`, and not checked into the repository.

Most UNIX C compilers offer built-in features to compute dependency lists. The most common option is the `-M` option to `cc` or the GNU C compiler.

mkmf — free makefile editor

Tool Name:	mkmf
Purpose:	makefile editor
Availability:	Linux sites: e.g., sunsite.unc.edu:/pub/Linux/devel/make/mkmf*
Authors:	Peter J. Nicklin, Michael F. Wilkinson

`mkmf` is a utility used to create `makefiles` for the `make` utility. This allows a more intuitive method of expressing dependencies and build commands.

pmake — free parallel make tool

This is a Linux port of the `pmake` utility. It offers the power to perform `make` commands in parallel for faster building.

Tool Name:	`pmake`
Purpose:	Parallel make tool
Availability:	Linux sites: e.g. sunsite.unc.edu:/pub/Linux/devel/make/pmake*
Author:	Karl London

cook — free build and dependency analysis tool

Tool Name:	`cook`
Purpose:	make-like dependency analysis and building
Platforms:	UNIX (many), Linux
Availability:	ftp.agso.gov.au /pub/Aegis (with the Aegis versioning system) Linux sites: e.g. sunsite.unc.edu:/pub/Linux/devel/make/cook*
Author:	Peter Miller

`cook` is a tool similar in purpose to `make`. It analyzes the dependencies to determine the need to rebuild files, and then executes the commands necessary to do so. Unfortunately, I have not had the time to evaluate how `cook` compares with the various `make` utilities.

Icmake — make utility using C-like syntax

Tool Name:	`Icmake`
Purpose:	Intelligent make with C-like syntax
Availability:	Linux sites: sunsite.unc.edu:/pub/Linux/devel/make/icmake*
Authors:	Frank B. Brokken and Karel Kubat

`Icmake` is a `make`-like utility that uses a C-like syntax rather than the usual `makefile` format. Hence, `Icmake` is an alternative to `make`, rather than an improved version.

WISH — UNIX GUI-based project definition

Being very UNIX-centric here, I'll wish for a GUI-based tool for building projects, with a lower price tag than the serious CASE tools. It seems a fairly simple application to write needing features such as:

- GUI-based mapping of files to libraries, libraries to executables, etc.
- GUI-based building of projects
- graphical display of dependencies
- automatic generation of dependencies (`makedepend` is somewhat slow)

PREPROCESSORS

The preprocessor is usually part of the compiler and gets little or no recognition as a tool. However, most compilers allow the preprocessor phase to run separately, typically with a "-E" option, which offers up its full power as a separate tool. In addition, there are a handful of tools that are similar to the standard C/C++ preprocessor in functionality, but have features specifically intended as a special purpose tool.

/lib/cpp — UNIX C preprocessor

Most UNIX platforms that offer a C compiler called "cc" also offer a separate executable called "cpp" (for C Pre-Processor). Typically the preprocessor is available as "/lib/cpp".

Compilers as preprocessors

Most compilers have some form of option to run the preprocessor phase separately and capture the output after preprocessing. The most common form is the "-E" option to the compiler, as is common for compilers on UNIX and also for Windows compilers when run in batch mode.

cccp — free GNU C preprocessor

The GNU C/C++ compiler comes with its own fully functional preprocessor called cccp. The preprocessor is a separate component that offers the usual options for a preprocessor, and some GNU extensions. cccp is available from GNU software archives as part of the gcc distribution.

unifdef — UNIX partial preprocessor

The unifdef utility allows the removal of #ifdef and other conditional compilation preprocessor directives. unifdef does not do file inclusion or expand any macros, and its only feature is to copy source code to standard output with the appropriate conditional compilation blocks included or elided. The -D option specifies which macros are to be considered when expanding conditional blocks. Any conditional code blocks that do not involve these macros are copied to output retaining the #ifdef, #else and #endif directives.

unifdef arose in the public domain, but I am not aware of an FTP site containing its sources or binaries. However, it is available as installed software with some UNIX variants, notably Solaris and HP-UX.

scpp — free selective C preprocessor

scpp is a special C preprocessor that does not perform macro expansion or conditional compilation by default. This allows it to be used to expand particular macros, or to remove blocks of code depending on a particular macro (e.g., for a particular platform). The -Mmacro option is used to specify a macro that should be expanded to its replacement value, and should have conditional compilation directives such as #if, #ifdef and #ifndef handled: scpp will

Tool Name:	scpp
Purpose:	Selective C preprocessor
Availability:	comp.sources.unix/volume3/scpp/
Author:	Brad Needham

only expand `#if` conditional compilation directives that do not depend on the value of any unspecified names (i.e., all macro names must be specified by `-M` to expand a `#if` expression and its code blocks). The set of options is rounded out by `-C` to retain comments and whitespace in the output, `-Idir` to specify the include file path, and the `-Dmacro=value` option that gives a value to a macro name (and implies `-M` for that macro).

Decus cpp — free C preprocessor for Decus C

Tool Name:	Decus cpp
Purpose:	Preprocessor for C
Platforms:	VAX/VMS, UNIX
Availability:	comp.sources.unix/volume1/cpp/
Author:	Martin Minow

Decus `cpp` is a public-domain implementation of the C preprocessor dating from 1985, conforming to what was then the draft ANSI C standard. Note that the extraction from the *comp.sources.unix* archive is a little involved as it is not shell archived, but the instructions are given. `cpp` acts similarly to the standard C preprocessor acting as a filter from `stdin` to `stdout` if no file arguments, taking input from a single file argument, and using any second file argument as a destination file (beware the pitfall that "cpp *.c" will overwrite the second C file!). The options to `cpp` are shown in Table 16–3.

Table 16–3 Options to cpp

Option	Meaning
-C	Comments are preserved in the output
-Dname,-Dname=value	Define macro for expansion
-E	Errors ignored in the cpp exit status
-Idirname	Add dirname to directories searched for include files
-N	Suppress builtin macro definitions
-Stext	Special platform type handling option
-Uname	Undefine macro name

cpp supports most ANSI C constructs including #elif, the '\xNN', '\a' and '\v' escapes, the __LINE__, __FILE__ and __DATE__ special macros, token concatenation # operator, and an extension to allow $ in identifiers. Some ANSI C cases are not handled correctly, such as unsigned values in #if expressions.

tpp — free preprocessor for TCL based on Decus cpp

tpp is a preprocessor for TCL adapted by Ken Edwards from the Decus cpp sources. Because of changes to the semantics, this tool is not of value for C or C++ preprocessing, but the reference may be of interest to anyone working with the Decus cpp sources. tpp is available from the standard TCL archives at *ftp.aud.alcatel.com/tcl/code/tpp**.

SOURCE CODE OBFUSCATORS

Tools for source code obfuscation or "shrouding" aim to change the source code so that it is not human readable, but is understood by the machine and will still compile and run. The main use of these tools is for commercial or shareware distribution of software in source code format but in a way that protects the intellectual property. Source code distribution simplifies the distribution of software for multiple platforms and is used successfully by a number of vendors.

The aim of obfuscation is to remove information that is useful to humans but unnecessary for the compiler. Typical transformations on the source code include removing comments, removing unnecessary whitespace, changing identifier names, and even modification of flow statements. Since the aim is for protection of useful information, the source code should resist attempts to use other tools such as pretty printers to reverse the changes. Although removing whitespace can be reversed, in a competition between obfuscators and pretty printers, the obfuscator will always win. Removal of comments is obviously nonreversible, changing loops to goto statements is almost impossible to resolve using a tool, and although identifier renaming can be automatically fixed, the more complex conversion of distinct identifiers in different scopes to the same identifier can make the process more difficult.

Obfuscated C contest

Although it doesn't really qualify as a "tool", there is a regular competition on the Internet for the most obfuscated C programs. The programs shown there are ingenious in the way their true intent is hidden. Some of my favorites have been a program with "main" declared as an array variable instead of a function, where the array contained data representing machine code (this actually works on some systems). And my favorite program used identifiers like _314 and _31459, was formatted in the shape of pi, and computed (can you guess?) the value of the mathematical constant *e*.

Name:	International Obfuscated C Contest
Availability:	FTP to ftp.uu.net as files pub/ioccc/* comp.sources.unix:volume15/ioccc/ comp.sources.unix:volume14/ioccc comp.sources.unix:volume9/old.bad.code comp.sources.misc:ioccc.1992/part0[1-5] comp.sources.misc:ioccc.1993/part0[1-4]

opqcp — free obfuscator for C

Tool Name:	opqcp
Status:	Free (commercial use unclear)
Availability:	comp.sources.misc/volume13/opqcp/
Author:	Russ Fish

opqcp is a preprocessor for C that obscures the meaning of C source code to protect intellectual property. Although the source distribution is quite old (from 1980!), the tool is still interesting although not nearly as polished as the commercial tool from Gimpel Software.

The standard C preprocessor is used to strip comments and whitespace, and to expand preprocessor macros and includes. A dictionary of global identifiers is used to translate identifiers to less readable names. This dictionary file must be created from the object files, such as by using the UNIX nm command, and is specifiable using the -d option to opqcp. The dictionary can specify a global to remain unchanged (e.g., printf) or to convert identically for all files (e.g., for a global typedef name). All identifiers not in the global dictionary are assumed to be local and are mapped uniquely within each file.

The C Shroud - source code obfuscation

Product Name:	The C Shroud
Purpose:	Source code protection for C
Platforms:	DOS, OS/2, UNIX
Languages:	ANSI C, K&R C
Status:	Commercial Product
Price:	$1298 (one-user / one-CPV license)
Company:	Gimpel Software
Address:	3207 Hogarth Lane, Collegeville, PA 19426, USA
Phone:	610-584-4261

Fax:	610-584-4266
Email:	gimpel@netaxs.com

The purpose of *The C Shroud* is to allow vendors the convenience of distribution of source code rather than binary but still protect intellectual property. Distribution of source has various advantages such as not requiring hardware on which to rebuild binary executables, easier support, and freedom from viruses.

The C Shroud achieves source code obfuscation by performing a number of translations that remove redundant information leaving only that required by the compiler. Some of the translations are removing comments, indentation removal, translating identifiers to random names (except for special library identifiers such as EOF or stdout), translating control flow structures such as if, if-else, for, while, do-while, continue and break into equivalent forms using the goto statement (goto considered useful!), and converting string and character constants to use hexadecimal or octal escape codes. Identifier translation is further confused by using the same strange names for different nonconflicting name spaces, which helps to thwart reverse-engineering by identifier renaming. Optional header file, conditional compilation and macro expansion are available, but not always desirable as they can often contain platform dependent information that is crucial.

The technique of source code shrouding is an interesting one. The idea for *The C Shroud* arose when Gimpel Software sought a cost-effective means to distribute the *PC-lint* source code checker for many non-PC platforms. *The C Shroud* is still used for distributing this checker product which is now called *FlexeLint*.

TEACHING TOOLS

Learning C or C++ is never a trivial task. Despite claims that C is a "small" language with few keywords, there are a myriad of special cases in the core language features, and plenty of standard library functions to cover. C++ is an even larger language and thus an even greater learning challenge.

Any tools that help this learning process are very welcome, and thankfully there are a few such tools. In this chapter we examine a few utilities to teach particular aspects of the language, including one particularly novel game playing method.

cparen: free tool to parenthesize expressions

cparen is a tool that parenthesizes C expressions, and is useful for those who don't want to memorize the 15 precedence levels of C's operators. cparen accepts a single expression (not an entire C file) from stdin and produces the parenthesized version on stdout.

I had some difficulty obtaining a copy of cparen via FTP; but after a search on the keyword "cparen" using the "archie" network searching tool, I found it at the site *pluto.ulcc.ac.uk* in the directory */convex_ug/us_archive_1992* as the file *cparen.tar.Z*. Note that cparen is primarily UNIX-based mainly because of its use of lex and yacc in the building process.

cdecl and c++decl: free tool to create and explain declarations

Tool Name:	cdecl and c++decl
Purpose:	Create and explain C/C++ declarations
Languages:	C and C++
Status:	Free
Availability:	FTP comp.sources.unix archive; volume14/cdecl2
	FTP comp.sources.unix archive; volume6/cdecl (original)
	FTP SimTel c:/cdecl.zip (DOS version)
Key Points:	Converts English to C or C++ declarations
	Converts C or C++ to English

cdecl is a UNIX-based free tool for converting C or C++ declarations into English text, and vice versa. Thus it can be used to explain complicated declarations and also to produce such declarations from an English explanation of a type.

There are three main commands which allow different conversions. The *declare* command takes an English-like type description and creates a C declaration. The *cast* command takes English and creates a C type cast. The *explain* command takes a C or C++ declaration and produces an Engish explanation.

cdecl is available via FTP as part of the *comp.sources.unix archive*. There are various archive sites including *ftp.uu.net* (USA) in the *usenet* directory, *archie.au* (Australia) in the *usenet* directory, or *gatekeeper.dec.com* (USA) in the *pub/usenet* directory; within these directories, the file appears in the sub-directory *comp.sources.unix/volume14/cdecl2* as a *shar* archive in two parts. The distribution includes *c++decl* for C++.

crobots and c++robots: free teaching game

Tool Name:	crobots, c++robots
Purpose:	Game for teaching C or C++
Availability:	SimTel archive c/crobots.zip
Authors:	Tom Pointdexter, Richard Rognlie

crobots is a game that teaches C in a novel way. Players compete by writing C programs that control their robots during a shootout with opposing robots. In this way students enhance their ability to write effective C programs and thereby learn the fundamentals of the language in a stimulating contest.

The crobots server consists of a C interpreter/compiler that accepts a large subset of the C language with only a few semantic differences (e.g., short-circuiting of the && operator is not properly handled). There are also many extensions to offer various built-in functions that offer control over the robot's direction, motion, and firing.

PORTING TOOLS

Porting a product written in C or C++ across many platforms is usually a grinding manual task involving resolution of issues including compiler feature differences and run-time library behavioral changes. Unless code has been written with portability in mind from the beginning, porting usually involves adding #ifdef's and implementing missing library functions. Fortunately there are a few tools that can help reduce the effort. Libraries of functions are available for many platforms.

Porting GUI code is a notoriously difficult task to perform by hand. A number of GUI tools make it possible to port a Motif GUI to a Windows environment and vice-versa — although the look-and-feel of the ported GUI is not identical to one that would arise from a native re-implementation, it can be a cost-effective solution. The most portable GUI development method when starting a new project is probably the use of one of the many commercial multi-platform GUI builder tools, many of them part of a 4GL-based development environment, but these are unfortunately beyond the scope of this book. This discussion is limited to those tools that help in the porting of existing C or C++ code to other platforms.

NuTCRACKER from DataFocus — UNIX to Windows porting

Product Name:	NuTCRACKER
Purpose:	Porting UNIX X/Motif programs to Windows 32-bit platforms
Platforms:	Windows NT (x86, Alpha, MIPS, PowerPC), Windows 95
Company:	DataFocus Inc.
Address:	12450 Fair Lakes Circle, Suite 400, Fairfax, VA 22033, USA
Phone:	1-800-637-8034, 703-631-6770
Fax:	703-818-1532
Web:	http://www.datafocus.com

NuTCRACKER aids in porting of Motif GUIs to Windows 32-bit native GUI platforms. In addition to GUI porting, *NuTCRACKER* provides implementations of basic UNIX system level operations to aid in porting non-GUI code. *NuTCRACKER* provides a suite of Windows DLLs that map the X/Motif API to the native Windows API. The X/Motif or character-based UNIX application can be ported to Windows by a recompilation of the UNIX source code on a Windows box. Microsoft Visual C++ is strongly supported as a development platform for the Windows version, although DataFocus also resells various MKS tools for those who want a UNIX-like environment. The resulting application has a Motif look-and-feel on Windows, or you can use the newer Wintif library for a native Windows look-and-feel.

NuTCRACKER is one tool I have no hesitation in recommending. We used it internally and got a Windows NT prototype up within a week. *NuTCRACKER* changes the GUI porting issue from a nightmare of recoding low-level X/Motif code in Windows API, to a process of resolving various minor non-GUI porting issues.

Wind/U from Bristol Technology — Windows to UNIX porting

Product Name:	Wind/U
Purpose:	Porting Windows API and MFC to UNIX or OpenVMS Motif
Platforms:	UNIX (HP, Sun, DEC, IBM, SGI, others), OpenVMS
Company:	Bristol Technology, Inc.
Address:	241 Ethan Allen Highway, Ridgefield, CT 06877, USA
Phone:	203-438-6969
Fax:	203-438-5013
Email:	info@bristol.com
Web:	http://www.bristol.com/

Wind/U is a porting tool for converting Windows C++ applications to UNIX or OpenVMS. Wind/U ports the Win16 and Win32 API sets and the Microsoft Foundation Classes (MFC) to use the Motif/X Windows interface on UNIX and OpenVMS. This makes porting a mere recompilation, and therefore allows a rapid development time with minimal code changes and identical functionality across platforms. Keeping the same source code tree is no longer out of the question.

Wind/U supports many Windows features on UNIX including OLE 2.0, MFC 4.0, MDI, GDI, DLLs, DDEML, WinSock, file I/O libraries, etc. Printing is supported via Post-Script support, and internationalization including DBCS support is enabled via Motif features. Hence, Wind/U supports porting of the GUI and non-GUI parts of your application. You can even convert your online help WinHelp files to UNIX using Bristol's HyperHelp tool. There are also a number of other useful utilities including a `makefile` generator, a source code checker for common portability pitfalls called "prepare_source", and Wind/U Spy, a message spying utility that runs on UNIX.

MainWin XDE— Windows to UNIX porting

Product Name:	MainWin XDE
Purpose:	Porting Windows applications to UNIX
Platforms:	SunOS, Solaris, Solaris-x86, HP, AIX, SCO, DEC, SGI
Company:	Mainsoft Corporation
Address:	1270 Oakmead Parkway, Suite 310, Sunnyvale, CA 94086, USA
Phone:	1-800-MAIN-WIN, 408-774-3400
Fax:	408-774-3404

Email:	info@mainsoft.com
Web:	http://www.mainsoft.com

MainWin XDE is a development tool for porting Windows applications to UNIX using the native X calls. This makes porting a recompilation with the MainWin libraries that map Windows API and MFC calls to native X API calls. Hence, the same source code base can be used on Windows and UNIX platforms with minimal differences.

The GUI resulting from a port can have either a Windows look-and-feel or a Motif look-and-feel. What is even more impressive is that this can be changed on-the-fly!

In addition to mapping of GUI API calls, MainWin XDE maps many other Windows features to UNIX. Supported features include low-level libraries, OLE, and printing via Post-Script generation. In addition to allowing source code sharing, various other application components can be converted. There is a resource compiler for porting resources to UNIX, and support for online help files via MainWin Help. Automated test scripts from Microsoft Test can be reused directly using MainWin Test, and the source code repository itself can be shared between Microsoft Visual SourceSafe and MainSoft's Visual SourceSafe for UNIX.

VERSIONING AND CONFIGURATION MANAGEMENT TOOLS

Versioning tools are also called revision control tools. Whatever you call them, versioning tools are a necessity for a multi-programmer project. Without them team coding is an atmosphere charged with cries of, "Hey Bob, do you have this file open?" Versioning tools prevent the lost changes problem automatically, provide historical logging of changes to files, allow rollback to previous versions of files or entire projects, and allow concurrent development of different versions of the product in the same source tree. Unfortunately, with some of the weaker locking-based versioning tools the atmosphere becomes charged with email messages of, "Hey Bob, can you *please* unlock this file!" However, with a good versioning tool, team coding can proceed with minimal disruption. That is, except for the occasional, "Bob, stop #@!^%$ reformatting my code!"

Configuration management tools are even more general than source code versioning tools, but not quite as general as CASE tools, although the distinction is becoming less clear. Versioning tools often handle versions of source code but not much else. A full-blown configuration management tool will coordinate all aspects of a product release, including source code, executables and binary files, and documentation files. Integration with a defect tracking system is another common feature whereby source code revisions can be tagged with a failure record, which allows better tracking of what fixes developers made (if any!) to resolve a support issue.

VERSIONING FEATURES TO LOOK FOR

Listed below are a number of the more advanced features that a good versioning tool may offer, some of which were already alluded to in the introduction. Although these features may not be so important for use in very small groups, these issues become increasingly important for larger groups of developers.

- Locking versus non-locking file modification checkout policy — In a locking policy each developer must "check out" a file to modify it, and no other developer can do the same until the first developer checks it back in. This prevents two developers working in the same file at the same time. While this policy encourages modularity, I prefer a non-locking policy where multiple developers can change a file, and the versioning tools resolve at check-in time any cases where a file has two concurrent changes.
- Remote developer support — handling long-distance development transparently. In these days of telecommuting the aim is to support developers in the remote geographical areas. The simplest policy is to have no special support and force developers to remotely access the file server. More advanced tools offer methods whereby a separate copy of the source files is maintained remotely, and regularly merged with the primary source code repository.
- Security/access control per file — This is desirable to enforce security, protect against inadvertent mistakes, and consolidate the build process. Sometimes it is preferable to prevent some developers from changing version or tag numbers, or even to prevent users from editing particular source code files. With this feature, you can even stop someone reformatting your code!
- Automated triggers — This refers to the automatic launching of commands on various actions. For example, a trigger on check-in should be able to apply a source code metric or error-checking tool, and reject the check-in if the module fails to meet standards. Another useful one is automated email to inform other developers or the administrators of changes to the repository.
- Defect tracking system integration — In an advanced maintenance procedure, developers should not be making changes other than those required for fixing reported defects. If the versioning tool integrates with defect tracking, it is possible to enforce the association of a defect record with every change. This offers complete auditing capability and discourages "tweaking" of code without due cause.
- Build process management — This is a general feature more in the area of configuration management tools than versioning. The simpler versioning tools usually provide a way to extract old versions of a project. More advanced build process management automates the creation of executables and archives all other aspects of the project from install scripts to icon bitmaps.

FREE VERSIONING TOOLS

There are a number of good tools freely available or bundled with the operating system. Although they are definitely not as fully featured as the more advanced commercial offerings, there are serious contenders available, particularly under UNIX.

sccs — UNIX version control system

sccs stands for "source code control system", and sccs is a long-standing UNIX tool for providing source code versioning features. Although it is not actually "free", sccs is usually bundled with the operating system on most UNIX variants. Although sccs has been and still is used successfully in many projects, the trend seems to be away from sccs toward more advanced tools such as those available freely from the GNU distributions or the various commercial versioning tools. Since I am not particularly familiar with sccs, and do not recommend it (based on experiences of others), I will refer the reader to the UNIX manual pages.

rcs — free GNU version control system

GNU initially offered rcs as an alternative to sccs and it provides the same level of functionality and more. rcs stands for "revision control system". There is support for a central source code repository with check-in and check-out of files. rcs maintains detailed logs of actions for auditing and rollback, and a common practice is to include these logs in the actual source files as C comments. Multiple branches of development are supported for larger development tasks.

My one tip about rcs is simply not to use it, since cvs is much better. If you use rcs on a non-trivial project you invariably end up writing scripts around rcs commands, usually to do things that cvs already does.

sccs2rcs — free tool to convert sccs repositories to rcs

Tool Name:	sccs2rcs
Purpose:	Convert sccs repositories to GNU rcs format
Platforms:	UNIX (many including this Linux port)
Availability:	Linux sites: e.g., sunsite.unc.edu:/pub/Linux/devel/ver_cont/sccs2rcs*
Authors:	Ken Cox, Eric S. Raymond

sccs2rcs is a migration tool for converting (upgrading?) from sccs to the GNU rcs version control tool. It converts the project repository to rcs format with preservation of change histories and delta comments.

cvs — free GNU version control system

Tool Name:	cvs
Purpose:	Source code version control

Platforms:	UNIX (many), Linux
Availability:	GNU archives as the CVS distribution Linux sites: e.g., sunsite.unc.edu:/pub/Linux/devel/ver_cont/ cvs*

cvs is the versioning tool with which I am the most familiar. Although I can tell you good and bad stories, cvs is mostly good news overall. cvs is a free versioning tool that sits on top of the more low-level GNU rcs tool. Since cvs uses GNU rcs to implement many of its low-level activities, it thereby provides a higher level view of the source code. This makes for a powerful versioning system with many features.

cvs works very well for small to medium size projects. It has a very broad set of features for tracking versions of files and entire project versions. Different strands of product development can go off on separate "branches" and then merge back into the main trunk later. The policy of allowing multiple developers to modify files, and then detecting and *merging* conflicting changes is very powerful and convenient.

So much for the good news. The bad news is that cvs has some pitfalls, some minor and some that occasionally required plumbing the depths of its repository. Although usually good, the algorithm used by cvs to fix editing conflicts is just an algorithm, rather than intelligence, and occasionally gets it wrong. Binary files such as executables and word processing documents are not handled well. Deleting files in the main trunk creates problems in the branches. Merging branches back into the main trunk becomes a manual process if there are any non-trivial changes.

Multiplatform development with cvs is particularly vulnerable to troubles. For example, cvs doesn't seem to handle UNIX/Windows newline/carriage return text file conversion and reports every line as "changed". In addition, the sharing of the repository presented problems with VMS and Windows NT where there was poor NFS file-system support. Without both NFS files and a cvs port, there is no easy way to share the repository across platforms, and developers are forced to copy files to and from UNIX and non-UNIX systems. This doesn't seem too bad but the manual process is: "cvs update", copy to non-UNIX, make porting changes, copy back to UNIX, remove carriage returns, "cvs commit". This is just a little tiresome and also risky, since cvs does not detect the "lost commit" that can result with non-UNIX developers interleaving the "cvs update" and copying operations wrongly. The best way to detect a lost commit (if something breaks and you suspect it) is to look for missing log entries in the files; the "cvs log" command does not help much here.

Another issue is that cvs offers only source code versioning and does not offer any fancy features of a configuration management tool. If you want to integrate cvs with your bug-tracking system, or you want to enforce a coding style standard on all committed files, you can probably do it, but you'll have to write the scripts.

However, having made all these negative comments, I am still impressed with cvs, especially the value for its price tag. cvs is high-quality software, is being maintained, and the next version may well fix most of the above-mentioned pitfalls. The bottom line is that for small to medium projects this is a very good tool.

pcl-cvs — free emacs front-end for cvs

Some of the distributions of cvs mentioned above, particularly the Linux archive distribution from *sunsite.unc.edu:/pub/Linux/devel/ver_cont/cvs**, includes an emacs front-end for cvs. This is called pcl-cvs, but unfortunately I have not had time to try it.

tkcvs — free GUI front-end for cvs using TCL

Tool Name:	tkcvs
Purpose:	Free GUI front-end for the GNU cvs versioning tool
Availability:	TCL archives: ftp://ftp.aud.alcatel.com/tcl/code/tkcvs*

tkcvs is a free GUI front-end for *cvs* that is distributed with the TCL archives. This is an impressive GUI that allows visualization of many aspects of source code versioning issues. The primary view is a list-based view of the files in the current directory showing file statuses and other attributes. This allows point-and-click navigation through the source code directory hierarchy. There are simple menu or button commands for almost any cvs commands including update, log viewing, committing, adding files, tagging, and more.

In addition to the many text-based features, there are a few notable graphical displays. Visual graph representations are used to display the branching sequence for any given file. Difference analysis of revisions is performed by automatic launching of the tkdiff TCL-based graphical file difference tool.

Aegis — free UNIX source code versioning tool

Tool Name:	Aegis
Purpose:	Software configuration management
Platforms:	UNIX (many), Linux
Availability:	ftp.nau.edu /pub/Aegis Linux sites: sunsite.unc.edu:/pub/Linux/devel/ver_cont/aegis*
Author:	Peter Miller

Aegis is a free tool for configuration management and source code versioning. It allows groups of developers to work on source code and will merge back their changes to the central repository. *Aegis* is a developers tool and offers no advanced management reports.

COMMERCIAL VERSIONING TOOLS

What follows are references to various providers of commercial versioning and configuration management tools. Full reviews were not possible due to time and space constraints. This is very unfortunate since a number of the commercial offerings are highly impressive with support for the more advanced desirable versioning features I mentioned above. But I'm afraid a detailed study of the various commercial tools will have to wait for the next edition.

Product Name:	ClearCase
Purpose:	Source code versioning
Platforms:	UNIX, Windows
Company:	Atria Software Inc.
Phone:	1-800-52-ATRIA
Email:	meg@atria.com
Web:	http://www.atria.com

Product Name:	MKS Source Integrity
Purpose:	Source code versioning
Company:	Mortice Kern Systems, Inc. (MKS)
Address:	185 Columbia Street W., Waterloo, Ontario N2L5Z5, Canada
Phone:	1-800-265-2797, 519-884-2251
Fax:	519-884-8861
Email:	sales@mks.com
CompuServe:	73260,1043
FTP:	ftp.mks.com
Web:	http://www.mks.com

Product Name:	Razor
Purpose:	Source code versioning, problem tracking
Platforms:	Solaris, SunOS, HP, SGI
Price:	$495 per floating license
Company:	Tower Concepts, Inc.

Address:	103 Sylvan Way, New Hartford, NY 13413, USA
Phone:	315-724-3540
Email:	razor-sales@tower.com or razor-manual@tower.com

Product Name:	INTERSOLV PVCS
Purpose:	Source code versioning
Company:	INTERSOLV Inc.
Phone:	1-800-547-4000
Email:	pvcsinfo@intersolv.com
Web:	http://www.intersolv.com

Product Name:	CCC/Harvest
Purpose:	Source code versioning
Company:	Softool Corporation
Address:	340 South Kellogg Ave., Goleta, CA 93117, USA
Phone:	1-800-723-0696, 805-683-5777
Email:	info@softool.com
Web:	http://www.softool.com

Product Name:	Microsoft SourceSafe & Microsoft Visual SourceSafe
Purpose:	Source code versioning
Platforms:	DOS, Windows 3.1, Windows 95, Windows NT, Macintosh
Company:	Microsoft Corporation
Address:	One Microsoft Way, Redmond, WA 98052-6399, USA
Phone:	1-800-426-9400,1- 800-727-3351
Fax:	206-635-2222, 206-936-7329
AutoFax:	1-800-426-9400
Web:	http://www.microsoft.com/

Product Name:	Visual SourceSafe 4.0 for UNIX
Purpose:	Project oriented version control

Platforms:	UNIX
Company:	Mainsoft Corporation
Address:	1270 Oakmead Parkway, Suite 310, Sunnyvale, CA 94086, USA
Phone:	1-800-MAIN-WIN, 408-774-3400
Fax:	408-774-3404
Email:	info@mainsoft.com
Web:	http://www.mainsoft.com

DEFECT TRACKING TOOLS

Defect tracking tools are an administrative aid for the product release process. They are used to trace the reported defects from entry to resolution. This provides auditing of reported defects, enhancement requests, fixes, workarounds, and documentation needs. Some of the typical features of a defect tracking tool include:

- allocation of defects to engineers, support staff, technical writers, etc.
- tracking of customer calls for support staff
- reporting capabilities (e.g., count defects by component or by severity)
- mapping defect reports to source code changes via integration with versioning systems

Some of the spin-off advantages include:

- support staff can avoid logging defects more than once
- tracking of if, when and how development fixed a problem logged by support
- common defects with workarounds can be extracted for product release notes
- defects fixed in each product release can be extracted
- defects and enhancement requests are in one place only
- documentation needs treated as a part of the overall product

The complexity of the defect tracking tool will depend on the budget. The simplest method is some sort of storage of all the information which could be just a shared text file, or preferably a front end to a set of forms on a database. This is adequate if the demands are not too high. However, a major project with multiple releases, many customers and a large staff begins to need a specialized tool with convenience features. Given enough time you can, of course, add all the features you want to a database application, but it gets to the point where you are redoing work that has already been done, and a better tool is cost-effective.

The human factor does affect the use of a defect tracking tool. The introduction of such a tool will have an initial learning curve, and it will take time before staff begin to follow the procedures needed by the tool. To minimize this, it is desirable to document the process, and to make sure to do this for all groups. Support and engineering have very different needs since support needs to track issues such as whether a customer has been called back, but engineering are interested only in whether any defects have been fixed.

Another recommendation I suggest is to *not* use the defect tracking tool as a staff evaluation tool. This should also be made clear to all staff. If used as an evaluation tool, some staff will tend to misuse the tool including: not logging defects against their product area, prematurely closing defects assigned to them, and ignoring other urgent tasks to resolve defects. Any of these problems can prevent the defect tracking tool from being an accurate model of reality.

The following is a list of the acquisition details of various defect tracking products. Unfortunately, time and space constraints prevented me from a more detailed analysis.

Free defect tracking tools

Tool Name:	GNATS
Purpose:	Free bug tracking tool
Availability:	GNU archives

Tool Name:	Open Track
Purpose:	Free bug tracking tool
Availability:	TCL archives at ftp://ftp.aud.alcatel.com/tcl/code/ot*.
Authors:	Robert Lent, John Bowe, Fred Dalrymple, Peter Harbo, Natalia Kogan

Tool Name:	TkGnats
Purpose:	Free GUI front-end for Gnats free GNU bug-tracking tool
Availability:	TCL archives: ftp://ftp.aud.alcatel.com/tcl/code/tkgnats*
Author:	Mike Hoegeman

Commercial and shareware defect tracking tools

Product Name:	Track Record
Purpose:	Issue tracking (bugs, features, schedules, documentation)
Company:	UnderWare, Inc.
Address:	321 Columbus Avenue, Boston, MA 02116, USA
Phone:	1-800-343-7308, 617-267-9743
Fax:	617-424-1839

Product Name:	BugBase
Purpose:	Defect tracking
Company:	Archimedes Software
Address:	303 Parkplace Center, Suite 125, Kirkland, WA 98033, USA
Phone:	1-800-338-1453, 415-567-4010, Europe: +41-42-72-04-84
FTP:	ftp.archimedesinc.com/pub/devtools
Web:	http://www.archimedesinc.com/devtools

Product Name:	Soffront TRACK
Company:	Soffront Software Inc.
Address:	238 S. Hillview Drive, Milpitas, CA 95035, USA
Phone:	1-800-SOF-FRONT, 408-263-2703
Fax:	408-263-7452

Product Name:	PR-TRACKER
Purpose:	Shareware bug tracking product
Platforms:	DOS, Windows
Availability:	ftp://oak.oakland.edu/SimTel/msdos/projmgr/prtrk131.zip ftp://ftp.halcyon.com/local/softwise/prtrk131.zip CompuServe:Software Development Forum:prtrk131.zip AOL:Development Forum:Utilities Library (search on Softwise)

Product Name:	Vantive
Platforms:	Windows, UNIX (includes Solaris, HP)
Company:	Vantive Corporation
Address:	1890 N. Shoreline Blvd., Mountain View, CA 94043, USA
Phone:	415-691-1500
Fax:	415-691-1515

Product Name:	Razor
Purpose:	Source code versioning, problem tracking
Platforms:	Solaris, SunOS, HP, SGI

Price:	$495 per floating license
Company:	Tower Concepts, Inc.
Address:	103 Sylvan Way, New Hartford, NY 13413, USA
Phone:	315-724-3540
Email:	razor-sales@tower.com or razor-manual@tower.com

P   A   R   T   **2**

LIBRARIES

The previous chapters have examined the various tools to help programmers put a new program together. The chapters that follow cover the use of ready-made building blocks as part of a new program. Using C function libraries or C++ class libraries allows the programmer to quickly build an advanced application based on existing code.

The market for code libraries has grown to offer a variety of different components ranging from basic data structures to GUI building libraries to mathematical and business components. Vendors of compilers or IDEs are rushing to add infrastructures that enable the storage and reuse of components with greater ease. Low-level operating system enhancements such as improved support for dynamic loading also increase the value that can be leveraged from off-the-shelf components.

There are also improvements in the pragmatic aspects of sharing code. Trust for vendors that produce code is an important issue since users of the code must cope with any defects or limitations that are present. Improvements in the quality process, including the use of many of the tools already covered, have meant that the quality of software is rising across the board. The future should therefore offer an even greater opportunity for sharing of software components freely or commercially.

Command-line argument processing

Extraction of command-line arguments from `argc` and `argv` is one of the worst instances of code reuse (or rather, lack thereof) in modern C and C++ programs. Almost every program I see explicitly processes `argc` and `argv` using some newly written code, and indeed, I am not exempt from this criticism in my own programs. However, processing arguments is a simple and usually repetitive coding problem and there are a variety of libraries available to make the coding burden quite small. All we have to do now is get into the habit of using these libraries!

There are many different types of options that you may wish to implement in a particular program. One of the most major issues is the character used to specify an option — under UNIX it is typically the minus sign -, under DOS it can be the forward slash /, but many DOS applications now also allow the minus sign. Some of the common styles (using the minus sign) are:

```
prog -i            # single-character
prog -ia           # groups of single characters
prog -longname     # word options
prog -DDEBUG       # single char with argument
prog -D DEBUG      # single char with following argument
prog -DDEBUG=VALUE # single char with argument and value
```

```
prog -D DEBUG=VALUE   # single char with argument and value
prog -arg=value       # word option with argument
```

Another common aspect is that many "boolean" options can be set on and off. This will apply to single options, but also to subsets of options under a given super-option (e.g., -Wname specifies the subset of -W options with the particular option identified by name). Hence there are various formats for negating options:

```
prog -n -p-        # n on, p off
prog -n+ -p-       # n on, p off
prog +n -p         # n on, p off
prog -noarg        # "arg" off (prefix "no")
prog -Wn -W-p      # -W subset: n on, p off
```

The various libraries support different types of common command-line argument formats, but typically do not support all the possible formats, which may be one explanation of their lack of widespread use.

The getopt Library Function

Although it is not part of the ANSI standard library, many implementations of C supply the getopt function to automate most of the details of testing for command line arguments. The getopt function allows the acceptance of the following forms of command-line argument:

```
prog -i            # single-character
prog -ia           # groups of single characters
prog -DDEBUG       # single char with argument
prog -D DEBUG      # single char with following argument
```

There are two important limitations of getopt:

1. only the minus sign is allowed to start an option and this cannot be altered; and
2. all options must appear before non-options.

The second restriction occurs because the first option without a prefix minus sign causes getopt to finish processing options and return EOF. If you have the source code for getopt (see next section), you have the opportunity to remove these limitations.

The getopt function is used like any other standard library function with its prototype declaration as follows:

```
int getopt(int argc, char *argv[], char *letters);
```

The argc and argv parameters are the usual arguments to main; letters is a string containing all the letters that are legal options to the program.

The getopt function also uses a number of external variables, which should be declared as below since some implementations require you to explicitly define them:

```
extern int optind;   /* Index into argv */
extern int opterr;   /* Error suppression flag */
extern char *optarg; /* Argument for an option */
```

A sequence of calls to getopt is used to extract each successive option, and each legal option is returned by getopt. If getopt detects an illegal option it produces an error message on stderr and returns the character '?'. The error message can be suppressed by setting the boolean flag opterr to zero.

The optind variable is used by getopt to keep track of which option it is up to. The fact that this variable is visible allows the programmer to use it in many ways such as to redo all options by setting optind to 1, or to redo some options by saving and resetting the value of optind.

When there are no more arguments, getopt returns EOF and either we are not at the end of the argument list or optind is an index into the first non-option argument. Note also that optind allows the opportunity to overcome this "options first" limitation when getopt returns EOF, by incrementing optind to skip the non-option (provided optind is less than argc) and continuing to call getopt for any further options.

The getopt function has a facility for more complicated options than the single character type. An option can be specified that requires an argument, such as below:

```
prog -DDEBUG
```

Such option letters are indicated by placing a colon after the option letter in the letters argument to getopt. When the option is found by getopt, the letter is returned by getopt and optarg is set to point to the string value of the argument. Note that the option can also have a space between the option letter and the argument. getopt would consider the two commands below as identical:

```
prog -DDEBUG
prog -D DEBUG
```

Let us now examine a full example of processing a program allowing the simple options -i and -a and also the -D option with a value.

```
#include <stdio.h>
#include <stdlib.h>

void process_options(int argc, char *argv[])
{
    int c;   /* NOTE: int type not char */
    extern char *optarg;

    for(;;) {  /* infinite loop */
        c = getopt(argc, argv, "iaD:");
        switch (c) {
            case 'i':     /* Process -i option */
                printf("-i option found\n");
                break;

            case 'a':     /* Process -a option */
                printf("-a option found\n");
                break;

            case 'D':  /* Process -D option */
```

```
                     /* value in optarg */
           printf("-D option, value '%s'\n",
                   optarg);
           break;

       case '?': /* Bad Option: do nothing */
           break;    /* getopt prints error */

       case EOF:  /* Non-minus sign */
                  /* or no more arguments */
           return;     /* Finished */

       default: /* Should never reach here */
           fprintf(stderr, "Internal error\n");
           exit(EXIT_FAILURE);
       }
   } /* forever */
}
```

Note that `getopt` returns `int` not `char` and the variable that the `getopt` return value is assigned to should be of type `int`; otherwise there is a portability problem when `EOF` is tested for because a `char` variable cannot always contain `EOF` properly.

GETOPT — FREE VERSIONS WITH SOURCE CODE

Because `getopt` is not an ANSI C standard library function, not all platforms will support it. Should you happen to meet a platform without `getopt`, you can retrieve a number of source code versions of `getopt` from various sites:

```
comp.sources.unix/volume3/att_getopt.Z
comp.sources.unix/volume1/getopt.Z
```

The public domain AT&T version is also available in print in Appendix F of Mark Horton's great book on portability:

HORTON, Mark, *Portable C Software*, Prentice Hall, New Jersey, 1990.

GETARGS — C LIBRARY BY ALLEN HOLUB

Tool Name:	getargs
Purpose:	Command-line processing C code library
Platforms:	K&R C compilers (ANSI C or C++ with some work)
Status:	Free
Availability:	FTP SimTel distributions as c/getargs.* and c/argtest.c (see also Dr Dobb's Journal, No. 103, May 1985)
Author:	Allen Holub (transcribed by James R. Van Zandt)

Key Points:	• specify flags as an array of structures • source code supplied — easy to modify
Limitations:	• Only five option formats allowed • Restricted to UNIX minus sign style

The `getargs` distribution consists of a C library of two files "`getargs.c`" and "`getargs.h`". The program should declare an array of structures which hold information about each option to be extracted. The forms of allowed options are shown in Table 17–1.

Table 17–1 getargs option type

Type	Example	Meaning
BOOLEAN	-b	Flag is either on or off
CHARACTER	-cx	Option has single character value
INTEGER	-n500	Option has integer value
STRING	-DDEBUG	Option has string value
PROC	-Panything	String passed to user-supplied function

The array of structures specifies a character for the option, the type of the option, the address of a variable to be used, and a string to be used by the automatically generated help message. A sample array of structures could be:

```
ARG Argtab[] = {
    { 'v', BOOLEAN, &verbose_flag, "set verbose mode on" },
    /* .... more options */
};
```

This array is passed, along with `argc` and `argv`, to the `getargs` function which processes all the arguments. Hence there is no need for any further code explicitly processing the -v or -verbose flags, as the call to `getargs` will correctly set the boolean variable `verbose_flag`.

A neat feature of the package is that processed options are removed from the `argv` array. The new value of `argc` is returned by the `getargs` function. This feature makes processing of non-option arguments a simple matter of iterating through the remaining arguments.

Unfortunately, the code in the distribution is quite old and requires a few changes for modern compilers including: conversion of functions to use prototyping; removal of explicit `islower/toupper` macros in favor of using `<ctype.h>`; including "getargs.h" not `<getargs.h>`; prototype of `stoi` at top of file; pointer-to-function type `PFI` requires argument type `char*`; and include `<stdlib.h>` to declare `exit`. Also to remove the ASCII dependence in the `stoi` function, I used `strtol(linep,&linep,0)` instead of calling `stoi`, since passing base zero to `strtol` supports the same octal and hexadecimal conversions.

One major portability problem that persists (because it is difficult to remove) with the PROC type is that the variable field of type int* is used to hold a pointer-to-function which is an illegal combination of pointer types that will fail on some architectures (e.g., if pointer-to-function types are smaller than ordinary pointers as in some DOS memory models). DOS users with 16-bit compilers should also beware that the INTEGER option type will only allow values up to 32,767 because of the use of the int type.

LIJNZAAD'S EXTENSION TO HOLUB'S GETARGS

Tool Name:	getargs (improved)
Purpose:	Command-line processing ANSI C library
Platforms:	ANSI C and C++ compilers
Status:	Free
Author:	Philip Lijnzaad, Allen Holub
Key Points:	• More types of common options • specify options in an array of structures • source code supplied — easy to modify

Philip Lijnzaad has extended Allen Holub's free getargs library to use ANSI C and to provide numerous extra features. The library also works as C++ code, but you have to fight the C++ type system about the pointer-to-function type of the checking function (e.g., the demonstration program might not compile as C++).

The basic mechanism of an array of structures remains the same, but there is now greater flexibility. The main change is that options are now specified as strings rather than a single character. Word options such as −verbose are now supported in a way that doesn't affect single character options (e.g., −ia is allowed to be treated as −i and −a, provided that "ia" is not a word option). A sample from the array of structures specifying the legal options is:

```
arg_t Argtab[] = {
/* option   type   address   comment     check_function */
    {"-v",BOOL,    &verbose, "verbose mode",   NULL },
    {"-verbose", BOOL, &verbose, "same as -v",   NULL },
    END_ARGTAB   /* NULL record terminates list */   };
```

In this example, −v and −verbose are both options setting a boolean variable. Note that the minus sign starting the option appears in the string representing the option. There is now also support for + signs to start options allowing −i and +i options to be supported with different meanings (i.e., turning a boolean flag on and off). There are now check functions to test options, such as checking whether an option's value or length is within satisfactory bounds.

Many of the original features of Holub's library remain supported in the new version. Most of the original formats are present, except that INTEGER has been renamed as INT. The

PROC format allowing procedure calls is present, but also extended with PROC1 allowing one argument to be passed to the function. Unfortunately, both PROC and PROC1 still have the portability problem of storing a pointer to a function in a void* type.

Another feature that is retained is that getargs removes processed options from the argv array and returns the new value of argc, so that processing of the unused arguments is achieved just by the "usual" processing of the updated argc/argv pair.

CLP — COMMAND LINE PROCESSOR FOR C

Product Name:	CLP
Version:	V1.1, September 1989
Purpose:	Command Line Processor
Platforms:	DOS (Turbo C, Microsoft C)
Languages:	ANSI C, K&R C (not C++)
Status:	Shareware
Availability:	FTP SimTel distributions as c/clp_v11.zip
Address:	Karl Keyte E.S.O.C. Robert-Bosch Strasse 5 6100 Darmstadt West Germany
Phone:	+(49) 6151 886783
Email:	ESC1332@ESOC.BITNET
Key Points:	• processes Command Line Definition file
Limitations:	• allows only DOS-style /arg=value switches

CLP can be used under DOS to process DOS-style command-line arguments (using the forward slash) of the form:

```
prog /arg=value
```

CLP allows quite a number of different formats for command-line switch including specified values (optional or required), default values, negatability (i.e., using prefix "no" as in /noverbose), and even run-time prompting for a value if absent.

Using CLP to process command-line arguments requires the creation of a Command Line Definition (CLD) file. The CLD file is processed by CLP to create a Command Line Library (CLL) file, which must be available to the program at run-time.

An API interface to CLP is used by the C program at run-time. First, a call to clp_accept must pass argc and argv to CLP, which then attempts to open the CLL file and process the arguments according to that description. Then for each argument the clp_get_spec function is called to determine whether a given option was in the command-line. If an option was present and was also given a value, the clp_get_value function can be used to retrieve the associated value. Finally, `clp_release` can be used after all arguments have been processed, to release any memory used by CLP.

PARSEARGS — FREE C ARGUMENT LIBRARY

Tool Name:	parseargs
Purpose:	Command-line processing in C
Platforms:	Any C compiler (UNIX, VAX/VMS, O2/2, MSDOS, Amiga-DOS) Not C++, although cleaning the source should be reasonably easy.
Status:	Free
Availability:	comp.sources.misc/volume29/parseargs/part[00-10] comp.sources.misc/volume22/parseargs/patch08 comp.sources.misc/volume26/parseargs/patch09[a-b] comp.sources.misc/volume26/parseargs/patch10 comp.sources.misc/volume30/parseargs/patch1[2-3]
Author:	Eric P. Allman, Peter da Silva, Brad Appleton
Key Points:	• Array of structures used to specify options • Supports different option styles for different platforms

The basic data structure used by the parseargs package is an array of structures, with one structure per legal option. The fields in each structure are shown in Table 17–2 in the order they are declared. Note the important portability improvement over the `getargs` package — the pointer-to-function type and the variable address are stored separately.

Table 17–2   parseargs structure fields

Type	Examples	Meaning
char	'c'	Character used for option
short	ARGOPT	Bit flags for actions
ptr-to-function	argBool	Function processing option
void*	&x	Variable storing option value
char*	"repetition counter"	Help/usage message

The list of allowed options becomes an array of these structures. One entry in the array of structures would be similar to:

```
{ 'd', ARGOPT, argBool, &debug, "debug: set debug level" }
```

The `argBool` function is one of many predefined functions in the package. Some of the other such primitives include: `argInt`, `argShort`, `argLong`, `argFloat`, `argChar`, and `argStr`. There are so many that it is easy to forget they are actually functions, and instead merely treat them as specifying the type of the option. However, the fact that they are functions gives greater flexibility to do more advanced option processing should the supplied primitives be inadequate.

Whereas these function primitives effectively determine the type of the option, there are the extra bit flags to set specific issues such as whether a value corresponding to an option is optional or required. ARGOPT is the default which specifies an optional argument; ARGREQ specifies a required option. There are many other flags — consult the documentation with the source distribution.

After the array of structures has been set up, the only other operation required to perform the parsing of command-line arguments is a call to the `parseargs` library function, such as:

```
int status = parseargs(argv, array_of_structs);
```

This single function call will parse the command-line arguments, extract any values and store them in the appropriate variable (i.e., using the address supplied in a structure). Errors are handled in various ways such as to print an error, or to ignore them. The bit flags are used to configure the behavior for individual options.

Overall, this is a really excellent C library with almost everything you would want (and lots that you probably wouldn't ever want!) for processing command-line arguments. `parseargs` may even be preferred by C++ programmers as it is likely to be slightly more efficient than the C++ class libraries that I have examined in this chapter, because it relies on compile-time initialization of an array. However, C++ usage will require some code modification, as the code does not currently compile for C++.

OPTIONS — FREE C++ ARGUMENT CLASS

Tool Name:	options
Purpose:	Command-line processing in C++
Platforms:	Any C++ compiler
Status:	Free
Availability:	FTP comp.sources.misc/volume31/options/part0[1-2] comp.sources.misc/volume36/options/patch01 (patch #1) comp.sources.misc/volume40/options/patch02 (patch #2)
Author:	Brad Appleton
Key Points:	• full C++ class, source supplied • automatic usage/help message generated

Limitations:	• Assumes UNIX-style minus signs
	• All arguments must be before other arguments

The `options` package is a medium-size C++ library for processing command-line arguments. It requires the definition of an array of strings (which is NULL terminated), where each string specifies one option using a particular encoding. This array of strings is used in a constructor call to initialize an object of the class `Options`. Also required is a related iterator object of type `OptArgvIter`. Once these objects are declared, the main loop processes options one at a time in a manner similar to the usual `getopt` loop. Thus a limitation of this class is that it still requires explicit code to process each argument. A typical sequence for processing options is:

```
Options opts(*argv, optv);
OptArgvIter iter(--argc, ++argv);
while( (optchar = opts(iter, optarg)) != 0 ) {
    switch (optchar) {
        case 'a' :
            /* process -a */
            break;
        case 'i' :
            /* process -i */
            break;
        default :   /* unknown option */
            break;
    } //switch
} // while
```

This code is using an overloaded version of `operator()` to iterate through the arguments. Since the `operator()` has return type `char`, every option must have a unique character by which it is identified. For single character options this is the character itself; for long options some character must be chosen.

This class supports a variety of command-line option formats with single characters and longer options including:

```
prog -a
prog -DDEBUG
prog -D DEBUG
prog --long_option
```

A notable feature is support for options with multiple corresponding arguments. An option can have a list of arguments terminated by a double minus (i.e., `--` option). For example, if the `-p` option required a list of files to be printed, an allowable call could be:

```
prog -p file1 file2 file3 -- other files here
```

Although there is a lot of flexibility, there are a few annoying limitations. The default method of specifying a word option at the command line is a `--` prefix. This can be changed by setting a `LONG_ONLY` control flag, but this creates some problems for single character options. Hence, short and long options do not mix well.

CMDLINE — FREE C++ ARGUMENT CLASS

Tool Name:	`cmdline`
Purpose:	Command-line processing in C++
Platforms:	C++ compiler (support for UNIX, VMS, MSDOS and OS/2)
Status:	Free
Availability:	comp.sources.misc/volume31/cmdline/part0[0-7] comp.sources.misc/volume36/cmdline/patch01[a-b] comp.sources.misc/volume39/cmdline/patch02 comp.sources.misc/volume40/cmdline/patch03
Author:	Brad Appleton
Key Points:	• No explicit code for processing common option formats • One object is created per legal option • Includes "cmdparse" for shell-script options
Limitations:	• Single character and word options do not mix well

This is a very large and impressive C++ library for command-line argument processing, and there is hardly space here to examine all its features. Its most elegant feature is that there is no need for any code to process each option once the set of allowed options has been initialized. Hence, this library is better than the UNIX `getopt` function and the free options class library, which require code processing each option (typically in a `case` clause within a `switch` statement). `cmdline` is similar in this respect to the `getargs` and `parseargs` packages, which use an array of structures containing pointers to the variables in which to store the values. However, instead of an array, all that is required is to create an object of the given argument class — one object per legal option.

Using `cmdline` requires a few steps:

1. create your objects for each option;
2. create a command-line object of class `CmdLine`;
3. create an iterator object from class `CmdArgvIter`; and
4. call `CmdLine::parse()` to do all the hard work.

There is usually no further processing of arguments needed, and this class even has an object to get all the non-option arguments (i.e., usually the filenames at the end of a command). A typical sequence to process arguments would be:

```
CmdArgInt count('c', "count", "number", "count times");
/* .. other CmdArg.. type declarations of option objects */
CmdLine cmd(*argv, &count, NULL);
CmdArgvIter iter(--argc, ++argv);

/* .. initialize any default option values */
count = 1;
cmd.parse(iter);
```

These steps require further explanation. The `CmdArgInt` declaration defines `count` as an object, and passes various parameters to its constructor; in this case they are single character option (i.e., `'c'`), equivalent word option (i.e., "count"), argument description for the help message, and the full description for the help message. Note that there are a variety of other option class types such as `CmdArgBool`, `CmdArgChar`, `CmdArgStr`, and others, each with their own particular constructor parameters.

The second step is to create cmd as an object representing the command line. The addresses of all option objects must be passed as a `NULL`-terminated list in the constructor. (Here is a potential improvement: could they register themselves automatically behind the scenes instead?)

The third step is to create an iterator object of type `CmdArgvIter` which is used by the `parse` operation. The option objects are then given initial values via assignment statements. (Another improvement: an extra constructor argument.) Finally, the `parse` function is called to process all the command-line arguments and set the appropriate values in the option objects.

After the arguments have been parsed, the values of the options can be extracted as if the option objects were in fact scalar variables. For example, the value specified as the count can be extracted as if `count` were an `int` variable. This is possible because class type `CmdArgInt` has an overloaded type cast operator to convert to `int`, which is applied whenever an `int` is required. The efficiency is unlikely to suffer greatly from this approach because small inline functions are used for these conversions.

Unfortunately, there are some restrictions on the option formats that are supported. These restrictions are similar to those that apply to the options package and relate mainly to long options. By default, long options require a `--` prefix; this can be removed but doing so creates difficulties with single character options. However, these minor difficulties do not detract greatly from what is a very impressive package.

GETLONGOPT — FREE C++ ARGUMENT CLASS

Tool Name:	GetLongOpt
Purpose:	Command-line processing C++ class
Platforms:	Any C++ compiler
Availability:	FTP comp.sources.misc/volume35/getlongopt/*
Status:	Free
Author:	S. Manoharan
Key Points:	• full C++ class, source supplied • changeable option character (defaults to minus sign) • automatic usage/help message generated
Limitations:	• Very little support for short options • Cannot make -ab the same as -a and -b • All options must appear before other arguments

The `GetLongOpt` package is a C++ class specifically for processing long options and their corresponding values. The library allows any character as an option specifier (e.g., UNIX would use minus signs whereas MSDOS users might prefer the slash), but has very little support for shorter options. The formats of options that are supported are:

```
prog -arg           # No value
prog -arg value     # Value after space
prog -arg=value     # Value after equals sign
```

There is no explicit support for short single-character options and in fact, there is no way to make `-ab` behave as `-a` and `-b` (although the latter form is supported as a special case of a "long" option with no value). There is also no way to have a `-DDEBUG` argument — instead it must use a space (`-D DEBUG`) or an equals sign (`-D=DEBUG`).

The overall usage method is a little disappointing in that it requires a number of steps. You must have explicit class member calls to "`enroll`" each option in the class database of legal options, then parse the options, and then perform a "`retrieve`" call to extract the information as to whether a given option was used on the command line. Thus, the method of using the class for a simple boolean "`-debug`" option is:

```
GetLongOpt option;

option.enroll("debug", GetLongOpt::NoValue,
              "turn on debugging", NULL);
/* ... more enroll calls for other options */

option.parse(argc, argv);     /* parse options */

if(option.retrieve("debug") != NULL) {
    // -debug was seen in command-line
}
/* ... more retrieve calls for other options */
```

A call to `retrieve` is required for every option. For options with values, the `retrieve` member function returns a character string pointing to the value.

Three types of options are allowed — no value, optional value, and mandatory value. Error messages are produced to standard error for problems such as failing to provide a value to one with a mandatory requirement.

Overall, although `GetLongOpt` is a neat package for handling a particular type of option, it requires many lines of code to handle simpler requirements. Although having multiple "`enroll`" calls wasn't any worse than multiple records in an array of structures (or similar), I felt it would have been better to pass the address of a variable in which to store the value (similar to use of variable addresses in getargs and parseargs), rather than requiring all the "`retrieve`" calls. In fact, this is reasonably trivial to add for string options, but it's more difficult to modify it so as to pass the address of an integer for a boolean option.

## CHAPTER 18

Exception handler macro libraries

This chapter presents a number of preprocessor macro libraries that hide the details of using `setjmp` and `longjmp` for exception handling in both C and C++. As far as C++ programs are concerned, this chapter may well be obsolete by the time you read these words, as the ANSI C++ exception handling should be available in the near future. However, the libraries presented herein should be useful when dealing with older C++ compilers, and for the implementation of exception handling in ANSI C. The libraries have been presented with names similar to the ANSI C++ exception handling keywords `try`, `catch`, and `throw`.

SETJMP AND LONGJMP IN C

The `setjmp` and `longjmp` ANSI C standard library functions are the only way to perform nonlocal jumps in C or pre-ANSI C++. The `goto` statement can jump only within the current function, and therefore `setjmp` and `longjmp` functions must be used when an exceptional condition is detected that necessitates a nonlocal jump. However, in ANSI C++ the preferred method is to throw an exception using the throw operator.

The setjmp and longjmp functions are companion functions. To use these functions it is necessary to include <setjmp.h> and to declare a variable of type jmp_buf (declared in <setjmp.h>) that is accessible to both setjmp and longjmp (usually a global variable). setjmp is called to set up the location where a later longjmp call will jump back to. When called the first time setjmp will return zero, indicating that it has been called normally. When longjmp is called later, the effect will be as if setjmp had just returned with a nonzero value. The longjmp function unwinds the stack and fixes up the system registers (whose previous values were stored in the jmp_buf) to mimic the effect of returning from a call to the setjmp function. Therefore, the standard method of calling setjmp is to test its return value:

```
#include <setjmp.h>
jmp_buf env;        /* global variable */
if (setjmp(env) != 0) {
    /* .. setjmp returns nonzero */
    /* .. exception has occurred */
    /* .. program has longjmp'd to get here */
}
else {
    /* .. normal start of program */
}
```

The manner of calling longjmp is to supply it with the env variable used by setjmp and a nonzero integer error code. The simplest method is:

```
longjmp(env, 1);
```

SETJMP AND LONGJMP IN C++

The setjmp and longjmp functions operate in exactly the same manner in C++ as they do in C. Because they are part of the ANSI standard C library, they are also part of the C++ standard library. Hence these functions are a useful alternative to proper exception handling in pre-ANSI C++ implementations that do not fully support exceptions.

However, there is one major problem with using longjmp in C++ — destructors are *not* called for local objects. In fact, the problem is worse in that whether destructors are called by longjmp is actually "undefined" and although most compilers don't call destructors, some implementations do so, and we have a portability problem across C++ implementations.

This failure to execute destructors is a major difference between the use of longjmp and the ANSI C++ throw statement, which does correctly destroy local automatic objects. Therefore the use of longjmp is more precarious, being prone to errors such as leaving files open or creating garbage memory.

There are a few solutions to this problem with destructors. An inelegant solution is to hand-code in the setjmp handling block any cleanup code that would have been performed by a destructor. Another possibility is to derive the class for objects requiring destruction by longjmp from a base class that helps longjmp to call the appropriate destructors. This is most easily achieved within a macro library, and Bengtsson's library discussed later is one example with its use of a Resource base class.

HORSMEIER'S C EXCEPTION HANDLING LIBRARY

The power of the C preprocessor can be used to create a suite of exception handling macros. The following method of using macros to hide setjmp and longjmp calls was communicated to me by Jos Horsmeier, and the macros and functions below are based upon those written by him in 1988.

The basis of the method is to use macros that cleverly extend the syntax of C to make it similar to the syntax of C++ exception handling. A block of code that must have its exceptions handled is surrounded by a TRY and ENDTRY pair, and followed by one or more CATCH blocks:

```
TRY {
    /* something */
} ENDTRY
CATCH(Exception1) {
    /* handle exception 1 */
}
```

Different exceptions are represented by int codes that are chosen by the user of the exception macros. When a (software) exception is found by the program, it uses the THROW function to raise an exception, which is "caught" by the exception handling code. The exception may be "thrown" in the current function, or in any function called by these functions:

```
THROW(MALLOC_FAILURE);
```

Implementing the exception handling macros

The macros work by hiding setjmp and longjmp calls from the user. A TRY block calls setjmp so as to store the location of where the exception returns to, and a later THROW call uses a longjmp call to return to the exception handling code. The most important macro definitions in the header file are:

```
#define TRY       if (setjmp(ExceptIst()) == 0) {
#define ENDTRY   ExceptRls(); }
#define CATCH(x)  else if (ExceptError == (x))
#define THISEXCEPT ExceptCode()
#define ALLOTHERS else
```

Note that THROW is a function, not a macro. Also needed is a C/C++ source file containing declarations of the functions that do most of the hard work.

Limitations of the exception handling macros

There are some unfortunate limitations of the macro approach to exception handling. The major problem is that flow of control must always fall through to the bottom of the TRY block, so that the CATCH macro can "clean up" the exception handling correctly. This means that the return statement cannot be used to return from the current function from within a block that has its exceptions handled:

```
TRY {
    ... return;    /* ERROR */
} ENDTRY
CATCH(...)
```

Similar restrictions apply to the use of other jump statements such as break, continue, and goto. If any of these statements cause the flow of control to bypass the closing ENDTRY macro, the exception handling for the rest of the program is corrupted, and will possibly cause a run-time failure.

   Another limitation is that it isn't portable to call THROW from within a signal handler, because it isn't portable to call longjmp from a signal handler. Although it will often behave correctly, a signal can occur at any moment, and could have left important data structures corrupted (e.g., the malloc internal free list). As always, the most portable method of handling signals is to print a message and exit. Therefore, although it is enticing to declare signal handlers that catch common signals (e.g., SIGINT) and THROW an exception, it isn't a portable solution.

AMSTERDAM'S EXCEPTION LIBRARY FOR C

Jonathan Amsterdam in the August 1991 issue of *Byte* magazine presented a method that differs slightly from Jos Horsmeier's method in that it avoids calling malloc to allocate jmp_buf records which is undesirable as malloc may fail. Instead, a stack of jmp_buf records is built on the C internal stack by using automatic jmp_buf variables. Each TRY macro declares a local jmp_buf variable after its opening left brace, and the address of this variable is threaded through a linked list of pointers. The advantages of this method are that stack allocation and deallocation should be faster than malloc and free, and also that there is no need to be concerned with malloc failure.

   Although the use of addresses of local variables may appear dangerous at first, it is safe because the addresses are removed from the linked list whenever control flow moves back up past the TRY macro. Thus these addresses can be used only by the exception handling library while they are currently active on the program stack. Of course, the safety of the method relies on consistent use of the exception handling library, and any form of failure might arise if the normal exception handling methods are bypassed.

   The idea of using automatic stack variables is a general solution to the problem of allocating jmp_buf records that applies to both C and C++ exception libraries. The stack-based solution has also been used by various implementations such as the C++ library of Leary and D'Souza, and Harald Winroth's library for C. In fact, Jos Horsmeier has modified his library to use this technique and it is available on the CDROM in the horsmeir directory.

HOOD'S EXCEPTION LIBRARY FOR C

Another interesting exception library has been shown to me by Stuart Hood and is available on the CDROM in the `hood` directory. The overall syntax is dissimilar to the ANSI C++ style, with separate "handle" and "unhandle" statements — the `EXHandle` macro instates some exception handler code, and the `EXUnhandle` macro removes the corresponding handler. A sample usage looks like:

```
EXHandle(free_array, EXCEPT_ALL, {free(array); });
/* code using the array that may raise exception */
free(array);
EXUnhandle(free_array);
```

The design of the paired macros is very clever, making good use of ANSI stringizing and token pasting (i.e., the # and ## macro operators). The requirement of explicit pairs of macros may seem error-prone, but there is support for run-time mismatch detection. The argument `free_array` above serves as a character string identifier for the handler, and must match in handle/unhandle macro pairs.

WINROTH'S EXCEPTION LIBRARY FOR C

Harald Winroth has presented a macro library for exceptions in ANSI C, with a number of neat features, including exception hierarchy support, unwind-protect, and callbacks. Let us examine the details of the method.

Winroth uses macro calls where code blocks are placed as arguments to the macro, leading to large macro calls. The TRY macro call has the form:

```
TRY( try_code_block , catch_code_block );
```

and the CATCH macro only has a code block as the second argument:

```
CATCH(exception , handler_block );
```

An example of this usage in practice shows that huge sequences of code are placed inside the macro arguments:

```
TRY (
    {
    /* try block:  do something useful */
    ......
    },   /* Note the comma! */
    {
    /* handler block ... one or more CATCH's */

    CATCH(lib_error, { /* handle lib_error */  } );

    CATCH(disk_full, { /* handle disk_full */  } ); }
);
```

All exceptions reach the start of the handler block. Therefore, code appropriate for all exceptions equivalent to `catch(...)` in ANSI C++ should be placed after all other CATCH macros. Code for all exceptions could be placed anywhere in the handler block, such as before all CATCH macros or between two, but this usage is more difficult to convert later to ANSI C++. Placing all default code after the CATCH calls simulates the idea that `catch(...)` must be the last handler. However, note that the default code must end with a `continue` statement to restart execution after the TRY block; otherwise the library doesn't know that the exception has been handled and will test for CATCH macros in outer run-time scopes.

Some other specific features of the macro library are:

- `continue` in a main or handler block will skip to after the TRY macro.
- `break` in a main block is a run-time error.
- `break` in a CATCH continues within the handler block after that CATCH.
- `break` in a handler block but not in a CATCH is a run-time error.
- CATCH in the wrong place is a run-time error.
- A successful CATCH will continue execution after the TRY macro.
- TRY blocks can be nested.
- `goto` into or out of blocks can corrupt the exception handling.
- `longjmp` usage can corrupt the exception handling.
- "THROW(exception)" causes rethrow.
- Rethrowing outside a handler block is a run-time error.

Limitations of large macro calls

In my opinion, the method of declaring exception handling code using Winroth's macros is far more cumbersome than some of the other macro methods, and also suffers because it is unlike the ANSI C++ exception syntax. There are also a few minor problems (other than its unusual syntax) with this use of macros. Some deficient compilers may have preprocessors that fail on such large macros, although good compilers should not have any problems for "reasonable" size code blocks.

Another minor problem is that any commas that are not nested inside brackets will start a new macro argument, and lead to compilation errors (hopefully). Note that braces do not hide commas from the preprocessor's macro argument collection process. Hence, consider the following code:

```
TRY (
    { int i,j;   // WHOOPS! Comma is an error!

    j = fn(i,i+1);   // This nested comma is ok
    },
{ .... }

);
```

Despite my complaints about its appearance, this method of large macros is a practical alternative to the C++-like syntax used by Horsmeier's method. It allows the treatment of entire code blocks as macro arguments, and they can be moved around or repeated within the macro replacement text.

Exception hierarchies using structs

The most strikingly useful feature of Winroth's method is a clever method of simulating C++ exception hierarchies using nested C `struct` definitions. Suppose you wish to represent a hierarchy of exceptions for library errors, which are divided into mathematical errors and I/O errors. Furthermore, mathematical errors include overflow and underflow, and I/O errors include disk full and open failure. In Winroth's exception library this would be represented as an "exception domain" by a nested `struct` definition, where each `struct` represents an exception domain, and each `int` member is a leaf in the hierarchy:

```
typedef struct {
    struct {
        int underflow;
        int overflow;
    } math_error;
    struct {
        int open_failed;
        int disk_full;
    } io_error;
} lib_error_type;
// declare exception object
extern lib_error_type lib_error;
```

This `struct` declaration and `extern` variable declaration can appear in a header file. `lib_error` must be defined as a global variable in one source file. Note that we cannot use a `static` variable because it is the address that is used by the CATCH macros, and using a `static` variable in the exception header file would lead to multiple addresses for the same exception.

The equivalent ANSI C++ exception hierarchy would be coded as:

```
class lib_error { };
class math_error : public lib_error { };
class underflow : public math error { };
class overflow : public math_error { };
class io_error : public lib_error { };
class open_failed : public io_error { }
class disk_full : public io_error { };
```

To use these exception domains with Winroth's library, the CATCH macro simply catches the appropriate variable or field. Some alternatives are:

```
// all library errors
CATCH(lib_error, {..})
// all math errors
CATCH(lib_error.math_error, {..})
// disk_full only
CATCH(lib_error.io_error.disk_full, {..})
```

In the C++ versions, these exceptions could be caught as below. The main difference is that there is no need to explicitly specify the outer domains:

```
catch(lib_error)       // all library errors
catch(math_error)      // all math errors
catch(disk_full)       // disk_full only
```

Note that Winroth's method permits more than one independent exception hierarchy (simply defined as a separate global `struct` variable). It is not a requirement that all exceptions be derived from one base group, as has been the case with other methods (e.g., Vidal's method). However, this is desirable for portability to platforms with nonlinear address spaces (see below). Also, Winroth's method cannot simulate multiple inheritance in the exception hierarchy, but then who needs it?

Although Winroth's exception library applies only to C, this idiom of simulating exception hierarchies using `struct` members can be applied to any of the C++ libraries. This makes it possible to design this exception facility using C++-like exception hierarchies, allowing the code to upgrade to ANSI C++ features *without changing the design*. Although there is significant change to the coding style, the exception hierarchy can remain the same. Therefore, this method is an important building block for an exception macro system.

Implementation details of Winroth's exception domains

The implementation trick used by the `CATCH` macro to ensure that it catches the correct domain is that it catches *addresses*. The exception y is handled by a `CATCH(x)` clause if the addresses satisfy:

```
&x <= &y <= &x + sizeof(x)
```

Therefore, the method requires special care if the memory organization is not linear. The danger is that of getting "false successes" from this test for pointers in different segments, and the wrong `CATCH` handler will be used. For example, for a segmented DOS architecture it becomes important what types of pointers are compared (i.e., huge pointers are needed). One safety method is that declaring all exception types within one struct declaration will ensure that all addresses can be meaningfully declared; alternatively, *defining* all exception objects in one source file will often ensure their addresses are within the same segment.

Implementation details of Winroth's run-time errors

Another very neat implementation trick is the method of ensuring run-time errors for various failures within the library. Let us examine how the trick is used to detect `return` statements inside a `TRY` block. The keyword `return` is defined as a self-referencing macro (legal in ANSI C and draft ANSI C++) that involves a compile-time test, conceptually similar to:

```
#define return if(sizeof(hidden) > 1) \
{ ERROR(); } else return
```

The trick is a hidden global variable name (i.e., hidden here) that is redefined as a different type in local scopes. The library defines the hidden variable globally with type `char`, and the

TRY macro defines a local variable of the same name as type `long`. Thus whenever a `return` occurs inside a TRY block it sees the local `long` variable that has size at least 4 and complains; but outside of any TRY blocks the compiler sees only the global `char` variable with size 1 and produces no error.

This clever use of two variables with the same name but different types allows the use of `sizeof` as a compile-time test. The efficiency of legitimate `return` statements should not be affected since any good optimizer will elide this test because it has constant value at compile-time.

All run-time errors in Winroth's exception library rely on this trick, which provokes a run-time error based on a compile-time test. In fact, it wouldn't be too hard to modify the method to ensure a *compile-time* diagnostic. One method would be to define the local version of the hidden variable as a `struct` and perform an impossible operation such as < upon the hidden variable. Unfortunately, the error message produced by such an error would probably be quite obscure, although this could be slightly improved by making the hidden variable name self-explanatory.

Unwind-protect

Another feature of Winroth's library is the `UNWIND_PROTECT` macro that provides a method of ensuring that a block of code is always executed, under both normal and exceptional control flows. The syntax of this macro is:

```
UNWIND_PROTECT( main_block, cleanup_block );
```

Limitations

One limitation of Winroth's method is that jump statements will corrupt the `jmp_buf` stack if improperly used. Because only C is used, the C++ popper class idiom of Bengtsson cannot be used. This problem is partially solved by requiring the use of a macro `tryreturn` inside TRY blocks; using `return` inside a TRY block should invoke a run-time error. However, the use of `goto` in and out of blocks is still dangerous.

All variables can be used as exceptions, but since it is actually their address being used, it is dangerous to use automatic local variables, as they may have been destroyed by the time the appropriate CATCH is reached. Exception variables should be global variables, typically declared in a single header file and defined in a single source file.

VIDAL'S LEX-BASED FILTER FOR C++

The library presented by Carlos Vidal is different from the other methods discussed in this chapter in that it is not a preprocessor macro library. Rather than use a library of macros, the idea is to use an extra filter tool in the compilation process, to convert the ANSI C++ exception style to C++ code using only pre-ANSI C++ features. Such a filter is presented in the paper as a script for lex, a lexical analyzer widely available under UNIX. The use of a filter increases flexibility by removing the limitations of the preprocessor.

The main novel features of Vidal's method are support for:

- function interface specifications (!)
- `unexpected` and `set_unexpected`
- `terminate` and `set_terminate`
- both `catch(type)` and `catch(type param_name)`

However, even with this extra flexibility, there are still many features of ANSI C++ exceptions that Vidal's method does not support. Some limitations are:

- exception classes must inherit from an `Exception` base class.
- exception classes must define size and type functions.
- stack unwinding does not call automatic object destructors.
- `return/goto/break/continue` in a `try` block may cause problems.

Regarding the last limitation, it seems that any jump statements, such as a `return` statement, inside a `try` block will skip past the `"Exh::stk--"` stack popping code and cause inconsistency of the stack of `jmp_buf` objects, causing unknown failure of this method.

Overall, Vidal's idea of the use of a filter is a great improvement over using preprocessor macros, although I believe some of the limitations of his implementation could be removed. For example, the execution of destructors and failure due to jump statements could perhaps be handled using Bengtsson's resource and popper class idioms. With these minor problems fixed, the use of a filter has incredible power, as evidenced by the fact that Vidal's method calls `unexpected` upon failure of built-in run-time checking of function interface specifications!

BENGTSSON'S EXCEPTION LIBRARY FOR C++

Johan Bengtsson presents an interesting exception handling library. His report first discusses the theory of various methods of handling exceptions, including using ANSI C++ exceptions, and then presents a macro library to simulate ANSI C++ exceptions using pre-ANSI C++ features.

This macro library uses the macro names TRY, CATCH, THROW, and RETHROW. The underlying method, as always, is the use of `setjmp` and `longjmp` by these macros. The syntax used by the method is:

```
TRY {
    // main block
}
CATCH(int throwCode) {
    // handler block
}
```

The syntax is quite limited in that only one CATCH block is allowed, which must handle all exceptions. Furthermore, there is no discrimination of CATCH blocks based on exception types; all exceptions have integer type. All failures cause execution of the closest CATCH, and the only way to handle the exception at a higher level is to RETHROW.

Popper class to avoid return problems

One notable feature of Bengtsson's method is the "popper" class that is used to avoid problems with jump statements (i.e., return, goto, break, and continue) skipping over destructors for objects declared in the TRY block.

The TRY macro declares a local automatic popper object, which has a destructor that pops the TRY-stack of jmp_buf variables. The definition of TRY and CATCH are effectively:

```
#define TRY if(setjmp(....) == 0) { Popper _popper;
#define CATCH(x) } else
```

Compare the CATCH macro with that of Horsmeier's method, which has an ExceptRls call before the closing right brace that pops the jmp_buf stack. The difference here is that the destructor Popper::~Popper() performs the jmp_buf stack pop operation implicitly. Using the popper class idiom, the destructor execution automatically ensures that the TRY/CATCH level is correct if either:

a) execution falls through the closing right brace of the TRY block; or

b) a jump statement skips past this right brace.

Only a) is guaranteed by an explicit pop operation before the CATCH's right brace, such as in Horsmeier's method. Unfortunately, this popper class idiom uses C++ features (i.e., destructors) and cannot be used by exception macros for C, such as Horsmeier's method.

Class for destructor calls in stack unwinding

Another interesting feature of Bengtsson's library is the method of calling destructors during stack unwinding using a Resource class. Although this method doesn't automatically ensure destructor calls, the programmer can ensure that a particular class has its objects deallocated by making it inherit from Resource (i.e., the new class becomes a derived class of Resource). The constructor and virtual destructor of the Resource base class then maintain a stack of objects to be destroyed when THROW is called. Note that a stack ensures destruction in reverse order to construction.

Unfortunately, this method of calling destructors from a common base class has disadvantages such as:

a) dynamically allocated objects are destroyed (not just automatic objects); and

b) objects inheriting from Resource should not be stored as data members.

Note that the dynamic object problem could be resolved nonportably using an InStack function as shown by Leary and D'Souza's method below. The restriction on storing any Resource-inheriting objects as data members of other objects (especially those that do not inherit from Resource) arises because the member object may be destroyed without destroying the outer object.

LEARY/D'SOUZA'S EXCEPTION LIBRARY FOR C++

Sean Leary and Desmond D'Souza have presented another method that uses C++ features to mimic ANSI C++ exceptions. The method uses the macros TRY, CATCH, ADNCATCH, END-CATCH, and THROW, with the basic syntax:

```
TRY {
    // main code
}
CATCH(type, var_name) {
    // handler code
}
ADNCATCH(type, var_name) {    // Additional catches
    // handler code
}
ENDCATCH
```

The method offers the flexibility to throw entire objects, with the minor restriction that exception class objects must be derived from an Exception class, which is common practice in any case.

Exception handling is based upon the character string representing the name of the exception object's type. All exception classes must define a unique name, and thus exception objects are distinguished using a simple form of run-time type inference. Unfortunately, this allows no possibility of defining exception hierarchies and catching classes of exceptions. The method used by Leary and D'Souza to destroy automatic objects during stack unwinding is the same as that used by Bengtsson, but has a new twist.

All object classes needing to be destroyed in this manner must inherit from the Unwind class; the idea is identical to Bengtsson's use of a Resource base class. The constructor and virtual destructor of Unwind maintain a stack of objects to be destroyed when an exception is thrown (a stack ensures destruction in reverse order of construction). The new twist is that they overcome the problem that dynamically allocated objects will be destroyed by defining an InStack function that determines whether an object is automatic. Unfortunately, the method is inherently nonportable, and the implementation presented works only for Borland C++ small model.

There are various other notable features of this implementation:

*   Throw(Obj) and Throw() are distinguished by overloading.
*   Throw() causes a rethrow operation.
*   catch(...) equivalent is CATCH(Exception, ptr_name).

LEE'S EXCEPTION LIBRARY FOR C

An interesting exception library is presented in the good technical paper by Lee, which is an early setjmp based exception library. The overall syntax is:

```
BEGIN
    ....
EXCEPTION
```

```
      . . .
   WHEN(Exception name)
      . . . .
   WHEN(Exception name)
      . . . .
END
```

Exceptions have `char*` type and are declared as variables. One minor caveat: The macro `NEW_EXCEPTION` relies on pre-ANSI macro parameter expansion within strings, and must be converted to use the # stringize operator for use with ANSI C/C++.

WILLIAM'S EXCEPTION LIBRARY FOR C

Another remarkable exceptions package is freely available via FTP. It was created by Ross N. Williams and publicly released in September 1993. The details are as follows:

Product:	William's Exception Library for C
Available:	by anonymous FTP to the site "ftp.adelaide.edu.au" in the directory pub/funnelweb/examples.
Author:	Ross N. Williams
Address:	Rocksoft Pty Ltd., 16 Lerwick Avenue, Hazelwood Park 5066, Australia
Voice:	+61-8-379-9217

Although distributed as an example of literate programming using the *FunnelWeb* literate programming tool, it is also a very useful package for C programmers in its own right.

BUILDING BLOCKS FROM THE LIBRARIES

All of the various exception handling macro libraries offer various features with advantages and disadvantages. However, the different authors have mixed these features in various ways, and it hasn't always been clear which ideas are compatible with each other. That is the purpose of this section — to identify the building blocks, and examine their orthogonality or lack thereof. This should help you to build your own exception handling library if none of the existing ones suffice. I have identified the following important building blocks for exceptions in both C and C++:

- Winroth's exception domains (hierarchies) using `structs` and addresses
- Winroth's run-time errors for bad `return` (macro trick with `sizeof`)
- allocation for `jmp_buf` stack — Horsmeier's `malloc` calls
- allocation for `jmp_buf` stack — Amsterdam's automatic variables
- allocation for `jmp_buf` stack — Hood's global fixed-size array

There are also some building blocks that require C++ features:

- Bengtsson's "popper" class to handle jump statements
- stack unwinding of destructors using Bengtsson's `Resource` class
- run-time type identification implemented in exception objects
- exception objects inheriting from a single `Exception` base class

There are also at least three styles of syntax for the exception handling code:

- Winroth style of large macros — i.e., code blocks in macro arguments
- ANSI C++ syntax imitation
- Hood's separate handle/unhandle macro syntax; dissimilar to C++ syntax

Some of these building blocks are orthogonal, and can be used in combination with others. For example, Winroth's exception domains using structs could be easily combined with a different macro style, such as the ANSI C++ imitation style used by Horsmeier and also Leary/ D'Souza.

However, other combinations of primitives are less compatible. For example, Winroth's `struct` method appears incompatible with the use of an `Exception` common base class, because the former requires treatment of addresses of objects, and the latter passes objects by reference at the throw-point.

One possibility that none of the authors used was to stringize the type argument to CATCH, and explicitly test for the string "..." as a special case. However, this is difficult to do; for example, the method of Leary and D'Souza does stringize the type argument in the CATCH macro, but also makes use of the same macro argument without stringizing, which would cause a compilation error from the CATCH(...) usage.

Another important issue to address is whether the method must use only the C/C++ preprocessor (as with the building blocks above) or whether the use of another tool in the compilation process is acceptable. For example, Vidal's method uses a separate language filter, built using a `lex` script, to preprocess the ANSI C++ code (using ANSI exception syntax) into pre-ANSI C++ code. Using an extra filter step provides much more flexibility, but the extra phase during compilation may be a headache.

FURTHER READING

This chapter has examined the work of a number of people, all presenting various methods of exception handling technique using macros in C or C++ to hide `setjmp` and `longjmp` calls. The bibliographic details of the relevant papers are listed below.

AMSTERDAM, Jonathan, "Some Assembly Required: Taking Exception to C", *Byte*, August 1991, pp. 259-264.

BENGTSSON, Johan, *C++, "Without Exceptions", Telia Research*, Lulea, Sweden. (available via FTP to `euagate.eua.ericsson.se` in directory *pub/eua/c++* with filename *Exceptions_920511.ps.Z*)

ERDELSKY, Philip J., "A Safer setjmp in C++", *C Users Journal*, Vol. 11, No. 1, January 1993, pp. 41-44.

LEARY, Sean, and D'SOUZA, Desmond, *Catch the Error: C++ Exception Handling*, Computer Language, October 1992, pp. 63-77.

LEE, P.A., "Exception Handling in C Programs", *Software — Practice & Experience*, Vol. 13, 1983, pp. 389-405.

MILLER, W.M., "Error Handling in C++", *Computer Language*, May 1988, pp. 43-52.

MILLER, W.M., "Exception Handling Without Language Support", *USENIX C++ Conference Proceedings*, Denver, Colorado, USENIX Press, 1988.

VIDAL, Carlos, "Exception Handling", *C Users Journal*, Vol. 10, No. 9, September 1992, pp. 19-28.

WINROTH, Harald, "Exception Handling in ANSI C", *Computational Vision and Active Perception Laboratory (CVAP)*, Royal Institute of Technology (KTH), Stockholm, Sweden (available via FTP to *ftp.bion.kth.se* in directory *cvap/2.0* as file *exception-1.2.tar.Z*).

Mathematical & scientific libraries

*F*or a long time Fortran was the single dominant programming language for any scientific or mathematical programs. Even the popularity of C as it rose to prominence did not really entice many scientists away from Fortran because of some fundamental problems with its use in mathematical programs, such as the absence of a `complex` type. However, C++ has been a different story. The class construct single-handedly resolved C's limitations and improved upon Fortran's capabilities with its ability to model complicated mathematical structures such as special forms of matrices and groups through well-defined abstractions and inheritance hierarchies. Although I will not venture to say that Fortran support is waning, C++ has become an established language in the scientific world for mathematical programming.

These days there is considerable activity in C++ programming of scientific algorithms. For example, the Internet newsgroup *hepnet.lang.c++* is used for discussion of C++ for High Energy Physics applications showing that C++ has made its way into some of the most theoretical areas of study. It is also no coincidence that this chapter contains more reviews of C++ libraries than C libraries.

M++ From Dyad Software

Product Name:	M++ 5.0
Platforms:	DOS, Windows 3.1, Windows 95, Windows NT, HP- UX, Solaris, Solaris-x86, SunOS
Price:	Starting at $495; educational discounts
Company:	Dyad Software Corporation
Address:	6947 Coal Creek Pkwy SE., Suite. 361, Newcastle, WA 98059-3159, USA
Phone:	1-800-366-1573, 206-637-9426
Fax:	206-637-9428
Email:	70724.2366@compuserve.com

M++ is a feature rich C++ library for scientific and engineering applications that makes multidimensional operations as easy to code as scalar operations. The basic classes implemented include vectors, matrices, multi-dimensional arrays, persistent and virtual arrays. Optional arrays bounds checking is available for debugging.

M++ includes a number of components with the VIS package for plotting graphs, the SUM package for statistics, LINPACK for linear system classes, and EISPACK for eigensystem classes. Features available include Bessel functions, Legendre polynomials, Elliptic Integrals, Householder and Givens rotations, correlation functions, coherence functions, spectral methods, FFT, piecewise approximation, numerical integration, least squares, ordinary differential equations, and unconstrained optimization. There is also support for common APL, MATLAB, and Mathematica features for easy "porting" of existing mathematical work.

Math Advantage from QTC

Product Name:	Math Advantage, Stat Advantage, Spec Advantage
Platforms:	DOS, Macintosh, PowerPC, UNIX, VMS
Company:	Quantitative Technology Corporation (QTC)
Address:	9305 SW Nimbus Ave, Beaverton, OR 97008, USA
Phone:	503-626-3081
Fax:	503-641-6012
Email:	QTC@IX.Netcom.Com

Math Advantage is an ANSI C library (Fortran also) implementing a huge number of mathematical routines. Available features include: vector operations, full and sparse matrix operations, complex operations, linear system solution, approximation and curve fitting, signal processing and FFT, polynomial operations, differentiation and integration, and Basic Linear Algebra Subprograms (BLAS)

Spec Advantage is another ANSI C (also Fortran) library implementing special functions. The functions available include: combinatorial functions, Bessel functions, Legendre polynomials, probability distributions, and various matrix conversion utilities (e.g., involving symmetric, Hermetian, banded or triangular matrices).

Stat Advantage is a library of statistics routines for ANSI C. Some of the features offered are: regression analysis, random number generation, probability distributions, descriptive statistics, and various utilities similar to those mentioned for Spec Advantage.

Math.h++, LAPACK.h++ from Rogue Wave

Product Name:	Math.h++, LAPACK.h++
Platforms:	DOS, Windows, NT, OS/2, UNIX
Price:	Math.h++: $299-$395; LAPACK.h++: $795-$1,195
Company:	Rogue Wave Software
Address:	P.O. Box 2328, Corvallis, OR 97339, USA
Phone:	1-800-487-3217, 541-754-3010
Fax:	541-757-6650
FTP:	FTP.Roguewave.com (user: anonymous)
Email:	sales@roguewave.com
Web:	http://www.roguewave.com

Math.h++ is a set of C++ classes for dealing with mathematical structures such as complex numbers, vectors and arrays. Classes and methods available include: complex numbers, FFT, linear algebra, histograms and linear regression. Optional array bounds checking can be enabled for debugging.

LAPACK.h++ is another separate product from Rogue Wave that uses Math.h++ and implements various linear algebra structures and algorithms as C++ classes and methods. This library implements all the features of the Lapack Fortran library. LAPACK.h++ offers classes for matrices, vectors, and factorization and decomposition objects, with methods for solving problems such as: systems of equations, determinants, inverses, condition numbers, eigenvalues, and decompositions.

## CHAPTER 20

Database libraries

The categories of programs and databases are already a grey area as almost all applications require some form of underlying database management. Database query languages now contain all the features of powerful programming languages combined with database access features (obviously). From the other end, the 3GLs like C and C++ now have a variety of methods of implementing database access.

Adding database features to an application can be done in a number of ways. There are a variety of application development environments using 4GLs on the market. There are also a number of products that support C/C++ programmers in adding database features to an application. Some of these products are pure C/C++ products, and others are interfaces to database components that support both C/C++ and 4GL accesses.

The two main types of database code libraries are front-ends to existing database tools and embedded database facilities. Front-end libraries allow the program to access an already existing database product. This means the database is not really part of the program, but that the program has been enabled with technology to access information through the avenues permitted by that database product. Some of these front-end products provide a way to execute SQL on the given database, and others provide API methods that are internally translated to SQL. Some of the more advanced front-end libraries support multiple databases, such as Oracle, Sybase, Informix and Ingres, and thereby form a level of abstraction above whichever RDBMS is being used.

The opposite to a front-end library is an embedded database library. This is a code library that implements all of the database-like features in the library itself, rather than leveraging the features from an existing database product. This usually offers advantages in performance because the code does not have to go through a general database interface. In addition, using an embedded database does not require purchase of a separate product, and is not vulnerable to failure in any external product. The disadvantage is that the general capabilities, many of them advanced, are not always available in an embedded database library.

C-INDEX/II FROM TRIO SYSTEMS

Product Name:	C-Index/II
Platforms:	DOS, Windows 3.1, Windows 95, Windows NT, OS/2, Linux, Macintosh, HP-UX, Ultrix, Solaris, Solaris-x86, SunOS, any UNIX system (generic UNIV V port supplied)
Languages:	K&R C, ANSI C (not C++)
Price:	$695 (no royalties)
Company:	Trio Systems
Address:	936 E. Green Street, Suite 105, Pasadena, CA 91106, USA
Fax:	818-584-0364
Phone:	818-584-9706
Email:	mail@triosystems.com
Web:	http://www.triosystems.com

C-Index/II is a C language library that adds file and database management capabilities to applications. The library uses fast B+tree indexing for advanced performance even with variable-length records. There are a large number of API functions for many features, and source code is fully supplied. There is support for single and multi-key access to records. There is also support for multiple users with locking and semaphore functions to avoid contention. Files up to 8.7 terabytes and 4 billion records are supported and all database files have a platform independent format that avoids byte ordering dependencies. European and Japanese character sets are supported to aid in writing international programs.

Also in the distribution are a number of standalone utilities: *rebuild* is used to rebuild corrupted files, *dump* is used to print database files in text, *compact* is used to reorder a file for space efficiency; *bcheck* is used to detect bad nodes in a file; and *convert* is used to resolve problems.

DBTOOLS.H++ FROM ROGUE WAVE

Product Name:	DBTools.h++
Platforms:	Windows, UNIX
Price:	$395-$3,995 (platform/database dependent)
Company:	Rogue Wave Software
Address:	P.O. Box 2328, Corvallis, OR 97339, USA
Phone:	1-800-487-3217, 541-754-3010
Fax:	541-757-6650
FTP:	FTP.Roguewave.com (user: anonymous)
Email:	sales@roguewave.com
Web:	http://www.roguewave.com

DBTools.h++ builds upon Rogue Wave's tools.h++ foundation classes to add database support to C++ programs using existing database products. This is a set of classes for database manipulation that serves to abstract the operations from the actual database used to implement the actions. The databases supported include Oracle, Sybase, Ingres and Informix. There is also ODBC support allowing the use of C++ classes to access information from any ODBC-enabled application.

ILOG DB LINK — RDBMS C++ LIBRARY

Product Name:	ILOG DB LINK
Platforms:	UNIX, PCs
Company:	ILOG, Inc.
Address:	2005 Landings Drive, Mountain View, CA 94043, USA
Phone:	415-390-9000
Fax:	415-390-0946
Email:	info@ilog.com
Web:	http://www.ilog.com

ILOG DB LINK is a C++ class library for connection to relational databases. A wide variety of commercial RDBMS systems are supported including Sybase, Oracle, Ingres and Informix on UNIX, and Oracle, SQL Base, and SQL Server on PC platforms. The classes for database access abstract the details of the database from the application, allowing generic cross-platform cross-database code to be written easily in a few lines. SQL requests are passed directly from the application to the RDBMS with support for transaction management, data manipulation and data dictionary access. This use of SQL offers many advantages over learning to use a new API-set for performing well-known database applications.

There are three main classes for implementing database applications. The `IdbDbms` class allows connection or disconnection to a database, creation of objects to handle SQL statements, and reading and using a schema or data dictionary. The `IdbRequest` class abstracts cursors in RDBMS systems and allows applying SQL queries to the connection via the `IdbDbms` object, selection of rows, and repeated data extraction. The `IdbRelation` class allows access to relational information such as column names, types, and null properties.

ILOG DB LINK allows multiple requests, database instances or database systems to be handled concurrently. Stored procedures are supported for connections to Oracle and Sybase databases. The library is also safe for multithreaded applications.

ILOG DB LINK also offers close integration with ILOG VIEWS for GUI or graphical use of the database information. Additional components from ILOG include ILOG SCHEDULE for scheduling capabilities, ILOG RULES for real-time data monitoring, and ILOG TALK for fast prototyping.

C-TREE PLUS — C DATABASE LIBRARY FROM FAIRCOM

Product Name:	c-tree Plus
Platforms:	DOS ,Windows 3.1, Windows 95, Windows NT, OS/2, Macintosh, PowerPC, Solaris, SunOS, Solaris-x86, HP-UX, OSF/1, AIX, SGI, Sequent, Ultrix, DG, NCR/AT&T, ICL, UniSys, Bull, QNX, Lynx
Price:	$895 per developer, no royalties
Company:	FairCom Corporation
Address:	4006 West Broadway, Columbia, MO 65203, USA
Phone:	573-445-6833
Fax:	573-445-9698
Email:	faircom@faircom.com
FTP:	ftp.faircom.com (user: anonymous)
BBS:	314-445-6318 (baud to 14,400; settings: N,8,1)

c-tree Plus is a cross-platform library distributed in C source that provides powerful data and file management capabilities. This is a library that allows management of large amounts of application data in files to provide database storage abilities with fast sequential or random file access. The volume of data that can be handled is massive with no limits on the number of records or indexes, but with some design limits that seem quite reasonable — 2 to 4 gigabytes for the maximum size of a variable length record seems adequate. The underlying technology is advanced B+tree data structures with support from indexes, hashing, and caching.

All features are provided as a C function API that provides both low-level access and high-level ISAM functionality to address all programmer needs. Many platforms are supported with the native I/O routines used for improved performance, and data files are portable across platforms despite byte ordering differences. Internationalization support is also available via collating sequence support at the file level and character set support such as Japanese Kanji. C-tree also supports ODBC access.

Three modes are supported by c-tree Plus for file access. Single user mode applies to applications with exclusive access to files and takes full advantage of this guarantee to improve performance. Multi-user mode applies when multiple processes need concurrent access to the database files and c-tree Plus uses file and record locking to resolve conflicts. The third mode is client/server mode where a separate product called the FairCom Server maintains control over the data files.

R-TREE REPORT GENERATOR LIBRARY FROM FAIRCOM

Product Name:	r-tree
Platforms:	DOS ,Windows 3.1, Windows 95, Windows NT, OS/2, Macintosh, PowerPC, Solaris, SunOS, Solaris-x86, HP-UX, OSF/1, AIX, SGI, Ultrix, DG, NCR/AT&T, QNX, Lynx
Price:	$445 per developer, no royalties
Company:	FairCom Corporation
Address:	4006 West Broadway, Columbia, MO 65203, USA
Phone:	573-445-6833
Fax:	573-445-9698
Email:	faircom@faircom.com
FTP:	ftp.faircom.com (user: anonymous)
BBS:	314-445-6318 (baud to 14,400; settings: N,8,1)

r-tree is a C library distributed in source form that reads data files produced by FairCom's c-tree Plus data manager and produces formatted reports. At the heart of r-tree is a report script language that is a textual description of data required by the report and its output format. Scripts can be distributed in text form or compiled into a proprietary format to protect intellectual property. The report script data manipulation commands allow specification of tables and keys from which to extract data, boolean set expressions to apply to the data including operators such as "for all" and "there exists", and arithmetic accumulators such as sums and averages.

The last section of the script is the IMAGE section which is a textual WYSIWYG display of how the output reports should appear, showing the positioning of all the relevant fields

in the output and specifying page breaks, footers and page numbering. In this way programmers and even customers can quickly develop custom textual reports of the data stored in
their c-tree Plus data files.

RAIMA DATABASE MANAGER++ — DATABASE LIBRARY

Product Name:	Raima Database Manager++
Platforms:	DOS, Windows 3.1, Windows 95, Windows NT, Macintosh, OS/2, UNIX (Solaris, Solaris-x86, SunOS, HP-UX, OSF/1, AIX, DG, NCR/AT&T, Bull, Pyramid, ICL, Sequent, MIPS, MIPS ABI, and QNX), VMS
Price:	$995 and up
Company:	Raima Corporation
Address:	1605 NW Sammamish Rd, Suite 200, Issaquah, WA 98027,USA
Phone:	1-800-327-2462, 206-557-0200
Fax:	206-557-5200
Email:	sales@raima.com
FTP:	hp_ux.raima.com (198.206.247.13), [username: anonymous]
Web:	http://www.raima.com

Raima Database Manager++ (RDM++), formerly called db_VISTA, is a C library that provides data and file management facilities for embedding database features in an application.
Multi-user access is supported and client/server access is available via the Raima Velocis
Database Server, a separate product from Raima that integrates embedded database technology into client/server architecture.

RDM++ provides efficient data access by combining the best features of the relational
model with the network model. Developers use a Database Definition Language (DDL) to
develop database schemas for the application. The underlying technology is fast B-tree indexing with improvements such as caching to reduce disk I/O needs.

Multi-user access to the database is supported by file and record locking using inbuilt
features or lock managers on various platforms. There is automatic logging and recovery of
database files, and timestamping of records can be used to determine the most recent change
or access to a record.

The primary feature of RDM++ is the C API functions, over 200 in number, for accessing and manipulating the database. The functions offer capabilities to open and close databases (including multiple databases at the same time), create, modify or read records,
searching through tables, and various administrative issues such as locking functions for
multi-user interactions. International character sets are also supported for localized use of the
database.

There are two important add-on products that enhance RDM++ facilities: db_REVISE and db_QUERY. The db_REVISE tool is a comprehensive database schema restructuring tool that is useful as the schema evolves. Various aspects of the database can be restructured including naming, organization of records across files, page sizes, and aspects such as whether records are timestamped.

The db_QUERY tool is used for ad-hoc or predefined queries of the database using SQL. Features such as searching, sorting, arithmetic operations and display options allow the development of powerful queries. Special report writing features include totalling, page break control, headers and footers, and column heading control. Using these features application developers can provide reports using data in RDM++ databases.

RAIMA OBJECT MANAGER — C++ DATABASE LIBRARY

Product Name:	Raima Object Manager
Platforms:	DOS, Windows 3.1, Windows 95, Windows NT, OS/2, UNIX (Solaris, Solaris-x86, SunOS, HP-UX, OSF/1, AIX, ICL, MIPS)
Price:	$495 and up
Company:	Raima Corporation
Address:	1605 NW Sammamish Road, Suite 200, Issaquah, WA 98027, USA
Phone:	1-800-327-2462, 206-557-0200
Fax:	206-557-5200
Email:	sales@raima.com
FTP:	hp_ux.raima.com (198.206.247.13), username: anonymous
Web:	http://www.raima.com

Raima Object Manager (ROM) is a C++ class library that provides an object-oriented interface to Raima Database Manager++ and Raima Velocis Database Server. This achieves many of the features desirable in an Object-oriented database with a fast embedded database engine. This allows C++ applications to take advantage of features such as transaction processing and Microsoft ODBC in a client/server architecture.

ROM includes numerous C++ classes for data and database management. Objects can be made persistent through a base class, and naturally there is control over their storage in the database. Overloaded operators such as the index operator allow convenient notations for database accesses. For example, with appropriate definitions the code fragment *customers["Mary Smith"]* will locate a client by searching the customer table. Concurrency of multi-user accesses is controlled automatically by the ROM classes. Ad hoc or stored SQL queries can be applied to the database via the ROM interface to the db_QUERY facilities for querying or reporting.

B-Tree Filer from TurboPower

Product Name:	B-Tree Filer
Platforms:	DOS, Windows
Price:	$249
Company:	TurboPower Software Co.
Address:	P.O. Box 49009, Colorado Springs, CO 80949-9009, USA
Phone:	1-800-333-4160, 719-260-9136
Fax:	719-260-7151
FTP:	tpower.com/pub/turbopower (user: anonymous)
Email:	info@tpower.com
Web:	http://www.tpower.com

B-Tree Filer is a library of C functions to build and maintain a database of records. The underlying data structure is the B+tree with support for variable-length records and large numbers of records per data file.

Single and multiple user network modes are supported by B-Tree Filer. Locking is supported on three levels of granularity: all databases, single database and per-record locking. Special read locks are supported that allow arithmetic over multiple records with the guarantee of no modification. The API offers low-level control over locks, indexes and records. Journalling is available, and there is automatic buffer flushing and a special safety mode that permits full recovery from faults.

In addition to the basic API there are add-on utilities. The virtual sort module sorts large amounts of data in limited space resources. An index rebuilder is available for automatic rebuilding of optimized indexes as the database grows. There is also the facility for importing or exporting of data to dBase format.

C/Database Toolchest from Mix Software

Product Name:	C/Database Toolchest
Platforms:	DOS, Windows 3.1, Windows 95, Windows NT, Linux, OS/2
Price:	$49.95 + $10.00 each additional platform
Company:	Mix Software, Inc.
Address:	1132 Commerce Drive, Richardson, TX 75081, USA
Phone:	1-800-333-0330, 214-783-6001
Fax:	214-783-1404
Email:	mixsoft@ibm.net

C/Database Toolchest has an attractive price tag for a product that offers a C library or C++ interface for file management that allows you to use sophisticated database access in your application. There is explicit support for Power C, Turbo C/C++, Borland C/C++, Microsoft C/C++ and Watcom C/C++. The C API offers low-level access to data records and indexes, or high-level ISAM interface to the data. The underlying technology is the B+tree data structure which is used for data files and indexes. The library allows records as large as 32K, and supports advanced features such as variable length keys, multiple keys per index and multiple indexes in single file. File and record locking is supported.

The distribution includes a database manager application as an example of how to use the ISAM library, with full source code supplied. All source code including the B+tree and ISAM libraries is also available from Mix Software for no additional charge.

A number of standalone utilities are supplied with C/Database Toolchest. Two utilities allow conversion to and from dBASE format. There are also utilities to dump data files and indexes to text output, and a utility to print labels from a database.

DATABASEPAK — MOTIF DATABASE-AWARE WIDGET LIBRARY

Product Name:	DatabasePak
Platforms:	UNIX (Solaris, SunOS, HP-UX, OSF/1, AIX, SGI)
Price:	$2,795 per developer
Company:	Integrated Computer Solutions, Inc.
Address:	201 Broadway, Cambridge, MA 02139, USA
Phone:	1-800 800 4271, 617-621-0060
Fax:	617-621-9555
Email:	info@ics.com
Web:	http://www.ics.com/

DatabasePak is a library of Motif widgets that can directly access relational databases. Oracle and Sybase are the currently supported databases. Using the DatabasePak widgets you can create a Motif application with automated database access for complicated operations.

There are four distinct types of widgets defined by DatabasePak: database access, query, data presentation and controls. Database access widgets connect to the database to permit queries. Query widgets submit a query to the database access widgets and manage the data resulting from a database query, transmitting it to data presentation widgets. Data presentation widgets display information on the GUI based on queries. Control widgets handle aspects such as moving to other records and performing SQL operations. Stored procedures are also supported including triggers.

The DatabasePak distribution also includes a schema browser. This connects to the database and allows browsing of the structure and data stored there. This is useful to determine the names of tables and columns to use in your DatabasePak SQL queries.

DATABASE XCESSORY — MOTIF DATABASE APPLICATION BUILDER

Product Name:	Database Xcessory
Platforms:	UNIX (Solaris, SunOS, HP-UX, OSF/1, AIX, SGI)
Price:	$5,995 per simultaneous user
Company:	Integrated Computer Solutions, Inc.
Address:	201 Broadway, Cambridge, MA 02139, USA
Phone:	1-800-800-4271, 617-621-0060
Fax:	617-621-9555
Email:	info@ics.com
Web:	http://www.ics.com/

Database Xcessory is a visual GUI builder that is tightly related to the DatabasePak widgets. Development of applications with database access is simplified by the use of the visual builder. Widgets are chosen from a Palette, and a special resource editor is used to customize their appearance and behavior. All of the features of DatabasePak widgets are available including stored procedure and trigger support.

There is also a "play" mode to view the current results of the GUI. This mode allows all visual elements of the GUI to behave with their usual dynamic behavior, although the full application code is not invoked at this stage.

The database schema browser supplied as a standalone utility with DatabasePak is an integrated window in Database Xcessory. This allows you to connect to the database and browse the structure and data stored there. Information from the browser can be drag-n-dropped into Database Xcessory to quickly create required database accesses.

Another component in Database Xcessory but not in DatabasePak is the GraphPak library of widgets for advanced graphical data display. These widgets offer the ability to plot data in line graphs, x-y graphs, bar graphs (including stacked bar and multibar graphs), histogram charts, and more. Many aspects of the data display can be customized and PostScript output is supported for printing.

POET — OBJECT DATABASE LIBRARY FOR C++

Product Name:	POET
Purpose:	Object database management system for C++
Platforms:	Windows 3.1, Windows 95, Windows NT, OS/2, Macintosh, PowerPC, Novell, NeXTStep, Solaris, Solaris-x86, SunOS, HP-UX, AIX, SGI, SCO
Price:	from $499
Company:	POET Software
Address:	999 Baker Way, Suite 100, San Mateo, CA 94404, USA
Phone:	1-800-950-8845, 415-286-4640
Fax:	415-286-4630
Email:	info@poet.com
Web:	http://www.poet.com

In contrast to those libraries that provide flat-file or relational database support, POET is an *object* management system. POET allows applications to store objects in a persistent database without any need to convert or "linearize" the objects into a file compatible format. POET avoids this conversion on saving and rebuilding on loading by storing objects directly. This use of an object-oriented database is a powerful addition to C++ applications.

POET offers a number of major features with single and multi-user versions. There is a single user POET engine, a multi-user POET personal server that handles concurrent accesses, and a POET workgroup server for client/server applications. POET's open architecture offers ODBC support and OLE 2.0 facilities.

There are a number of tools provided with the POET database. The POET Developer toolset includes a schema builder that creates the data dictionary from C++ header files, a class explorer for examining C++ classes, and the POET Object Explorer for interrogating object databases. The POET Administrator offers a suite of database tools including authorization and access control, schema versioning, transaction rollback, backup and recovery, and reorganization facilities. POET has its own Object Query Language (OQL) for SQL-like queries on the database. Hence POET is an advanced database with many features, and the C++ class API allows that power to be incorporated into C++ programs.

Component libraries

One of the most useful types of libraries of C functions or C++ classes is one offering various data structures for organizing data. Some of the most common data structures that are provided include linked lists, stacks, queues, sets, binary trees, B-trees, hash tables, and many more.

TOOLS.H++ FROM ROGUE WAVE

Product Name:	Tools.h++
Platforms:	Windows 3.1, Windows 95, Windows NT, OS/2, Macintosh, UNIX (OSF/1, HP-UX, SunOS, Solaris, SGI, AIX)
Price:	$395 (source code included)
Company:	Rogue Wave Software

Address:	P.O. Box 2328, Corvallis, OR 97339, USA
Phone:	1-800-487-3217, 541-754-3010
Fax:	541-757-6650
FTP:	FTP.Roguewave.com (user: anonymous)
Email:	sales@roguewave.com
Web:	http://www.roguewave.com

Tools.h++ is a huge library of foundation classes for C++ with many features. Over 100 classes are available for a variety of programmer needs. Some of the classes included are: dates, time, files, B-trees, collections, linked lists, queues, stacks, hash tables, sets, vectors, regular expressions, tokenizers, DDE/clipboard buffer classes, and more.

Advanced string manipulation is available with various string classes. Supported features include concatenation, comparison, indexing, substring operations, regular expressions, and tokenization of strings.

There are a variety of container or collection classes available for operating on groups of objects in three main areas: template-based collection classes, generic collection classes, and Smalltalk-like collection classes. There is support for both value-based and reference-based collections. Some of the offerings are bags, sets, dictionaries, binary trees, ordered lists, hash tables, and more.

Internationalization is supported by a `RWLocale` class. The RWZone class allows easy calculations involving times across borders. In addition, string functions support multibyte and wide-character manipulation for internationalization.

Persistence of objects allows storage of objects on disk, even exchange of objects via DDE on Windows. All objects can be stored in this way on persistent storage.

Threaded programs can use Tools.h++ safely by turning on a compile-time define. This causes the library to both use thread-safe low-level primitives, and its own internal locking.

The performance philosophy of Rogue Wave class libraries is the same as the general C++ implementation philosophy: only the user pays. Code that does not use a particular feature is not degraded by the need to test for other features. In addition, some Rogue Wave classes use copy-on-write via reference counts to reduce object copying. Tools.h++ can also be built as a Windows DLL.

C++ DATA OBJECT LIBRARY FROM CODE FARMS

Product Name:	C/C++ Data Object Library
Platforms:	DOS, Windows, Windows NT, Mac, UNIX, OS/2, VMS
Status:	Commercial product
Price:	$299 DOS/WIN/NT/MAC; $599 UNIX
Company:	Code Farms Inc.

Address:	7214 Jock Trail, Richmond, Ontario, K0A2Z0, Canada
Phone:	613-838-4829
Fax:	613-838-3316
Email:	info@CodeFarms.com
Web:	http://www.CodeFarms.com

Dr. Jiri Soukup is the founder of Code Farms and his original ideas on how C and C++ librar-ies should be used appear in his product. His techniques aim to prevent spaghetti++ and are described in his book:

> SOUKUP, Jiri, *Taming C++. Patterns Classes and Persistence for Large Projects*, Addison Wesley, 1994, ISBN 0-201-52826-6.

The C++ Data Object Library uses these ideas to offer various advantages: elimination of ref-erences and pointer-members to prevent pointer errors, orthogonal design of object classes, and use of code generation rather than templates.

The features offered in the classes include single and double linked lists, heterogeneous hierarchies and aggregates, trees, directed and undirected graphs, stacks and queues, binary heaps, hash tables, reference counting, and dynamic arrays. Entity-relationship diagrams can be represented with support for 1-1, 1-*n*, *m*-1, and *m*-*n* mappings.

An important feature is automatic saving to disk of objects and inter-dependent object structures to achieve persistent storage of objects and data structures. Stored objects can use binary format for minimal disk space or ASCII format for platform independence.

The collection classes offer a number of useful features. Collections can be added to, deleted from, scanned via iterators, split into separate collections, or two collections can be merged into one larger collection. There is a timestamp facility which can be enabled to record the creation or last modification time. Run-time error checking can be optionally enabled for debugging. Dangling pointers are eliminated by a form of reference counting that does not release objects until all pointers to it have been destroyed or nulled. The library also includes a data browser for traversing data structures at run-time for debugging.

WIN/SYS LIBRARY FROM TURBOPOWER

Product Name:	Win/Sys Library
Platforms:	Windows
Price:	$149
Company:	TurboPower Software Co.
Address:	P.O. Box 49009, Colorado Springs, CO 80949-9009, USA
Phone:	1-800-333-4160, 719-260-9136
Fax:	719-260-7151

FTP:	tpower.com/pub/turbopower (user: anonymous)
Email:	info@tpower.com
Web:	http://www.tpower.com

Win/Sys Library provides a variety of functions and classes for different programming needs. Data structures provided include linked lists, stacks, queues, trees, bit sets, hashed dictionaries and large collections. There are functions for string manipulation, date and time manipulations and fast sorting.

The library also supports a number of features for low-level Windows or DOS programming. There is support for DOS Protected Mode Interface (DPMI) programming and an error trapping feature that intercepts fatal errors such as divide by zero and floating pointer overflow to allow graceful application termination. There are also heap analysis, time delay, sound, and DOS access routines that complement existing compiler run-time libraries by providing easier access and additional features.

Most of the functions of the Win/Sys Library are provided in DLL form for access from many programming languages. Some C++ specific classes are provided in true C++ form rather than direct calls to the DLL.

CHAPTER **22**

Heap allocation libraries

*I*n Chapter 5 we examined a large number of tools for detecting errors in memory allocation such as double frees or memory leaks. In this chapter we'll examine a number of code libraries which, although often providing quite a lot of non-trivial error detection, are not really directed centrally toward debugging. Instead, these libraries are designed for programmers seeking to improve performance of programs that heavily use dynamic memory by offering faster servicing of allocation requests, reduced memory overhead, and less heap fragmentation.

These libraries typically re-implement the underlying allocation algorithms with tuning capabilities for getting the best for your application's memory usage patterns. In addition, there is usually support for small objects in these libraries, as significant gains are possible when the size and distribution of allocation requests are known in advance. In this way you can relink with the new libraries for an effort-free gain, or use the API to tune the performance even further. By taking control of the method used for memory allocation you can improve application performance, and no longer be at the mercy of the vendor's `malloc` library in cross-platform coding. I will politely refrain from naming the UNIX platforms where I know the vendor libraries can cause process size growth via memory fragmentation.

SMARTHEAP FROM MICROQUILL

Product Name:	SmartHeap
Platforms:	MS-DOS, Windows 3.1, Windows 95, Windows NT, OS/2, Mac, PowerMac, UNIX (SGI, AIX, HP-UX, Solaris, SunOS)
Company:	MicroQuill Software Publishing, Inc.
Address:	4900 25th Ave. NE, Ste 206, Seattle, WA, 98105
Phone:	1-800-441-7822/206-525-8218
Fax:	206-525-8309
Email:	info@microquill.com
Compuserve:	70751,2443

SmartHeap is a library that solves two important problems related to heap allocation: perfor-mance and debugging. SmartHeap offers huge improvements in performance of programs relying on heap allocated memory. Along the way SmartHeap will detect a variety of com-mon coding errors related to the heap. However, note that SmartHeap's error detection capa-bilities appear somewhat secondary to its performance enhancements, as MicroQuill distributes a separate tool called HeapAgent specifically for heap error checking with more features in this area. Hence we'll focus on the performance improvement in this discussion.

SmartHeap improves performance in a number of ways. It improves locality of accesses to reduce memory page faults and page swapping by maintaining the representation of free blocks in as few pages as possible (this avoids the multi-page scanning of the free list as performed by some vendor libraries), and by mapping consecutive allocation requests to the same page where possible. The overhead of allocation from SmartHeap is very low, and the fixed size block allocation facilities will be faster still, even without changing your code to use a new fixed size allocation API. Naturally, SmartHeap does have various API functions including support for multiple memory pools to improve locality and further eliminate frag-mentation, and handle-based allocation. The API is identical across all platforms, but each implementation behind the scenes is tuned for the particular platform.

HEAP.H++ FROM ROGUE WAVE

Product Name:	Heap.h++
Platforms:	UNIX
Price:	$995
Company:	Rogue Wave Software
Address:	P.O. Box 2328, Corvallis, OR 97339, USA

Phone:	1-800-487-3217, 541-754-3010
Fax:	541-757-6650
FTP:	FTP.Roguewave.com (user: anonymous)
Email:	sales@roguewave.com
Web:	http://www.roguewave.com

Heap.h++ works with C and C++ and replaces the allocation primitive behind `malloc` and `new` with a faster allocator that also reduces heap fragmentation. The algorithm used by Heap.h++ avoids linear searches of free lists and involves vector lookup for common block sizes and tree lookup for larger blocks. Using a technique called "page tagging" overhead of small blocks is reduced by a compacted representation of their header information. These combined methods serve to reduce the overall use of heap memory by reduced header overhead, and less fragmentation.

The above techniques apply automatically without any code changes. Heap.h++ also offers a high-level interface allowing the programmer to create private heaps and control allocation policies while coexisting with existing allocation schemes. This gives you the ability to change your application to best use allocated memory.

GUI/UI libraries

*D*evelopment of GUIs is one area where software development is still moving rapidly. There are a variety of rapid prototyping tools based on 4GLs, as well as the numerous "visual" tools where developers build the GUI visually with the GUI tool generating the code automatically. Originally I intended this chapter to cover neither of these advanced forms of GUI tools since they reach beyond C and C++ into a more general arena. However, a few GUI building tools found their way to my desk and I decided to mention them. In addition, we'll examine the many libraries available that programmers can use to build GUIs the old fashioned way — by writing code.

VIEW.H++ — MOTIF CLASSES FROM ROGUE WAVE

Product Name:	View.h++
Platforms:	UNIX
Price:	$795 object code; $2,995 source

Company:	Rogue Wave Software
Address:	P.O. Box 2328, Corvallis, OR 97339, USA
Phone:	1-800-487-3217, 541-754-3010
Fax:	541-757-6650
FTP:	FTP.Roguewave.com (user: anonymous)
Email:	sales@roguewave.com
Web:	http://www.roguewave.com

View.h++ is a C++ class library that simplifies C++ Motif coding. There is support for Motif 1.2 and Common Desktop Environment (CDE). Both Motif and X Intrinsics libraries are wrapped in C++ classes for object oriented GUI programming. Notable areas of Motif feature encapsulation include: drag-and-drop, menus, frame constraints, and wide character strings. Some common GUI patterns that are offered include dialog boxes for information or notification, and lists of filenames.

Encapsulation of X Intrinsics features is also achieved by the C++ classes. Event management is encapsulated, with events such as key, mouse and exposure events handled internally, but they are also available through the API if needed. Another remarkable feature is that View.h++ has been integrated into a number of visual GUI builders including UIM/X, TeleUSE, and iXBUILD, to yield a visual development environment for Motif C++ code.

ILOG VIEWS — C++ GUI BUILDER AND CLASS LIBRARY

Product Name:	ILOG Views
Platforms:	UNIX/X, Windows 3.1, Windows 95, Windows NT, OS/2
Price:	$10,000: UNIX; $6,500: other
Company:	ILOG Inc.
Address:	2005 Landings Drive, Mountain View, CA 94043, USA
Phone:	415-390-9000
Fax:	415-390-0946
Email:	info@ilog.com
Web:	http://www.ilog.com

ILOG Views is a rich suite of C++ classes for high powered GUI development. ILOG calls this VGUI (Very Graphical User Interface) development and this attitude shines through with support for advanced graphics, animation, and a number of "power" objects including a spreadsheet, graph editor, drawing editor, cartographic primitives, and a Gantt chart editor.

The performance of the graphical objects is impressive with quad-trees behind the scenes to give fast screen update and double-buffering for flicker-free animation.

The library can run on top of Motif or directly over X, and under Microsoft Windows with MFC and Borland OWL support. There are a variety of classes involved including simpler GUI component gadgets (e.g., menu bar, buttons, scrollbar, etc.), behavior objects to abstract the object interactions, and manager objects to control large numbers of other objects. All of the objects respond to actions such as resizing and zooming, and PostScript output is supported. Applications are fully portable across UNIX, OS/2 and Windows.

One very impressive feature is the "active values" feature where components can be dynamically linked together based on formulae expressed in C/C++ expression syntax. By mapping a GUI component to another this way, the GUI can be automatically updated without any code on your part. ILOG Views uses an expression interpreter behind the scenes to automatically update any objects as needed when something changes in the expression.

ILOG Views comes with a complete VGUI Editor called Studio for standard interface design. Studio offers multi-lingual message support and is customizable and extensible to fit specific development needs.

OBJECT PROFESSIONAL FOR C++ FROM TURBOPOWER

Product Name:	Object Professional for C++
Platforms:	DOS
Price:	$279
Company:	TurboPower Software Co.
Address:	P.O. Box 49009, Colorado Springs, CO 80949-9009, USA
Phone:	1-800-333-4160, 719-260-9136
Fax:	719-260-7151
FTP:	tpower.com/pub/turbopower (user: anonymous)
Email:	info@tpower.com
Web:	http://www.tpower.com

Object Professional simplifies the development of DOS text-mode user interfaces. The package includes visual interface builder tools and powerful windowing classes. This allows the development of interfaces interactively using tools or via direct coding.

The *makemenu* utility offers interactive development of the menu part of the interface. It offers control over the content, color, behavior and appearance of the menus. Once completed, the menu design can be written out as source code to add to the application.

The *makescrn* utility is similar, and allows interactive development of data entry screens. By choosing a component and setting its position and appearance, you can quickly develop screens. The final result is source code output to integrate into the application.

There are many components accessible as GUI object classes. There are powerful classes that control where text-based windows appear and how they behave. Windows have features such as title and border, mouse hot spots, scroll bars and transparent shadows. Other components include a file browser, text editor, calendar and pick list file selector. The offering is rounded out by printer classes and context-sensitive help support. The printer classes provide access to the printer port and control over fonts and emphasis. The help features include help viewing with hypertext links and a supplied help compiler to create the help files. Using all these features of Object Professional it is possible to build a powerful text-based GUI for DOS.

ENHANCEMENTPAK — MOTIF WIDGET LIBRARY FROM ICS

Product Name:	EnhancementPak
Platforms:	UNIX (Solaris, SunOS, HP-UX, OSF/1, AIX, SGI, SCO), VMS
Price:	$2,495
Company:	Integrated Computer Solutions, Inc.
Address:	201 Broadway, Cambridge, MA 02139, USA
Phone:	1-800-800-4271, 617-621-0060
Fax:	617-621-9555
Email:	info@ics.com
Web:	http://www.ics.com/

EnhancementPak is a collection of widgets for OSF/Motif GUI programming. These can be used directly from the library or alternatively, the fully available source code can be used to write your own more advanced widgets. Some of the useful widgets for simple GUI elements include a button box, color selector, font selector, paned windows and icon button. There are also panner and porthole widgets that allow scrolling over a large object through a small view area. The larger GUI elements that are offered include an icon box to lay out icons according to a grid, a toolbar to contain icons and popup menus, and a fully functional pixmap editor with abilities such as draw lines, draw circles, fill, copy and move. There is also support for business graphs for viewing data in a variety of 2D graphs, and a tab widget for a tab interface commonly seen in Windows 95.

To show tree structural information there are three widget classes: Hierarchy, Outline and Tree. The Hierarchy widget is the base widget of the other two and contains fundamental information. The Outline widget shows tree structure by indenting its children, just like an outline of the contents of a document. The Tree widget shows a drawn tree with lines between nodes, and icons or text for nodes, and the correct tree structure shown by positioning the nodes.

BUILDER XCESSORY — MOTIF GUI BUILDER FROM ICS

Product Name:	Builder Xcessory
Platforms:	UNIX (Solaris, SunOS, HP-UX, OSF/1, AIX, SGI, SCO), VMS
Price:	$3,200 floating single user license
Company:	Integrated Computer Solutions, Inc.
Address:	201 Broadway, Cambridge, MA 02139, USA
Phone:	1-800-800-4271, 617-621-0060
Fax:	617-621-9555
Email:	info@ics.com
Web:	http://www.ics.com/

Builder Xcessory is an interactive GUI builder for Motif interfaces. There are two modes: build mode and play mode. During build mode, you create the GUI through the various dialogs and interfaces offered by Builder Xcessory. The first step is usually to choose widgets from the Palette and add them to the GUI. These widgets can then be customized for location, size, and many resources (i.e., color, fonts, geometry, etc). The hierarchical structure of all the widgets is maintained and modified by the user within Builder Xcessory. There are a great many other features including support for large interfaces and internationalization support.

Once the GUI is constructed, you can use the play mode to play with the GUI you have developed. All of the GUI-specific dynamic behavior will be shown including any pre-defined callbacks, although application callbacks will not be hooked in at this stage.

Builder Xcessory can output C, C++ or Motif UIL code when the GUI is completed. By linking your application code with the GUI code to resolve callbacks, the result is a fully functional GUI on top of your application code.

VIEWKIT OBJECTPAK — MOTIF C++ APPLICATION FRAMEWORK

Product Name:	ViewKit ObjectPak
Platforms:	UNIX (Solaris, SunOS, HP-UX, AIX, OSF/1, SGI, SCO)
Price:	$1,995 per developer
Company:	Integrated Computer Solutions, Inc.
Address:	201 Broadway, Cambridge, MA 02139, USA
Phone:	1-800-800-4271, 617-621-0060
Fax:	617-621-9555

| Email: | info@ics.com |
| Web: | http://www.ics.com/ |

ViewKit ObjectPak is a C++ application development framework for Motif. Rather than a set of widgets or a visual GUI builder tool, it is a set of C++ classes that encapsulate much of the Motif functionality and offer higher level GUI components. This simplifies the development of a Motif GUI in C++ by allowing the programmer to operate at a higher level.

The basic GUI classes are windows, menus and dialogs. Medium level GUI components include preference dialogs, check boxes, radio boxes, tab panels, meter displays and auto-repeating push buttons. Higher level components include a graph viewer/editor with arcs and nodes, an outliner class for indented "outlines" showing structure, an interprocess message facility via ToolTalk and support for integrating online help. All of these classes are added to your application by creating objects in the class or deriving new classes from the ViewKit classes.

P A R T **3**

RESOURCES

*T*here is always the need for the programmer
to remain current with the latest advances in areas of expertise. The traditional resources of
the printed word in books and magazines continue to strengthen the programming arena.
Those who predicted a downturn in hardcopy publishing as computers became widely used
are still waiting for this to happen. In fact, the computer industry has caused a boom in publishing because of the increased need for the provision of up-to-date information to computer
users in a timely fashion. There are now printed books on every topic and software package
imaginable. Trade magazines are also thriving and continue to offer a combination of tutorial articles, current news items, and advertising from software vendors.

In addition to traditional hardcopy, there are now modern methods of reaching
advanced information through various Online resources. There are many Internet newsgroups for group discussions of particular topics. The many sites on the World Wide Web
offer great volumes of information on all areas of interest. Only through adept use of all these
resources can the serious programmer maintain an advantage.

Books and magazines

*T*he growth of computers has brought a boom to technical publishing, rather than the widely predicted paperless office. C and C++ books are certainly no exception and the variety of topics is stupendous. This chapter attempts to present book citations grouped by category, rather than one long list. We'll also look at the numerous magazines available that cover C and C++ programming, and examine some of the journal articles they contain.

TEXTS AND TEACHING BOOKS ON C AND C++

There are so many books that teach C programming that it is hard to keep up with the latest developments. The textbook written by two of the C language designers, Brian Kernighan and Dennis Ritchie, became a classic and made publishing history as the biggest selling technical book, with millions of copies in print. Whether you like the terse writing style or not, you're not a true C programmer unless you know what "K&R" stands for. Since then everyone else has got into the act, and the market for C textbooks is crowded.

Introductory C books fall into a number of categories including textbooks for course-work, self-teaching manuals and those that introduce C with a particular focus such as business programming or a particular platform such as Visual C++. Even the general textbooks differ in their level of coverage with some aimed at teaching new students of Computer Science the theory of programming using C as the vehicle, and others aimed at teaching students already proficient in programming in another language such as Pascal. In the category of books that teach C to later-year computing students, here is my personal list of books that deserve an honorable mention:

> BARCLAY, Kenneth A., *C Problem Solving and Programming (ANSI edition)*, Prentice Hall, 1991.

> KELLEY, Al, and POHL, Ira, *A Book on C (2nd edition)*, Benjamin/Cummings Publishing Company, 1990.

> KERNIGHAN, Brian W., and RITCHIE, Dennis M., *The C Programming Language (2nd edition)*, Prentice Hall, 1989.

> KOCHAN, Stephen G., *Programming in ANSI C*, Hayden Books, 1988.

> PURDUM, Jack, *C Programming Guide (3rd edition)*, Que Corporation, 1988.

> PUGH, Ken, *All on C*, Scott, Foresman/Little, Brown Higher Education, 1990.

> SCHILDT, Herbert, *C: The Complete Reference*, Osborne-McGraw-Hill, 1987.

There are just as many C++ teaching books as C books on the market and perhaps even more. As with C, there are now books with C++ as a first language, teaching C++ to competent programmers, and a variety of platform specific introductory books and self-teaching manuals. As with C, the textbook written by the designer of the language, Bjarne Stroustrup, is a classic textbook for C++ programming:

> STROUSTRUP, Bjarne, *The C++ Programming Language (2nd edition)*, Addison-Wesley, 1991.

The books listed above are far from the end of it. A full listing of C and C++ textbooks would expand this chapter out to far too many pages and the information in the list would be of limited value anyway. Instructors seeking a course textbook are advised to contact various publishers for information on their most recent offerings. Readers seeking introductory self-teaching manuals should request recent catalogs from publishers and/or drive to the nearest bookstore and examine the offerings.

PROFESSIONAL C AND C++ BOOKS

There are books written on any and every topic you can imagine for C and C++ programming, from program portability to computer game coding. In this section we'll examine all those books that are not general textbooks or self-teaching manuals for C and C++. Publishers call these books professional or technical reference books. The book you're holding falls into this category as do two of my previous efforts.

Technical reference and classics for C

HARBISON, Samuel P., and STEELE, Guy L. Jr., *C: A Reference Manual (4th edition)*, Prentice Hall, 1995.

KERNIGHAN, Brian W., and RITCHIE, Dennis M., *The C Programming Language (1st edition)*, Prentice Hall, 1978. (Classic pre-ANSI C textbook).

KERNIGHAN, Brian W., and RITCHIE, Dennis M., *The C Programming Language (2nd edition)*, Prentice Hall, 1989. (Classic ANSI C textbook).

PLAUGER, P. J., *The Standard C Library*, Prentice Hall, 1991.

PLUM, Thomas, *Notes on the C Draft Standard*, Plum Hall Inc., 1987.

Technical reference and classics for C++

ELLIS, Margaret A., and STROUSTRUP, Bjarne, *The Annotated C++ Reference Manual*, Addison-Wesley, 1990. (Known as the "ARM")

PLAUGER, P. J., *The Standard C++ Library*, Prentice Hall, 1995.

STROUSTRUP, Bjarne, *The C++ Programming Language (2nd edition)*, Addison-Wesley, 1991.

Advanced C topics

ANDERSON, Paul, and ANDERSON, Gail, *Advanced C: Tips and Techniques*, Hayden Books, 1988.

KELLEY, Al, and POHL, Ira, *A Book on C (2nd edition)*, Benjamin/Cummings Publishing Company, 1990.

KOCHAN, Stephen G., and WOOD, Patrick H., *Topics in C Programming (revised edition)*, John Wiley and Sons, 1991.

Advanced C++ topics

COPLIEN, James O., *Advanced C++ Programming Styles and Idioms*, Addison-Wesley, 1992.

MEYERS, Scott, *Effective C++: 50 Specific Ways to Improve Your Programs and Designs*, Addison-Wesley, 1992.

SHAPIRO, Jonathan S., *A C++ Toolkit*, Prentice Hall, 1991.

Efficiency and performance improvement for C and C++

ABRASH, Michael, *Zen of Code Optimization*, Coriolis Group Books, 1995.

GULUTZAN, Peter, and PELZER, Trudy, *Optimizing C with Assembly Code*, ISBN 0-13- 234567-5

HELLER, Steve, *Efficient C/C++ Programming*, ISBN: 0-12-339095-8.

PLUM, Thomas, and BRODIE, Jim, *Efficient C*, Plum Hall Inc., 1985.

SPULER, David, *C++ and C Efficiency*, Prentice Hall, Sydney, 1992.

YOUNG, Douglas A., *Motif Debugging and Performance Tuning*, Prentice Hall, New Jersey, 1995.

Coding style and standards for C and C++

KERNIGHAN Brian W., and PLAUGER, P. J., *The Elements of Programming Style*, McGraw-Hill, 1974.

KORSH, James F., and GARRETT, Leonard J., Data Structures, *Algorithms and Program Style Using C*, PWS-Kent publishing, 1988.

PLUM, Thomas, *C Programming Guidelines*, Prentice Hall, 1984.

RANADE, Jay, and NASH, Alan, *The Elements of C Programming Style*, McGraw-Hill, 1995.

STRAKER, David, *C Style: Standards and Guidelines*, Prentice Hall, 1992.

Debugging and testing in C and C++

DARWIN, Ian F., *Checking C Programs with lint*, O'Reilly & Associates, 1988.

DAVIS, Stephen R., *C++ Programmer's Companion: Designing, Testing and Debugging*, Addison-Wesley, 1993.

KOENIG, Andrew, *C Traps and Pitfalls*, Addison-Wesley, 1989.

MAGUIRE, Steve, *Writing Solid Code*, Microsoft Press, 1995.

McCONNELL, Steve, *Code Complete*, Microsoft Press, 1995.

SPULER, David, *C++ and C Debugging, Testing and Reliability: The prevention, detection and correction of program errors*, Prentice Hall, 1994.

THIELEN, David, *NO BUGS: Delivering Error-Free Code in C and C++*, Addison-Wesley, 1992.

WARD, Robert, *Debugging C*, Que Corporation, 1988.

YOUNG, Douglas A., *Motif Debugging and Performance Tuning*, Prentice Hall, New Jersey, 1995.

Portability and multi-platform coding in C and C++

HORTON, Mark, *Portable C Software*, Prentice Hall, 1990.

JAESCHKE, Rex, *Portability and the C Language*, Hayden Books, 1989.

LAPIN, J. E., *Portable C and UNIX System Programming*, Prentice Hall, 1987.

RABINOWITZ, Henry, and SCHAAP, Chaim, *Portable C*, Prentice Hall, 1990.

Reusability in C and C++

SESSIONS, Roger, *Reusable Data Structures in C*, Prentice Hall, 1989.

SMITH, Jerry D., *Reusability and Software Construction: C and C++*, John Wiley and Sons, 1990.

Algorithms and Data Structures in C

AMMERAAL, Leendert, *Programs and Data Structures in C*, John Wiley and Sons, 1987.

ESAKOV, Jeffrey, and WEISS, Tom, *Data Structures: An Advanced Approach Using C*, Prentice Hall, 1989.

GONNET, G. H., and BAEZA-YATES, R., *Handbook of Algorithms and Data Structures (2nd edition)*, Addison-Wesley, 1991.

KORSH, James F., and GARRETT, Leonard J., *Data Structures, Algorithms and Program Style Using C*, PWS-Kent publishing, 1988.

KRUSE, Robert L., LEUNG, Bruce P., and TONDO, Clovis L., *Data Structures and Program Design in C*, Prentice Hall, 1991.

SESSIONS, Roger, *Reusable Data Structures in C*, Prentice Hall, 1989.

TENENBAUM, Aaron, LANGSAM, Yedidyah, and AUGENSTEIN, Moshe J., *Data Structures Using C*, Prentice Hall, 1990.

VAN WYK, Christopher J., *Data Structures and C Programs*, Addison-Wesley, 1988.

Algorithms and Data Structures in C++

FLAMIG, Bryan, *Practical Algorithms in C++*, Coriolis Group Books, 1995.

SENGUPTA, Saumyendra, and KOROBKIN, Carl Philip, *C++: Object Oriented Data Structures*, Springer-Verlag, 1994.

UNIX Systems Programming in C

BOURNE, Stephen R., *The UNIX System*, Addison-Wesley, 1983.

HORSPOOL, R. Nigel, *C Programming in the Berkeley UNIX Environment*, Prentice Hall, 1986.

KERNIGHAN, Brian W., and PIKE, Rob, *The UNIX Programming Environment*, Prentice Hall, 1984.

LAPIN, J. E., *Portable C and UNIX System Programming*, Prentice Hall, 1987.

Compiler Design

HOLUB, Allen I., *Compiler Design in C*, Prentice Hall, 1990.

SCHREINER, A.T., and FRIEDMAN, H.G., *Introduction to Compiler Construction with UNIX*, Prentice Hall, 1985.

Numerical Programming

KEMPF, James, *Numerical Software Tools in C*, Prentice Hall, 1987.

KEMPF, James, *Numerical Software Tools in C++*, Prentice Hall, 1995.

PRESS, William H., FLANNERY, Brian P., TEUKOLSKY, Saul A., and VETTER-LING, William T., *Numerical Recipes in C: The Art of Scientific Computing*, Cambridge University Press, 1988.

Graphics and GUI in C and C++

ABRASH, Michael, *Zen of Graphics Programming*, 1995.

FOWLER, Susan L, and STANWICK, Victor R., *The GUI Style Guide*, 1995.

HEINY, Loren, *Windows Graphics Programming With Borland C++*, Coriolis Groups, 1995.

HEINY, Loren, *Advanced Graphics Programming Using C/C++*, Coriolis Group, 1995.

TAYLOR, Philip, *3-D Graphics Programming in Windows*, 1995.

Games Programming and Animation

ROBERTS, Dave, *PC Game Programming Explorer*, 1995.

MYERS, Lary, *Amazing 3-D Games Adventure Set*, 1995.

GRUBER, Diana, *Action Arcade Adventure Set*, 1995.

LAMOTHE, Andre, *Tricks of the Game Programming Gurus*, SAMS Publishing, 1995

LAMPTON, Christopher, *Gardens of Imagination: Programming 3D Maze Games in C/C++*, Waite Group Press, 1994.

LAMPTON, Christopher, *Flights of Fantasy: Programming 3D Video Games in C/C++*, Waite Group Press, 1994.

THOMPSON, Nigel, *Animation Techniques in Win32*, Microsoft Press, 1995.

Miscellaneous topics in C and C++

BIGGERSTAFF, Ted J., *Systems Software Tools*, Prentice Hall, 1986

CAMPBELL, Joe, *Crafting C Tools for IBM PCs*, Prentice Hall, 1986.

CAMPBELL, Joe, *C Programmer's Guide to Serial Communications*, 1995.

EMBREE, P.M and KIMBLE, B., *C Language Algorithms for Digital Signal Processing*, Prentice Hall, 1990.

FEUER, Allan R., *C Puzzle Book (2nd edition)*, Prentice Hall, 1989.

GODFREY, J.T., *Applied C*, Prentice Hall, 1990

MILLER, Webb, *A Software Tools Sampler*, Prentice Hall, 1987.

OGILVIE, John W. L., *Advanced C Struct Programming*, John Wiley and Sons, 1990.

PINSON, James, *Designing Screen Interfaces in C*, Prentice Hall, 1991.

ROCHKIND, Marc J., *Advanced C Programming for Displays*, Prentice Hall, 1988.

ROETZHEIM, William H., *A C Programmer's Guide to the IBM Token Ring*, Prentice Hall, 1991.

SCHREINER, A.T., *Using C with curses, lex and yacc*, Prentice Hall, 1990.

TONDO, Clovis L., and GIMPEL, Scott E., *The C Answer Book (2nd edition)*, Prentice Hall, 1988.

TRAISTER, Robert J., *Mastering C Pointers*, Academic Press, 1990.

JOURNAL ARTICLES ON TOOLS, C AND C++

AMSTERDAM, Jonathan, *Some Assembly Required: Taking Exception to C*, Byte, August 1991, pp. 259-264.

BATES, Rodney M., *Debugging with Assertions*, The C Users Journal, Vol. 10, No. 10, October 1992.

CAHILL, Conor P., *The Art of Debugging C Programs*, X Journal, March/April 1993.

ERDELSKY, Philip J., *A Safer setjmp in C++*, C Users Journal, Vol. 11, No. 1, January 1993, pp. 41-44.

HORSTMANN, Cay, *Memory management and smart pointers*, C++ Report, Vol. 5, No. 3, March/April 1993, pp. 28-34.

LADD, Scott Robert, *Debugging Dynamic Memory in C++*, PC Techniques, Vol. 3, No. 5, December/January 1993, pp. 38-43.

LEARY, Sean, and D'SOUZA, Desmond, *Catch the Error: C++ Exception Handling*, Computer Language, October 1992, pp. 63-77.

LEE, P.A., *Exception Handling in C Programs, Software* — Practice & Experience, Vol. 13, 1983, pp. 389-405.

MILLER, W.M., *Error Handling in C++*, Computer Language, May 1988, pp. 43-52.

MILLER, W.M., *Exception Handling Without Language Support*, USENIX C++ Conference Proceedings, Denver, Colorado, USENIX Press, 1988. PIETREK, Matt, *Postmortem Debugging*, Dr Dobbs Journal, September 1992, pp. 18-31.

SMITH, William M., *Debugging with Macro Wrappers*, The C Users Journal, Vol. 10, No. 10, October 1992.

VIDAL, Carlos, *Exception Handling*, C Users Journal, Vol. 10, No. 9, September 1992, pp. 19-28.

WILSON, C., and OSTERWEIL, L.J., *Omega — A Data Flow Analysis Tool for the C Programming Language*, IEEE Transactions on Software Engineering, Vol. 11, No. 9, 1985, pp. 832-838.

JOHNSON, S.C., *Lint: a C Program Checker*, Computer Science Technical Report No. 65, Bell Laboratories, 1978.

SHIMOMURA, Takao, and ISODA, Sadahiro, *Linked-List Visualization for Debugging*, IEEE Software, May 1991, pp. 44-51 (discusses VIPS).

ONLINE BOOK LISTS AND CATALOGS

Catalog of O'Reilly Books: FTP from *ftp.ora.com as book.catalog.Z*; also available via gopher: telnet *gopher.ora.com* login: *gopher* or *gopher gopher.ora.com*

X Technical Bibliography: by Ken Lee, FTP from *gatekeeper.dec.com* in */pub/X11/contrib* or from *export.lcs.mit.edu* in */contrib* as filename *Xbibliography*.

cbooks.zip on SimTel: look for the file *cbooks.zip* in the *c* subdirectory at your favorite SimTel archive site.

Yet another book list: by Mitch Wright, an annotated list of C books, FTP *ftp.rahul.net* in directory *pub/mitch/YABL*.

ANSI/ISO C STANDARD — ACQUISITION DETAILS

Perhaps the most important reference for C is the ANSI/ISO C standard, although the majority of people won't need to read it. The ANSI C standard is more properly called American National Standard ANS-X3.159-1989 "Programming Languages—C", and has also been adopted as the international standard ISO/IEC 9899:1990 (which differs only in section and page numbering). The standard is not a public domain document and can be purchased from:

Company:	American National Standards Institute
Address:	1430 Broadway, New York, NY 10018,USA
Phone:	(+1) 212 642 4900

and also from:

Company:	Global Engineering Documents
Address:	2805 McGaw Avenue, Irvine, CA 92714, USA

Phone:	(+1) 714 261 1455
	1-800-854 7179 (within USA and Canada only)

ANSI and ANSI equivalent ISO standards are available from:

Company:	ASQC Quality Press, Customer Service Department
Address:	P.O. Box 3066, Milwaukee, WI 53201-3066, USA
Phone:	1-800-248-1946
FAX:	414-272-1734

And also:

Company:	National Technical Information Service (NTIS),
Address:	5284 Port Royal Rd.,Springfield, VA 22161, USA
Phone:	703-487-4650.

The standard is also available on CD-ROM from:

Company:	Omnicom, Inc.
Address:	115 Park St. SE, Vienna, VA 22180-4607, USA
Phone:	1-800-OMNICOM

FTP retrieval of the ANSI C Rationale

Although the full ANSI C standard is not available freely, the "rationale" document associated with the standard is available via FTP as shown below. This document explains the reasons behind many of the decisions made in producing the standard. Note that the rationale is no longer shipped with the standard by many standards organizations, and thus FTP is the simplest way to obtain it.

ANSI, *Rationale for the ANSI/ISO C standard*, FTP from *ftp.uu.net* in directory *doc/standards/ansi/X3.159-1989*.

Acquiring ANSI C in Australia

Within Australia, a version of the standard (equivalent to ISO/IEC 9899:1990) can be purchased from Standards Australia, and is called Australian Standard AS 3955-1991 *Programming Languages — C*. The mailing address of the National Sales Center is:

Company:	Standards Australia, National Sales Center
Address:	P.O. Box 1055, Strathfield 2135, AUSTRALIA
Phone:	(02) 746 4600 (within Australia only)

Acquiring ANSI C in Canada

In Canada, the standard is available from:

Company:	Standards Council of Canada / Conseil canadien des normes
Address:	1200-45 O'Connor, Ottawa K1P 6N7
Phone:	613-238-3222
Fax:	613-995-4564

MAGAZINES ON C AND C++

No doubt there are plenty of computer magazines at your local newsstand. This section presents details on the magazines that focus on issues related to programming rather than on hardware or user issues. A handful of magazines are specific to the language. Others cover programming on a particular platform with C or C++ cropping up in almost all articles, except for those on the new breed of 4GL application development frameworks.

C/C++ Users Journal

Summary — All C/C++ programming issues; varied articles and columns. Subscriptions:

Address:	R&D Publications, Suite 200, 1601 West 23rd Street, Lawrence, KS 66046, USA
Phone:	913-841-1631
Fax:	913-841-2624
Email:	cujsub@rdpub.com
Price:	$34.95; Canada/Mexico $US46; foreign: $US65

C++ Report

Summary — All C/C++ programming issues; varied articles and columns. Subscriptions:

Address:	SIGS PUBLICATIONS, Subscriber Services Dept. Cpr, P.O. Box 3000, Denville NJ 07834-9979, USA

Phone:	212-274-0640
Fax:	212-274-0646

Journal of Object-Oriented Programming (JOOP)
Summary — Object oriented programming issues; plenty of C++ coverage. Subscriptions:

Address:	SIGS PUBLICATIONS
Voice:	212-274-0640
Fax:	212-274-0646

Object Magazine
Summary — Object oriented programming issues; plenty of C++ coverage. Subscriptions:

Address:	SIGS PUBLICATIONS
Phone:	212-274-0640
Fax:	212-274-0646

PC Techniques
Summary — Programming for PC (Windows, OS/2, etc.); C++ often used. Subscriptions:

Address:	7721 E Gray Rd, Suite 204, Scottsdale, AZ 85260, USA
Phone:	602-483-0192
Fax:	602-483-0193
Price:	USA: $21.95; Canada: $US29.95; other: $US39.95

Dr Dobb's Journal
Subscriptions: Programming (mainly PC platforms); C and C++ dominate

Address:	P.O. Box 105843, Atlanta, GA 30348-9523, USA
Phone	1-800-283-9455

Fax:	404-426-1044

UNIX Review
Summary — General UNIX issues; frequent C/C++ articles and columns. Subscriptions:

Address:	P.O. Box 420029, Palm Coast, FL 32142-0029, USA
Phone:	1-800-829-5475
Price:	USA: $55; Canada: US$75, Other: $US 119 (surface)

Software Development
Summary — Programming on all platforms; C/C++ often used. Subscriptions:

Address:	P.O. Box 5032, Brentwood, TN 37204-5032, USA
Phone:	1-800-950-0523, 615-377-3322
CompuServe:	71572,341 (email: 71572.341@compuserve.com)
Price:	USA: $39; Canada/Mexico: $45; foreign: $54 or $79

Windows/DOS Development Journal
Summary — Microsoft Windows and DOS programming; C++ often used. Subscriptions:

Address:	R&D Publications, Suite 200, 1601 West 23rd Street, Lawrence, KS 66046, USA
Phone:	913-841-1631
Fax:	913-841-2624

Windows Tech Journal
Summary — Microsoft Windows programming; C++ often used. Subscriptions:

Address:	Oakley Publishing Co., 150 N. Fourth St., Springfield, OR 97477, USA
Phone:	1-800-234-0386
Fax:	503-746-0071
Price:	USA: $29.95; Canada/Mexico: $39.95; other: $69.95 (air)

Microsoft Systems Journal

Summary — Microsoft Windows and DOS programming; C++ often used. Subscriptions:

Address:	Circulation Department, MSJ, P.O. Box 56621, Boulder, CO 80322-6621, USA
Phone:	1-800-666-1084 (24 hours), 303-447-9330
Fax:	415-905-2233
CompuServe:	71572,341 (email: 71572.341@compuserve.com)
Price:	USA: $50; Canada/Mexico: $65; foreign: $70

## CHAPTER 25

Internet resources

C and C++ have a large presence on the Internet because of their widespread usage in real world projects. Hence the Internet contains many resources that are of interest to the programmer. There are many free documents, interesting WWW sites, news groups for interactions, and commercial tool vendors are also beginning to offer their wares via the Internet.

INTERNET NEWS GROUPS ON C AND C++

There are many news groups worth perusing for gems of insight into C and C++ programming. The ones I visit the most often are listed in Table 25–1. It's easy enough to spend a few hours reading news daily because of the high volume in some of the groups. Just be careful you still get enough work done!

Table 25–1 C/C++ news groups

comp.lang.c	C programming issues in general
comp.lang.c++	C++ programming issues in general
comp.std.c	C standardization issues
comp.std.c++	C++ standardization issues
comp.lang.software-eng	Software engineering; any language
comp.software.testing	Testing (any programming language)
comp.software.config-mgt	Configuration management, bug tracking, etc.
comp.os.msdos.programmer	MS-DOS programming (often C/C++)
comp.unix.questions	UNIX programming (including C/C++)

FREE FTP DOCUMENTS ON TOOLS, C AND C++

FAQ documents

SUMMIT, Steve, "comp.lang.c FAQ", the current version should be in *news.answers*, else see regular news postings or FTP to *rtfm.mit.edu/pub/usenet/comp.lang.c* as files *C-FAQ**.

CLINE, Marshall, "comp.lang.c++ FAQ", the current version should be in *news.answers*, else see regular news postings or FTP to *rtfm.mit.edu/pub/usenet/comp.lang.c++*.

LEVINE, John R., "comp.compilers FAQ", the current version should be in *news.answers*, else see regular news postings or FTP to *rtfm.mit.edu/pub/usenet/comp.compilers*.

BROWN, Stan, "comp.os.msdos.programmer FAQ", the current version should be in *news.answers*, else see regular news postings in the group itself, or FTP to *rtfm.mit.edu/pub/usenet/comp.os.msdos.programmer*.

"comp.software-eng", *comp.software-eng* archives, available via FTP to *ftp.qucis.queensu.ca/pub/archive* as various filenames, including *inspect*, *fault*, *verification*, *testTools*, *horror*.

Catalogs

DUTTA, Saumen K., "C++ Products List and Description", FTP to *ftp.th-darmstadt.de* as file *pub/programming/languages/C++/c++-products/**.

ROBENALT, Steven A., and SHARNOF, David M., "Catalog of compilers, interpreters, and other language tools", the current version should be posted to *news.answers*, else see regular news postings in *comp.compilers*, or FTP to *rtfm.mit.edu/pub/usenet/comp.compilers*.

SHAH, Ajay, "Index of resources for numerical computation in C or C++", see regular news postings to *comp.lang.c* or FTP to *rtfm.mit.edu:pub/usenet/comp.lang.c* as various files.

Coding style standards and code inspection checklists

BALDWIN, John T., "An Abbreviated C++ Code Inspection Checklist", Testing Foundations, 1992 (available via FTP to the site *cs.uiuc.edu* in directory *pub/testing* as filename *baldwin-inspect.ps*; also part of *giza.cis.ohio-state.edu:pub/style-guide/ style.shar.part.0[1-5].gz*).

CANNON, L.W., ELLIOTT, R.A., KIRCHHOFF, L.W., MILLER, J.H., MILNER, J.M., MITZE, R.W., SCHAN, E.P., WHITTINGTON, N.O., SPENCER, Henry, KEPPEL, David, and BRADER, Mark, (Indian Hill) "C Style and Coding Standards", FTP to *cs.washington.edu:pub/cstyle.tar.Z* or *cs.toronto.edu:doc/programming/ihstyle** or *giza.cis.ohio-state.edu:pub/style-guide/**.

COTTAM, Ian D., "idC: A Subset of Standard C for Initial Teaching", Tech Report UMCS-92-12-3, Department of Computer Science, University of Manchester, England, 1992 (available via FTP from *ftp.cs.man.ac.uk* in directory *pub/TR* as file *UMCS-92-12-3.ps.Z*).

DICHTER, Carl R., "Two Sets of Eyes", FTP to *cs.toronto.edu:doc/programming/dichter.inspection* (summary of article on code inspections from Unix Review, Vol. 10, No. 1, January 1992).

Expert Solutions Australia Pty Ltd., "C Coding Standard", FTP to *giza.cis.ohio-state.edu:pub/style-guide/style.shar.part.0[1-5].gz*.

Free Software Foundation, "Gnu coding standards", FTP to anywhere GNU stuff is archived; also part of *giza.cis.ohio-state.edu.pub/style-guide/style.shar.part.0[1-5].gz*.

HENRICSON, Mats, and NYQUIST, Erik, "Programming in C++: Rules and Recommendations", Technical Report, Ellemtel Telecommunication Systems Laboratories, Sweden, 1990-1992; available via anonymous FTP to the site *euagate.eua.ericsson.se* in directory *pub/eua/c++* as numerous files including *rules.ascii.Z*, or to *giza.cis.ohio-state.edu:pub/style guide/**.

MARICK, Brian, "A Question Catalog for Code Inspections", Testing Foundations, 1992 (available via FTP to *cs.uiuc.edu* in directory *pub/testing* as filenames *inspect.n* and *inspect.ps*).

PIKE, Rob, "Notes on Programming in C", FTP to *cs.toronto.edu:doc/programming/ pikestyle.**; also part of *giza.cis.ohio-state.edu:pub/style-guide/style.shar.part.0[1-5].gz*.

Compiler and debugger design

RAMSEY, Norman, "PhD thesis", FTP from *bellcore.com:pub/norman/thesis.ps.Z*.

PAXSON, Vern, "A Survey of Support For Implementing Debuggers", FTP from *ftp.ee.lbl.gov* as filename *debugger-support.ps.Z*.

COPPERMAN, Max, "Debugging Optimized Code Without Being Misled: Currency Determination", Technical Report UCSC-CRL-93-24, University of California at Santa Cruz, FTP to *ftp.cse.ucsc.edu* in */pub/tr as* filename *ucsc-crl-93-24.ps.Z.*

COPPERMAN, Max, and THOMAS, Jeff, "Poor Man's Watchpoints", (discusses debugger design) Technical Report UCSC-CRL-93-12, University of California at Santa Cruz, FTP to *ftp.cse.ucsc.edu:pub/tr/ucsc-crl-93-12.ps.Z.*

KEPPEL, David, "Fast Data Breakpoints", (discusses debugger design) FTP to *ftp.cs.washington.edu:tr/1993/04/UW-CSE-93-04-06.PS.Z.*

PIZZI, Robert, "GNU Debugger Internal Architecture", FTP to *sisal.llnl.gov* (128.115.19.65) in the *pub/gdbDocument* directory; main file is *gdbdoc.ps.*

SRIVASTAVA, Amitabh, and WALL, David W., "A Practical System for Intermodule Code Optimization at Link-Time", Technical Report 92/6, Digital Western Research Laboratory, FTP to *gatekeeper.dec.com* in directory *pub/Digital/WRL/research-reports* as file *WRL-TR-92.6.ps.*

WALL, David W., "Link-Time Code Modification", Technical Report 89/17, Digital Western Research Laboratory, FTP to *gatekeeper.dec.com* in directory *pub/Digital/ WRL/research-reports* as file *WRL-TR-89.17.ps.*

Testing techniques

MARICK, Brian, "Testing Software That Reuses", Testing Foundations, 1992 (available via FTP to *cs.uiuc.edu/pub/testing/reuse-note.txt*).

MARICK, Brian, "Three Ways To Improve Your Testing", Testing Foundations, 1992 (available via FTP to *cs.uiuc.edu/pub/testing/three.ps*).

MARICK, Brian, "Experience With The Cost of Different Coverage Goals For Testing", Testing Foundations, 1992 (available via FTP to *cs.uiuc.edu* in directory *pub/testing* as filename *experience.ps*).

MARICK, Brian, "A Summary of Subsystem Testing", Testing Foundations, 1992 (available via FTP to *cs.uiuc.edu/ pub/testing/subsystem.ps*).

MARICK, Brian, "The Craft of Software Testing, Testing Foundations", 1994 (this is a full book (!) that is available via FTP to *cs.uiuc.edu* in directory *pub/testing/book* as various files).

OVERBECK, Jan, "Testing Object-Oriented Software — State of the Art and Research Directions", FTP to *mira.dbai.tuwien.ac.at:pub/overbeck/survey.ps*.

TURNER, C. D., and ROBSON, D. J., "The Testing of Object-Oriented Programs", Technical Report TR-13/92, Computer Science Division, School of Engineering and Computer Sciences (SECS), University of Durham, England, FTP to *vega.dur.ac.uk* in */ pub/papers* as *toop.ps.Z* (A4) or *toopus.ps.Z* (US letter).

TURNER, C. D., and ROBSON, D. J., "A Suite of Tools for the State-Based Testing of Object-Oriented Programs", Technical Report TR-14/92, Computer Science Division, School of Engineering and Computer Science (SECS), University of Durham, Durham,

England, FTP to *vega.dur.ac.uk* in */pub/papers* as *tools.ps.Z* (A4) or *toolsus.ps.Z* (US letter).

TURNER, C. D., and ROBSON, D. J., "Guidance for the Testing of Object-Oriented Programs", Technical Report TR-2/93, Computer Science Division, School of Engineering and Computer Science (SECS), University of Durham, Durham, England, FTP to *vega.dur.ac.uk* in */pub/papers* as *guide.ps.Z* (A4) or *guideus.ps.Z* (US letter).

TURNER, C. D., and ROBSON, D. J., "State-Based Testing and Inheritance", Technical Report TR-1/93, Computer Science Division, School of Engineering and Computer Science (SECS), University of Durham, Durham, England, FTP to *vega.dur.ac.uk* in */pub/papers* as *toopinht.ps.Z* (A4) or *toopinhtus.ps.Z* (US letter).

TURNER, C. D., and ROBSON, D. J., "A Framework for Testing Object-Oriented Programs", (also in JOOP, Vol. 5, No.3, pp. 45-53, June 1992), FTP to *vega.dur.ac.uk* in */pub/papers* as *foot.dvi*.

NOLL, Landon Curt, and BASSEL, Larry, "comp.lang.c, International Obfuscated C Code Contest" , FTP to *ftp.uu.net* as files *pub/ioccc/**.

Code checker tools

DUBY, Carolyn K., MEYERS, Scott, and REISS, Steven P., "CCEL: A Metalanguage for C++", Technical Report CS-92-51, Department of Computer Science, Brown University, Providence, Rhode Island, October 1992; available via FTP to *wilma.cs.brown.edu*; directory: */pub/techreports/92*, file: *cs92-51.ps.Z*.

GHIYA, Rakesh, "Interprocedural Analysis in the Presence of Function Pointers", ACAPS Technical Memo62, McGill University, December 1992, FTP to *wally.cs.mcgill.ca* in the directory *pub/doc/memos* as filename *memo62.ps.gz*.

HENDREN, L., EMAMI, M., GHIYA, R., and VERBRUGGE, C., "A Practical Context-Sensitive Interprocedural Analysis Framework for C Compilers", ACAPS Technical Memo72, McGill University, July 1993, FTP to *wally.cs.mcgill.ca* in the directory *pub/doc/memos as filename memo72.ps.gz*.

MEYERS, Scott, and LEJTER, Moses, "Automatic Detection of C++ Programming Errors: Initial Thoughts on a lint++", Technical Report CS-91-51, Department of Computer Science, Brown University, Providence, Rhode Island, August 1991 (also published USENIX C++ Conference Proceedings, April 1991, p29-40); available via FTP to *wilma.cs.brown.edu*; directory:*/pub/techreports/91*, file: *cs91-51.ps.Z*.

SPULER, David A., "Check: A Better Checker for C", Honors Thesis, Department of Computer Science, James Cook University, Townsville, Australia, 1991 (FTP to *coral.cs.jcu.edu.au* in the directory *pub/techreports* as the file *spuler-hons.ps.gz*).

SPULER, D., and SAJEEV, A.S.M., "Static Detection of Preprocessor Macro Errors in C", Technical Report 92/7, Department of Computer Science, James Cook University, Townsville, Australia, July 1992/7 (available via FTP to the site *coral.cs.jcu.edu.au* as file *pub/techreports/92-7.ps.gz*).

Exceptions

BENGTSSON, Johan, "C++, Without Exceptions", Telia Research, Lulea, Sweden (available via FTP to the site *euagate.eua.ericsson.se* in directory *pub/eua/c++* with filename *Exceptions_920511.ps.Z*).

WILLIAMS, Ross N., "A C Exceptions Package Written Using the FunnelWeb Literate Programming Tool", available via FTP to *ftp.adelaide.edu.au* in the directory *pub/funnelweb/examples*.

WINROTH, Harald, "Exception Handling in ANSI C", Computational Vision and Active Perception Laboratory (CVAP), Royal Institute of Technology (KTH), Stockholm, Sweden (available via FTP to *ftp.bion.kth.se* in directory *cvap/2.0/* as file *exception-1.2.tar.Z*).

Debugging tools and techniques

AUSTIN, Todd M., BREACH, Scott E., and SOHI, Gurindar S., "Efficient Detection of All Pointer and Array Access Errors", FTP to *ftp.cs.wisc.edu* as file *tech-reports/reports/93/tr1197.ps.Z*.

DUNHAM, Alan, "Crash Tracebacks in UNIX", Dr Dobbs Journal, September 1992 (code via FTP to ftp.mv.com in *pub/ddj/1992/1992.09* as file *trace.arc*).

Coding quality, debugging and reliability techniques

DARWIN, Ian, and COLLYER, Geoff, "Can't Happen or /*NOTREACHED*/ or Real Programs Dump Core", FTP to *ftp.th-darmstadt.de* as file *pub/programming/languages/C/style-guides/canthappen.PS.Z* or FTP to *cs.toronto.edu:doc/programming/canthappen.PS*.

KOENIG, Andrew, "C Traps & Pitfalls" (the original paper), FTP from *netlib.att.com: /netlib/att/cs/cstr/123.ps.Z*.

ISO 9000 News, "ISO-9000 Quality Standards in 24 Questions", available via FTP to *ftp.uni-erlangen.de* in the directory *pub/doc/ISO/english* as file *ISO-9000-summary*.

MORAES, Mark, "Some notes on defensive programming", FTP to *cs.toronto.edu:doc/programming/defensive*.

SAKKINEN, Markku, "The darker side of C++ revisited", FTP to *ftp.ifi.unizh.ch* as file *c++_dark_sides.ps.Z*.

SAKKINEN, Markku, "A critique of the inheritance principles of C++", FTP to *ftp.ifi.unizh.ch* as file *c++_inherit_critique.ps.Z*.

SAKKINEN, Markku, "Correction to: A critique of the inheritance principles of C++", FTP to ftp.ifi.unizh.ch as file *correction.ps.Z*.

SAKKINEN, Markku, "How should virtual bases be initialized (and finalised)?", FTP to *ftp.ifi.unizh.ch* as file *virtual_basecl.ps.Z*.

SPENCER, Henry, "The Ten Commandments for C Programmers", FTP to *cs.toronto.edu:doc/programming/ten-commandments*; also part of *giza.cis.ohio-state.edu:pub/style-guide/style.shar.part.0[1-5].gz*.

Standards documents

ANSI, "Rationale for the ANSI C standard", FTP from *ftp.uu.net* in directory *doc/standards/ansi/X3.159-1989/*.

ISO, "ANSI/ISO Resolutions" (discusses ANSI C++), FTP to *world.std.com* as file *pub/AW/*_Stroustrup*.

Portability

BUTTERWORTH, Ray, "TRUE or FALSE" (quiz on portability), FTP to *cs.toronto.edu:doc/programming/c.quiz*.

C News, "Portability Coding Issues", in C News newsletter (see LYNCH), issue 19, FTP to SimTel [*oak.oakland.edu/SimTel/msdos/*] *c/cnews019.zip*.

DOLENC, A., LEMMKE, A., KEPPEL, D., and REILLY, G. V., "Notes on Writing Portable Programs in C", FTP to *cs.washington.edu:pub/cport.tar.Z*.

Reusability

SPENCER, Henry, "How To Steal Code or Inventing The Wheel Only Once", FTP to *cs.toronto.edu:doc/programming/steal.**; also part of *giza.cis.ohio-state.edu:pub/styleguide/style.shar.part.0[1-5].gz*.

Security

Sun, "setuid — checklist for security of setuid programs", FTP to *cs.toronto.edu:doc/programming/setuid.**.

General C/C++ discussions

BROWNING, Roy, "Migrating From C to C++", in C News newsletter (see LYNCH), issue 18, FTP to SimTel [*oak.oakland.edu/SimTel/msdos/*] *c/cnews018.zip*.

GIGUERE, Eric, "The ANSI Standard: A Summary for the C Programmer", FTP to *cs.toronto.edu:doc/programming/ansi-c.summary*.

JOYNER, Ian, "C++ — A Critique of C++", FTP to *euagate.eua.ericsson.se* in the *pub/c++* directory as file *cpp.crit.ps*.

LYNCH, Barry, SINGLETON, Jim, KOZAK, Dan, and DERNOCOURT, Wayne, "C News", FTP to SimTel as files *c/cnews*.zip* (Issues 1 to 19 only; there is no 20th issue as the newsletter stopped with issue 19).

RITCHIE, Dennis, "Errata to K&R 2nd edition", FTP to *cs.toronto.edu:doc/programming/KR2.errata*.

SMITH, Sidney L., and MOSIER, Jane N., "Guidelines For Designing User Interface Software", FTP to *ftp.uu.net as files doc/style/uis*.Z*.

Garbage collection

ELLIS, John R., and DETLEFS, David L., Safe, "Efficient Garbage Collection for C++", May, 1993, FTP to *parcftp.xerox.com:/pub/ellis/gc*; main file is *gc.ps*.

EDELSON, Daniel R., "Comparing Two Garbage Collectors for C++", Technical Report UCSC-CRL-93-20, University of California at Santa Cruz, FTP to *ftp.cse.ucsc.edu:pub/tr/ucsc-crl-93-20.ps.Z*.

Command line arguments

CASTLE, Paul E., "Toggles and Command-Line Parsing", in C News newsletter (see LYNCH), issue 18, FTP to SimTel *c/cnews018.zip*.

SINGLETON, Jim, "Command Line Arguments in C", in C News newsletter (see LYNCH), issue 17, FTP to SimTel *c/cnews017.zip*.

Teaching tools

SINGLETON, Jim, "C Tutors: Shareware and Public Domain", in C News newsletter (see LYNCH), issue 18, FTP to SimTel *c/cnews018.zip*.

Obfuscator tool

SINGLETON, Jim, "PEPTO: A ShareWare Source Code Compressor", in C News newsletter (see LYNCH), issue 17, FTP to SimTel *c/cnews017.zip*.

Data structures

CHERDAK, Arnold, "Sets in C", in C News newsletter (see LYNCH), issue 16, FTP to SimTel *c/cnews016.zip*.

LANDER, A., "Linked Lists: An Introduction", in C News newsletter (see LYNCH), issue 15, FTP to SimTel *c/cnews015.zip*.

Understanding tool design

This appendix examines the technical ideas upon which most tools are based. Understanding how the various tools operate is useful to evaluate how effective they will be, and to understand how to use them best.

CODE ANALYSIS TECHNIQUES

There are many tools that operate upon C and C++ source code files to measure various properties or detect anomalies. Some such types of tools are metric computation, checkers, and even pretty printers. All of these tools operate in a manner similar to one or more passes of a compiler, and thus compiler design issues are most important to designing these tools. The logical levels in which these tools can operate include:

- character stream
- lexical level — token stream
- preprocessing — modified token stream

- parsing — syntax analysis
- symbol table
- expressions — expression tree
- type checking
- call graph — function call hierarchy
- flow graph — statement control flow
- data flow analysis

Character stream

The lowest level is to treat source code as a stream of single characters, like any other text file. Any tools based on the `grep`, `sed` or `awk` text processing tools work at this level because character patterns is all that these tools understand. However, very few useful operations that can be performed by a source code analysis tool at this level. The characters need to be processed in a more useful way to show their relationships to each other.

Lexical

The next level is the lexical level where the character stream has been broken up into logical tokens. Longer groups of characters forming one item, such as identifiers, string literals and numeric constants, become one token rather than a group of characters. For example, the code sequence "count+=1" contains three tokens: `count`, `+=`, and `1`. The token level is useful for looking for localized patterns. For example, analyzing single tokens can be useful to warn about `int` constants that are so large they should be `long` constants.

Perhaps surprisingly, another example of using the token level is analysis of comments (e.g., extraction, removal, or whatever the tool is doing to comments). It appears that comment detection is most easily achieved by looking for the two-character sequences `/*` or `//` and then for their delimiting pattern `*/` or newline, respectively. However, operating this way at character level is dangerous if a comment starting sequence appears in a string literal. Thus, comment processing must also account for *tokens* such as string literals and character constants.

Analyzing sequences of tokens can also be useful. For example, the sequence `fprintf("hello",...)` is obviously a common error of a missing `FILE*` argument to `fprintf`, and this error can be detected lexically by the token sequence of `"fprintf"`, `"("`, string literal, and `","`. However, analyzing sequences of tokens has many limitations for detecting more complicated patterns, and it is often better to perform parsing and then analyze the resulting expression tree or flow graph. After parsing, this bug can be found by strict type checking on the first argument to `fprintf` because it is a `char*` type instead of a `FILE*` pointer.

Preprocessing

The action of the preprocessor is to take an input token stream and output a modified token stream. Changes to the token stream involve file inclusion, macro expansions and conditional compilation. A tool can make use of the preprocessing level in two ways:

1. the tool can have its own preprocessor which performs the desired function (e.g., detect errors in macro expansion); or
2. the tool can operate on the token stream produced by the preprocessor.

In the latter case, all of the comments relevant to the lexical level apply. The only difference is that the token sequence is changed, having no preprocessor directives or comments.

Parsing

The central action of the compiler is to "parse" the input sequence of tokens into a more usable form. This process involves syntax analysis, where the token sequence is tested for acceptability subject to the syntax rules of the language, and syntax errors (parse errors) usually cause diagnostics. If the syntax is correct, the result of parsing consists of various data structures such as a syntax tree (includes expression trees), a symbol table, and a flow graph.

Expression trees

Expressions are most easily analyzed in terms of a tree representation of their actions. An example of an expression tree for the expression "a*b+3" is shown in Fig. 26–1.

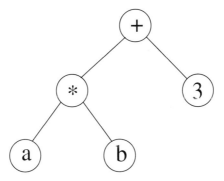

Fig. 26–1 Expression tree for a*b+3

This represents the evaluation of an expression in a form of bottom-up (postorder) tree traversal. Working from the leaves upwards, nodes are combined according to the operator in the internal node, and the result propagated up the tree for use in the evaluation of another operator higher in the tree.

The main convenience of this internal representation of an expression, rather than a linear sequence of tokens, is that the precedence and associativity have been automatically handled. An operation closer to the leaves has higher precedence (or brackets have been used to get that effect). For example, because * has higher precedence than +, the * node is closer to the leaves, and thus occurs earlier in the evaluation sequence.

When the parser generates this form of expression tree representation, this can be operated upon by the tool for various reasons. For example, a static checker can look for possible operator precedence errors where two operators that are adjacent nodes in the tree (i.e., one is the immediate child of the other) are a dangerous pair, such as mixing << and + without using parentheses.

Symbol table

The symbol table contains all identifiers used in a program. In fact, a C compiler usually has quite a few different symbol tables: The preprocessor has a separate symbol table for macro names, and the parser must deal with four different name spaces (e.g., labels, tags, types and variable names in C). In C++ the extra scope levels introduced by classes and even nested classes creates even more complexities in the handling of symbols.

The use of the symbol table is often an integral part of any nontrivial C or C++ tool. Some of the tools that need to use a symbol table include cross-reference generators, function call tree generators, and even source code checkers (e.g., to check for unused variables).

Type checking

The process of type checking involves both expressions and the symbol table. The symbol table is used to find the type corresponding to a given identifier, whether it be a variable name or a type name. Then in expressions there is also the need to keep track of type conversions, such as knowing what the type of x op y is, which typically depends on the types of x and y in a manner dependent on the operator. The process of determining the types and the process of checking that types are correct are inseparable.

Not all tools will need to know about types. Many tools like cross-referencers, prototype extractors, don't bother with type checking, and instead assume that the input has been checked by the compiler. Examples of tools where type checking is crucial are compilers, interpreters, and source code checkers.

Call graph

The program's call graph is a graph data structure representing the relationship between functions, showing how they call each other. The root of the graph is typically the `main` function, as this is where program execution begins. For example, consider the following code block:

```
void fn3() { /*...*/  }
void fn1() { /*...*/  }
void fn2() { fn3(); fn1(); }
main() {  fn1(); fn2(); }
```

The corresponding call graph is shown in Fig. 26–2. A call graph is a directed graph where the arrows can either show the direction of function call (as here), or can point to the caller, so as to give inverse information. In this case the graph is acyclic because there is no recursion.

The call graph is itself a useful output, and many documentation tools exist to produce this graph from a given set of C/C++ files. In addition, tools can use the call graph for various reasons: finding recursion (infinite or otherwise), or measuring maximum possible call depth (ignoring recursion).

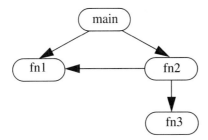

Fig. 26–2 Call graph

Flow graph

An important data structure for more complicated analysis of programs is the graph representing the flow of control through a single function. This graph shows the possible branching points at if statements, loops and jump statements. For example, consider the following code block:

```
void print_file(FILE *fp)
{
    if (fp != NULL) {
        int ch;
        while ((ch = getc(fp) != EOF) {
            putchar(ch);
        }
    }
}
```

The flow graph is shown in Fig. 26–3, with some indication of what each node is for. The internal flow graph data structure would typically require some information associated with each node, although what information would depend on the application. The graph is directed, with arrows showing where control can flow from a given node; the graph is cyclic if there are any loops.

Unfortunately, it is common to say "flow" graph, when really "call" graph is meant, since the function call hierarchy is a more common tool requirement.

The flow graph can be useful to check for irregularities in the flow of control through a program. This is typically how a compiler will detect problems such as unreachable code, a function not returning a value on all paths, or even a missing break in a switch statement. The flow graph can also be a useful documentation, maintenance, and debugging tool in itself.

Data flow analysis

This is a very advanced technique where the flow graph is augmented with information about variables at given points in the graph. For example, every point of use or assignment to each variable can be grouped with the relevant node in the flow graph. Data flow analysis can then iteratively propagate this information around the flow graph to determine various properties

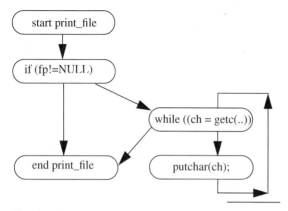

Fig. 26–3   Flow graph

of variables, such as their "lifetime" (i.e., at what point their value is no longer needed), and where a variable's value has been computed from.

Data flow analysis is usually associated with the code optimization of a compiler because it can be applied to problems such as register allocation, but it can also be used to detect common coding errors such as used-before-set variables and dead assignments. Although it is a powerful technique, the practical disadvantages of data flow analysis are that it is quite expensive in terms of time (and thus can slow down compilation) and is difficult to implement correctly, especially in C and C++ which have far too many operators that must be treated as special cases.

RUN-TIME TOOL TECHNIQUES

There are many tools available that perform work at run-time to inform you about the execution of your program. Some of the types of tools that use run-time techniques are:

- memory allocation debugging tools
- code coverage testing tools
- profilers

All of these tools are implemented using similar basic methods, but using these underlying methods to achieve different effects. The fundamental idea is *interception* of run-time operations. The run-time tool must know when a certain run-time event has occurred, and is then called into action. For example, a memory allocation debugging library must intercept all calls to allocation primitives, and perform debugging checks. Typically, the interception occurs at only a few specific levels (pre-compilation, compile-time, or link-time) and relies on one of the following techniques:

- macro interception during preprocessing
- linker interception
- object code modification

- executable code modification
- source code modification
- class/overloading interception (C++ only)

Macro interception

Macro interception is by far the most common method of intercepting calls to functions, because it is the simplest and most portable method. The method relies on the inbuilt power of the C/C++ preprocessor, and thus requires no special changes to the compilation phase. The typical method of implementing this idea is to place all the macro definitions in a header file, which is then included in all the C/C++ source files using a #include directive.

An important advantage of macro interception is the ability to extract the line number and filename where the macro expansion occurred by using the special macros ___LINE___ and ___FILE___. A typical usage is to pass these values to the intercepted version of the function, such as:

```
#define malloc(size)   \
    debug_malloc(size, __LINE__, __FILE__)
```

Recent versions of the GNU C/C++ compiler gcc also allow the use of ___FUNCTION___ to get the current function name. However, this is not allowed in standard C/C++ and is therefore not portable.

Limitations of macro interception

Third party libraries not intercepted: any libraries that are linked with the code, but have no source code and are not compiled (and hence not preprocessed) during a project build will not have their methods intercepted. This can be both a bane and a blessing; for example, it means that with a malloc debugging package using macro interception you cannot find errors in uses of a third-party library (e.g., passing bad memory addresses to X windows, or your compiler's standard libraries), but can be a blessing as you are not told about memory leaks in the third-party library, which is something you may not have any interest in, because you can't fix them anyway!

Function call interception only: only functions are intercepted with this method, simply because only identifiers can be macro expanded. Hence other operations such as pointer dereferences and array accesses are not intercepted using this method. This is why some memory allocation debugging libraries cannot find situations where an array reference has too large an index.

Non-immediate error detection: to make up for the previous failing, many debugging libraries check for array overruns at every intercepted function. Thus although an array index overflow may not be detected where it occurred, it may be detected at the next call to an intercepted function (if it has caused some obvious damage, such as overwriting a magic value). Thus although error checking that is performed at each intercepted function is good, it does not report the error immediately, but only a symptom of its prior occurrence.

Macros affect all identifier uses, ignoring scope: the preprocessor does not understand other scope levels, and hence it will replace all occurrences of an identifier, even if it is a local variable or (more annoyingly) a local member function of a C++ class. However, there are only rare problems with local variables, structure fields or labels as these usually do not resemble parameterized macros. The preprocessor does use a parameterized macro definition such as `malloc(x)` to expand occurrences without a parameter list such as a declaration of a local variable:

```
int malloc;   // Not expanded (has no argument)
```

Thus the scope problems occur mainly with class-local functions in C++, and cases where a non-parameterized macro definition is used. Fortunately, most problems will cause a compilation diagnostic rather than a run-time failure.

Cannot have both parameterized and parameter-less macros: It is not possible to define a macro with two definitions, one for the parameterized case and one for the non-parameterized case. Attempting to produce two such definitions via:

```
#define malloc(sz)   debug_malloc(sz)
#define malloc        debug_malloc
```

will cause only the second definition to take effect, and probably provoke a compilation warning about "redefining" a macro name. Although it seems it should be possible to allow both forms of definition to coexist peacefully, this is not supported in (standard) C or C++, and we must work around the limitation. One of the main problems this limitation creates is the possibility to subvert the macros, in which case see the next point.

Macro interceptions can be subverted: a minor problem is that the interception can be prevented, either accidentally or intentionally, by the programmer. There are a few ways to avoid having a macro expanded by the preprocessor:

a) #undef preprocessor directive (obviously)
b) Brackets around the function name: `ptr = (malloc)(sz);`
c) Pointers to functions: `pfn=&malloc; ... ptr = pfn(size);`

In older preprocessors the placement of a space after the identifier could prevent macro expansion — that is, "`ptr=malloc (sz);`" would not macro expand the identifier "`malloc`". However, this feature is no longer sanctioned by modern ANSI C preprocessors, although it may represent a problem with very old (deficient) compilers.

Note that in some cases this subversion can be an advantage as it provides you with an easy workaround if the run-time tool is not performing adequately. For example, you could hide a `malloc` call which you know is never freed (and don't care!), so as to prevent warnings about leaked blocks.

Variable argument macro calls are not supported: The interception of calls to variable argument functions is made difficult by the absence of variable argument macros in standard C or C++. The GNU C/C++ compiler, `gcc`, supports a non-standard extension for specifying variable argument macros, but most compilers have no such facility. The typical solution is to use a non-parameterized macro definition which contains some clever form of expression, usually using the comma operator or the ternary conditional operator. For example, consider intercepting `printf` to call a `debug_printf` function; the obvious method is simply:

```
#define printf debug_printf
```

but this will not pass along the line number and filename. This is where the prevention of variable argument macros is annoying, as we wish to do something like:

```
#define printf(fmt, ...) \
    debug_printf(__LINE__, __FILE__, fmt, ...)
```

but this is not allowed in standard C/C++. There are various possible solutions using non-parameterized macros, the comma operator or ternary conditional operator, and passing the line number and filename via global variables:

```
#define printf \
    (g_line = __LINE__, \
     g_file = __FILE__), debug_printf

#define printf \
    (g_line = __LINE__, \
     g_file = __FILE__, 0) ? 0 : debug_printf
```

The use of the ternary conditional operator is probably preferred as the first macro will cause problems if `printf` is ever used directly in a call to another function (the roles of the commas become conflicting). Naturally there are alternatives to use global variables, such as passing __LINE__ and __FILE__ to some initialization function:

```
#define printf \
  _fn(__LINE__, __FILE__), debug_printf
#define printf \
  (_fn(__LINE__,__FILE__),0) ? 0 : debug_printf
```

Linker interception

Linker interception of function calls is similar to macro interception, except it is the linker that performs the interception, not the preprocessor. This is achieved by supplying a linkable library with definitions of those functions you wish to intercept. The linker will then use your function definitions rather than those in the standard libraries.

The main advantage of this method over macro interception is that third-party libraries are now intercepted. Because interception does not rely on code passing through the preprocessor, all function calls that the linker detects are intercepted. In addition, the problems with macros and scope levels disappear and there is also no way to subvert the method by preventing the linker from intercepting a function.

Limitations of linker interception

- **Linker replacement of functions is less portable:** some linkers will not allow standard library functions to be replaced at link-time. The ANSI C standard explicitly states that defining your own version of a standard library function causes undefined behavior, and thus this method of interception can cause any manner of failure. In addition, attempting to intercept C++ functions at link-time requires knowledge of the manner of name "mangling" used by the C++ compiler. However, many platforms successfully allow link-time replacement of functions.

- **Line numbers and filename information absent:** since the preprocessor has not been used, linker interception does not permit easy extraction of the line number and filename using __LINE__ and __FILE__. In theory it is possible to extract the return address from the stack and use the object code information to map this to a line number and filename. In practice, this is non-portable, and requires much more knowledge than is easily available. Some commercial tools will do this, but there's no easy way for a portable tool to do so. The alternative, which is commonly used, is for a combination of macro and linker interception to be used. This means that any intercepted calls in source code will be sent the macro expanded information, but any calls via third-party libraries will not have line number and filename information.

- **Hard to mimic platform-specific functions:** it is difficult to implement some of the replacement functions you would use to replace the standard versions. Linker replacement intercepts all calls to these functions, and once you intercept a standard function, there is no way at all to access the original function. Although you could quite easily write a version of strcpy that works correctly, it is more difficult to write a version of malloc, which relies on platform-specific information (e.g., it probably uses sbrk on UNIX, but not in DOS implementations).

- **Function call interception only:** as with macro interception, this method can only intercept function calls, and any operations between intercepted function calls are not intercepted.

- **Non-immediate error detection:** because only functions are intercepted, errors such as array index overruns (which occurs in an assignment expression) will not be immediately detected, and will only be detected at the next call to an intercepted function (if at all).

Link-time interception of new and delete

Intercepting calls to the global new and delete operators at link-time is a special situation. It differs from the usual link-time interception of functions in that these functions are actually operators, and these operators are the only ones that standard C++ allows to be overloaded at a global scope level. Hence there is explicit compiler support for this form of interception and it should be fully portable to all standard C++ platforms.

Handling new and delete with a linkable malloc library

One especially useful technique for extending linkable libraries that intercept malloc and free to C++ is to redefine global new and delete operators to call malloc and free. In this way, blocks allocated using new and deallocated using delete are error checked in the same manner as the C library functions. The simplest definitions are:

```
void* operator new (size_t size)
{
    if (size == 0) size = 1;
    return ::malloc(size);
}
void operator delete(void *p)
{
    if (p != NULL) ::free(p);
}
```

Depending on the library being used, you might wish to raise some diagnostic messages to warn about `delete` of `NULL` (although legal C++ code, it is still unusual) or allocating a zero-sized block.

Object code modification

An effective but difficult method of intercepting operations is to explicitly modify the object code prior to the link phase. A few commercial memory debugging tools (notably the Purify debugging tool) operate on this principle. Typically this method requires the linker phase to be replaced with a call to some other tool which instruments the object code and then links it (using either the system linker or a substitute linker). There is much greater accuracy at this level of modification, and it is the most effective method of implementing low-level tools such as profilers.

The main advantage of this method is that absolutely everything can be intercepted. The interception can occur much more frequently than just at some function calls. For example, Purify examines all memory reads and writes, and will thus find a memory error from array accesses immediately, rather than at the next intercepted function call.

The main disadvantage of this method is that it is non-portable because it relies on very specific information about the format of object and executable files. Hence it is impossible to do portably, and quite difficult to do even for a single platform. This complexity explains why this method is mainly seen in commercial tools.

Executable code modification

This method is very similar to object code modification. However, rather than accept the object files as input, the method modifies the executable file after it has already been linked. The advantages and limitations of this method are almost identical to those for object code modification. An example of a tool that works on this principle is the `pixie` profiler under UNIX.

Source code modification

Whereas the object and executable code modification methods work at the end of compilation, the source code modification technique operates at the beginning of the compilation phase. The source code files are modified, such as to add extra code for error checking or timing instrumentation, and replaced with these augmented source code files. The compilation process must first build these augmented source files and then compile and link them.

The tool that modifies the source files could be as simple as an `awk` or `sed` regular expression modifier, or could be a full-blown parsing tool that examines the code in detail. An example is Brian Marick's `gct` code coverage testing tool which relies on instrumenting source code with extra code indicating whether a given path was taken during execution.

This technique is highly powerful and offers many advantages. The obvious limitations are the extra compilation phase (although this can be made to disappear if the source code modification tool implicitly calls the compiler on the resulting code), and the difficulty of writing a compiler front end with which to achieve the full benefits of the method.

C++ class overloading interception

An interesting technique is that C++ classes allow the overloading and interception of almost all operations in expressions. This allows a very powerful technique whereby a class object can be substituted for an ordinary object, and all the usual operations are routed through the class object's member functions. This can be used to detect a number of errors at run-time. For example, bad pointer dereferences can be found by replacing a declaration:

```
int *ptr;
```

with a class declaration that mimics all the usual actions but also performs error checking:

```
SmartPtr<int> ptr;
```

By careful definition of `SmartPtr` as a template class with all the right constructors, operators and type conversions, we can make the smart pointer class act just like an ordinary pointer in all respects, but also apply error checks. Another similar idea is a "`DebugInt`" class which replaces an "`int`" type, complaining about arithmetic overflows and other errors.

CODE GENERATION TECHNIQUES

We've looked at tools that analyze source code; we've looked at tools that work inside running code; now let's look at tools that *produce* C/C++ source code. The basic idea here is that some form of description file, which makes sense in terms of the given application domain, is analyzed and used to create a C or C++ program to perform the required actions.

The `yacc` and `lex` tools are probably the best-known examples of such tools. The `lex` tool takes a description file of regular expressions and produces a C library to create a lexical analyzer; similarly `yacc` takes a formal language grammar and creates a language recognizer in C. Versions that produce C++ classes are also now widely available.

In addition, the variety of commercial multi-platform development environments include a number of examples. GUI builder tools typically allow the user to specify the GUI design visually, and then produce C or C++ code to implement the design.

CDROM Information

On the CDROM attached to this book, you will find software that I wrote, and freely distributable software written by others. My own material consists of a variety of small tools that I have evolved for practical use, and while they're not perfect, they are a good starting point for thinking about what sort of tools you want in your environment.

Although this is the only place you will find my own work, most of the other software is freely available over the Internet. This CDROM should help you avoid time downloading and building tools from the various Internet sites just to try them out. Some of these source distributions such as the GNU distributions or the X11 contributions are regularly maintained and you should periodically check for newer releases available via the Internet or other vendor distributions.

The remainder of the chapter consists of notices that seemed necessary to comply with the various copyright and distribution arrangements of software included on the CDROM. It is my sincere hope that the CDROM is fair to authors of the software, and at the same time useful to the reader. It was not possible to include some powerful free tools mentioned in the book on the CDROM because the tools' distribution rights are limited or unclear in some cases.

GNU General Public License Version 2

Preamble

The licenses for most software are designed to take away your freedom to share and change it. By contrast, the GNU General Public License is intended to guarantee your freedom to share and change free software--to make sure the software is free for all its users. This General Public License applies to most of the Free Software Foundation's software and to any other program whose authors commit to using it. (Some other Free Software Foundation software is covered by the GNU Library General Public License instead.) You can apply it to your programs, too.

When we speak of free software, we are referring to freedom, not price. Our General Public Licenses are designed to make sure that you have the freedom to distribute copies of free software (and charge for this service if you wish), that you receive source code or can get it if you want it, that you can change the software or use pieces of it in new free programs; and that you know you can do these things.

To protect your rights, we need to make restrictions that forbid anyone to deny you these rights or to ask you to surrender the rights. These restrictions translate to certain responsibilities for you if you distribute copies of the software, or if you modify it.

For example, if you distribute copies of such a program, whether gratis or for a fee, you must give the recipients all the rights that you have. You must make sure that they, too, receive or can get the source code. And you must show them these terms so they know their rights.

We protect your rights with two steps: (1) copyright the software, and (2) offer you this license which gives you legal permission to copy, distribute and/or modify the software.

Also, for each author's protection and ours, we want to make certain that everyone understands that there is no warranty for this free software. If the software is modified by someone else and passed on, we want its recipients to know that what they have is not the original, so that any problems introduced by others will not reflect on the original authors' reputations.

Finally, any free program is threatened constantly by software patents. We wish to avoid the danger that redistributors of a free program will individually obtain patent licenses, in effect making the program proprietary. To prevent this, we have made it clear that any patent must be licensed for everyone's free use or not licensed at all.

The precise terms and conditions for copying, distribution and modification follow.

GNU GENERAL PUBLIC LICENSE
TERMS AND CONDITIONS FOR COPYING, DISTRIBUTION AND MODIFICATION

0. This License applies to any program or other work which contains a notice placed by the copyright holder saying it may be distributed under the terms of this General Public License. The "Program", below, refers to any such program or work, and a "work based on the Program" means either the Program or any derivative work under copyright law: that is to say, a work containing the Program or a portion of it, either verbatim or with modifications and/or translated into another language. (Hereinafter, translation is included without limitation in the term "modification".) Each licensee is addressed as "you".

Activities other than copying, distribution and modification are not covered by this License; they are outside its scope. The act of running the Program is not restricted, and the output from the Program is covered only if its contents constitute a work based on the Program (independent of having been made by running the Program). Whether that is true depends on what the Program does.

1. You may copy and distribute verbatim copies of the Program's source code as you receive it, in any medium, provided that you conspicuously and appropriately publish on each copy an appropriate copyright notice and disclaimer of warranty; keep intact all the notices that refer to this License and to the absence of any warranty; and give any other recipients of the Program a copy of this License along with the Program.

You may charge a fee for the physical act of transferring a copy, and you may at your option offer warranty protection in exchange for a fee.

2. You may modify your copy or copies of the Program or any portion of it, thus forming a work based on the Program, and copy and distribute such modifications or work under the terms of Section 1 above, provided that you also meet all of these conditions:

a) You must cause the modified files to carry prominent notices stating that you changed the files and the date of any change.

b) You must cause any work that you distribute or publish, that in whole or in part contains or is derived from the Program or any part thereof, to be licensed as a whole at no charge to all third parties under the terms of this License.

c) If the modified program normally reads commands interactively when run, you must cause it, when started running for such interactive use in the most ordinary way, to print or display an announcement including an appropriate copyright notice and a notice that there is no warranty (or else, saying that you provide a warranty) and that users may redistribute the program under these conditions, and telling the user how to view a copy of this License. (Exception: if the Program itself is interactive but does not normally print such an announcement, your work based on the Program is not required to print an announcement.)

These requirements apply to the modified work as a whole. If identifiable sections of that work are not derived from the Program, and can be reasonably considered independent and separate works in themselves, then this License, and its terms, do not apply to those sections when you distribute them as separate works. But when you distribute the same sections as part of a whole which is a work based on the Program, the distribution of the whole must be on the terms of this License, whose permissions for other licensees extend to the entire whole, and thus to each and every part regardless of who wrote it.

Thus, it is not the intent of this section to claim rights or contest your rights to work written entirely by you; rather, the intent is to exercise the right to control the distribution of derivative or collective works based on the Program.

In addition, mere aggregation of another work not based on the Program with the Program (or with a work based on the Program) on a volume of a storage or distribution medium does not bring the other work under the scope of this License.

3. You may copy and distribute the Program (or a work based on it, under Section 2) in object code or executable form under the terms of Sections 1 and 2 above provided that you also do one of the following:

a) Accompany it with the complete corresponding machine-readable source code, which must be distributed under the terms of Sections 1 and 2 above on a medium customarily used for software interchange; or,

b) Accompany it with a written offer, valid for at least three years, to give any third party, for a charge no more than your cost of physically performing source distribution, a complete machine-readable copy of the corresponding source code, to be distributed under the terms of Sections 1 and 2 above on a medium customarily used for software interchange; or,

c) Accompany it with the information you received as to the offer to distribute corresponding source code. (This alternative is allowed only for noncommercial distribution and only if you received the program in object code or executable form with such an offer, in accord with Subsection b above.)

The source code for a work means the preferred form of the work for making modifications to it. For an executable work, complete source code means all the source code for all modules it contains, plus any associated interface definition files, plus the scripts used to control compilation and installation of the executable. However, as a special exception, the source code distributed need not include anything that is normally distributed (in either source or binary form) with the major components (compiler, kernel, and so on) of the operating system on which the executable runs, unless that component itself accompanies the executable.

If distribution of executable or object code is made by offering access to copy from a designated place, then offering equivalent access to copy the source code from the same place counts as distribution of the source code, even though third parties are not compelled to copy the source along with the object code.

4. You may not copy, modify, sublicense, or distribute the Program except as expressly provided under this License. Any attempt otherwise to copy, modify, sublicense or distribute the Program is void, and will automatically terminate your rights under this License. However, parties who have received copies, or rights, from you under this License will not have their licenses terminated so long as such parties remain in full compliance.

5. You are not required to accept this License, since you have not signed it. However, nothing else grants you permission to modify or distribute the Program or its derivative works. These actions are prohibited by law if you do not accept this License. Therefore, by modifying or distributing the Program (or any work based on the Program), you indicate your acceptance of this License to do so, and all its terms and conditions for copying, distributing or modifying the Program or works based on it.

6. Each time you redistribute the Program (or any work based on the Program), the recipient automatically receives a license from the original licensor to copy, distribute or modify the Program subject to these terms and conditions. You may not impose any further restrictions on the recipients' exercise of the rights granted herein. You are not responsible for enforcing compliance by third parties to this License.

7. If, as a consequence of a court judgment or allegation of patent infringement or for any other reason (not limited to patent issues), conditions are imposed on you (whether by court order, agreement or otherwise) that contradict the conditions of this License, they do not excuse you from the conditions of this License. If you cannot distribute so as to satisfy simultaneously your obligations under this License and any other pertinent obligations, then as a consequence you may not distribute the Program at all. For example, if a patent license would not permit royalty-free redistribution of the Program by all those who receive copies directly or indirectly through you, then the only way you could satisfy both it and this License would be to refrain entirely from distribution of the Program.

If any portion of this section is held invalid or unenforceable under any particular circumstance, the balance of the section is intended to apply and the section as a whole is intended to apply in other circumstances.

It is not the purpose of this section to induce you to infringe any patents or other property right claims or to contest validity of any such claims; this section has the sole purpose of protecting the integrity of the free software distribution system, which is implemented by public license practices. Many people have made generous contributions to the wide range of software distributed through that system in reliance on consistent application of that system; it is up to the author/donor to decide if he or she is willing to distribute software through any other system and a licensee cannot impose that choice.

This section is intended to make thoroughly clear what is believed to be a consequence of the rest of this License.

8. If the distribution and/or use of the Program is restricted in certain countries either by patents or by copyrighted interfaces, the original copyright holder who places the Program under this License may add an explicit geographical distribution limitation excluding those countries, so that distribution is permitted only in or among countries not thus excluded. In such case, this License incorporates the limitation as if written in the body of this License.

9. The Free Software Foundation may publish revised and/or new versions of the General Public License from time to time. Such new versions will be similar in spirit to the present version, but may differ in detail to address new problems or concerns.

Each version is given a distinguishing version number. If the Program specifies a version number of this License which applies to it and "any later version", you have the option of following the terms and conditions either of that version or of any later version published by the Free Software Foundation. If the Program does not specify a version number of this License, you may choose any version ever published by the Free Software Foundation.

10. If you wish to incorporate parts of the Program into other free programs whose distribution conditions are different, write to the author to ask for permission. For software which is copyrighted by the Free Software Foundation, write to the Free Software Foundation; we sometimes make exceptions for this. Our decision will be guided by the two goals of preserving the free status of all derivatives of our free software and of promoting the sharing and reuse of software generally.

NO WARRANTY

11. BECAUSE THE PROGRAM IS LICENSED FREE OF CHARGE, THERE IS NO WARRANTY FOR THE PROGRAM, TO THE EXTENT PERMITTED BY APPLICABLE LAW. EXCEPT WHEN OTHERWISE STATED IN WRITING THE COPYRIGHT HOLDERS AND/OR OTHER PARTIES

PROVIDE THE PROGRAM "AS IS" WITHOUT WARRANTY OF ANY KIND, EITHER EXPRESSED OR IMPLIED, INCLUDING, BUT NOT LIMITED TO, THE IMPLIED WARRANTIES OF MERCHANTABILITY AND FITNESS FOR A PARTICULAR PURPOSE. THE ENTIRE RISK AS TO THE QUALITY AND PERFORMANCE OF THE PROGRAM IS WITH YOU. SHOULD THE PROGRAM PROVE DEFECTIVE, YOU ASSUME THE COST OF ALL NECESSARY SERVICING, REPAIR OR CORRECTION.

12. IN NO EVENT UNLESS REQUIRED BY APPLICABLE LAW OR AGREED TO IN WRITING WILL ANY COPYRIGHT HOLDER, OR ANY OTHER PARTY WHO MAY MODIFY AND/OR REDISTRIBUTE THE PROGRAM AS PERMITTED ABOVE, BE LIABLE TO YOU FOR DAMAGES, INCLUDING ANY GENERAL, SPECIAL, INCIDENTAL OR CONSEQUENTIAL DAMAGES ARISING OUT OF THE USE OR INABILITY TO USE THE PROGRAM (INCLUDING BUT NOT LIMITED TO LOSS OF DATA OR DATA BEING RENDERED INACCURATE OR LOSSES SUSTAINED BY YOU OR THIRD PARTIES OR A FAILURE OF THE PROGRAM TO OPERATE WITH ANY OTHER PROGRAMS), EVEN IF SUCH HOLDER OR OTHER PARTY HAS BEEN ADVISED OF THE POSSIBILITY OF SUCH DAMAGES.

END OF TERMS AND CONDITIONS

Appendix: How to Apply These Terms to Your New Programs

If you develop a new program, and you want it to be of the greatest possible use to the public, the best way to achieve this is to make it free software which everyone can redistribute and change under these terms.

To do so, attach the following notices to the program. It is safest to attach them to the start of each source file to most effectively convey the exclusion of warranty; and each file should have at least the "copyright" line and a pointer to where the full notice is found.

<one line to give the program's name and a brief idea of what it does.>

Copyright (C) 19yy <name of author>

This program is free software; you can redistribute it and/or modify it under the terms of the GNU General Public License as published by the Free Software Foundation; either version 2 of the License, or (at your option) any later version.

This program is distributed in the hope that it will be useful, but WITHOUT ANY WARRANTY; without even the implied warranty of MERCHANTABILITY or FITNESS FOR A PARTICULAR PURPOSE. See the GNU General Public License for more details.

You should have received a copy of the GNU General Public License along with this program; if not, write to the Free Software Foundation, Inc., 675 Mass Ave, Cambridge, MA 02139, USA.

Also add information on how to contact you by electronic and paper mail.

If the program is interactive, make it output a short notice like this when it starts in an interactive mode:

Gnomovision version 69, Copyright (C) 19yy name of author

Gnomovision comes with ABSOLUTELY NO WARRANTY; for details type 'show w'.

This is free software, and you are welcome to redistribute it

under certain conditions; type 'show c' for details.

The hypothetical commands 'show w' and 'show c' should show the appropriate parts of the General Public License. Of course, the commands you use may be called something other than 'show w' and 'show c'; they could even be mouse-clicks or menu items--whatever suits your program.

You should also get your employer (if you work as a programmer) or your school, if any, to sign a "copyright disclaimer" for the program, if necessary. Here is a sample; alter the names:

> Yoyodyne, Inc., hereby disclaims all copyright interest in the program 'Gnomovision' (which makes passes at compilers) written by James Hacker.

> <signature of Ty Coon>, 1 April 1989

> Ty Coon, President of Vice

This General Public License does not permit incorporating your program into proprietary programs. If your program is a subroutine library, you may consider it more useful to permit linking proprietary applications with the library. If this is what you want to do, use the GNU Library General Public License instead of this License.

GNU LIBRARY GENERAL PUBLIC LICENSE

GNU LIBRARY GENERAL PUBLIC LICENSE

Version 2, June 1991

Copyright (C) 1991 Free Software Foundation, Inc., 675 Mass Ave, Cambridge, MA 02139, USA. Everyone is permitted to copy and distribute verbatim copies of this license document, but changing it is not allowed.

[This is the first released version of the library GPL. It is numbered 2 because it goes with version 2 of the ordinary GPL.]

Preamble

The licenses for most software are designed to take away your freedom to share and change it. By contrast, the GNU General Public Licenses are intended to guarantee your freedom to share and change free software--to make sure the software is free for all its users.

This license, the Library General Public License, applies to some specially designated Free Software Foundation software, and to any other libraries whose authors decide to use it. You can use it for your libraries, too.

When we speak of free software, we are referring to freedom, not price. Our General Public Licenses are designed to make sure that you have the freedom to distribute copies of free software (and charge for this service if you wish), that you receive source code or can get it if you want it, that you can change the software or use pieces of it in new free programs; and that you know you can do these things.

To protect your rights, we need to make restrictions that forbid anyone to deny you these rights or to ask you to surrender the rights. These restrictions translate to certain responsibilities for you if you distribute copies of the library, or if you modify it.

For example, if you distribute copies of the library, whether gratis or for a fee, you must give the recipients all the rights that we gave you. You must make sure that they, too, receive or can get the source code. If you link a program with the library, you must provide complete object files to the recipients so that they can relink them with the library, after making changes to the library and recompiling it. And you must show them these terms so they know their rights.

Our method of protecting your rights has two steps: (1) copyright the library, and (2) offer you this license which gives you legal permission to copy, distribute and/or modify the library.

Also, for each distributor's protection, we want to make certain that everyone understands that there is no warranty for this free library. If the library is modified by someone else and passed on, we want its recipients to know that what they have is not the original version, so that any problems introduced by others will not reflect on the original authors' reputations.

Finally, any free program is threatened constantly by software patents. We wish to avoid the danger that companies distributing free software will individually obtain patent licenses, thus in effect transforming the program into proprietary software. To prevent this, we have made it clear that any patent must be licensed for everyone's free use or not licensed at all.

Most GNU software, including some libraries, is covered by the ordinary GNU General Public License, which was designed for utility programs. This license, the GNU Library General Public License, applies to certain designated libraries. This license is quite different from the ordinary one; be sure to read it in full, and don't assume that anything in it is the same as in the ordinary license.

The reason we have a separate public license for some libraries is that they blur the distinction we usually make between modifying or adding to a program and simply using it. Linking a program with a library, without changing the library, is in some sense simply using the library, and is analogous to running a utility program or application program. However, in a textual and legal sense, the linked executable is a combined work, a derivative of the original library, and the ordinary General Public License treats it as such.

Because of this blurred distinction, using the ordinary General Public License for libraries did not effectively promote software sharing, because most developers did not use the libraries. We concluded that weaker conditions might promote sharing better.

However, unrestricted linking of non-free programs would deprive the users of those programs of all benefit from the free status of the libraries themselves. This Library General Public License is intended to permit developers of non-free programs to use free libraries, while preserving your freedom as a user of such programs to change the free libraries that are incorporated in them. (We have not seen how to achieve this as regards changes in header files, but we have achieved it as regards changes in the actual functions of the Library.) The hope is that this will lead to faster development of free libraries.

The precise terms and conditions for copying, distribution and modification follow. Pay close attention to the difference between a "work based on the library" and a "work that uses the library". The former contains code derived from the library, while the latter only works together with the library.

Note that it is possible for a library to be covered by the ordinary General Public License rather than by this special one.

GNU LIBRARY GENERAL PUBLIC LICENSE
TERMS AND CONDITIONS FOR COPYING, DISTRIBUTION AND MODIFICATION

0. This License Agreement applies to any software library which contains a notice placed by the copyright holder or other authorized party saying it may be distributed under the terms of this Library General Public License (also called "this License"). Each licensee is addressed as "you".

A "library" means a collection of software functions and/or data prepared so as to be conveniently linked with application programs (which use some of those functions and data) to form executables.

The "Library", below, refers to any such software library or work which has been distributed under these terms. A "work based on the Library" means either the Library or any derivative work under copyright law: that is to say, a work containing the Library or a portion of it, either verbatim or with modifications and/or translated straightforwardly into another language. (Hereinafter, translation is included without limitation in the term "modification".)

"Source code" for a work means the preferred form of the work for making modifications to it. For a library, complete source code means all the source code for all modules it contains, plus any associated interface definition files, plus the scripts used to control compilation and installation of the library.

Activities other than copying, distribution and modification are not covered by this License; they are outside its scope. The act of running a program using the Library is not restricted, and output from such a program is covered only if its contents constitute a work based on the Library (independent of the use of the Library in a tool for writing it). Whether that is true depends on what the Library does and what the program that uses the Library does.

1. You may copy and distribute verbatim copies of the Library's complete source code as you receive it, in any medium, provided that you conspicuously and appropriately publish on each copy an appropriate copyright notice and disclaimer of warranty; keep intact all the notices that refer to this License and to the absence of any warranty; and distribute a copy of this License along with the Library.

You may charge a fee for the physical act of transferring a copy, and you may at your option offer warranty protection in exchange for a fee.

2. You may modify your copy or copies of the Library or any portion of it, thus forming a work based on the Library, and copy and distribute such modifications or work under the terms of Section 1 above, provided that you also meet all of these conditions:

a) The modified work must itself be a software library.

b) You must cause the files modified to carry prominent notices stating that you changed the files and the date of any change.

c) You must cause the whole of the work to be licensed at no charge to all third parties under the terms of this License.

d) If a facility in the modified Library refers to a function or a table of data to be supplied by an application program that uses the facility, other than as an argument passed when the facility is invoked, then you must make a good faith effort to ensure that, in the event an application does not supply such function or table, the facility still operates, and performs whatever part of its purpose remains meaningful.

(For example, a function in a library to compute square roots has purpose that is entirely well-defined independent of the application. Therefore, Subsection 2d requires that any application-supplied function or table used by this function must be optional: if the application does not supply it, the square root function must still compute square roots.)

These requirements apply to the modified work as a whole. If identifiable sections of that work are not derived from the Library, and can be reasonably considered independent and separate works in themselves, then this License, and its terms, do not apply to those sections when you distribute them as separate works. But when you distribute the same sections as part of a whole which is a work based on the Library, the distribution of the whole must be on the terms of this License, whose permissions for other licensees extend to the entire whole, and thus to each and every part regardless of who wrote it.

Thus, it is not the intent of this section to claim rights or contest your rights to work written entirely by you; rather, the intent is to exercise the right to control the distribution of derivative or collective works based on the Library.

In addition, mere aggregation of another work not based on the Library with the Library (or with a work based on the Library) on a volume of a storage or distribution medium does not bring the other work under the scope of this License.

3. You may opt to apply the terms of the ordinary GNU General Public License instead of this License to a given copy of the Library. To do this, you must alter all the notices that refer to this License, so that they refer to the ordinary GNU General Public License, version 2, instead of to this License. (If a newer version than version 2 of the ordinary GNU General Public License has appeared, then you can specify that version instead if you wish.) Do not make any other change in these notices.

Once this change is made in a given copy, it is irreversible for that copy, so the ordinary GNU General Public License applies to all subsequent copies and derivative works made from that copy.

This option is useful when you wish to copy part of the code of the Library into a program that is not a library.

4. You may copy and distribute the Library (or a portion or derivative of it, under Section 2) in object code or executable form under the terms of Sections 1 and 2 above provided that you accompany it with the complete corresponding machine-readable source code, which must be distributed under the terms of Sections 1 and 2 above on a medium customarily used for software interchange.

If distribution of object code is made by offering access to copy from a designated place, then offering equivalent access to copy the source code from the same place satisfies the requirement to distribute the source code, even though third parties are not compelled to copy the source along with the object code.

5. A program that contains no derivative of any portion of the Library, but is designed to work with the Library by being compiled or linked with it, is called a "work that uses the Library". Such a work, in isolation, is not a derivative work of the Library, and therefore falls outside the scope of this License.

However, linking a "work that uses the Library" with the Library creates an executable that is a derivative of the Library (because it contains portions of the Library), rather than a "work that uses the library". The executable is therefore covered by this License. Section 6 states terms for distribution of such executables.

When a "work that uses the Library" uses material from a header file that is part of the Library, the object code for the work may be a derivative work of the Library even though the source code is not. Whether this is true is especially significant if the work can be linked without the Library, or if the work is itself a library. The threshold for this to be true is not precisely defined by law.

If such an object file uses only numerical parameters, data structure layouts and accessors, and small macros and small inline functions (ten lines or less in length), then the use of the object file is unrestricted, regardless of whether it is legally a derivative work. (Executables containing this object code plus portions of the Library will still fall under Section 6.)

Otherwise, if the work is a derivative of the Library, you may distribute the object code for the work under the terms of Section 6. Any executables containing that work also fall under Section 6, whether or not they are linked directly with the Library itself.

6. As an exception to the Sections above, you may also compile or link a "work that uses the Library" with the Library to produce a work containing portions of the Library, and distribute that work under terms of your choice, provided that the terms permit modification of the work for the customer's own use and reverse engineering for debugging such modifications.

You must give prominent notice with each copy of the work that the Library is used in it and that the Library and its use are covered by this License. You must supply a copy of this License. If the work during execution displays copyright notices, you must include the copyright notice for the Library among them, as well as a reference directing the user to the copy of this License. Also, you must do one of these things:

a) Accompany the work with the complete corresponding machine-readable source code for the Library including whatever changes were used in the work (which must be distributed under Sections 1 and 2 above); and, if the work is an executable linked with the Library, with the complete machine-readable "work that uses the Library", as object code and/or source code, so that the user can modify the Library and then relink to produce a modified executable containing the modified Library. (It is understood that the user who changes the contents of definitions files in the Library will not necessarily be able to recompile the application to use the modified definitions.)

b) Accompany the work with a written offer, valid for at least three years, to give the same user the materials specified in Subsection 6a, above, for a charge no more than the cost of performing this distribution.

c) If distribution of the work is made by offering access to copy from a designated place, offer equivalent access to copy the above specified materials from the same place.

d) Verify that the user has already received a copy of these materials or that you have already sent this user a copy.

For an executable, the required form of the "work that uses the Library" must include any data and utility programs needed for reproducing the executable from it. However, as a special exception, the source code distributed need not include anything that is normally distributed (in either source or binary form) with the major components (compiler, kernel, and so on) of the operating system on which the executable runs, unless that component itself accompanies the executable.

It may happen that this requirement contradicts the license restrictions of other proprietary libraries that do not normally accompany the operating system. Such a contradiction means you cannot use both them and the Library together in an executable that you distribute.

7. You may place library facilities that are a work based on the Library side-by-side in a single library together with other library facilities not covered by this License, and distribute such a combined library, provided that the separate distribution of the work based on the Library and of the other library facilities is otherwise permitted, and provided that you do these two things:

a) Accompany the combined library with a copy of the same work based on the Library, uncombined with any other library facilities. This must be distributed under the terms of the Sections above.

b) Give prominent notice with the combined library of the fact that part of it is a work based on the Library, and explaining where to find the accompanying uncombined form of the same work.

8. You may not copy, modify, sublicense, link with, or distribute the Library except as expressly provided under this License. Any attempt otherwise to copy, modify, sublicense, link with, or distribute the Library is void, and will automatically terminate your rights under this License. However, parties who have received copies, or rights, from you under this License will not have their licenses terminated so long as such parties remain in full compliance.

9. You are not required to accept this License, since you have not signed it. However, nothing else grants you permission to modify or distribute the Library or its derivative works. These actions are prohibited by law if you do not accept this License. Therefore, by modifying or distributing the Library (or any work based on the Library), you indicate your acceptance of this License to do so, and all its terms and conditions for copying, distributing or modifying the Library or works based on it.

10. Each time you redistribute the Library (or any work based on the Library), the recipient automatically receives a license from the original licensor to copy, distribute, link with or modify the Library subject to these terms and conditions. You may not impose any further restrictions on the recipients' exercise of the rights granted herein. You are not responsible for enforcing compliance by third parties to this License.

11. If, as a consequence of a court judgment or allegation of patent infringement or for any other reason (not limited to patent issues), conditions are imposed on you (whether by court order, agreement or otherwise) that contradict the conditions of this License, they do not excuse you from the conditions of this License. If you cannot distribute so as to satisfy simultaneously your obligations under this License and any other pertinent obligations, then as a consequence you may not distribute the Library at all. For example, if a patent license would not permit royalty-free redistribution of the Library by all those who receive copies directly or indirectly through you, then the only way you could satisfy both it and this License would be to refrain entirely from distribution of the Library.

If any portion of this section is held invalid or unenforceable under any particular circumstance, the balance of the section is intended to apply, and the section as a whole is intended to apply in other circumstances.

It is not the purpose of this section to induce you to infringe any patents or other property right claims or to contest validity of any such claims; this section has the sole purpose of protecting the integrity of the free software distribution system which is implemented by public license practices. Many people have made generous contributions to the wide range of software distributed through that system in reliance on consistent application of that system; it is up to the author/donor to decide if he or she is willing to distribute software through any other system and a licensee cannot impose that choice.

This section is intended to make thoroughly clear what is believed to be a consequence of the rest of this License.

12. If the distribution and/or use of the Library is restricted in certain countries either by patents or by copyrighted interfaces, the original copyright holder who places the Library under this License may add an explicit geographical distribution limitation excluding those countries, so that distribution is permitted only in or among countries not thus excluded. In such case, this License incorporates the limitation as if written in the body of this License.

13. The Free Software Foundation may publish revised and/or new versions of the Library General Public License from time to time. Such new versions will be similar in spirit to the present version, but may differ in detail to address new problems or concerns.

Each version is given a distinguishing version number. If the Library specifies a version number of this License which applies to it and "any later version", you have the option of following the terms and conditions either of that version or of any later version published by the Free Software Foundation. If the Library does not specify a license version number, you may choose any version ever published by the Free Software Foundation.

14. If you wish to incorporate parts of the Library into other free programs whose distribution conditions are incompatible with these, write to the author to ask for permission. For software which is copyrighted by the Free Software Foundation, write to the Free Software Foundation; we sometimes make exceptions for this. Our decision will be guided by the two goals of preserving the free status of all derivatives of our free software and of promoting the sharing and reuse of software generally.

NO WARRANTY

15. BECAUSE THE LIBRARY IS LICENSED FREE OF CHARGE, THERE IS NO WARRANTY FOR THE LIBRARY, TO THE EXTENT PERMITTED BY APPLICABLE LAW. EXCEPT WHEN OTHERWISE STATED IN WRITING THE COPYRIGHT HOLDERS AND/OR OTHER PARTIES PROVIDE THE LIBRARY "AS IS" WITHOUT WARRANTY OF ANY KIND, EITHER EXPRESSED OR IMPLIED, INCLUDING, BUT NOT LIMITED TO, THE IMPLIED WARRANTIES OF MERCHANTABILITY AND FITNESS FOR A PARTICULAR PURPOSE. THE ENTIRE RISK AS TO THE QUALITY AND PERFORMANCE OF THE LIBRARY IS WITH YOU. SHOULD THE LIBRARY PROVE DEFECTIVE, YOU ASSUME THE COST OF ALL NECESSARY SERVICING, REPAIR OR CORRECTION.

16. IN NO EVENT UNLESS REQUIRED BY APPLICABLE LAW OR AGREED TO IN WRITING WILL ANY COPYRIGHT HOLDER, OR ANY OTHER PARTY WHO MAY MODIFY AND/OR REDISTRIBUTE THE LIBRARY AS PERMITTED ABOVE, BE LIABLE TO YOU FOR DAMAGES, INCLUDING ANY GENERAL, SPECIAL, INCIDENTAL OR CONSEQUENTIAL DAMAGES ARISING OUT OF THE USE OR INABILITY TO USE THE LIBRARY (INCLUDING BUT NOT LIMITED TO LOSS OF DATA OR DATA BEING RENDERED INACCURATE OR LOSSES SUSTAINED BY YOU OR THIRD PARTIES OR A FAILURE OF THE LIBRARY TO OPERATE WITH ANY OTHER SOFTWARE), EVEN IF SUCH HOLDER OR OTHER PARTY HAS BEEN ADVISED OF THE POSSIBILITY OF SUCH DAMAGES.

END OF TERMS AND CONDITIONS

Appendix: How to Apply These Terms to Your New Libraries

If you develop a new library, and you want it to be of the greatest possible use to the public, we recommend making it free software that everyone can redistribute and change. You can do so by permitting redistribution under these terms (or, alternatively, under the terms of the ordinary General Public License).

To apply these terms, attach the following notices to the library. It is safest to attach them to the start of each source file to most effectively convey the exclusion of warranty; and each file should have at least the "copyright" line and a pointer to where the full notice is found.

<one line to give the library's name and a brief idea of what it does.>

Copyright (C) <year> <name of author>

This library is free software; you can redistribute it and/or modify it under the terms of the GNU Library General Public License as published by the Free Software Foundation; either version 2 of the License, or (at your option) any later version.

This library is distributed in the hope that it will be useful, but WITHOUT ANY WARRANTY; without even the implied warranty of MERCHANTABILITY or FITNESS FOR A PARTICULAR PURPOSE. See the GNU Library General Public License for more details.

You should have received a copy of the GNU Library General Public License along with this library; if not, write to the Free Software Foundation, Inc., 675 Mass Ave, Cambridge, MA 02139, USA.

Also add information on how to contact you by electronic and paper mail.

You should also get your employer (if you work as a programmer) or your school, if any, to sign a "copyright disclaimer" for the library, if necessary. Here is a sample; alter the names:

Yoyodyne, Inc., hereby disclaims all copyright interest in the library 'Frob' (a library for tweaking knobs) written by James Random Hacker.

<signature of Ty Coon>, 1 April 1990

Ty Coon, President of Vice

That's all there is to it!

f2c Copyright Notice

Copyright 1990 by AT&T Bell Laboratories and Bellcore.

Permission to use, copy, modify, and distribute this software and its documentation for any purpose and without fee is hereby granted, provided that the above copyright notice appear in all copies and that both that the copyright notice and this permission notice and warranty disclaimer appear in supporting documentation, and that the names of AT&T Bell Laboratories or Bellcore or any of their entities not be used in advertising or publicity pertaining to distribution of the software without specific, written prior permission.

AT&T and Bellcore disclaim all warranties with regard to this software, including all implied warranties of merchantability and fitness. In no event shall AT&T or Bellcore be liable for any special, indirect or consequential damages or any damages whatsoever resulting from loss of use, data or profits, whether in an action of contract, negligence or other tortious action, arising out of or in connection with the use or performance of this software.

Index

Symbols

__cplusplus standard C++ macro 172
__FUNCTION__ GNU extension 20
__GNUC__ GNU macro 175
__STDC__ macro 172, 183, 184

Numerics

100% coverage 217
4GLs 227, 231, 313, 333

A

A2C (assembler to C) 167
AARD toolset (vmon/vmemcheck) 86
ABR/ABW, Purify tip 77
Abraxas Software, Inc. 51, 244, 248
Absoft C/C++ compiler (Macintosh) 34
Absoft Corporation 34
access-level run-time error checking 70
adb, UNIX debugger 6, 103
Aegis free versioning tool 270
AiB Software Corp. (SENTINEL) 73
algorithm animation 79
allocation failure 216
American National Standards Institute 348
Amiga 10
Amsterdam's exception library for C 296
animation books 346
ANSI/ISO C standard 348
ANSI/ISO C++ standard 19
ansi2knr prototype conversion tool 183

ape programmers 3
API calls
    checking Windows compliance 84
    debugger usage 68, 103
    run-time checking 84, 85
    static checking 53
Apogee C/C++ Compiler Package 22
ar, UNIX library archiver 25
Archimedes Software (BugBase) 274
argc and argv 279
argument processing 279–291, 362
ARM (Annotated C++ Reference Manual) 343
asedit free X11 editor 196
assert macro 102, 238
Atari 10
Atria Software Inc. (ClearCase) 271
attach to a running process 95, 104, 105, 121, 122
Automated Test Facility, testing tool 7, 234
awk 178, 212, 364, 373
    awkcheck, simple source checker 58
aXe free X11 editor 197

B

B+tree indexing 314, 317, 318, 320
BAS_C, BASIC to C conversion 166
BASIC 165, 166
basic block 126, 129, 221
Battlemap Analysis Tool 239
bba, HP test coverage tool 223
bdiff, UNIX big file differencing 252

391

LICENSE AGREEMENT AND LIMITED WARRANTY

READ THE FOLLOWING TERMS AND CONDITIONS CAREFULLY BEFORE OPENING THIS DISK PACKAGE. THIS IS AN AGREEMENT BETWEEN YOU AND PRENTICE-HALL, INC. (THE "COMPANY"). BY OPENING THIS SEALED PACKAGE, YOU ARE AGREEING TO BE BOUND BY THESE TERMS AND CONDITIONS. IF YOU DO NOT AGREE WITH THESE TERMS AND CONDITIONS, DO NOT OPEN THE DISK PACKAGE. PROMPTLY RETURN THE DISK PACKAGE AND ALL ACCOMPANYING ITEMS TO THE COMPANY.

1. **GRANT OF LICENSE:** In consideration of your adoption of textbooks and/or other materials published by the Company, and your agreement to abide by the terms and conditions of this Agreement, the Company grants to you a nonexclusive right to use and display the copy of the enclosed software program (hereinafter the "SOFTWARE") so long as you comply with the terms of this Agreement. The Company reserves all rights not expressly granted to you under this Agreement. This license is not a sale of the original SOFTWARE or any copy to you.

2. **USE RESTRICTIONS:** You may not sell or license copies of the SOFTWARE or the Documentation to others. You may not transfer or distribute copies of the SOFTWARE or the Documentation, except to instructors and students in your school who are users of the adopted Company textbook that accompanies this SOFTWARE. You may not reverse engineer, disassemble, decompile, modify, adapt, translate, or create derivative works based on the SOFTWARE or the Documentation without the prior written consent of the Company.

3. **LIMITED WARRANTY AND DISCLAIMER OF WARRANTY:** Because this SOFTWARE is being given to you without charge, the Company makes no warranties about the SOFTWARE, which is provided "AS-IS." THE COMPANY DISCLAIMS ALL WARRANTIES, EXPRESS OR IMPLIED, INCLUDING WITHOUT LIMITATION, THE IMPLIED WARRANTIES OF MERCHANTABILITY AND FITNESS FOR A PARTICULAR PURPOSE. THE COMPANY DOES NOT WARRANT, GUARANTEE, OR MAKE ANY REPRESENTATION REGARDING THE USE OR THE RESULTS OF THE USE OF THE SOFTWARE. IN NO EVENT, SHALL THE COMPANY OR ITS EMPLOYEES, AGENTS, SUPPLIERS, OR CONTRACTORS BE LIABLE FOR ANY INCIDENTAL, INDIRECT, SPECIAL, OR CONSEQUENTIAL DAMAGES ARISING OUT OF OR IN CONNECTION WITH THE LICENSE GRANTED UNDER THIS AGREEMENT, NOR FOR LOSS OF USE, LOSS OF DATA, LOSS OF INCOME OR PROFIT, OR OTHER LOSSES, SUSTAINED AS A RESULT OF INJURY TO ANY PERSON, OR LOSS OF OR DAMAGE TO PROPERTY, OR CLAIMS OF THIRD PARTIES, EVEN IF THE COMPANY OR AN AUTHORIZED REPRESENTATIVE OF THE COMPANY HAS BEEN ADVISED OF SUCH DAMAGES.
SOME JURISDICTIONS DO NOT ALLOW THE LIMITATION OF IMPLIED WARRANTIES OR LIABILITY FOR INCIDENTAL, INDIRECT, SPECIAL, OR CONSEQUENTIAL DAMAGES, SO THE ABOVE LIMITATIONS MAY NOT ALWAYS APPLY. THE WARRANTIES IN THIS AGREEMENT GIVE YOU SPECIFIC LEGAL RIGHTS AND YOU MAY ALSO HAVE OTHER RIGHTS WHICH VARY IN ACCORDANCE WITH LOCAL LAW.

ACKNOWLEDGMENT

YOU ACKNOWLEDGE THAT YOU HAVE READ THIS AGREEMENT, UNDERSTAND IT, AND AGREE TO BE BOUND BY ITS TERMS AND CONDITIONS. YOU ALSO AGREE THAT THIS AGREEMENT IS THE COMPLETE AND EXCLUSIVE AGREEMENT BETWEEN YOU AND THE COMPANY.

Should you have any questions concerning this Agreement or if you wish to contact the Company for any reason, please contact in writing at the address below or call the at the telephone number provided.

PTR Customer Service
Prentice Hall PTR
One Lake Street
Upper Saddle River, New Jersey 07458
Telephone: 201-236-7105